shiho. sugiura's Silver diamond

7: Stone Wolf

By Shiho Sugiura

TOKYOPOP®

HAMBURG // LONDON // LOS ANGELES // TOKYO

SILVER DIAMOND Vol. 7
Created by Shiho Sugiura

Translation - Angela Liu
English Adaptation - Karen S. Ahlstrom
Copy Editor - Joseph Heller
Retouch and Lettering - Star Print Brokers
Production Artist - Michael Paolilli
Graphic Designer - Christian Lownds

Editor - Lillian Diaz-Przybyl
Print Production Manager - Lucas Rivera
Managing Editor - Vy Nguyen
Senior Designer - Louis Csontos
Art Director - Al-Insan Lashley
Director of Sales and Manufacturing - Allyson De Simone
Associate Publisher - Marco F. Pavia
President and C.O.O. - John Parker
C.E.O. and Chief Creative Officer - Stu Levy

A 🐢 TOKYOPOP® Manga

TOKYOPOP Inc.
5900 Wilshire Blvd. Suite 2000
Los Angeles, CA 90036

E-mail: info@TOKYOPOP.com
Come visit us online at www.TOKYOPOP.com

ISBN: 978-1-4278-0971-1

First TOKYOPOP printing: September 2010
10 9 8 7 6 5 4 3 2 1
Printed in the USA

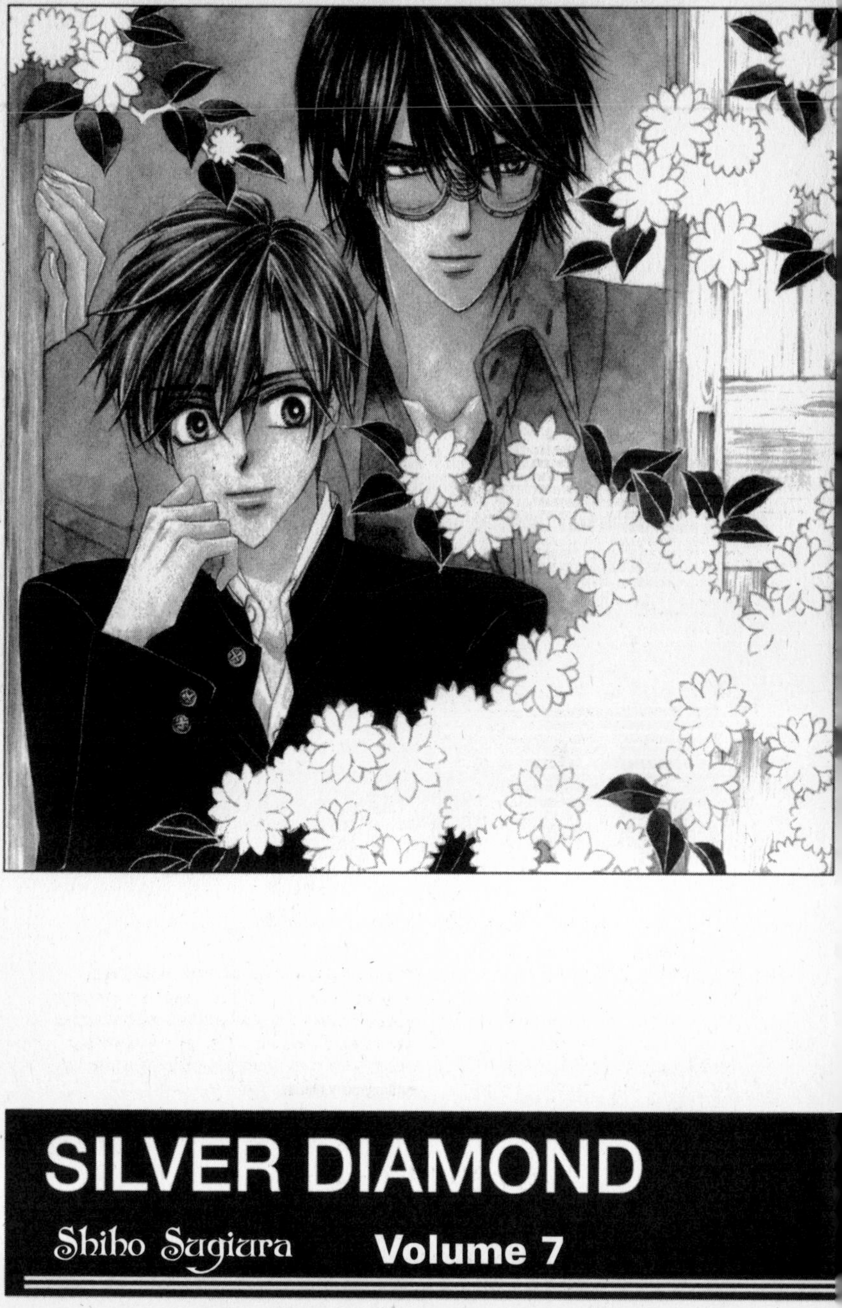

SILVER DIAMOND

Shiho Sugiura

Volume 7

Contents

Silver Diamond

TO KEEP SILVER DIAMOND AS AUTHENTIC AS POSSIBLE, JAPANESE
NAME ORDER (FAMILY NAME FIRST) AND HONORIFICS WILL BE
MAINTAINED THROUGH OUT THE TEXT. FOR FURTHER EXPLANATIONS,
PLEASE CHECK THE GLOSSARY AT THE END OF THE VOLUME.

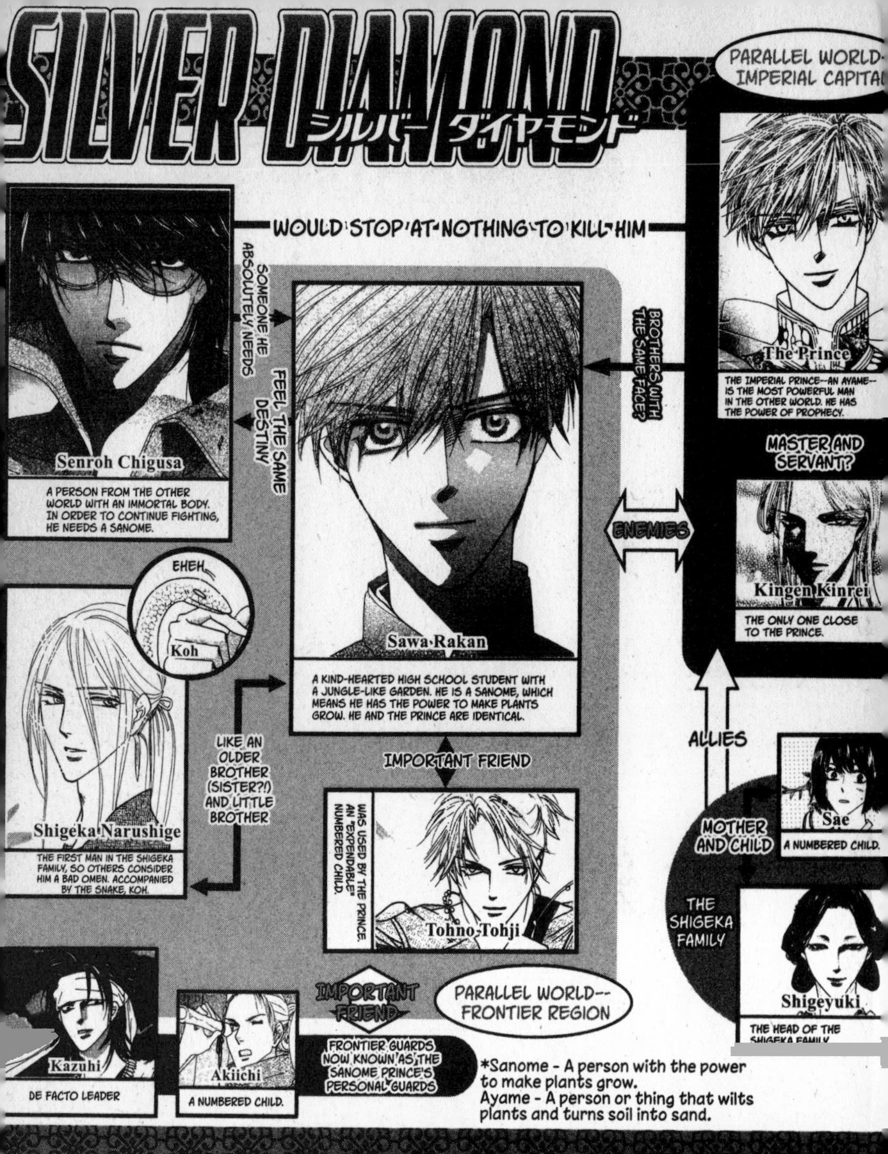
SILVER DIAMOND
シルバーダイヤモンド
PARALLEL WORLD-- IMPERIAL CAPITAL
The Prince
THE IMPERIAL PRINCE--AN AYAME--IS THE MOST POWERFUL MAN IN THE OTHER WORLD. HE HAS THE POWER OF PROPHECY.
MASTER AND SERVANT?
Kingen Kinrei
THE ONLY ONE CLOSE TO THE PRINCE.
WOULD STOP AT NOTHING TO KILL HIM
BROTHERS WITH THE SAME FACE?
ENEMIES
Senroh Chigusa
A PERSON FROM THE OTHER WORLD WITH AN IMMORTAL BODY. IN ORDER TO CONTINUE FIGHTING, HE NEEDS A SANOME.
SOMEONE HE ABSOLUTELY NEEDS
FEEL THE SAME DESTINY
Sawa Rakan
A KIND-HEARTED HIGH SCHOOL STUDENT WITH A JUNGLE-LIKE GARDEN. HE IS A SANOME, WHICH MEANS HE HAS THE POWER TO MAKE PLANTS GROW. HE AND THE PRINCE ARE IDENTICAL.
ALLIES
EHEH
Koh
Shigeka Narushige
THE FIRST MAN IN THE SHIGEKA FAMILY, SO OTHERS CONSIDER HIM A BAD OMEN. ACCOMPANIED BY THE SNAKE, KOH.
LIKE AN OLDER BROTHER (SISTER?!) AND LITTLE BROTHER
IMPORTANT FRIEND
Tohno Tohji
WAS USED BY THE PRINCE. AN "EXPENDABLE" NUMBERED CHILD.
Sae
A NUMBERED CHILD.
MOTHER AND CHILD
THE SHIGEKA FAMILY
Shigeyuki
THE HEAD OF THE SHIGEKA FAMILY
PARALLEL WORLD-- FRONTIER REGION
IMPORTANT FRIEND
Kazuhi
DE FACTO LEADER
Akiichi
A NUMBERED CHILD.
FRONTIER GUARDS NOW KNOWN AS THE SANOME PRINCE'S PERSONAL GUARDS
*Sanome - A person with the power to make plants grow.
Ayame - A person or thing that wilts plants and turns soil into sand.

WHEN CHIGUSA, A PERSON FROM ANOTHER WORLD, FALLS INTO RAKAN'S GARDEN, HE CALLS RAKAN, WHO CAN MAKE PLANTS GROW, A SANOME AND CLAIMS TO NEED HIM. LATER, NARUSHIGE AND KOH, AND ALSO TOHJI, AN ASSASSIN SENT BY KINREI, DROP IN AS WELL. AFTER RAKAN AND THE OTHERS CAPTURE TOHJI, THEY FIND OUT THAT ALL FOUR OF THEM WERE SENT TO THIS WORLD BECAUSE THEY WERE DEEMED TROUBLESOME. SUDDENLY, THE IMPERIAL PRINCE OF THE PARALLEL WORLD AND KINREI APPEAR. BECAUSE RAKAN FEELS STRONG TIES TO THE OTHER WORLD, HE GOES THERE TO FIND OUT MORE ABOUT HIMSELF AND HELP CHIGUSA RECOVER HIS MISSING EMOTIONS. THE FIRST PEOPLE HE MEETS THERE ARE KAZUHI AND HIS BANDITS. RAKAN BEFRIENDS THEM, AND THEY BEGIN THEIR QUEST TOGETHER TO COVER THE WORLD WITH GREEN PLANTS AGAIN. MEANWHILE, AT THE IMPERIAL CAPITAL, THE PRINCE HAS MADE ANOTHER PROPHECY. AS THE PROPHECY, "THE LAND WILL SHATTER..." IS FULFILLED, RAKAN AND THE OTHERS FIND THEMSELVES UNDER ATTACK. AFTER FINALLY BEING ABLE TO CONFIRM THE SAFETY OF KAZUHI AND THE GUARDS WHO FELL INTO A CREVASSE, RAKAN CONTINUES FORWARD. THE LANTERN FLOWERS BLOOMING ALONG THE PATH HE WALKS BECOME A ROAD OF LIGHT.

FOR MORE DETAILS, PLEASE READ VOLUMES 1-6!!

—STORY & CAST—

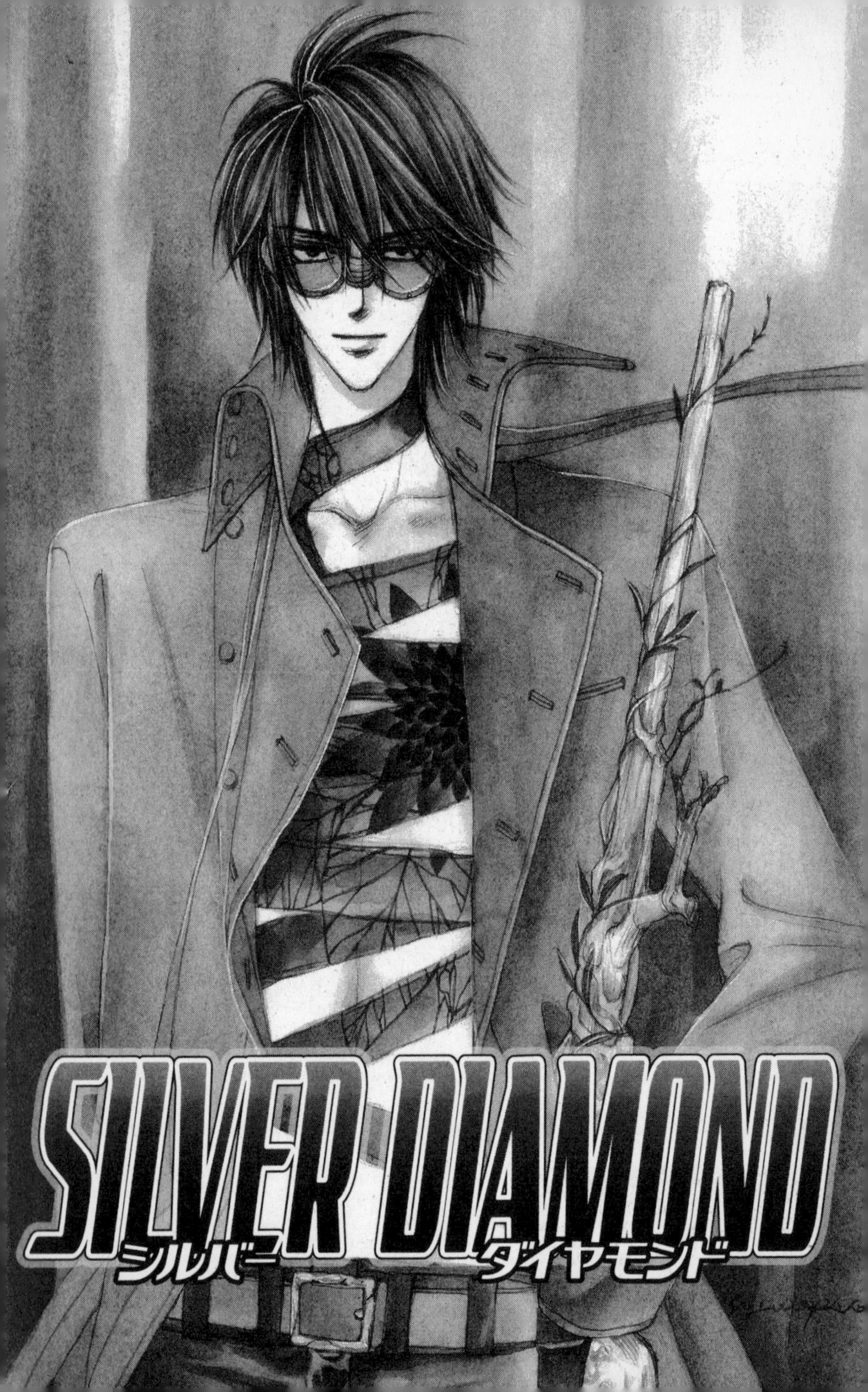
SILVER DIAMOND
シルバーダイヤモンド

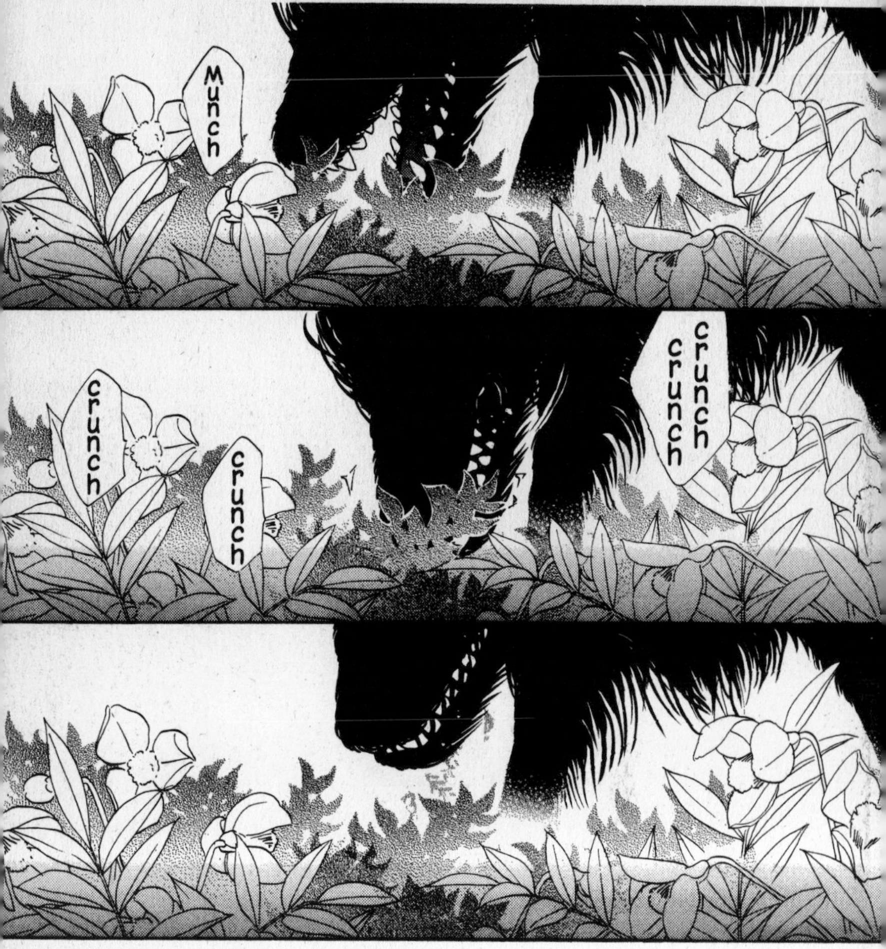
Munch
crunch crunch
crunch
crunch

Stone Wolf

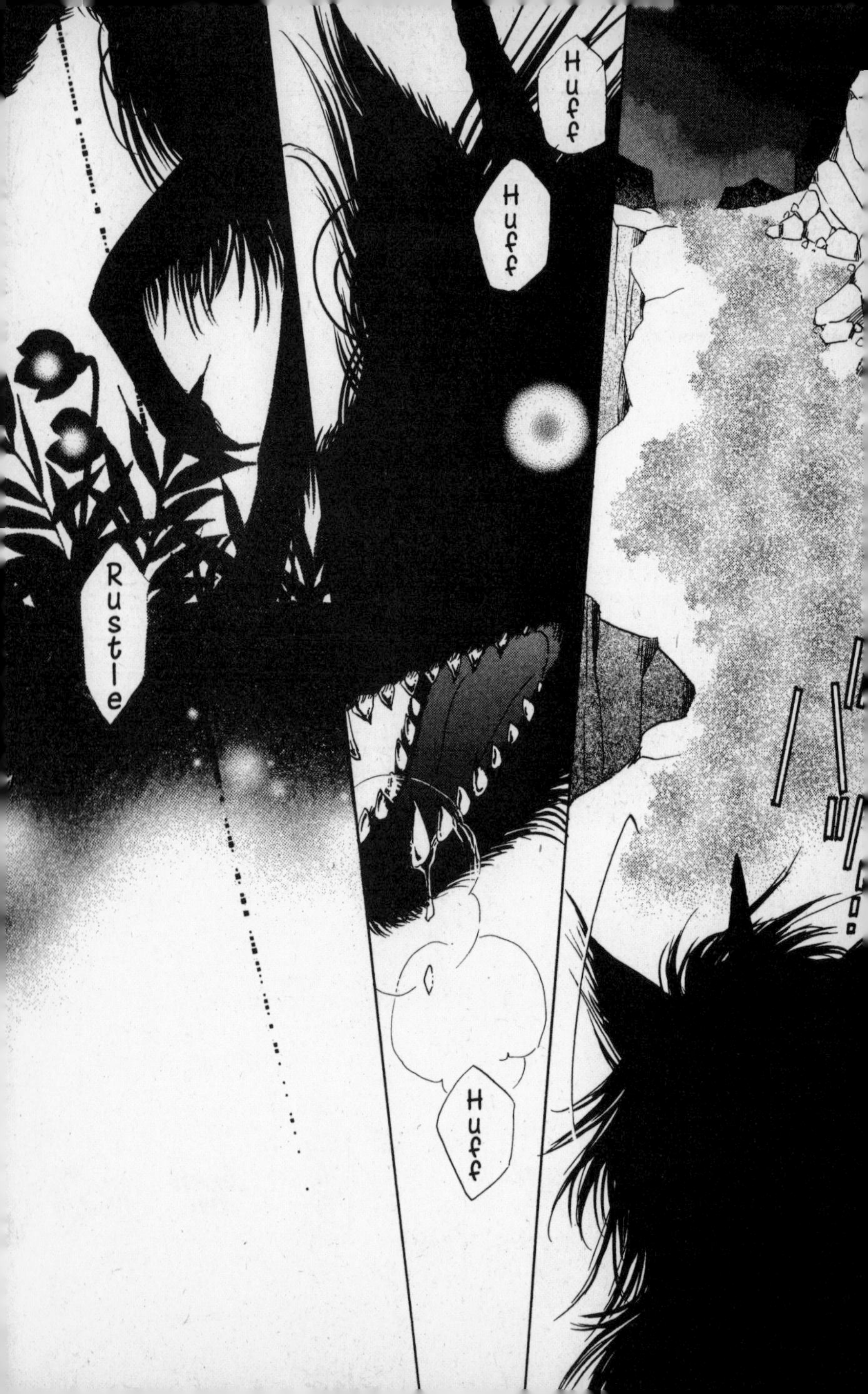
Huff
Huff
Huff
Rustle

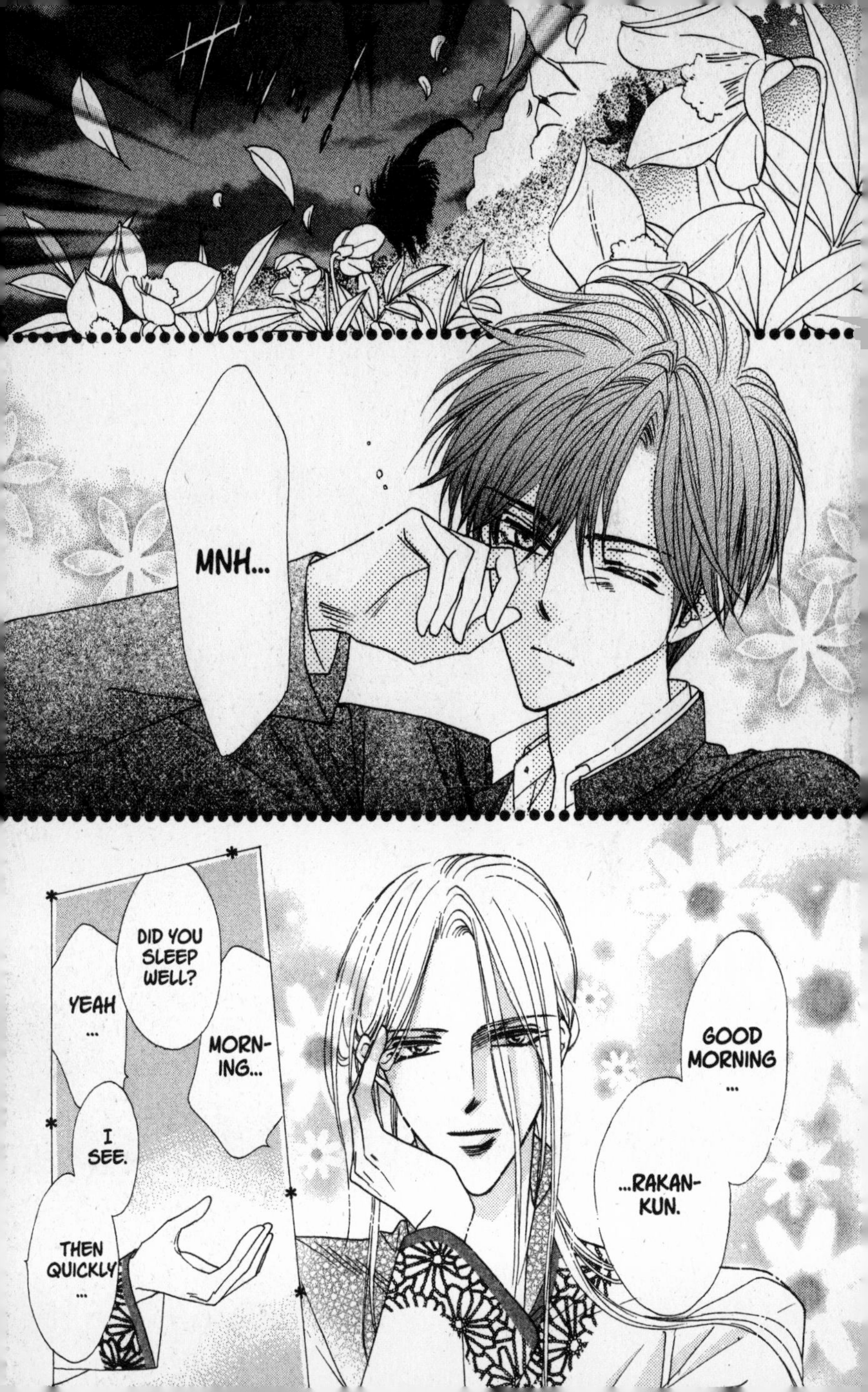
MNH...
GOOD MORNING ...
...RAKAN-KUN.
MORN-ING...
DID YOU SLEEP WELL?
YEAH ...
I SEE.
THEN QUICKLY ...

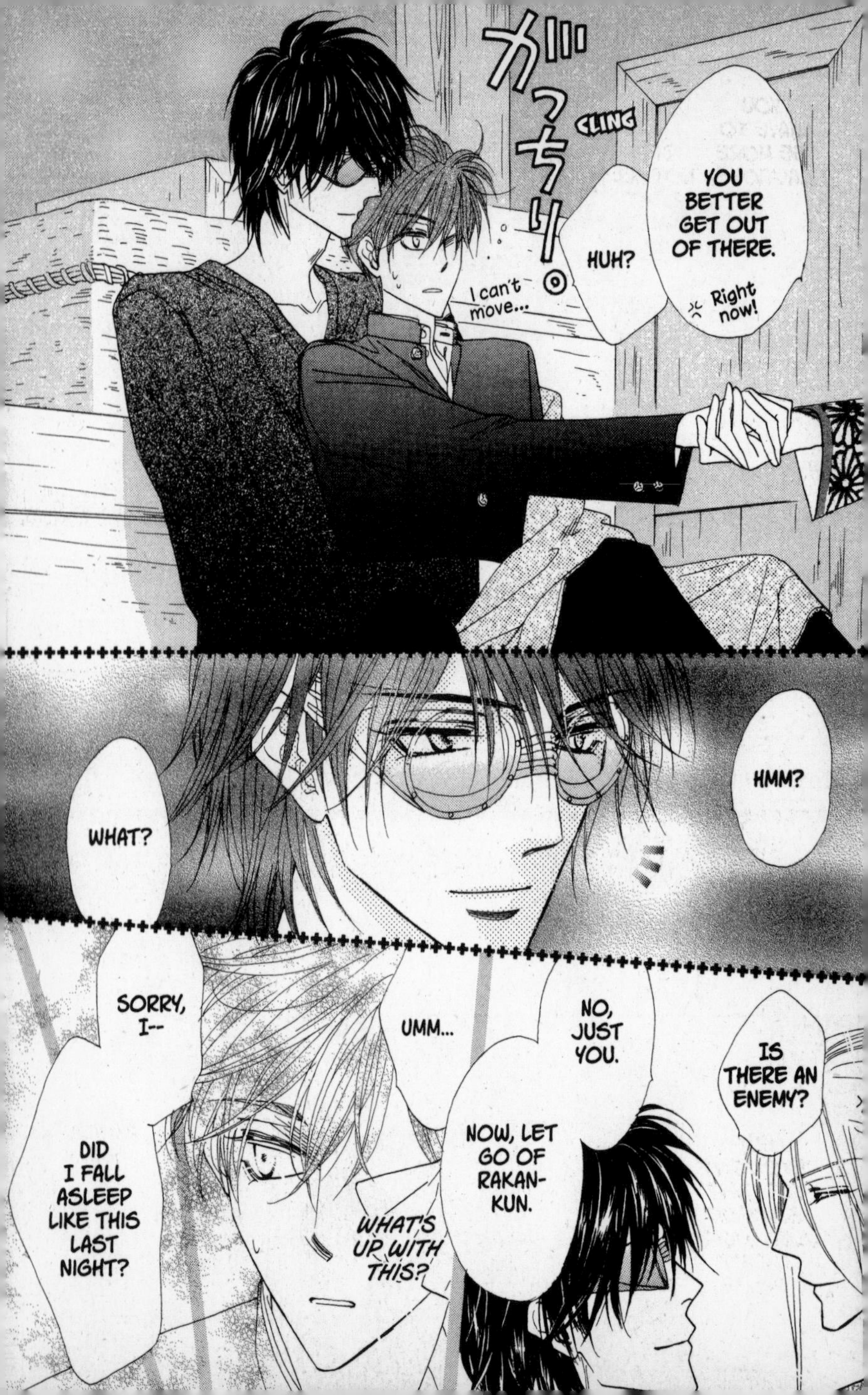
ガっちり
CLING
YOU BETTER GET OUT OF THERE.
Right now!
HUH?
I can't move...
HMM?
WHAT?
IS THERE AN ENEMY?
NO, JUST YOU.
NOW, LET GO OF RAKAN-KUN.
UMM...
SORRY, I--
WHAT'S UP WITH THIS?
DID I FALL ASLEEP LIKE THIS LAST NIGHT?

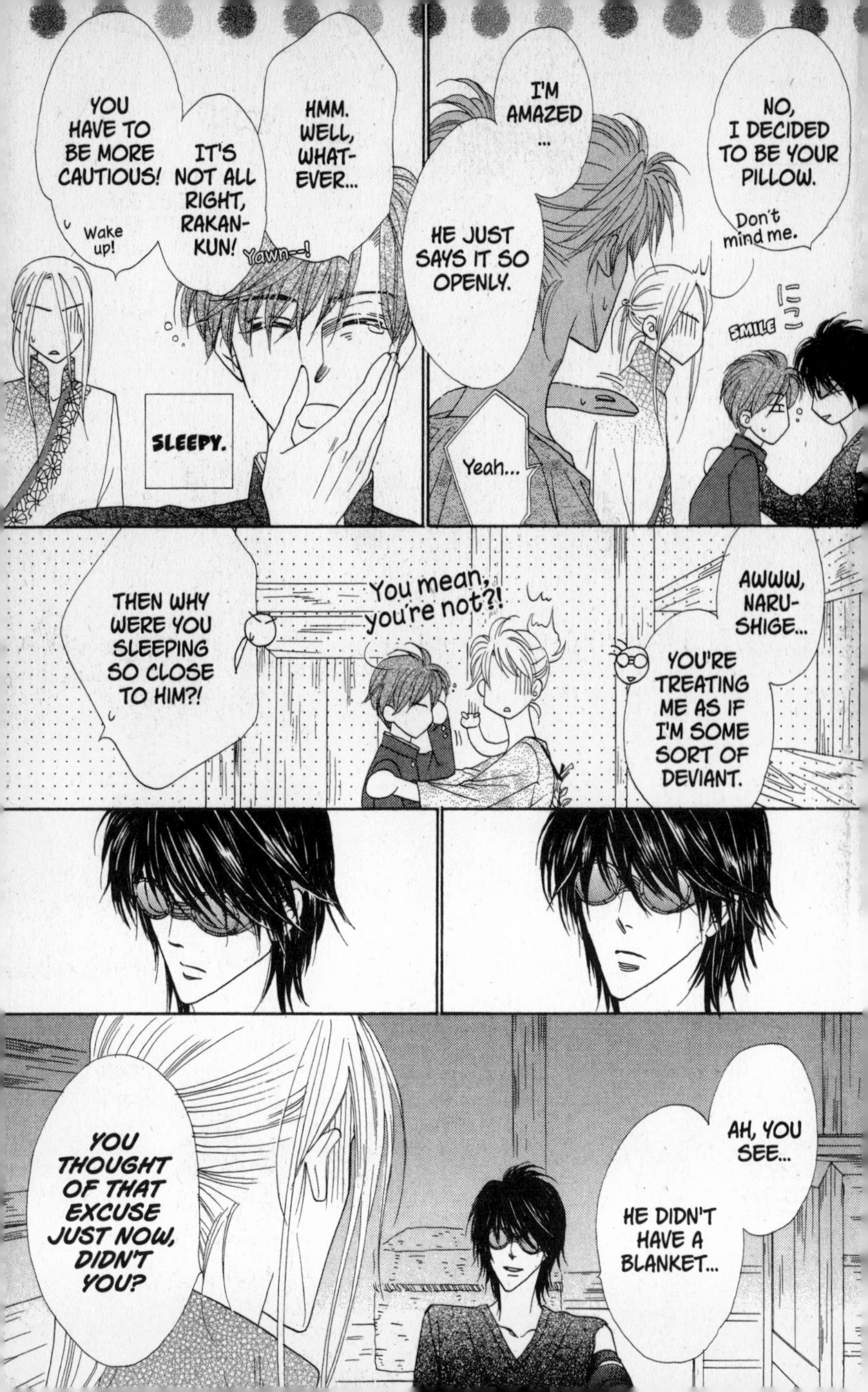
NO, I DECIDED TO BE YOUR PILLOW.
Don't mind me.
SMILE
I'M AMAZED...
HE JUST SAYS IT SO OPENLY.
Yeah...
HMM. WELL, WHAT-EVER...
IT'S NOT ALL RIGHT, RAKAN-KUN!
YOU HAVE TO BE MORE CAUTIOUS!
Yawn--!
Wake up!
SLEEPY.
AWWW, NARU-SHIGE...
YOU'RE TREATING ME AS IF I'M SOME SORT OF DEVIANT.
You mean, you're not?!
THEN WHY WERE YOU SLEEPING SO CLOSE TO HIM?!
AH, YOU SEE...
HE DIDN'T HAVE A BLANKET...
YOU THOUGHT OF THAT EXCUSE JUST NOW, DIDN'T YOU?

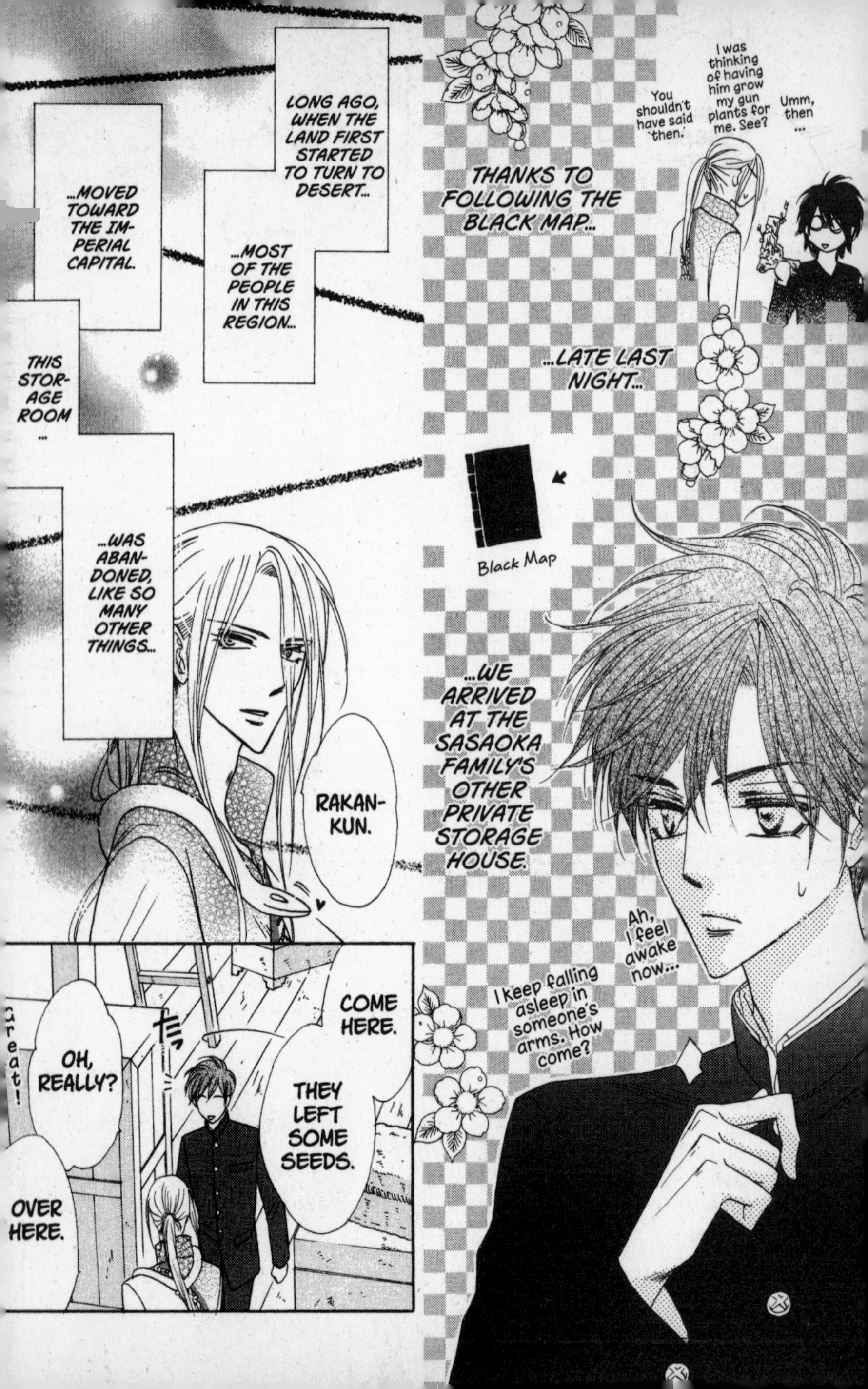

Umm, then ...
I was thinking of having him grow my gun plants for me. See?
You shouldn't have said 'then.'
THANKS TO FOLLOWING THE BLACK MAP...
...LATE LAST NIGHT...
Black Map
...WE ARRIVED AT THE SASAOKA FAMILY'S OTHER PRIVATE STORAGE HOUSE.
Ah, I feel awake now...
I keep falling asleep in someone's arms. How come?
LONG AGO, WHEN THE LAND FIRST STARTED TO TURN TO DESERT...
...MOST OF THE PEOPLE IN THIS REGION...
...MOVED TOWARD THE IMPERIAL CAPITAL.
THIS STORAGE ROOM ...
...WAS ABANDONED, LIKE SO MANY OTHER THINGS...
RAKAN-KUN.
COME HERE.
THEY LEFT SOME SEEDS.
OH, REALLY?
OVER HERE.
Great!

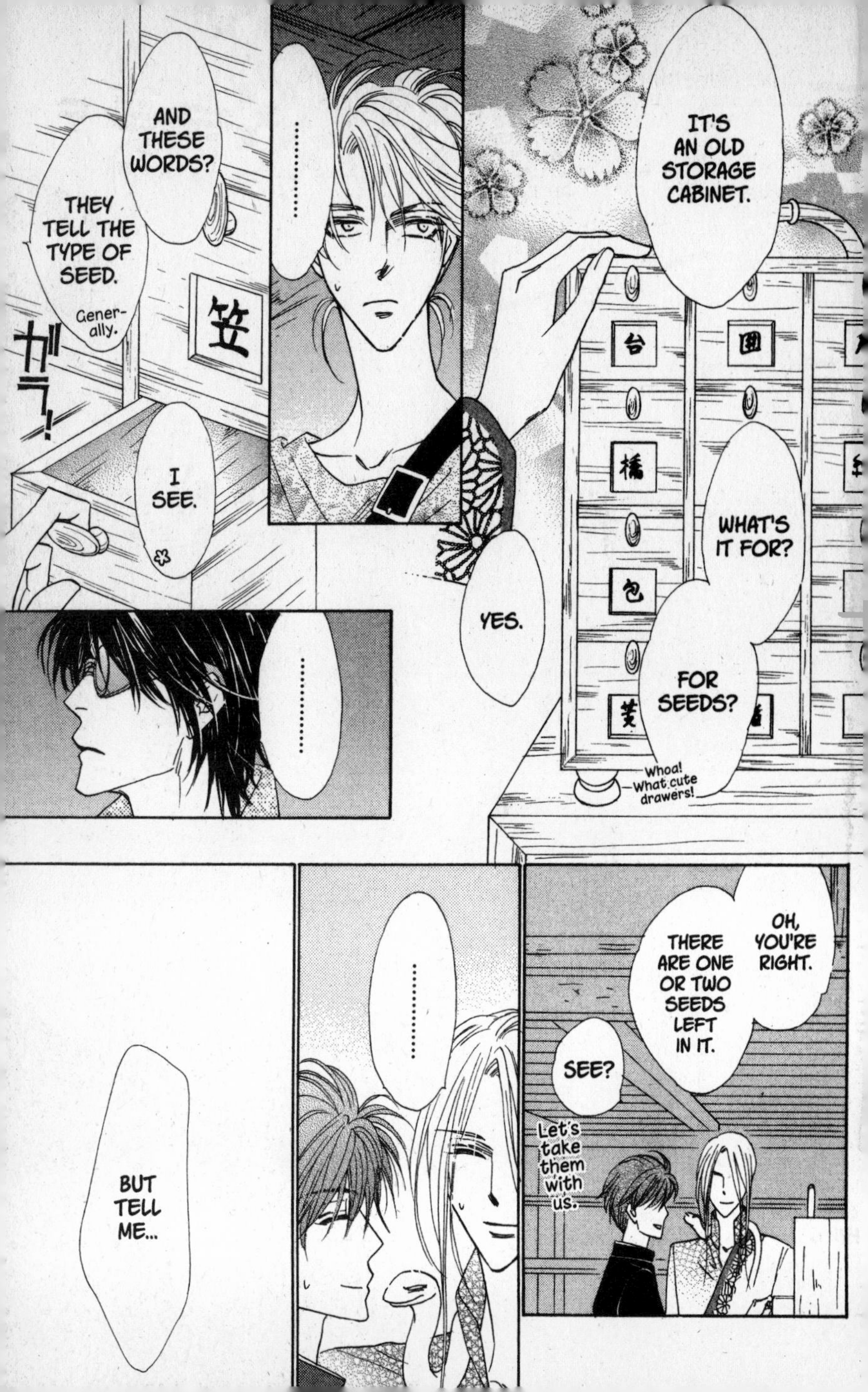
IT'S AN OLD STORAGE CABINET.
WHAT'S IT FOR?
FOR SEEDS?
YES.
Whoa! What cute drawers!
......
AND THESE WORDS?
THEY TELL THE TYPE OF SEED.
Gener-ally.
ガラ!
笠
I SEE.
......
OH, YOU'RE RIGHT.
THERE ARE ONE OR TWO SEEDS LEFT IN IT.
SEE?
Let's take them with us.
......
BUT TELL ME...

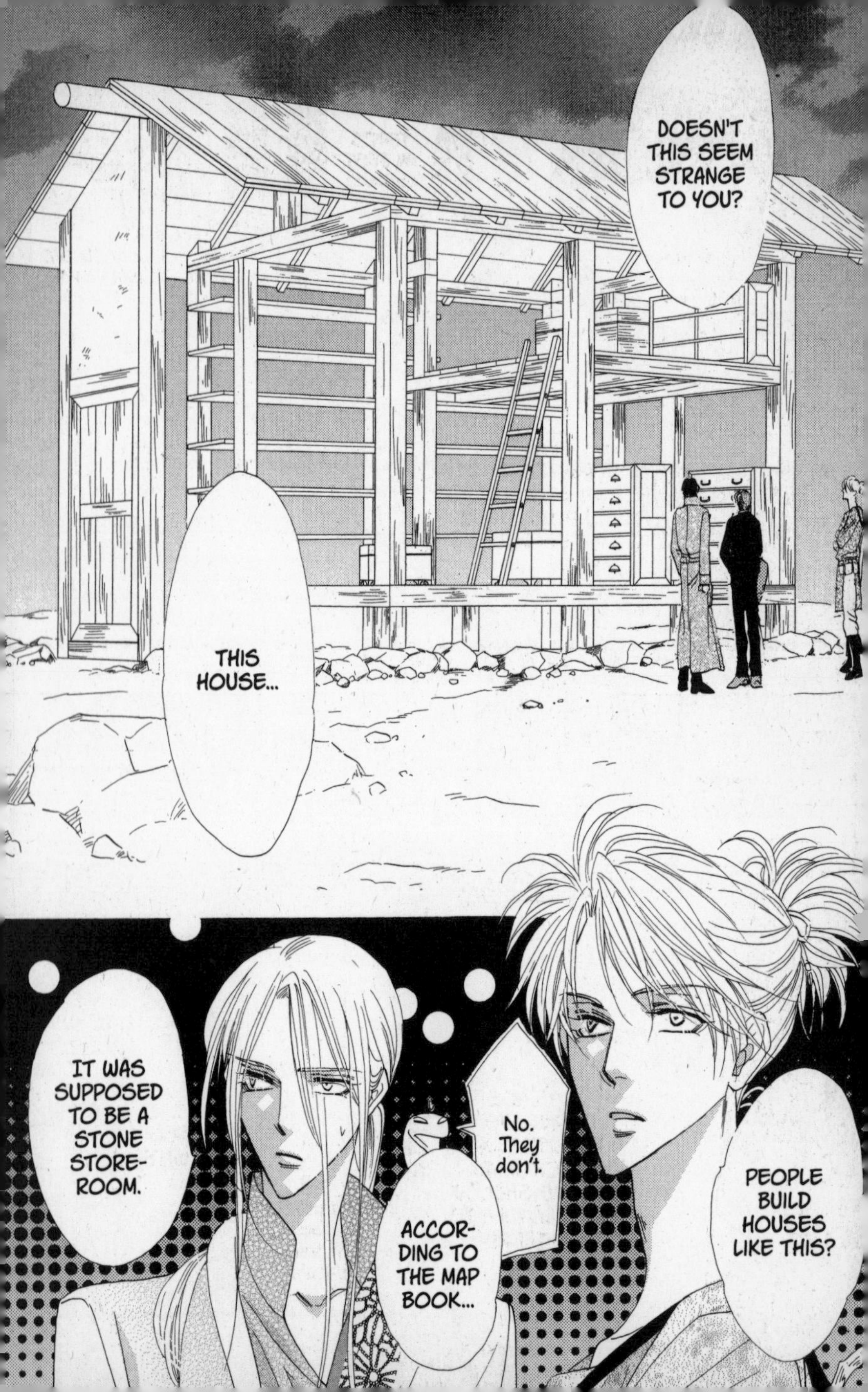
DOESN'T THIS SEEM STRANGE TO YOU?
THIS HOUSE...
PEOPLE BUILD HOUSES LIKE THIS?
No. They don't.
ACCORDING TO THE MAP BOOK...
IT WAS SUPPOSED TO BE A STONE STOREROOM.

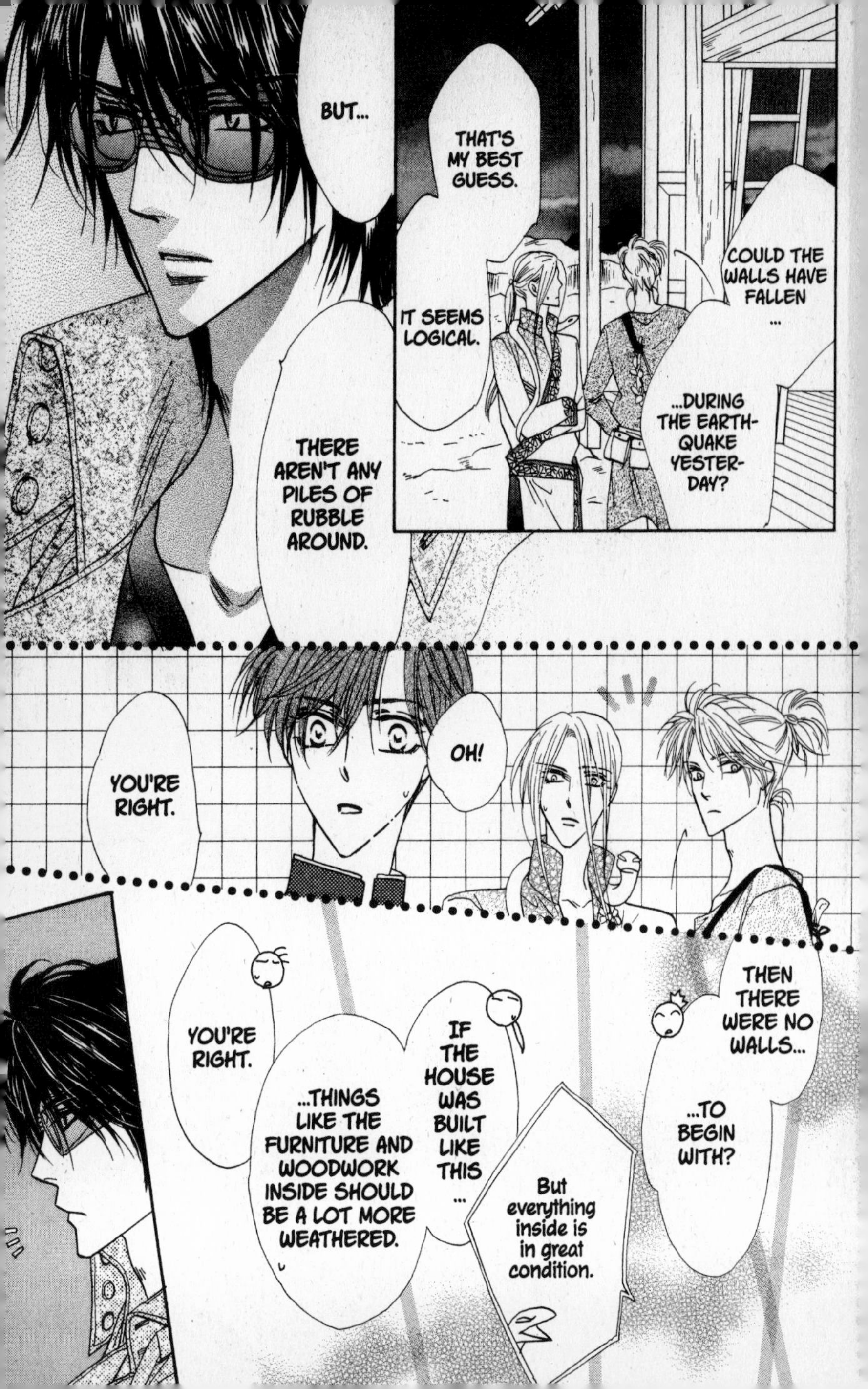
COULD THE WALLS HAVE FALLEN ...
...DURING THE EARTH-QUAKE YESTER-DAY?
THAT'S MY BEST GUESS.
IT SEEMS LOGICAL.
BUT...
THERE AREN'T ANY PILES OF RUBBLE AROUND.
OH!
YOU'RE RIGHT.
THEN THERE WERE NO WALLS...
...TO BEGIN WITH?
But everything inside is in great condition.
IF THE HOUSE WAS BUILT LIKE THIS ...
...THINGS LIKE THE FURNITURE AND WOODWORK INSIDE SHOULD BE A LOT MORE WEATHERED.
YOU'RE RIGHT.

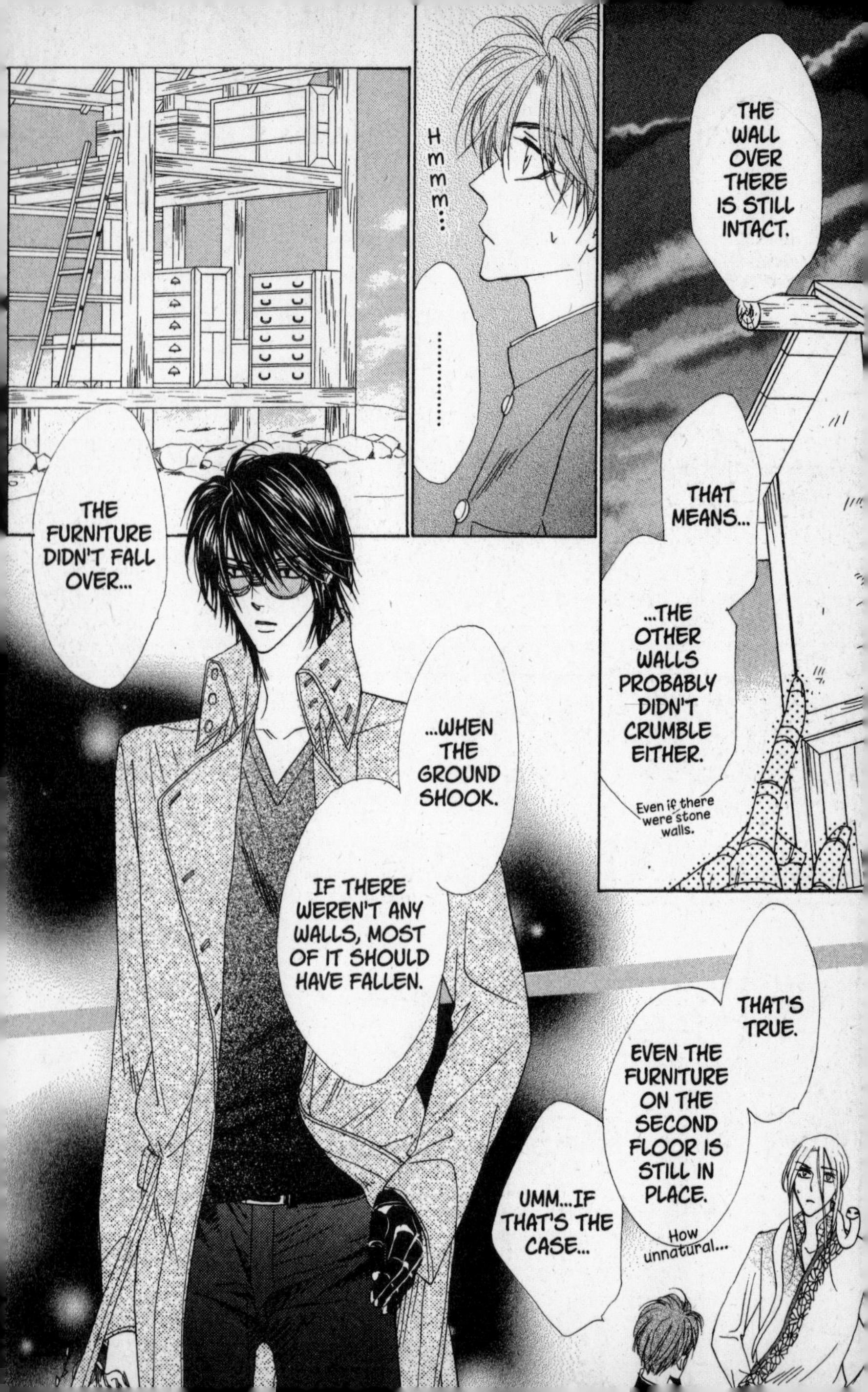
THE WALL OVER THERE IS STILL INTACT.
THAT MEANS...
...THE OTHER WALLS PROBABLY DIDN'T CRUMBLE EITHER.
Even if there were stone walls.
Hmmm...
....
THAT'S TRUE.
EVEN THE FURNITURE ON THE SECOND FLOOR IS STILL IN PLACE.
How unnatural...
UMM...IF THAT'S THE CASE...
THE FURNITURE DIDN'T FALL OVER...
...WHEN THE GROUND SHOOK.
IF THERE WEREN'T ANY WALLS, MOST OF IT SHOULD HAVE FALLEN.

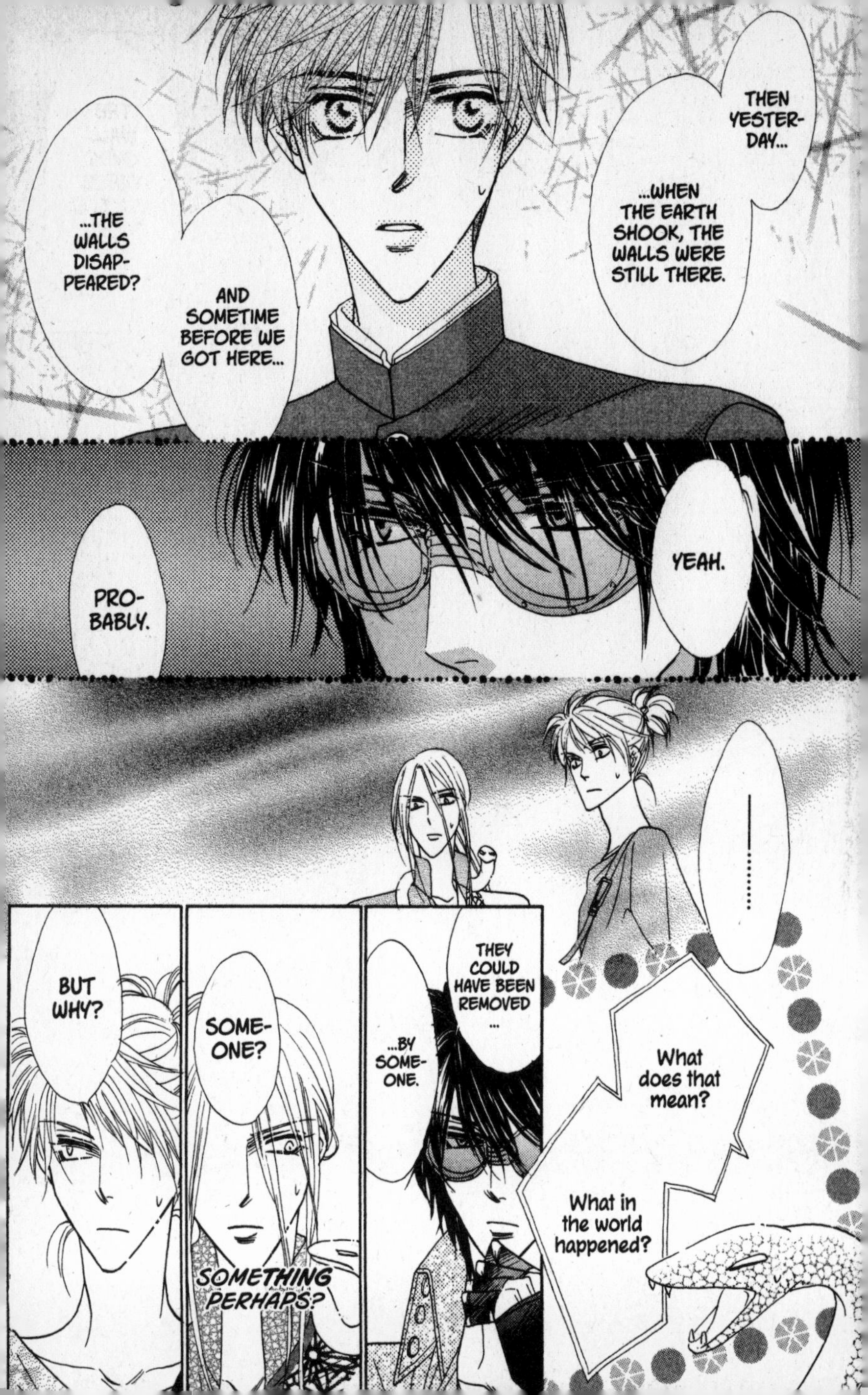
THEN YESTER-DAY...
...WHEN THE EARTH SHOOK, THE WALLS WERE STILL THERE.
AND SOMETIME BEFORE WE GOT HERE...
...THE WALLS DISAP-PEARED?
YEAH.
PRO-BABLY.
—......
What does that mean?
What in the world happened?
THEY COULD HAVE BEEN REMOVED...
...BY SOME-ONE.
SOME-ONE?
SOMETHING PERHAPS?
BUT WHY?

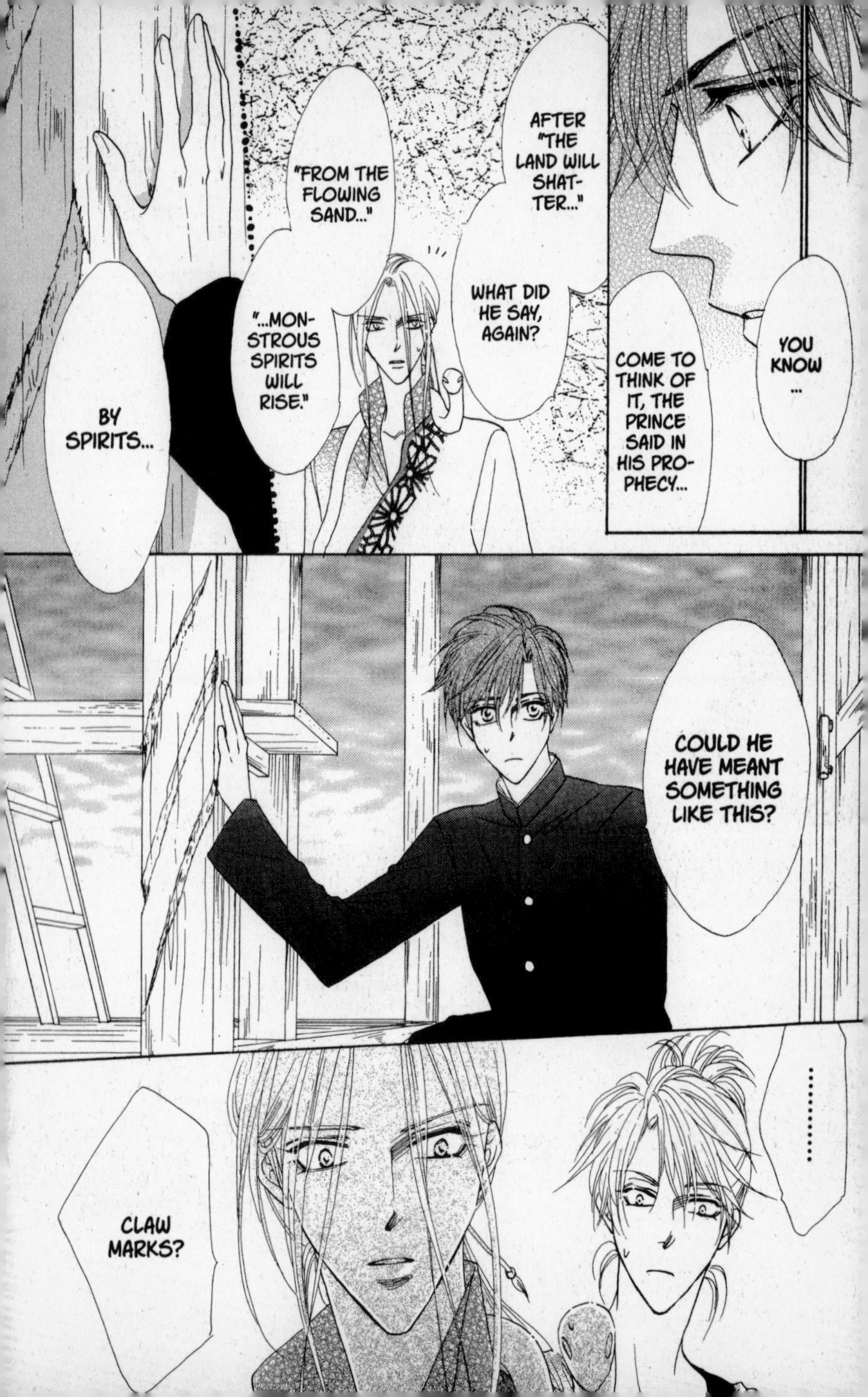
YOU KNOW ...
COME TO THINK OF IT, THE PRINCE SAID IN HIS PROPHECY...
AFTER "THE LAND WILL SHATTER..."
WHAT DID HE SAY, AGAIN?
"FROM THE FLOWING SAND..."
"...MONSTROUS SPIRITS WILL RISE."
BY SPIRITS...
COULD HE HAVE MEANT SOMETHING LIKE THIS?
......
CLAW MARKS?

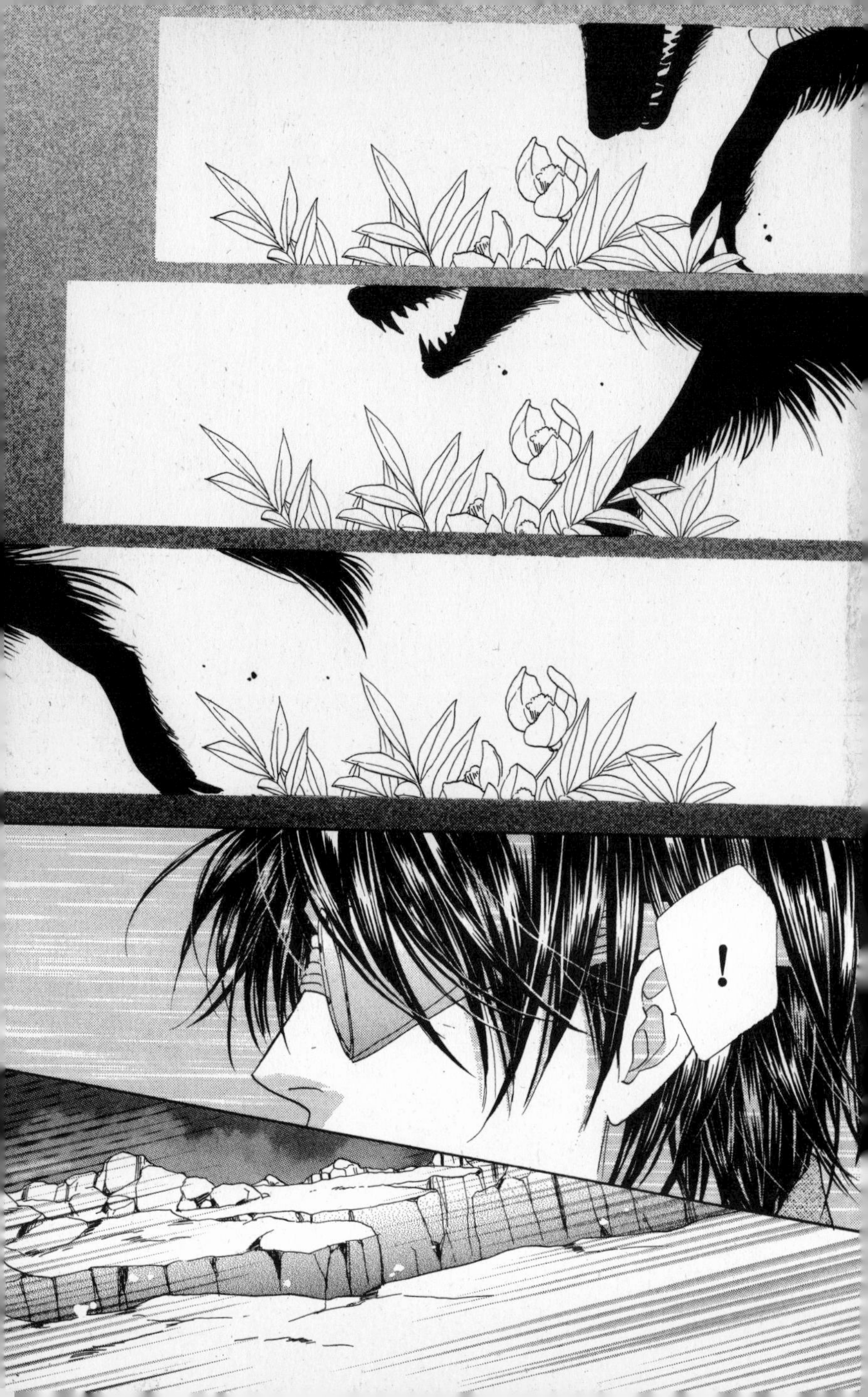
!

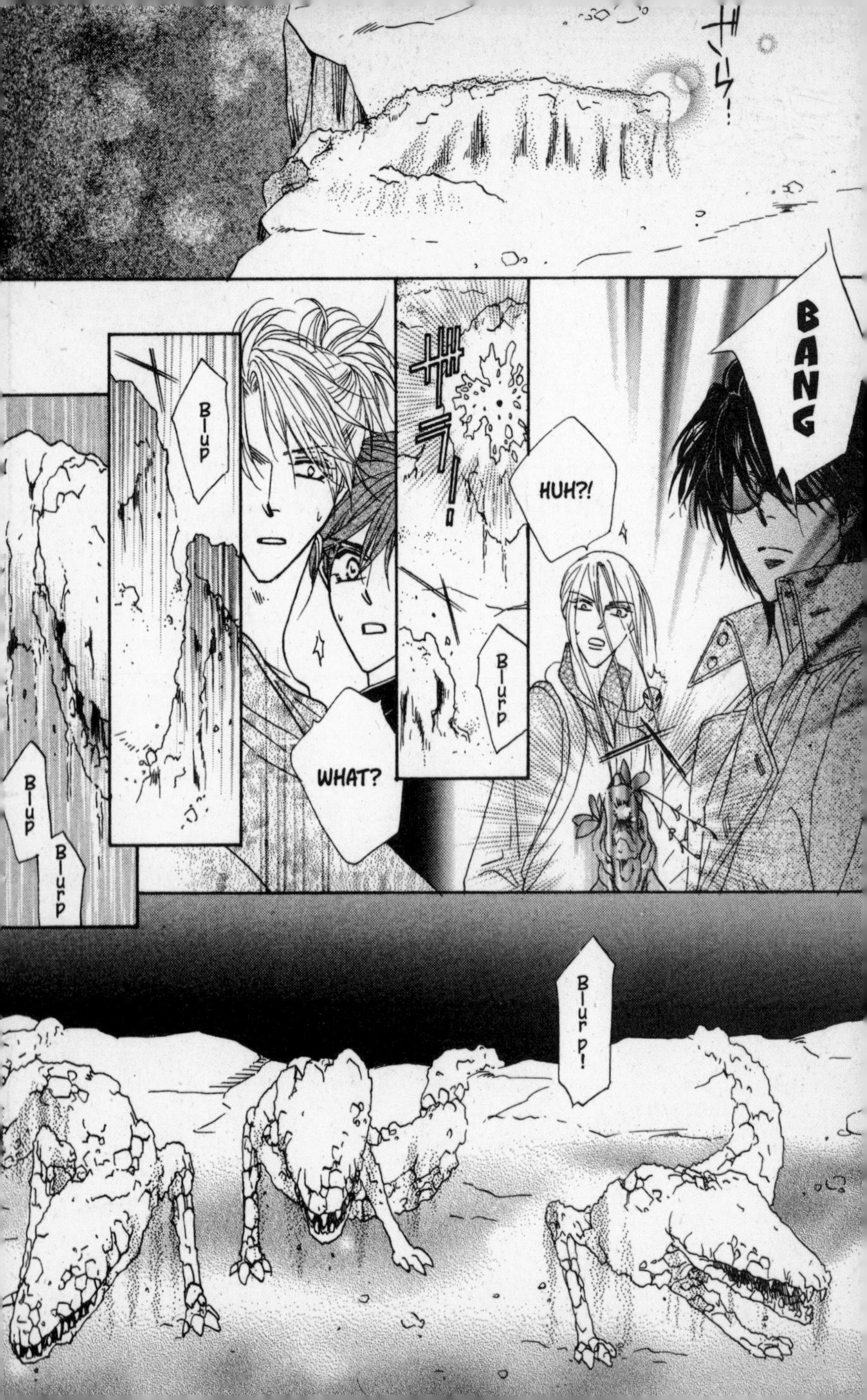

BANG
HUH?!
Blurp
WHAT?
Blup
Blup
Blurp
Blurp!

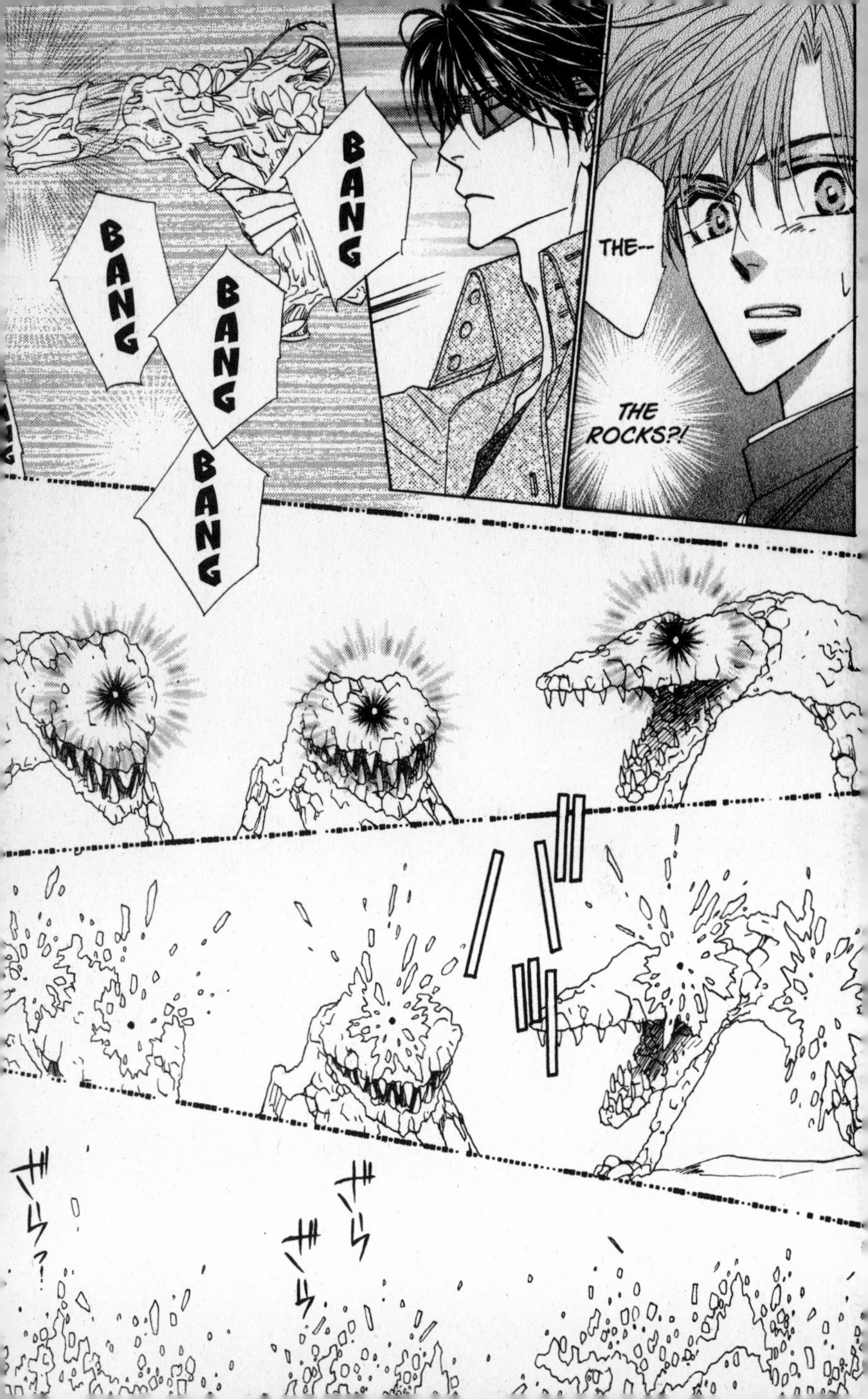
THE--
THE ROCKS?!
BANG
BANG
BANG
BANG

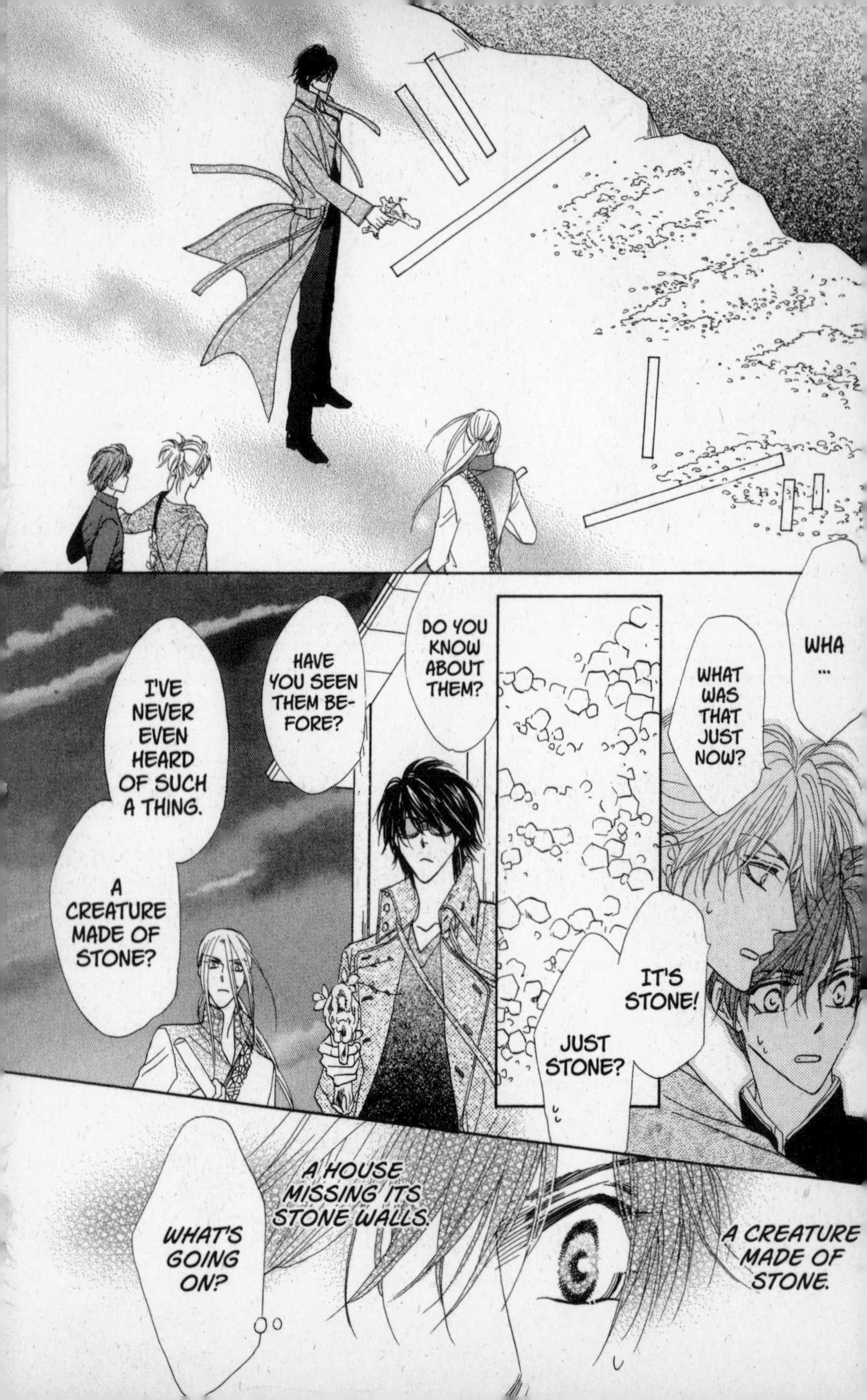
WHA ...
WHAT WAS THAT JUST NOW?
DO YOU KNOW ABOUT THEM?
HAVE YOU SEEN THEM BE-FORE?
I'VE NEVER EVEN HEARD OF SUCH A THING.
IT'S STONE!
JUST STONE?
A CREATURE MADE OF STONE?
A CREATURE MADE OF STONE.
A HOUSE MISSING ITS STONE WALLS.
WHAT'S GOING ON?

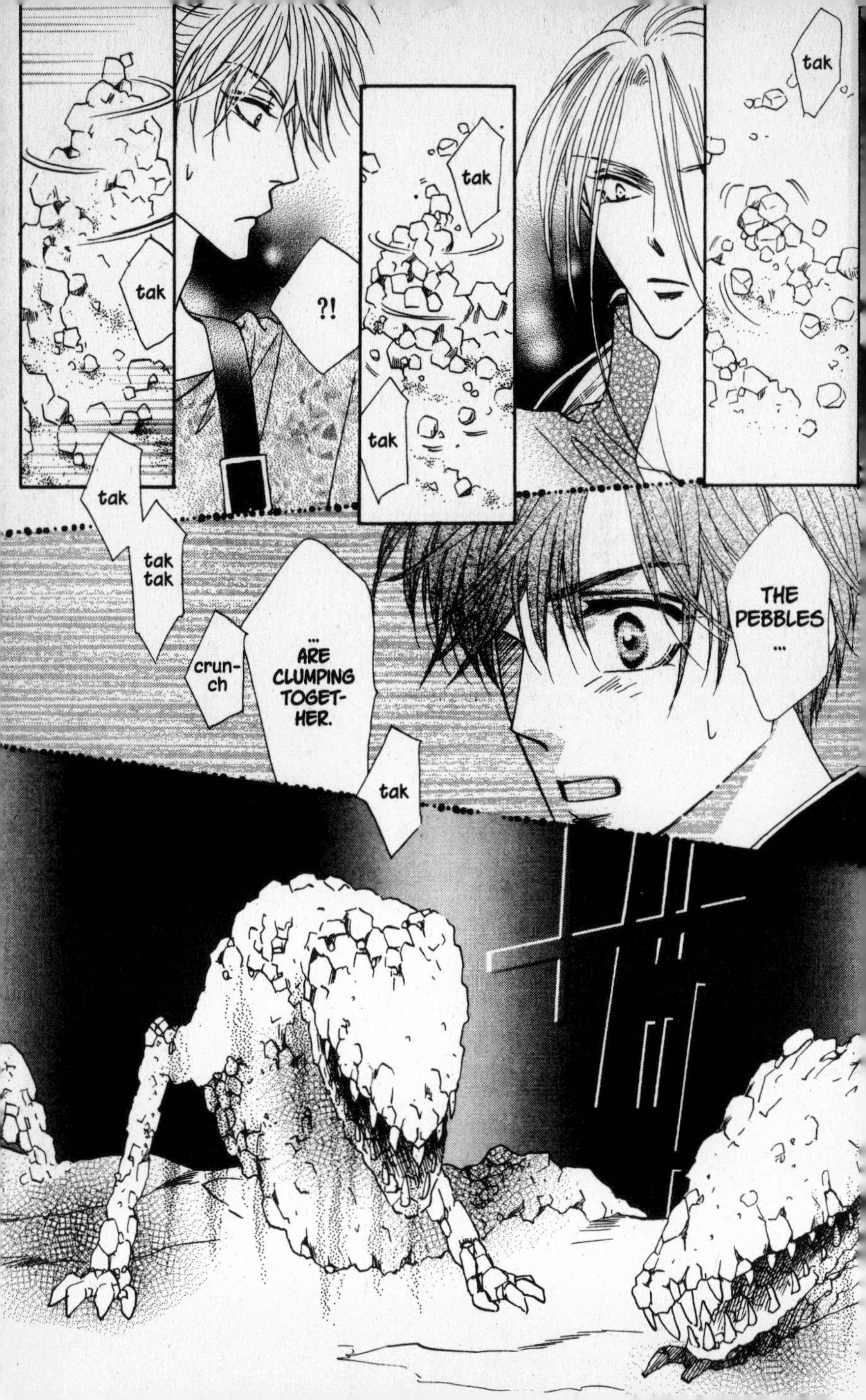
tak
tak
tak
?!
tak
tak
tak
tak
THE PEBBLES ...
... ARE CLUMPING TOGET-HER.
crun-ch
tak

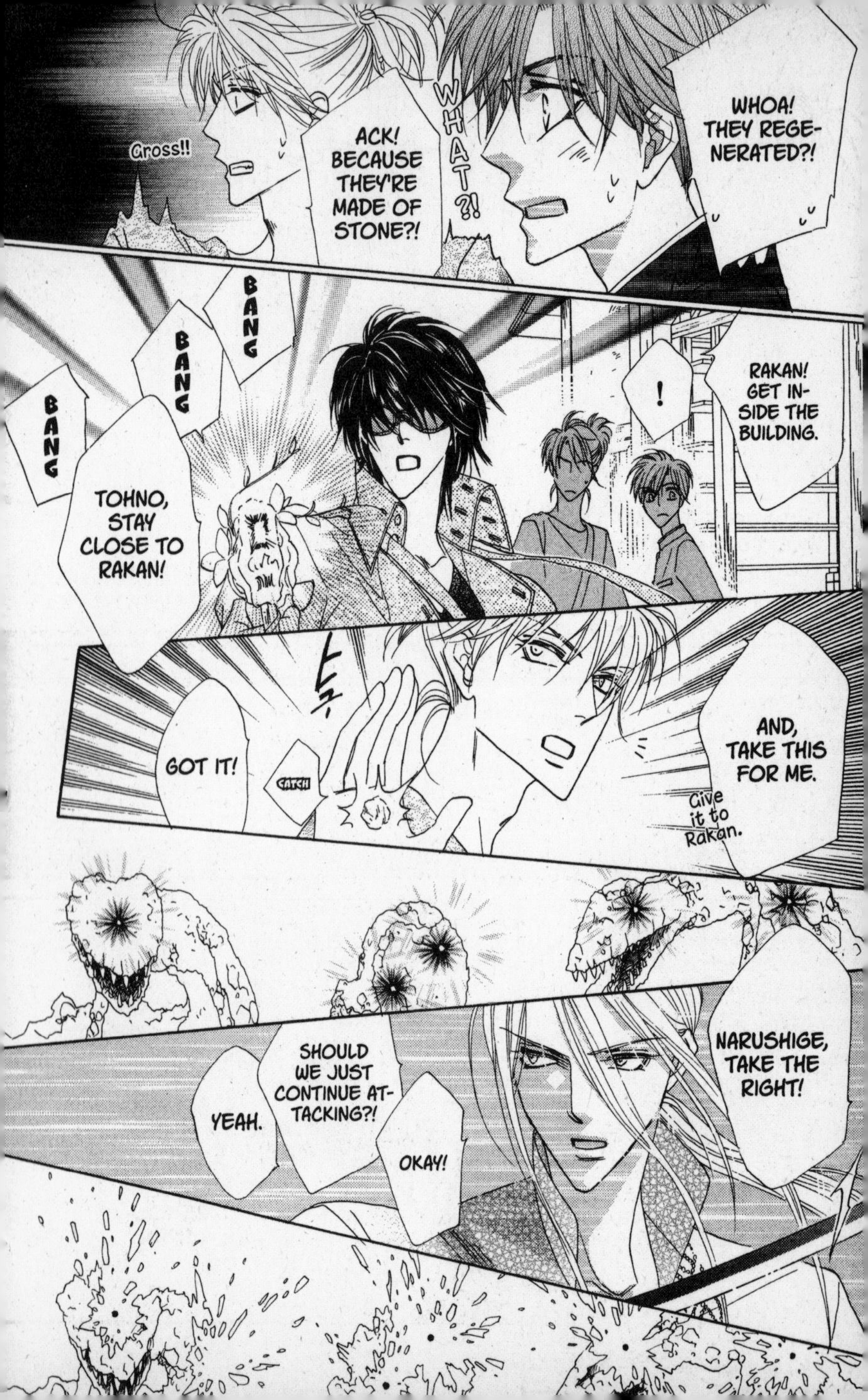
WHOA! THEY REGE- NERATED?!
WHAT?!
ACK! BECAUSE THEY'RE MADE OF STONE?!
Gross!!
RAKAN! GET IN- SIDE THE BUILDING.
!
BANG
BANG
BANG
TOHNO, STAY CLOSE TO RAKAN!
AND, TAKE THIS FOR ME.
Give it to Rakan.
CATCH
GOT IT!
NARUSHIGE, TAKE THE RIGHT!
OKAY!
SHOULD WE JUST CONTINUE AT- TACKING?!
YEAH.

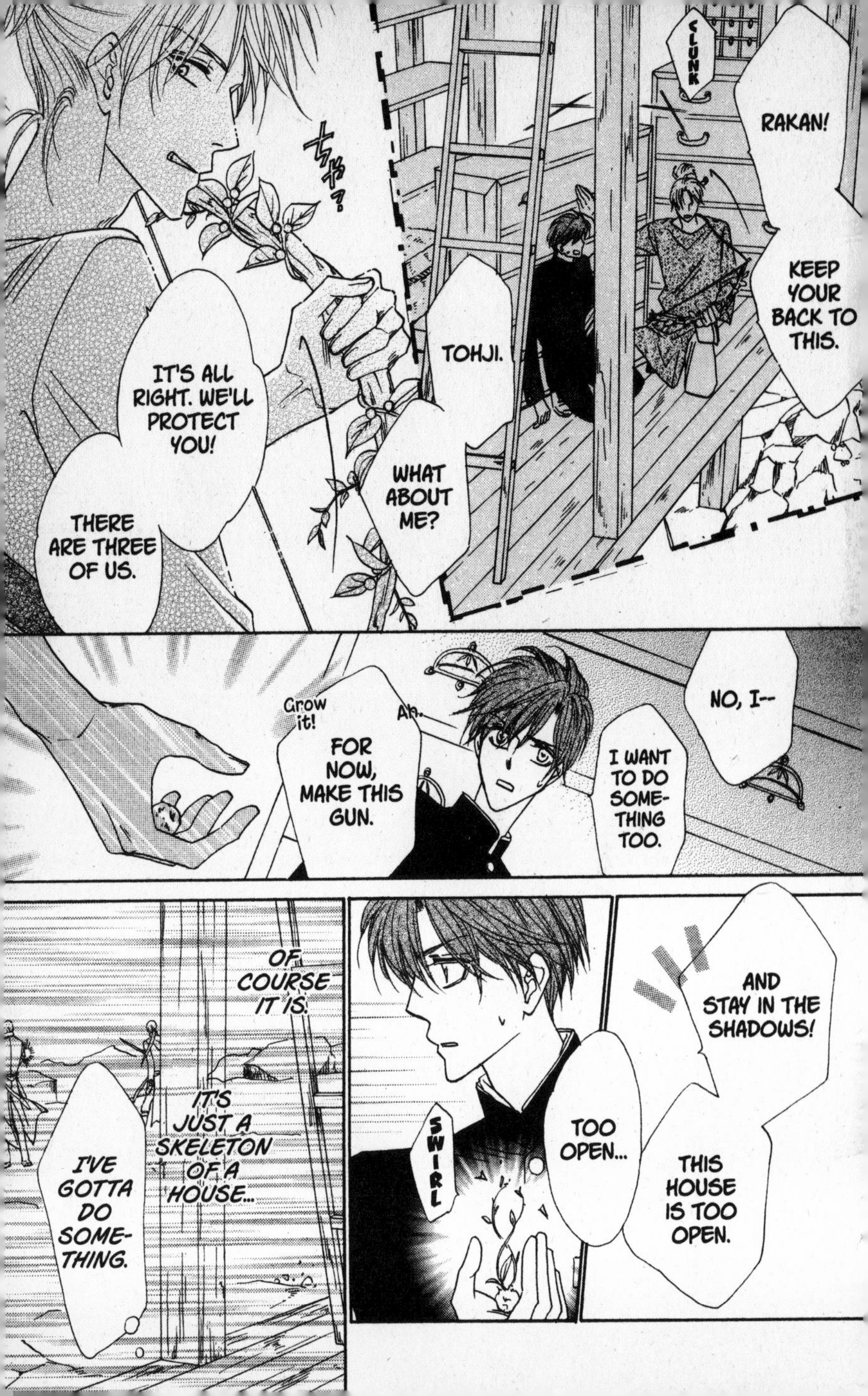
CLUNK
RAKAN!
KEEP YOUR BACK TO THIS.
TOHJI.
WHAT ABOUT ME?
IT'S ALL RIGHT. WE'LL PROTECT YOU!
THERE ARE THREE OF US.
NO, I--
I WANT TO DO SOME-THING TOO.
Ah.
FOR NOW, MAKE THIS GUN.
Grow it!
AND STAY IN THE SHADOWS!
THIS HOUSE IS TOO OPEN.
TOO OPEN...
SWIRL
OF COURSE IT IS.
IT'S JUST A SKELETON OF A HOUSE...
I'VE GOTTA DO SOME-THING.

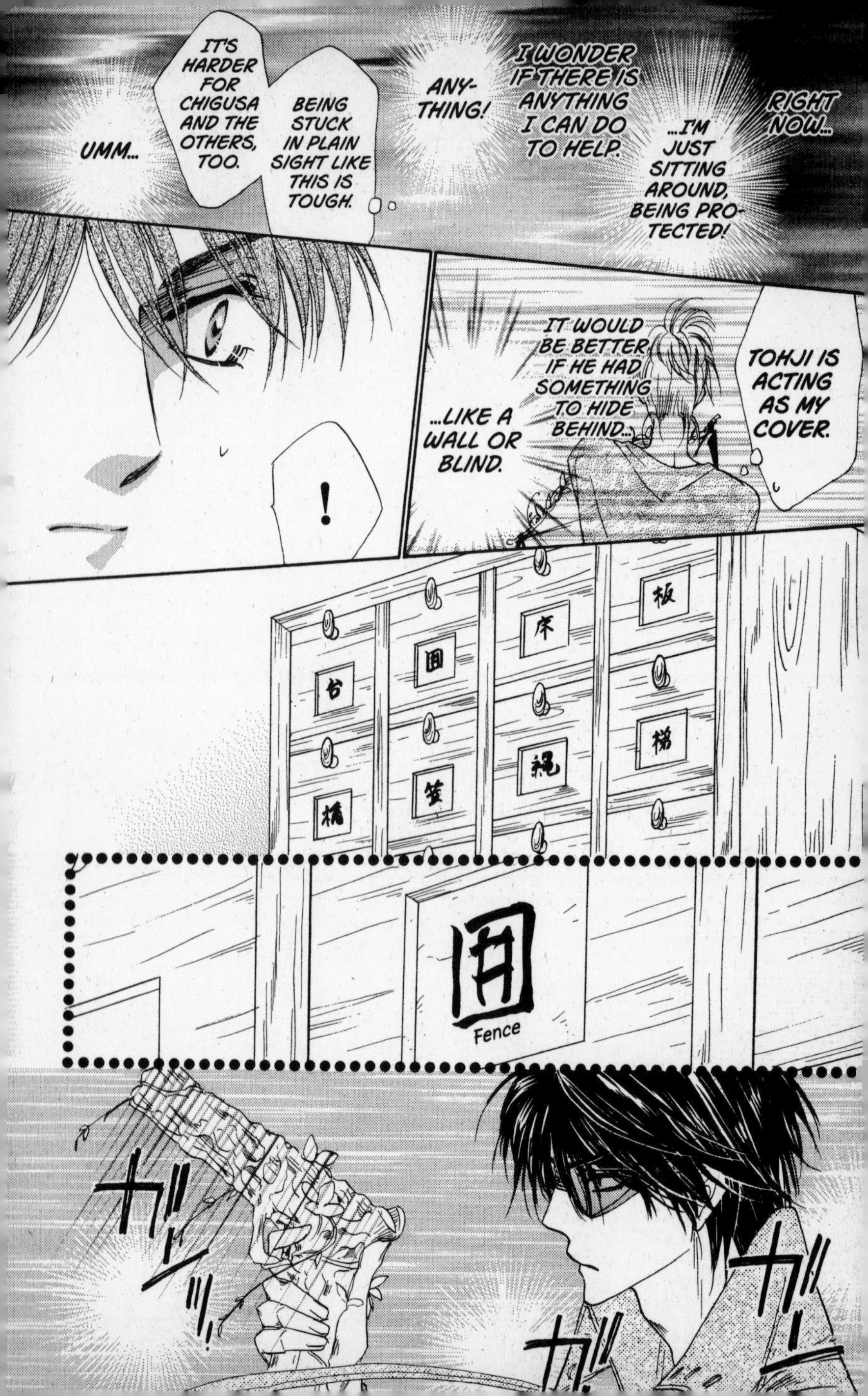
RIGHT NOW...
...I'M JUST SITTING AROUND, BEING PROTECTED!
I WONDER IF THERE IS ANYTHING I CAN DO TO HELP.
ANY-THING!
BEING STUCK IN PLAIN SIGHT LIKE THIS IS TOUGH.
IT'S HARDER FOR CHIGUSA AND THE OTHERS, TOO.
UMM...
TOHJI IS ACTING AS MY COVER.
IT WOULD BE BETTER IF HE HAD SOMETHING TO HIDE BEHIND...
...LIKE A WALL OR BLIND.
!
囲
Fence

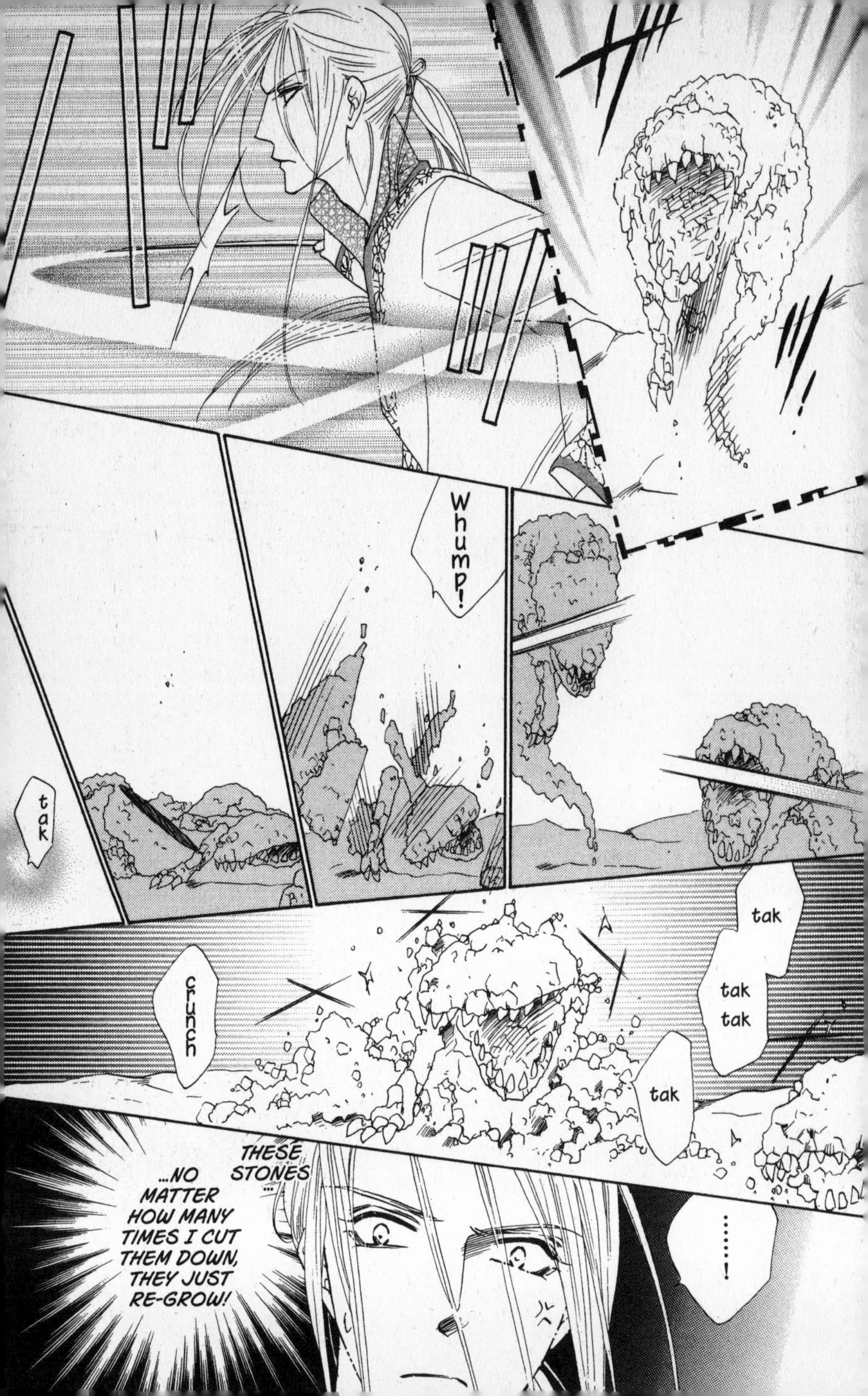
Whump!
tak
tak
tak tak
tak
crunch
......!
THESE STONES...
...NO MATTER HOW MANY TIMES I CUT THEM DOWN, THEY JUST RE-GROW!

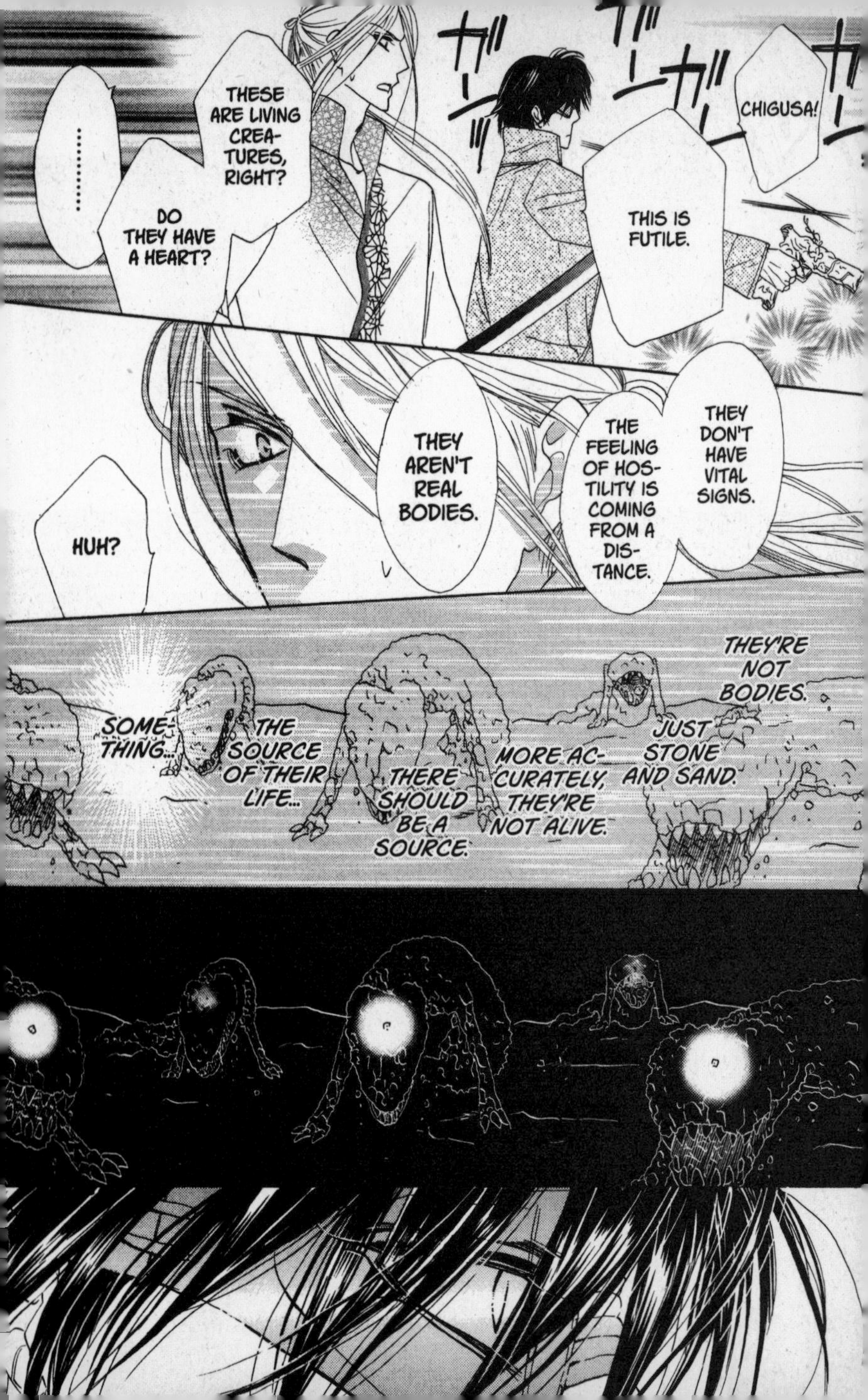

CHIGUSA!
THIS IS FUTILE.
THESE ARE LIVING CREA-TURES, RIGHT?
DO THEY HAVE A HEART?
......
THEY DON'T HAVE VITAL SIGNS.
THE FEELING OF HOS-TILITY IS COMING FROM A DIS-TANCE.
THEY AREN'T REAL BODIES.
HUH?
THEY'RE NOT BODIES.
JUST STONE AND SAND.
MORE AC-CURATELY, THEY'RE NOT ALIVE.
THERE SHOULD BE A SOURCE.
THE SOURCE OF THEIR LIFE...
SOME-THING...

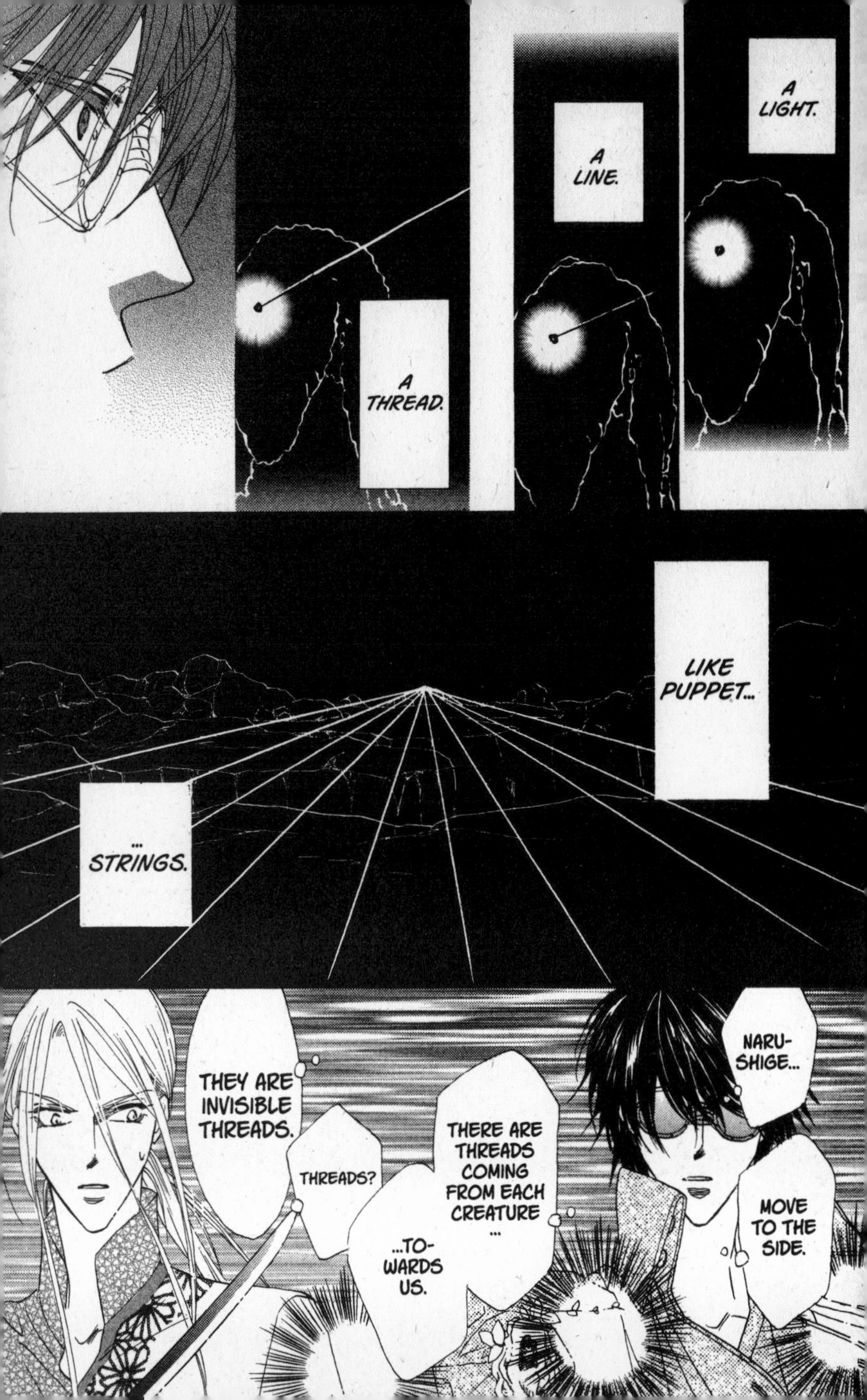
A LIGHT.
A LINE.
A THREAD.
LIKE PUPPET...
...STRINGS.
NARU-SHIGE...
MOVE TO THE SIDE.
THERE ARE THREADS COMING FROM EACH CREATURE ...
...TO-WARDS US.
THREADS?
THEY ARE INVISIBLE THREADS.

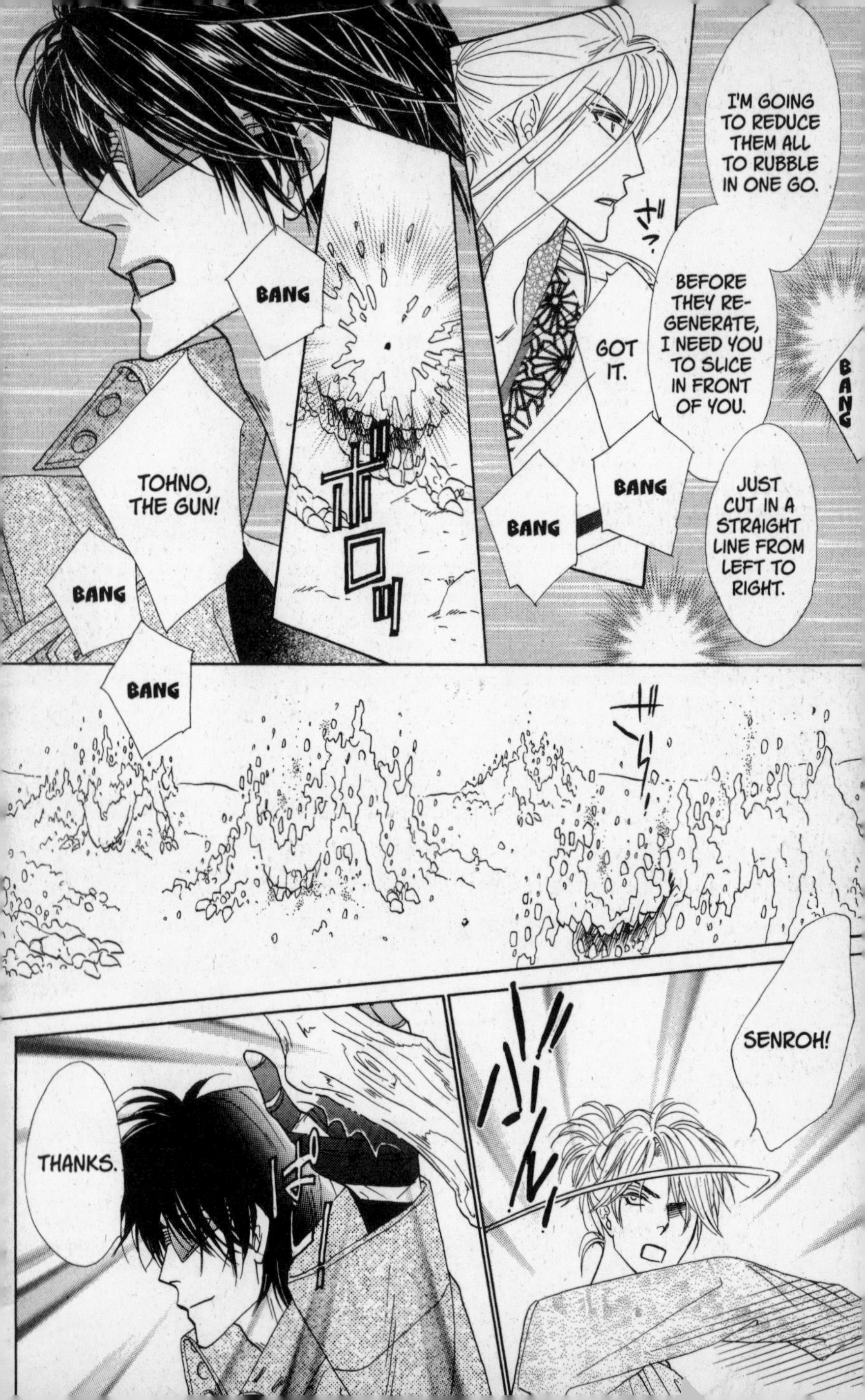

I'M GOING TO REDUCE THEM ALL TO RUBBLE IN ONE GO.
BANG
BEFORE THEY RE-GENERATE, I NEED YOU TO SLICE IN FRONT OF YOU.
GOT IT.
JUST CUT IN A STRAIGHT LINE FROM LEFT TO RIGHT.
BANG
BANG
BANG
TOHNO, THE GUN!
BANG
BANG
SENROH!
THANKS.

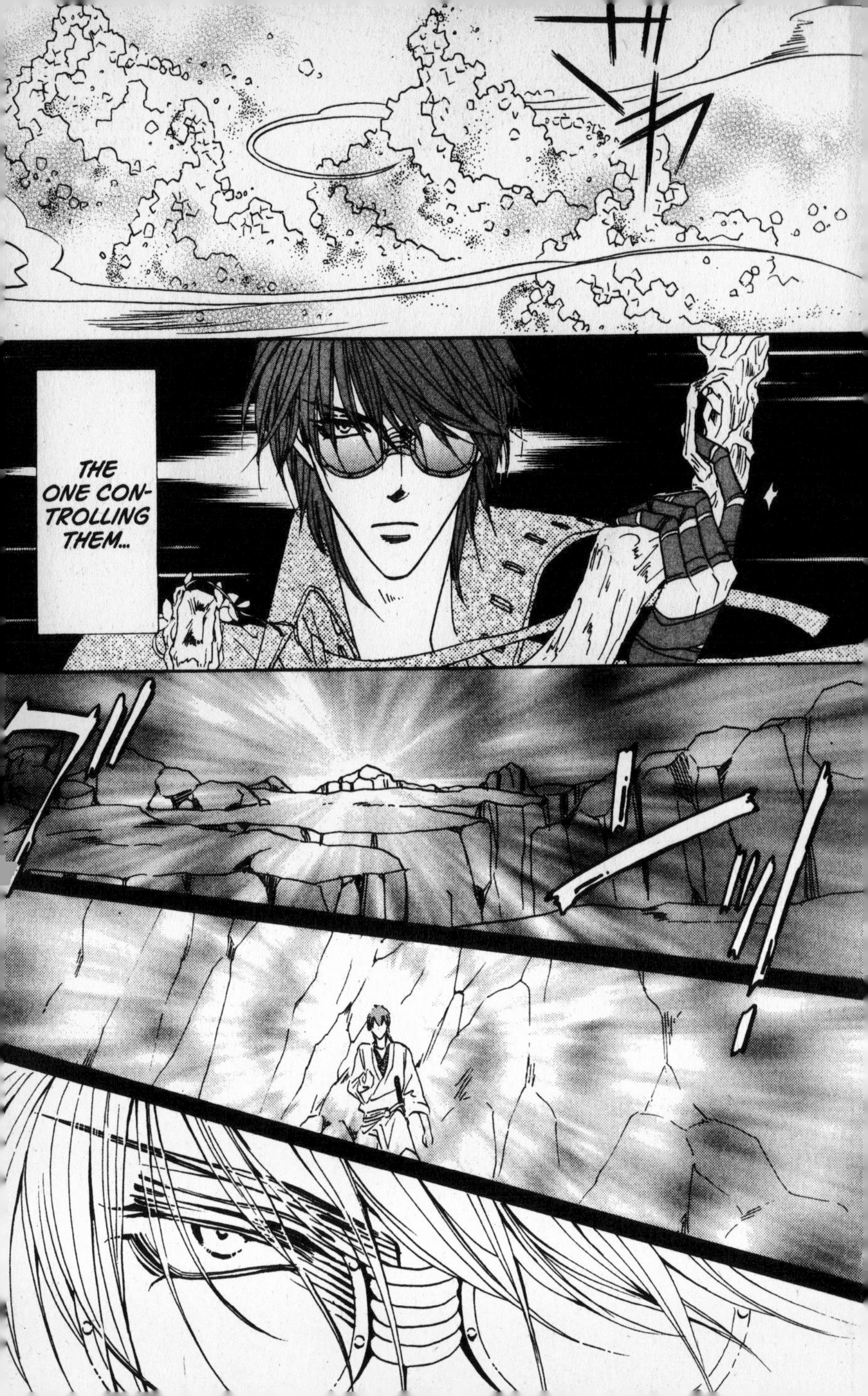
THE ONE CON-TROLLING THEM...

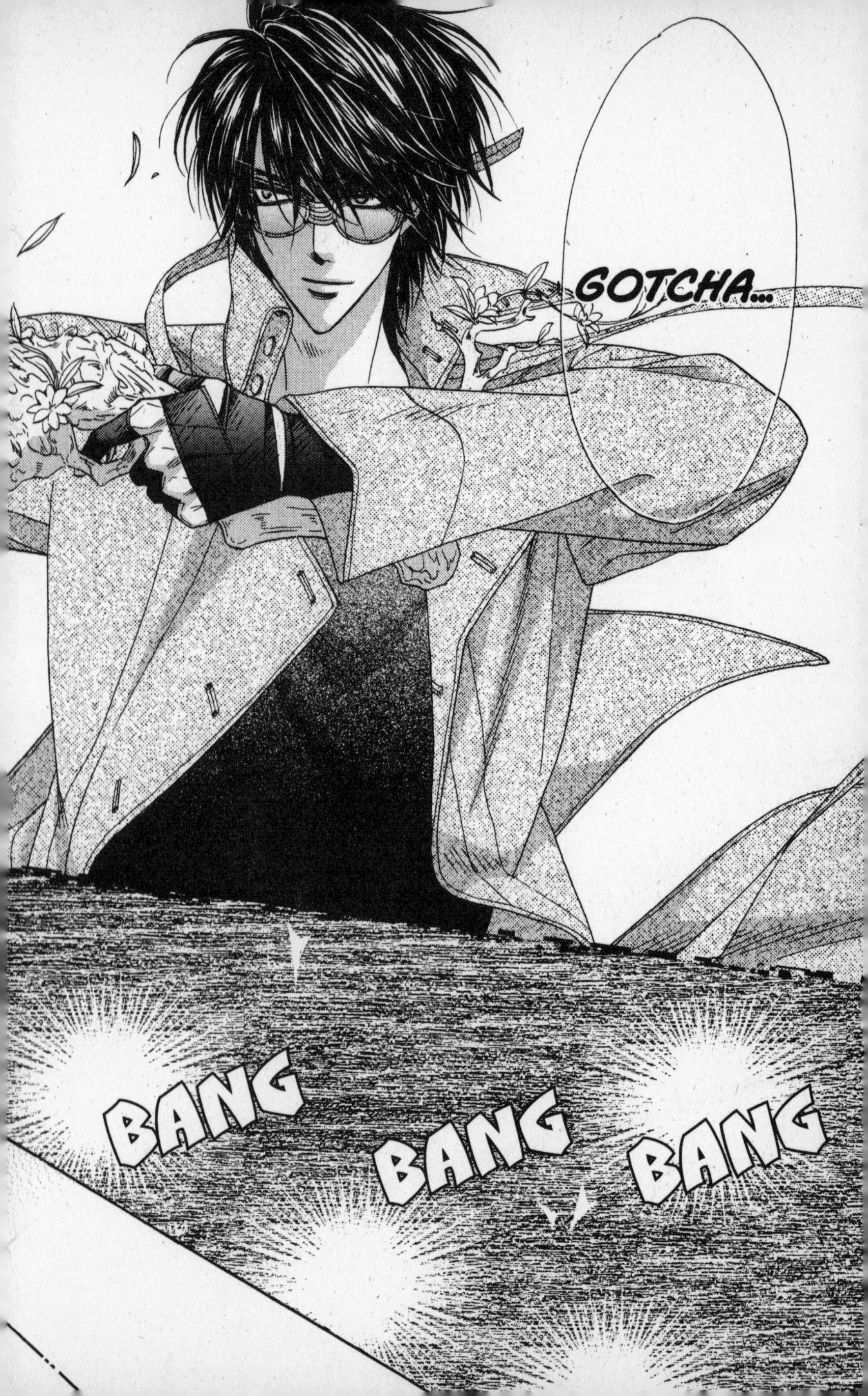
GOTCHA...
BANG
BANG
BANG

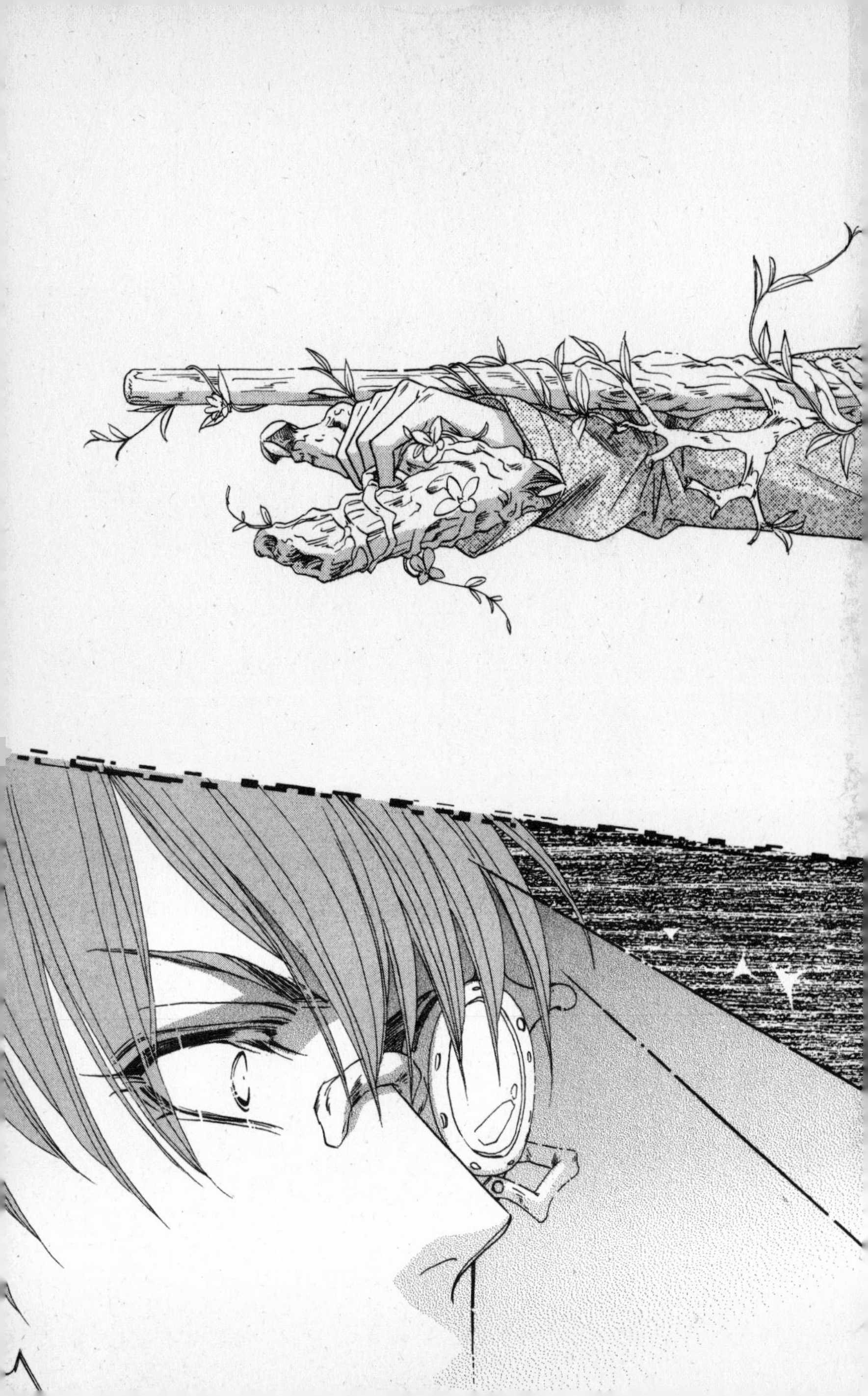

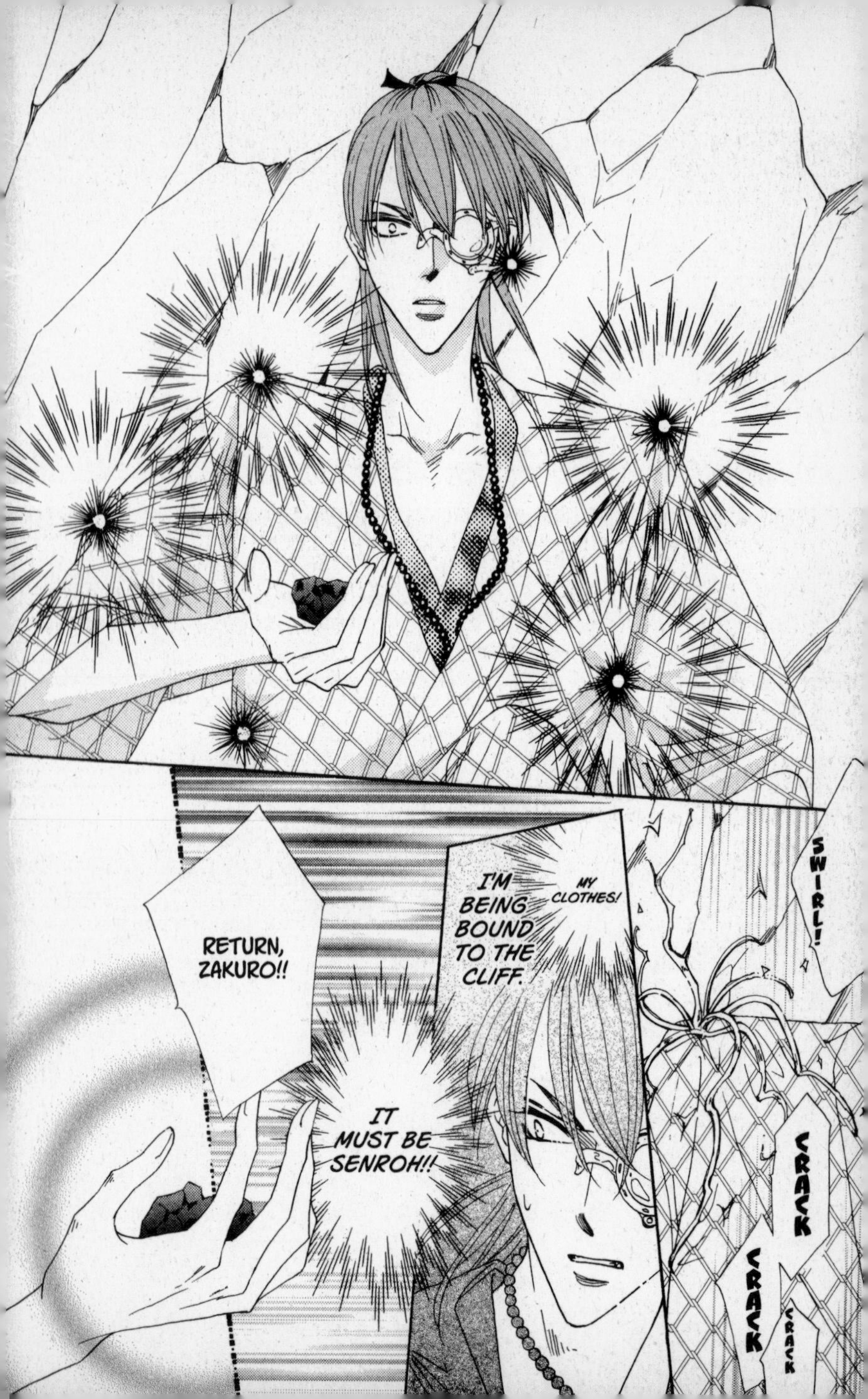
SWIRL!
MY CLOTHES!
I'M BEING BOUND TO THE CLIFF.
RETURN, ZAKURO!!
CRACK
CRACK
CRACK
IT MUST BE SENROH!!

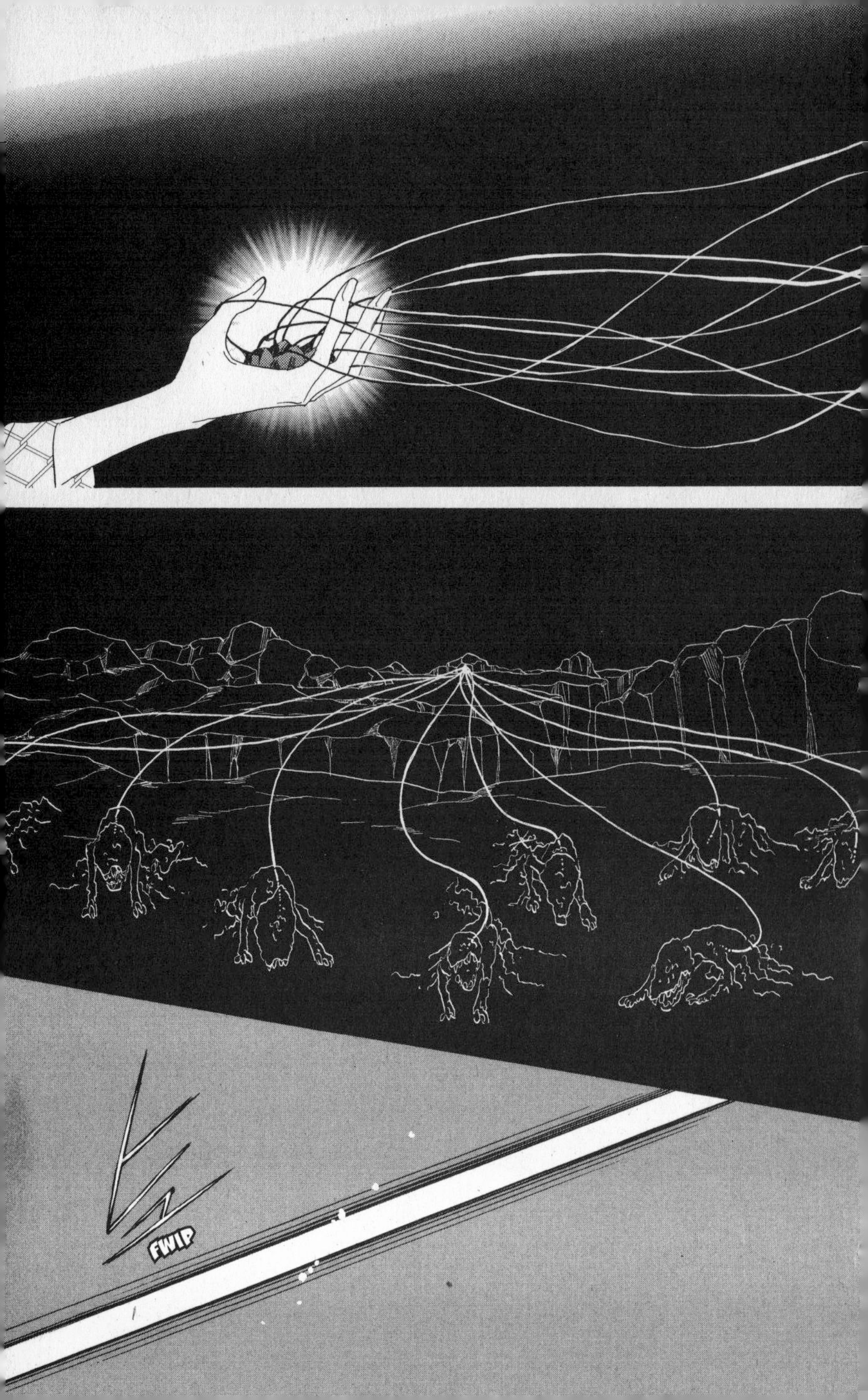
FWIP

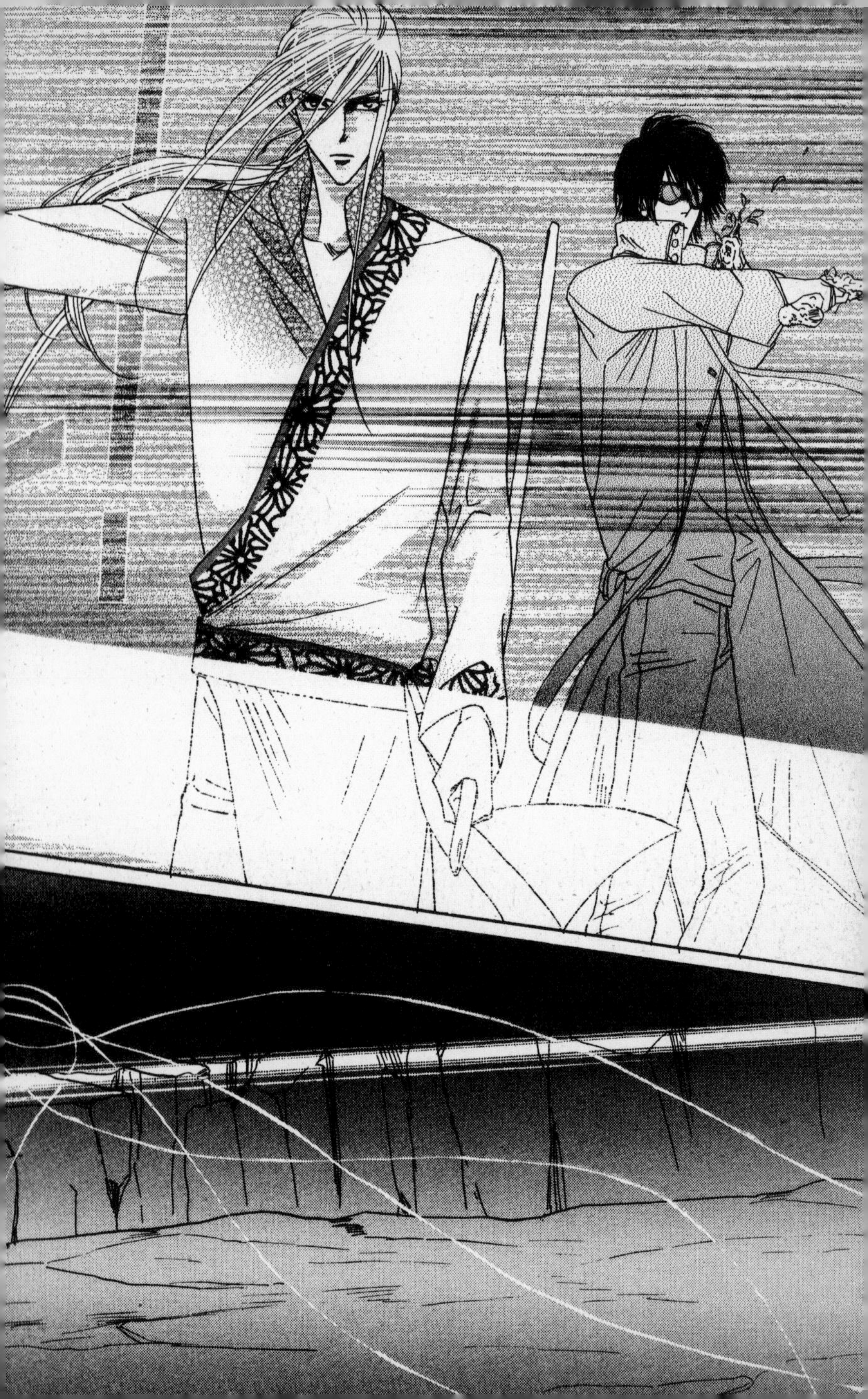

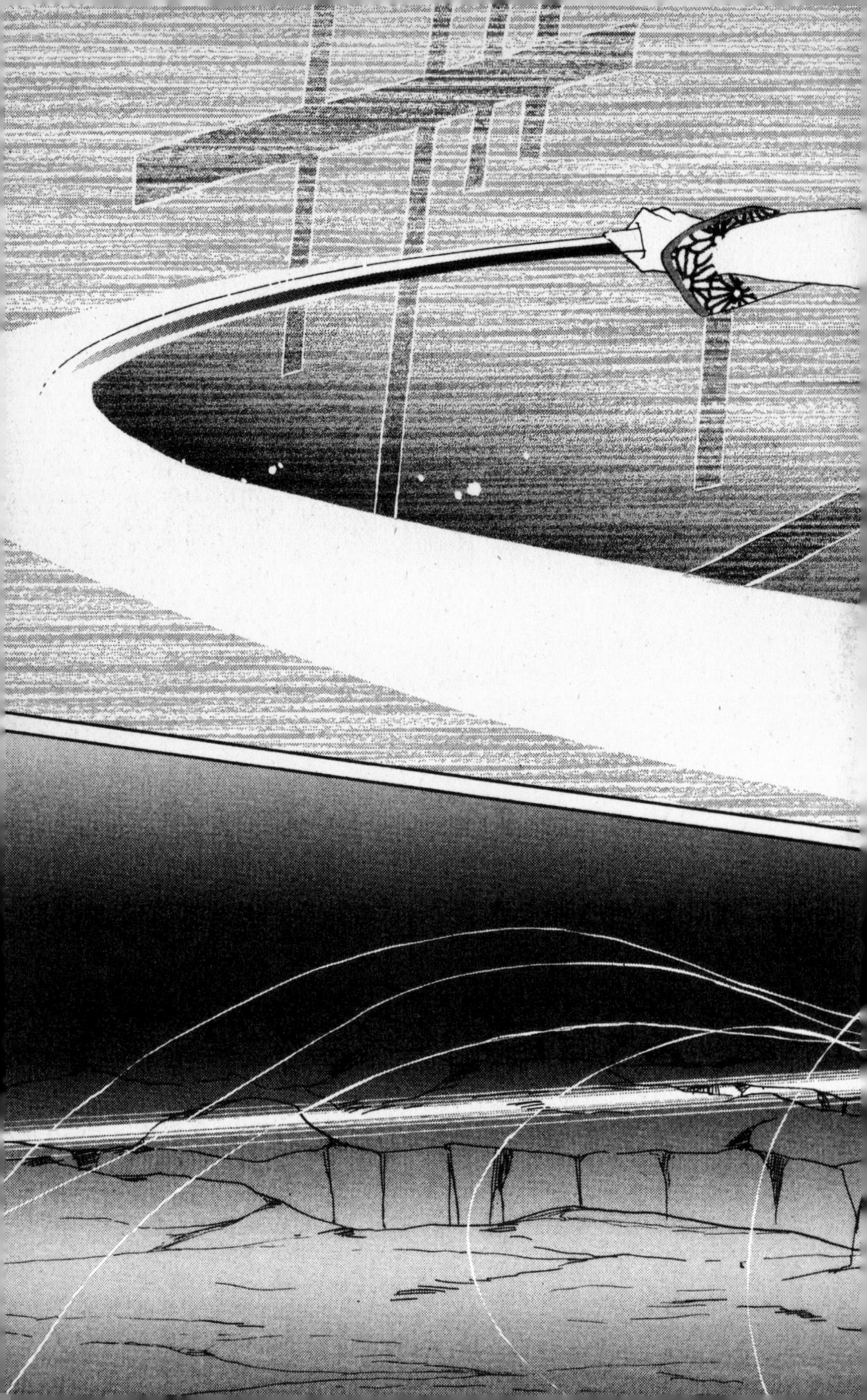

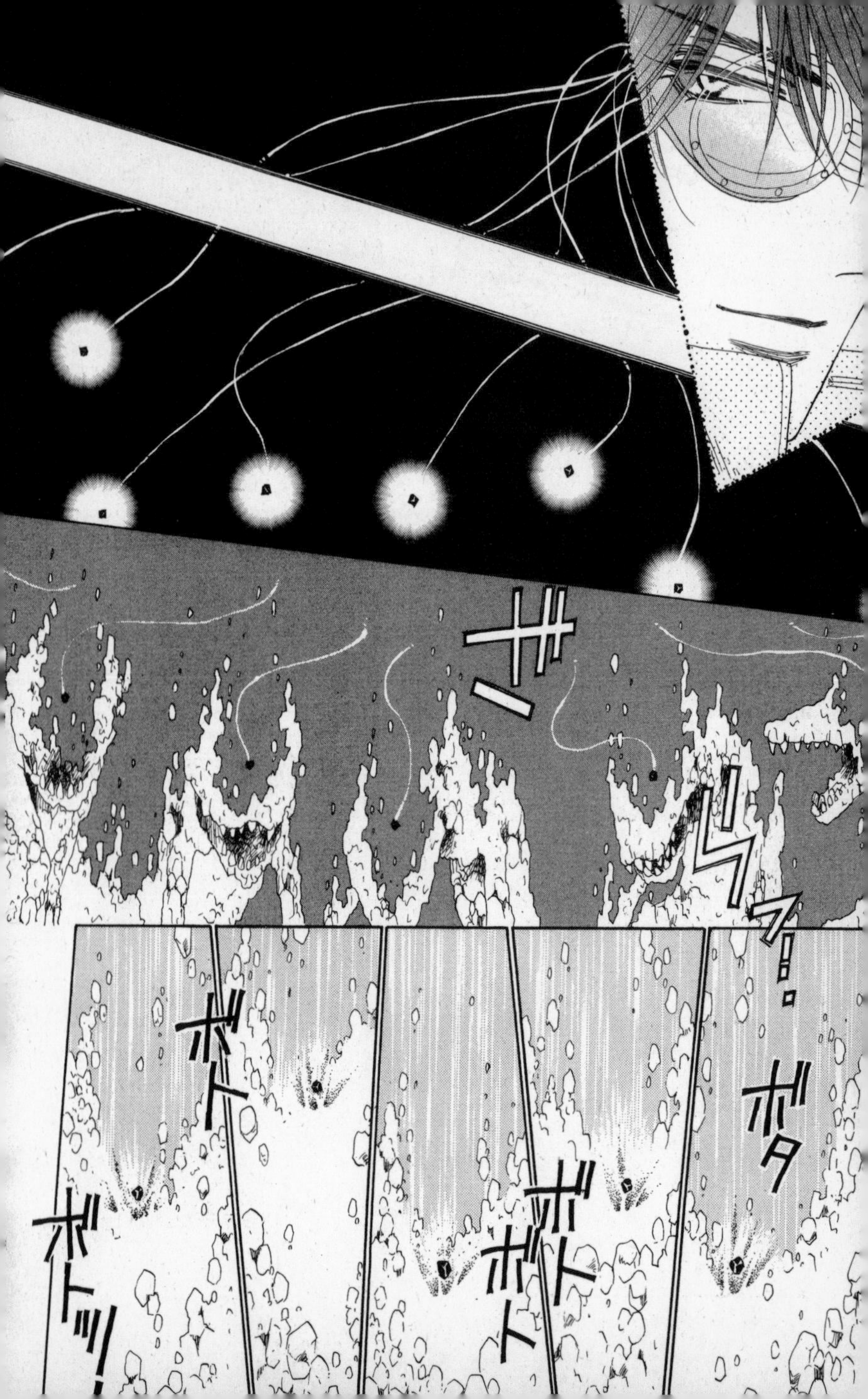
ザー
ボタ
ボトボト
ボトッ
ボトッ!

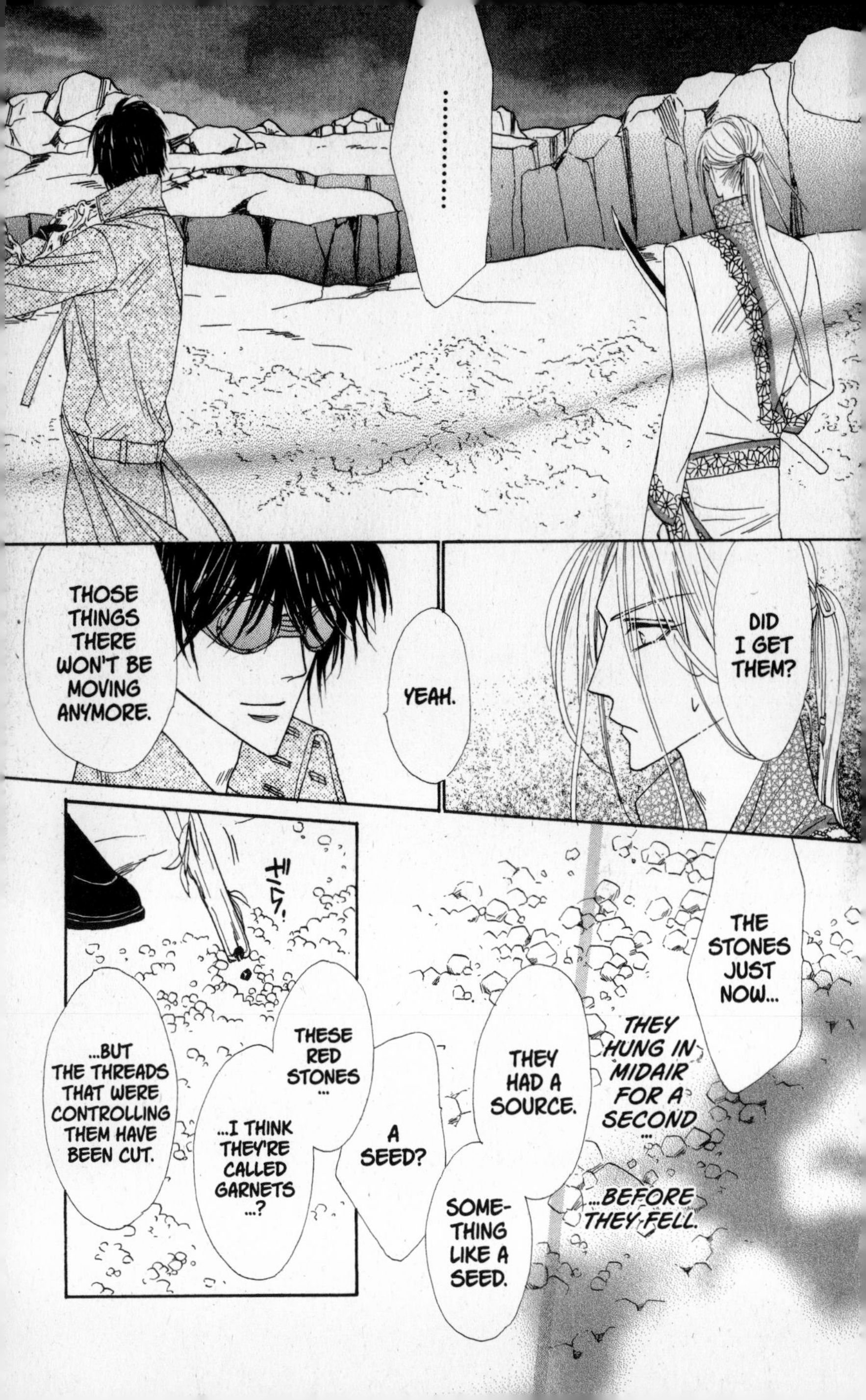
......
DID I GET THEM?
YEAH.
THOSE THINGS THERE WON'T BE MOVING ANYMORE.
THE STONES JUST NOW...
THEY HUNG IN MIDAIR FOR A SECOND...
...BEFORE THEY FELL.
THEY HAD A SOURCE.
SOMETHING LIKE A SEED.
A SEED?
THESE RED STONES...
...I THINK THEY'RE CALLED GARNETS...?
...BUT THE THREADS THAT WERE CONTROLLING THEM HAVE BEEN CUT.

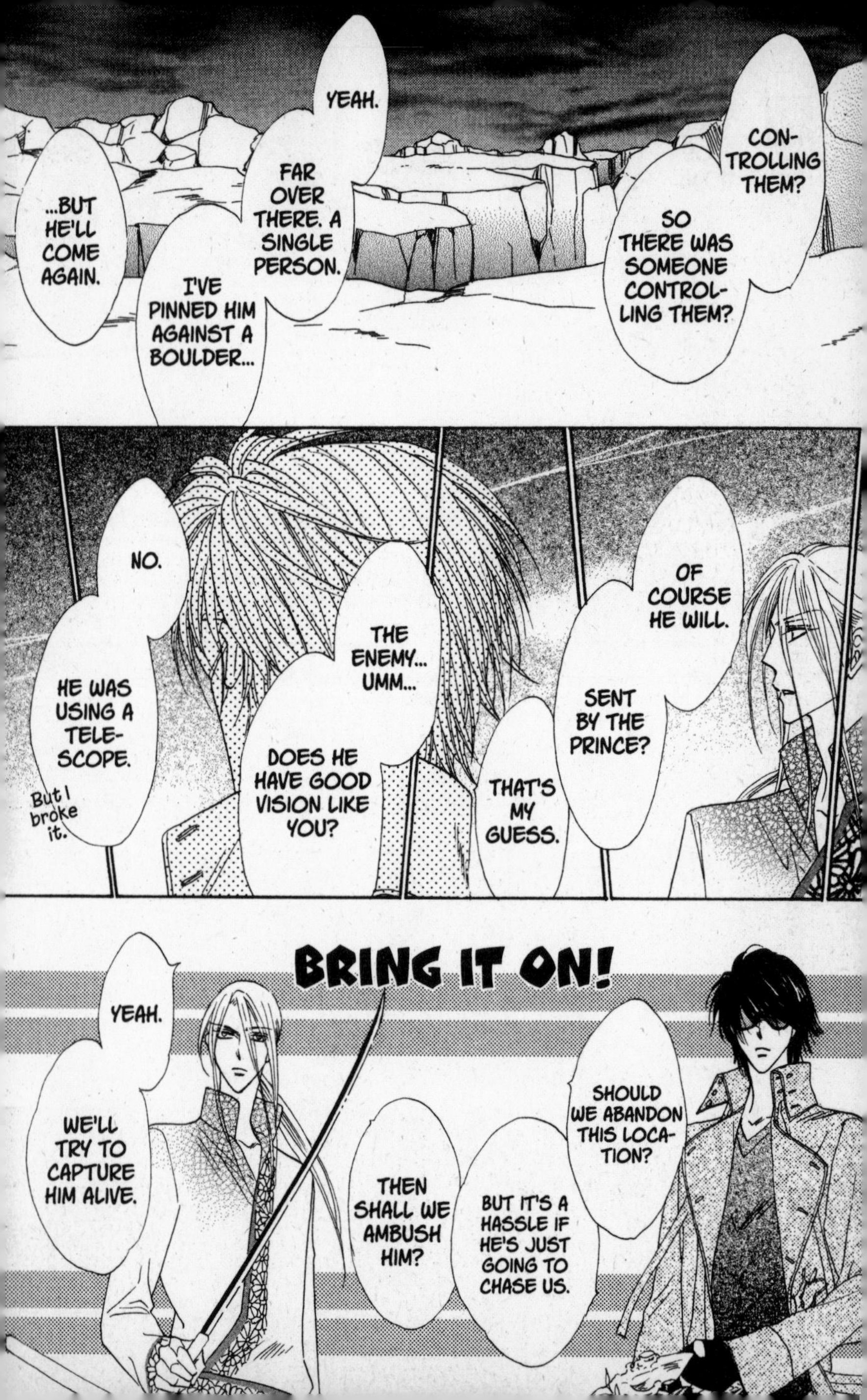
CON-TROLLING THEM?
SO THERE WAS SOMEONE CONTROL-LING THEM?
YEAH.
FAR OVER THERE. A SINGLE PERSON.
I'VE PINNED HIM AGAINST A BOULDER...
...BUT HE'LL COME AGAIN.
OF COURSE HE WILL.
SENT BY THE PRINCE?
THAT'S MY GUESS.
THE ENEMY... UMM...
DOES HE HAVE GOOD VISION LIKE YOU?
NO.
HE WAS USING A TELE-SCOPE.
But I broke it.
BRING IT ON!
SHOULD WE ABANDON THIS LOCA-TION?
BUT IT'S A HASSLE IF HE'S JUST GOING TO CHASE US.
THEN SHALL WE AMBUSH HIM?
YEAH.
WE'LL TRY TO CAPTURE HIM ALIVE.

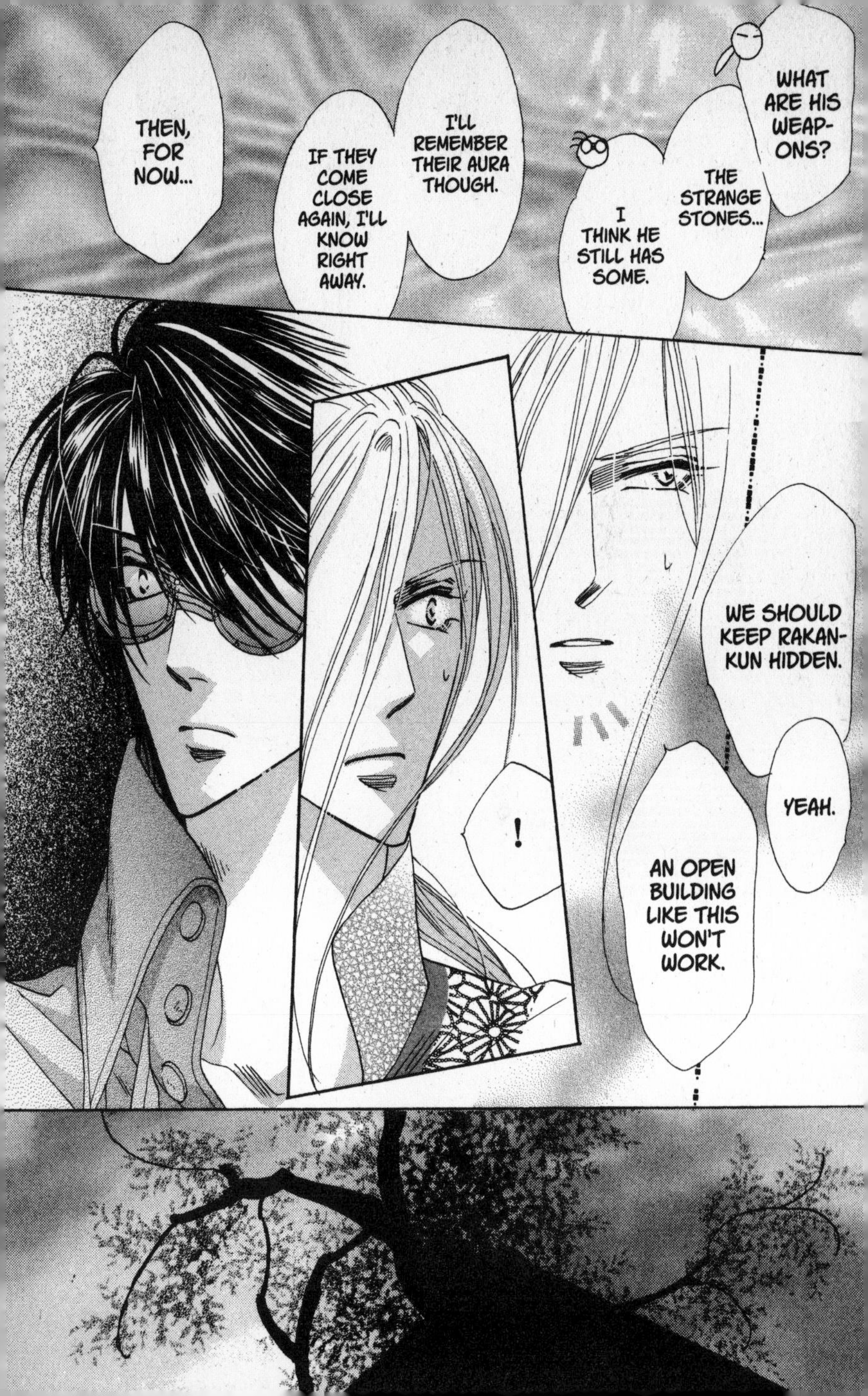
WHAT ARE HIS WEAPONS?
THE STRANGE STONES...
I THINK HE STILL HAS SOME.
I'LL REMEMBER THEIR AURA THOUGH.
IF THEY COME CLOSE AGAIN, I'LL KNOW RIGHT AWAY.
THEN, FOR NOW...
WE SHOULD KEEP RAKAN-KUN HIDDEN.
YEAH.
AN OPEN BUILDING LIKE THIS WON'T WORK.
!

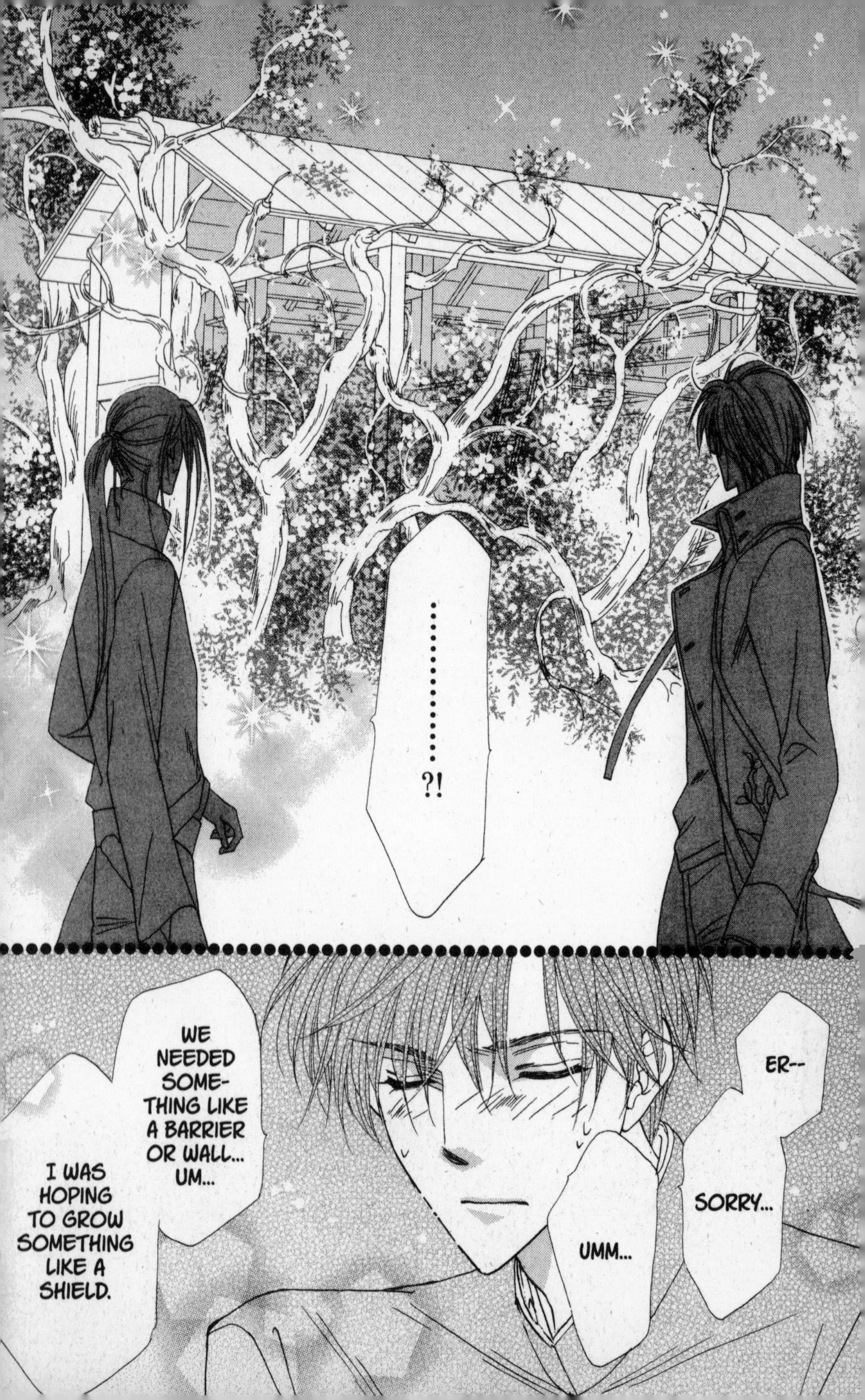
……?!
ER--
SORRY...
UMM...
WE NEEDED SOME-THING LIKE A BARRIER OR WALL... UM...
I WAS HOPING TO GROW SOMETHING LIKE A SHIELD.

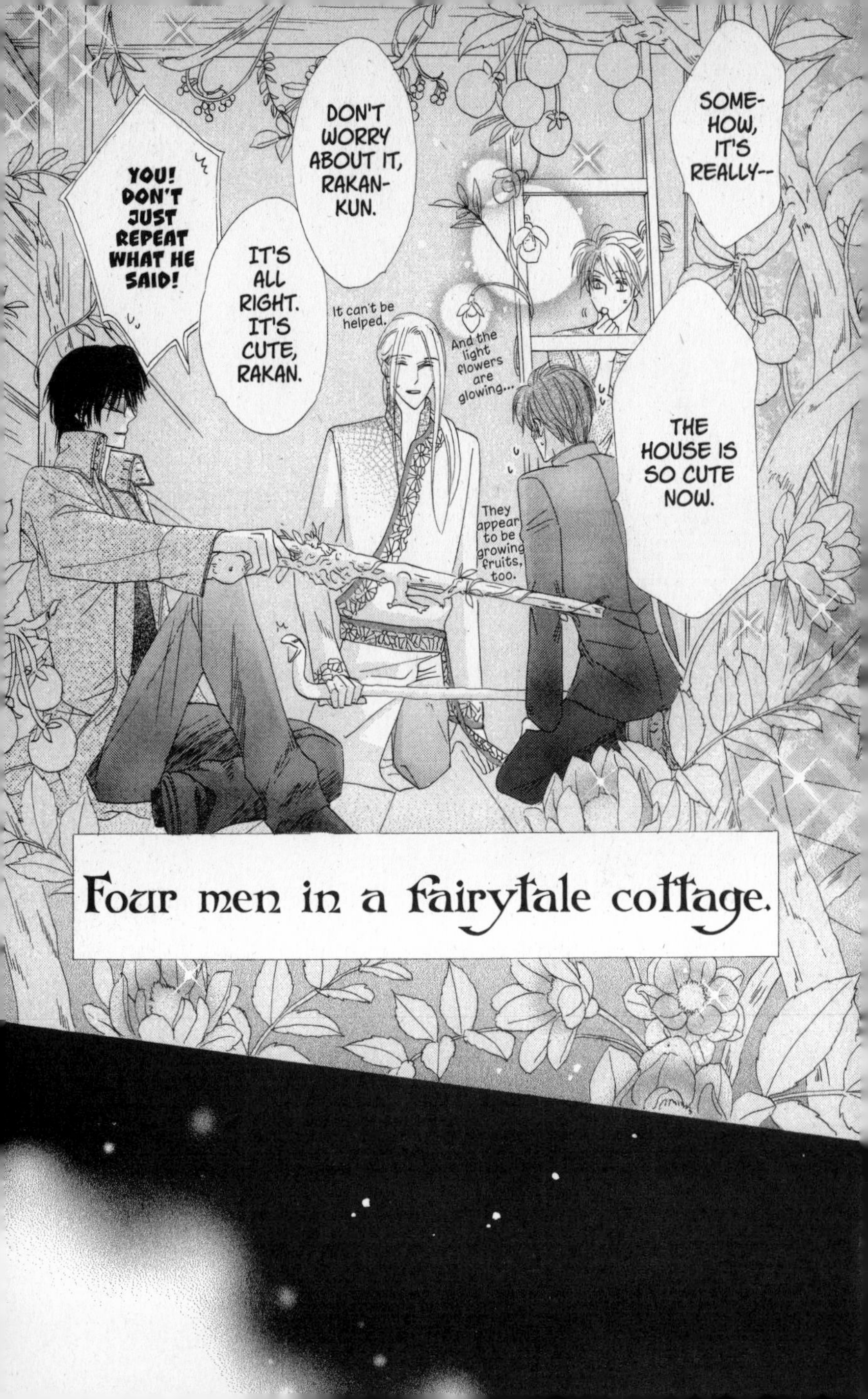
SOME-HOW, IT'S REALLY--
THE HOUSE IS SO CUTE NOW.
DON'T WORRY ABOUT IT, RAKAN-KUN.
It can't be helped.
And the light flowers are glowing...
They appear to be growing fruits, too.
IT'S ALL RIGHT. IT'S CUTE, RAKAN.
YOU! DON'T JUST REPEAT WHAT HE SAID!
Four men in a fairytale cottage.

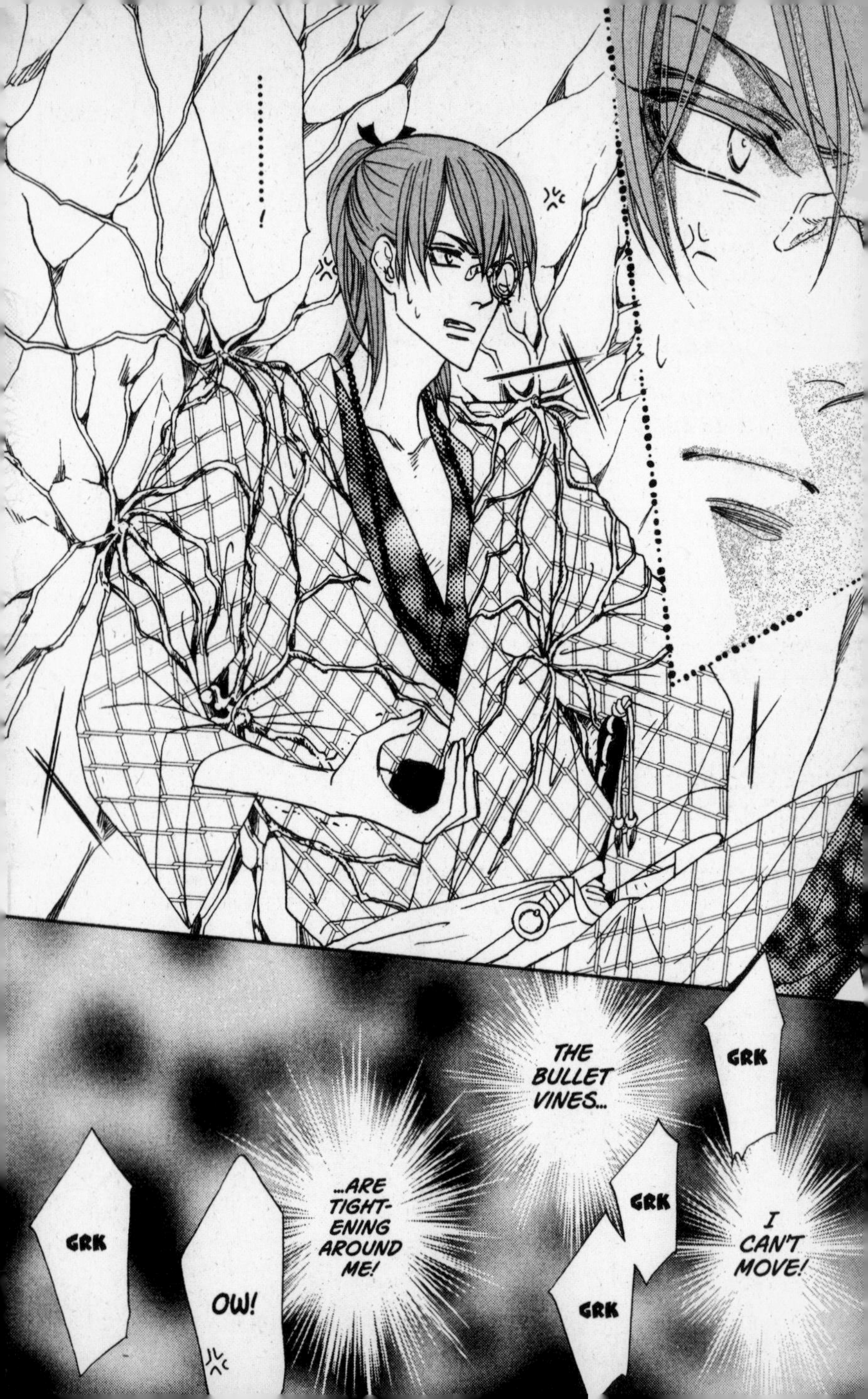

......!
GRK
THE BULLET VINES...
GRK
I CAN'T MOVE!
GRK
...ARE TIGHTENING AROUND ME!
OW!
GRK

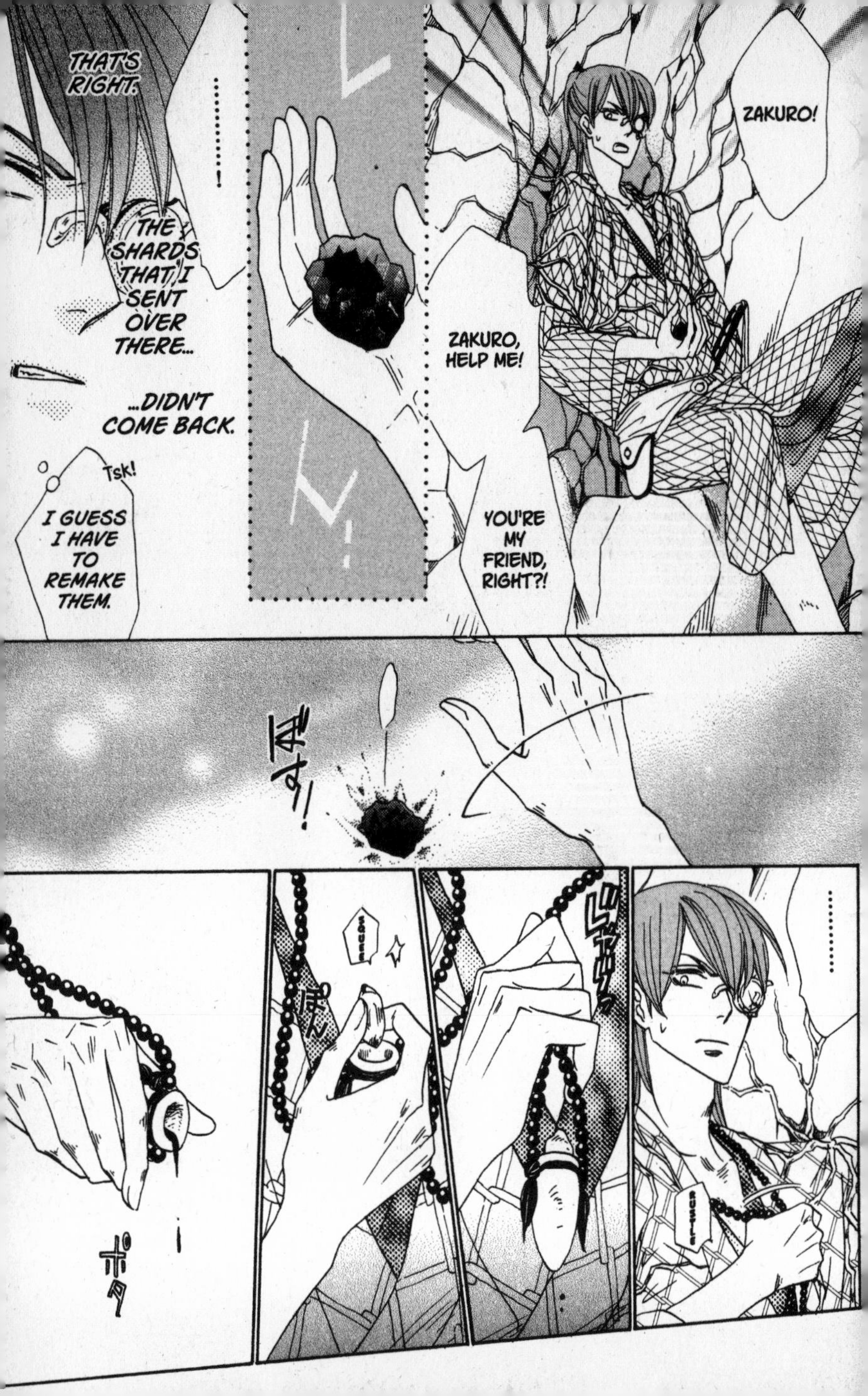
ZAKURO!
ZAKURO, HELP ME!
YOU'RE MY FRIEND, RIGHT?!
......!
THAT'S RIGHT.
THE SHARDS THAT I SENT OVER THERE...
...DIDN'T COME BACK.
Tsk!
I GUESS I HAVE TO REMAKE THEM.
......
RUSTLE
ぽん
ポタ

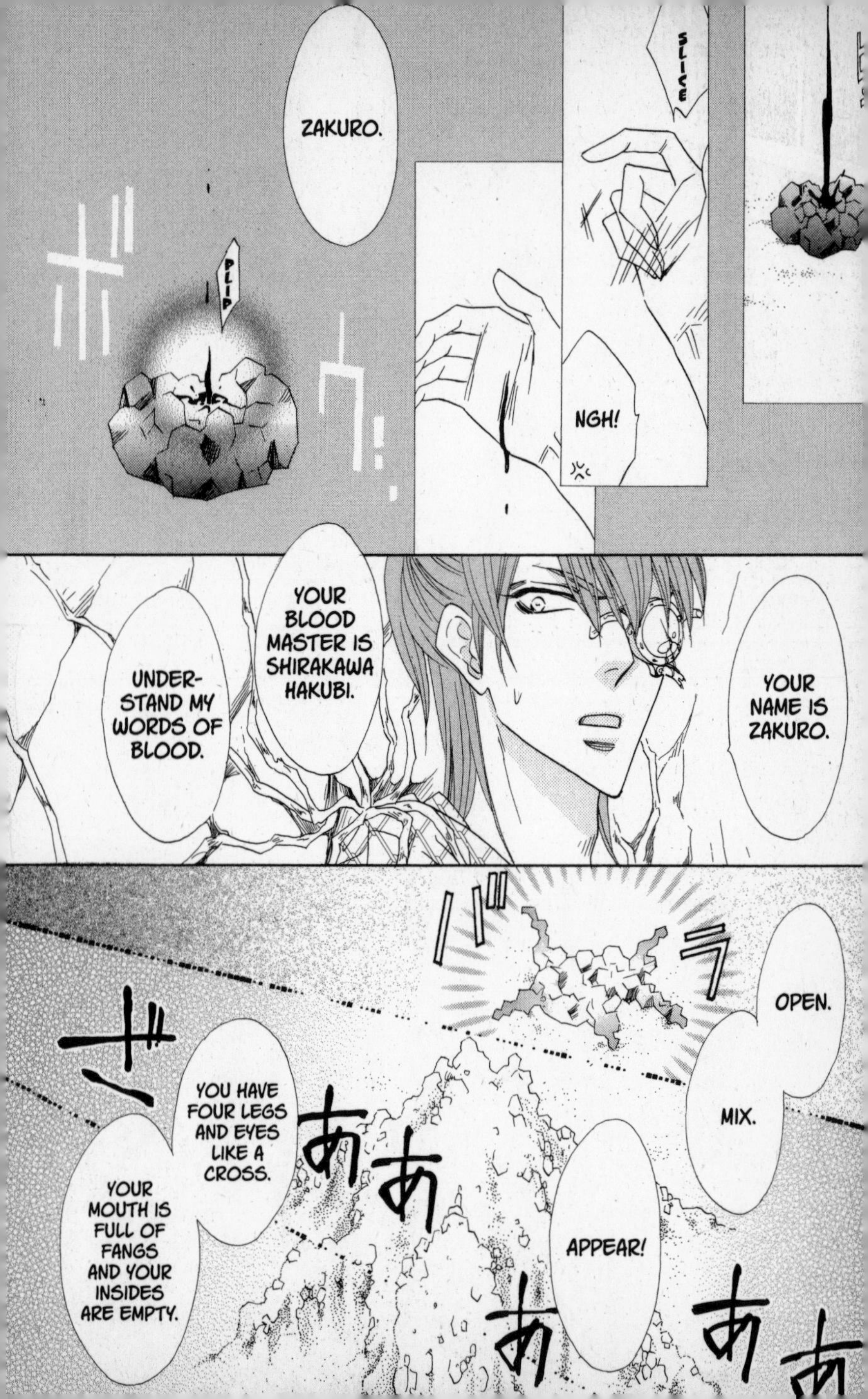
SLICE
NGH!
ZAKURO.
PLIP
ボウ!!
YOUR NAME IS ZAKURO.
YOUR BLOOD MASTER IS SHIRAKAWA HAKUBI.
UNDER-STAND MY WORDS OF BLOOD.
バラ
OPEN.
MIX.
APPEAR!
ああああ
YOU HAVE FOUR LEGS AND EYES LIKE A CROSS.
ざ
YOUR MOUTH IS FULL OF FANGS AND YOUR INSIDES ARE EMPTY.

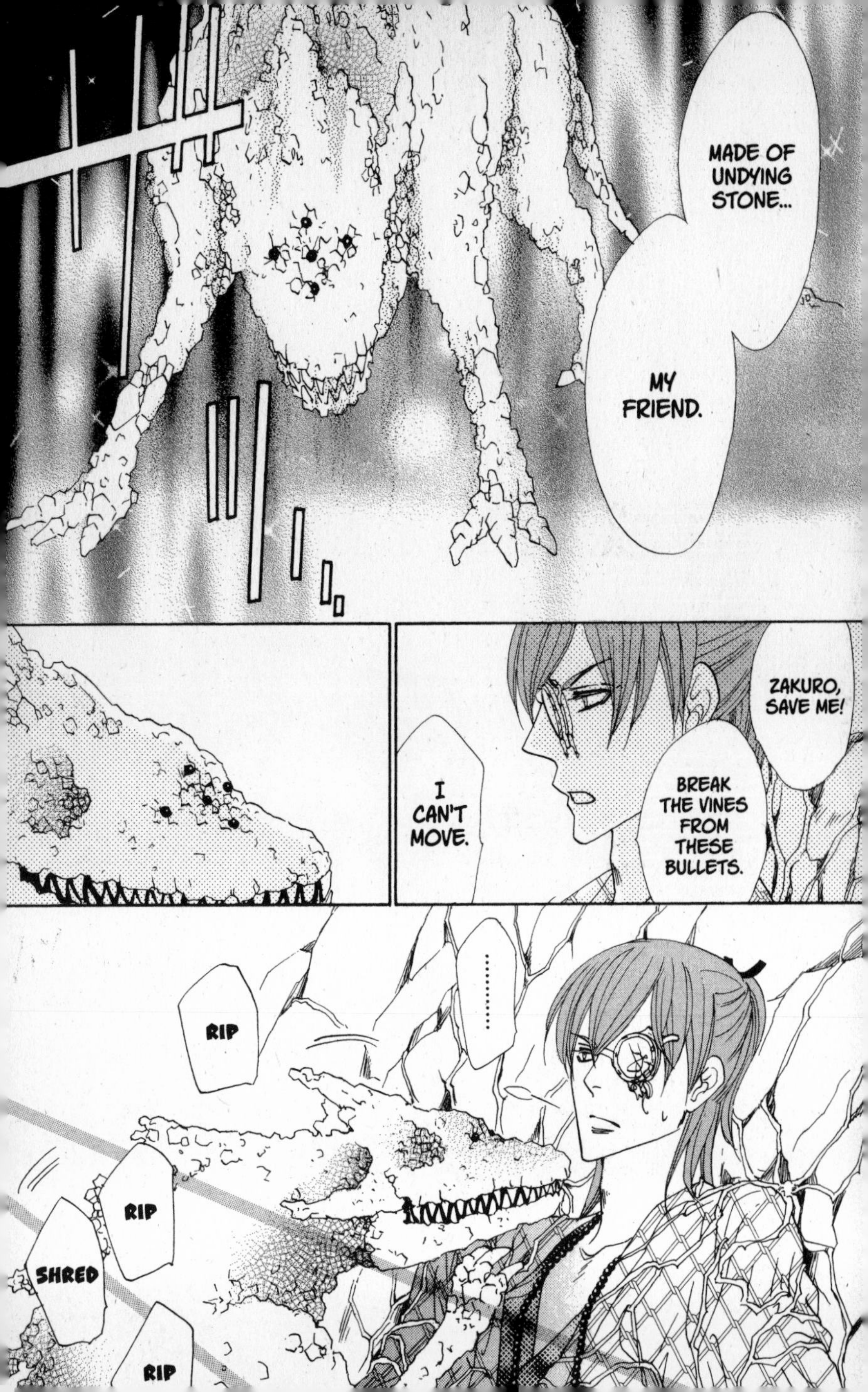
MADE OF UNDYING STONE...
MY FRIEND.
ZAKURO, SAVE ME!
BREAK THE VINES FROM THESE BULLETS.
I CAN'T MOVE.
......
RIP
RIP
SHRED
RIP

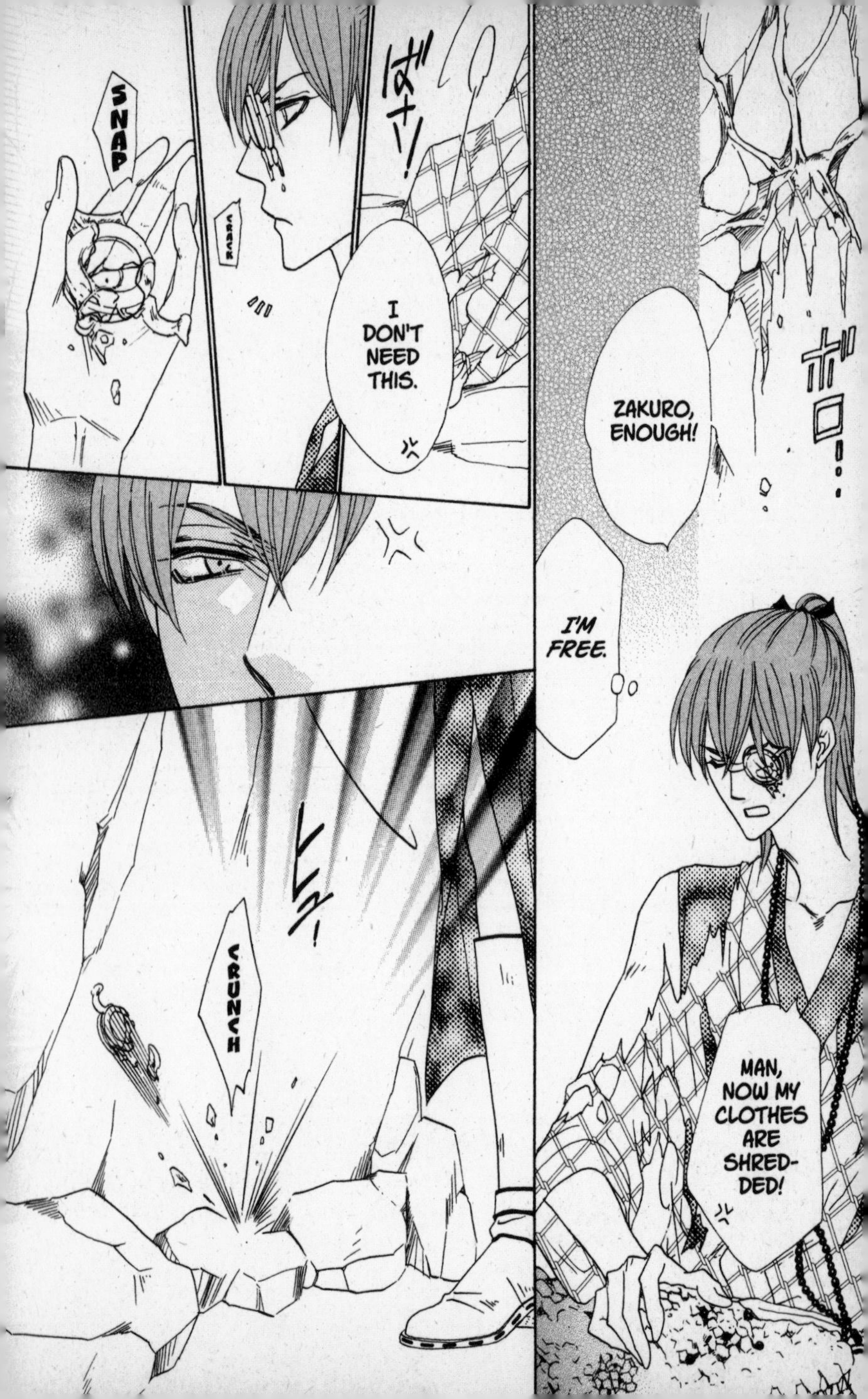
ボロ!
ZAKURO, ENOUGH!
I'M FREE.
MAN, NOW MY CLOTHES ARE SHRED-DED!
ばサ!
I DON'T NEED THIS.
CRACK
SNAP
ヒュ!
CRUNCH

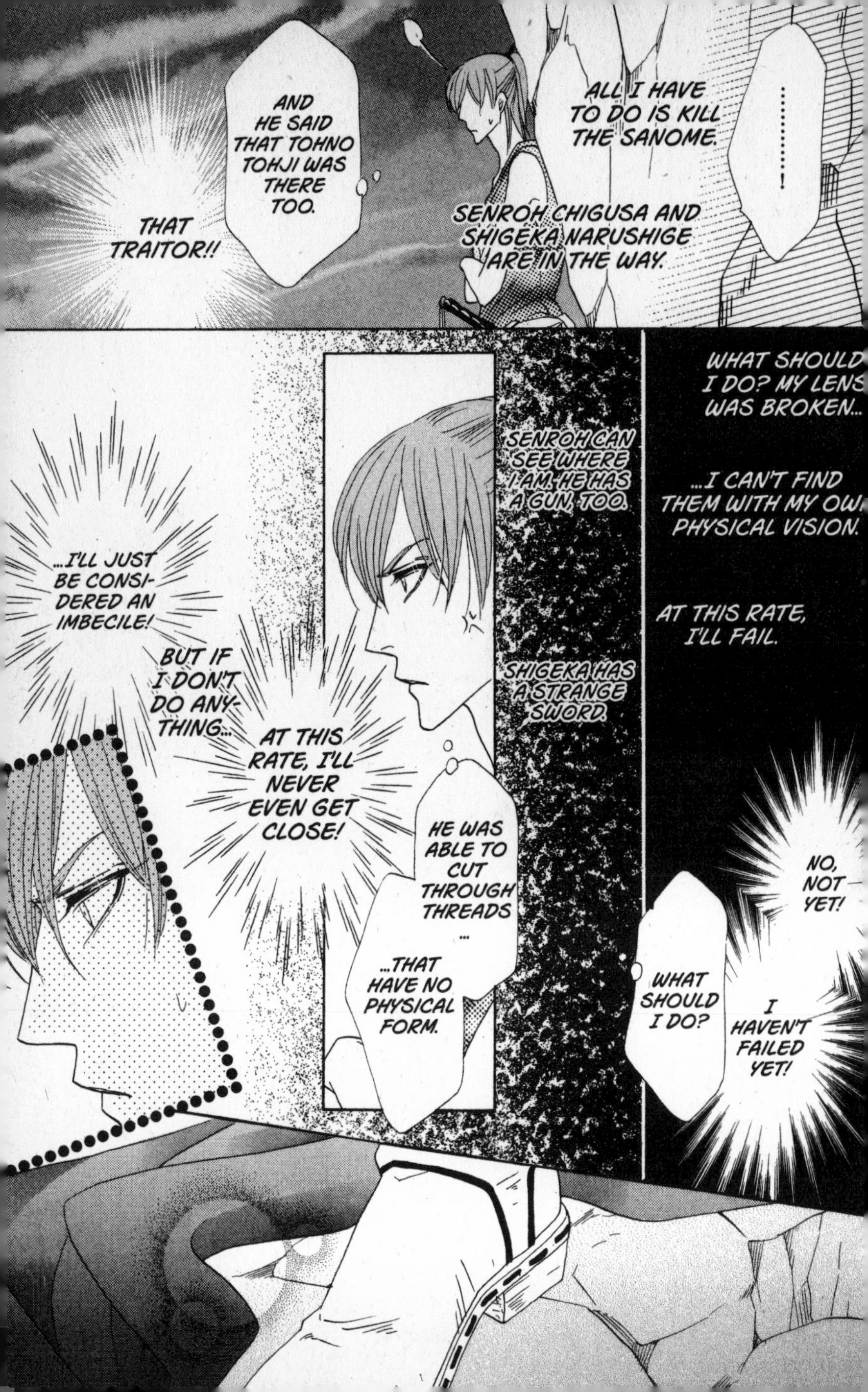
......!
ALL I HAVE TO DO IS KILL THE SANOME.
SENROH CHIGUSA AND SHIGEKA NARUSHIGE ARE IN THE WAY.
AND HE SAID THAT TOHNO TOHJI WAS THERE TOO.
THAT TRAITOR!!
WHAT SHOULD I DO? MY LENS WAS BROKEN...
...I CAN'T FIND THEM WITH MY OW PHYSICAL VISION.
AT THIS RATE, I'LL FAIL.
SENROH CAN SEE WHERE I AM. HE HAS A GUN, TOO.
SHIGEKA HAS A STRANGE SWORD.
HE WAS ABLE TO CUT THROUGH THREADS...
...THAT HAVE NO PHYSICAL FORM.
NO, NOT YET!
WHAT SHOULD I DO?
I HAVEN'T FAILED YET!
AT THIS RATE, I'LL NEVER EVEN GET CLOSE!
BUT IF I DON'T DO ANYTHING...
...I'LL JUST BE CONSIDERED AN IMBECILE!

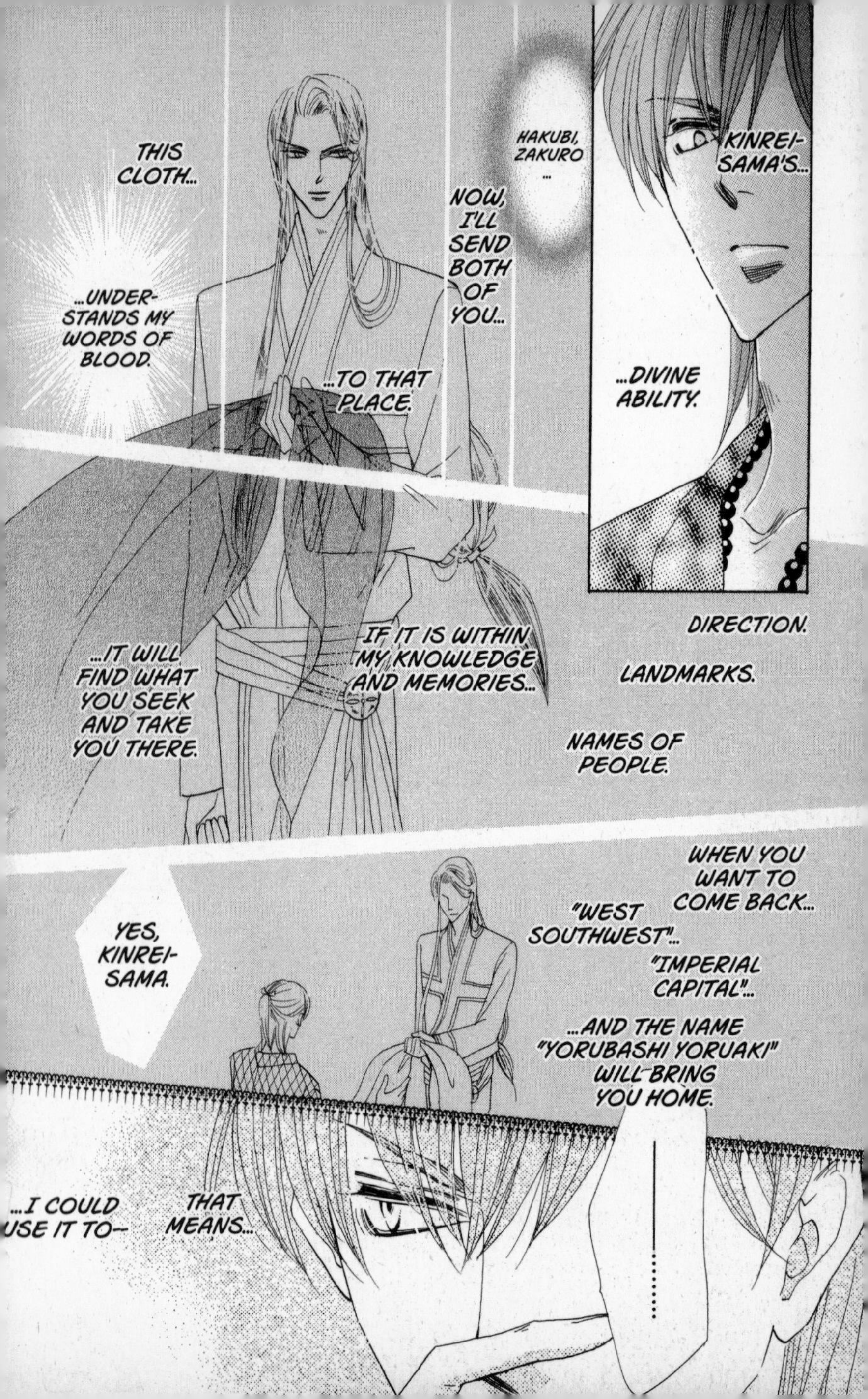
KINREI-SAMA'S...
...DIVINE ABILITY.
HAKUBI, ZAKURO ...
THIS CLOTH...
...UNDER-STANDS MY WORDS OF BLOOD.
NOW, I'LL SEND BOTH OF YOU...
...TO THAT PLACE.
DIRECTION.
LANDMARKS.
NAMES OF PEOPLE.
IF IT IS WITHIN MY KNOWLEDGE AND MEMORIES...
...IT WILL FIND WHAT YOU SEEK AND TAKE YOU THERE.
WHEN YOU WANT TO COME BACK...
"WEST SOUTHWEST"...
"IMPERIAL CAPITAL"...
...AND THE NAME "YORUBASHI YORUAKI" WILL BRING YOU HOME.
YES, KINREI-SAMA.
......
THAT MEANS...
...I COULD USE IT TO--

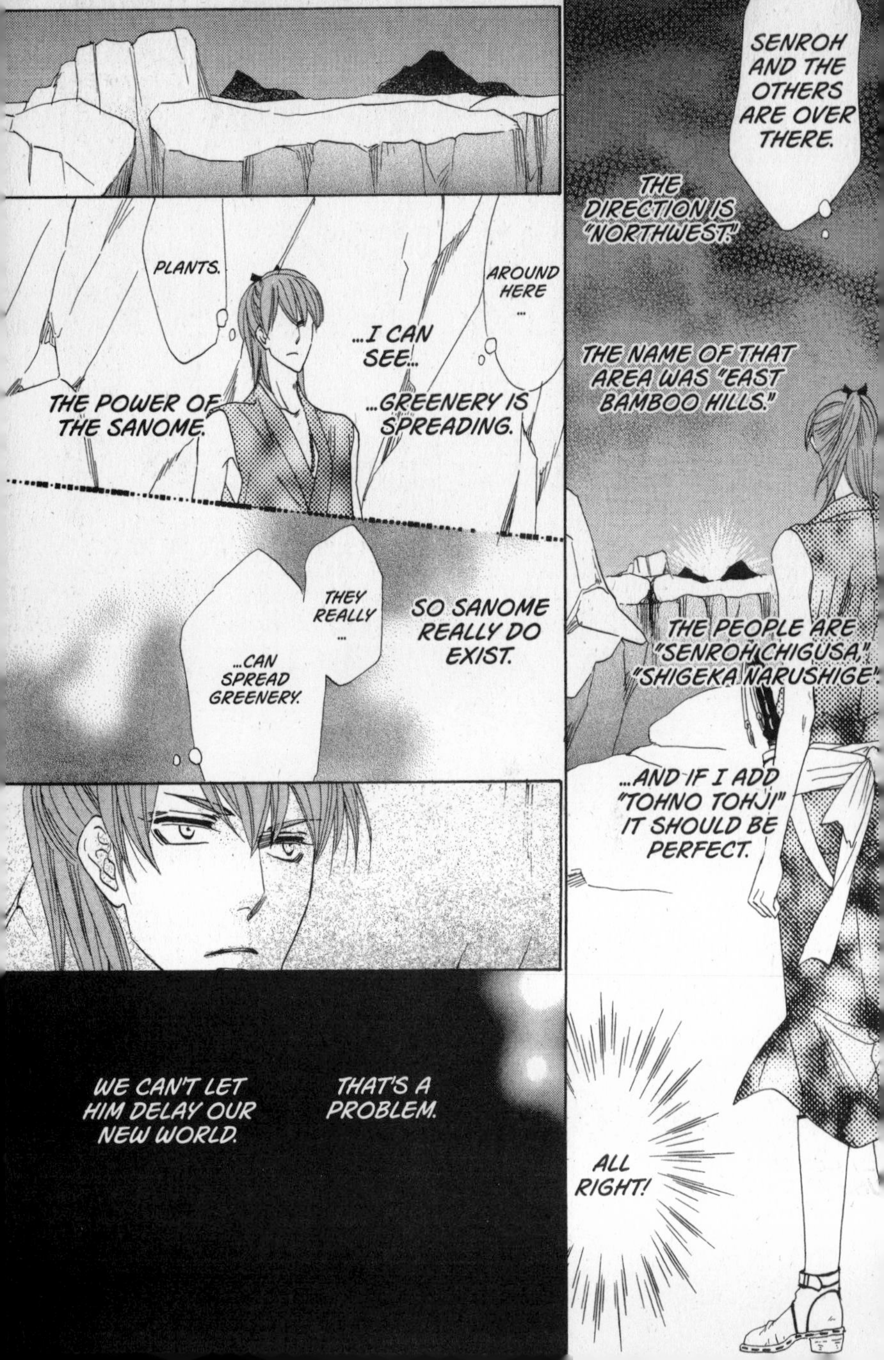
SENROH AND THE OTHERS ARE OVER THERE.
THE DIRECTION IS "NORTHWEST."
THE NAME OF THAT AREA WAS "EAST BAMBOO HILLS."
THE PEOPLE ARE "SENROH CHIGUSA," "SHIGEKA NARUSHIGE"
...AND IF I ADD "TOHNO TOHJI" IT SHOULD BE PERFECT.
ALL RIGHT!
AROUND HERE...
...I CAN SEE...
...GREENERY IS SPREADING.
PLANTS.
THE POWER OF THE SANOME.
SO SANOME REALLY DO EXIST.
THEY REALLY...
...CAN SPREAD GREENERY.
THAT'S A PROBLEM.
WE CAN'T LET HIM DELAY OUR NEW WORLD.

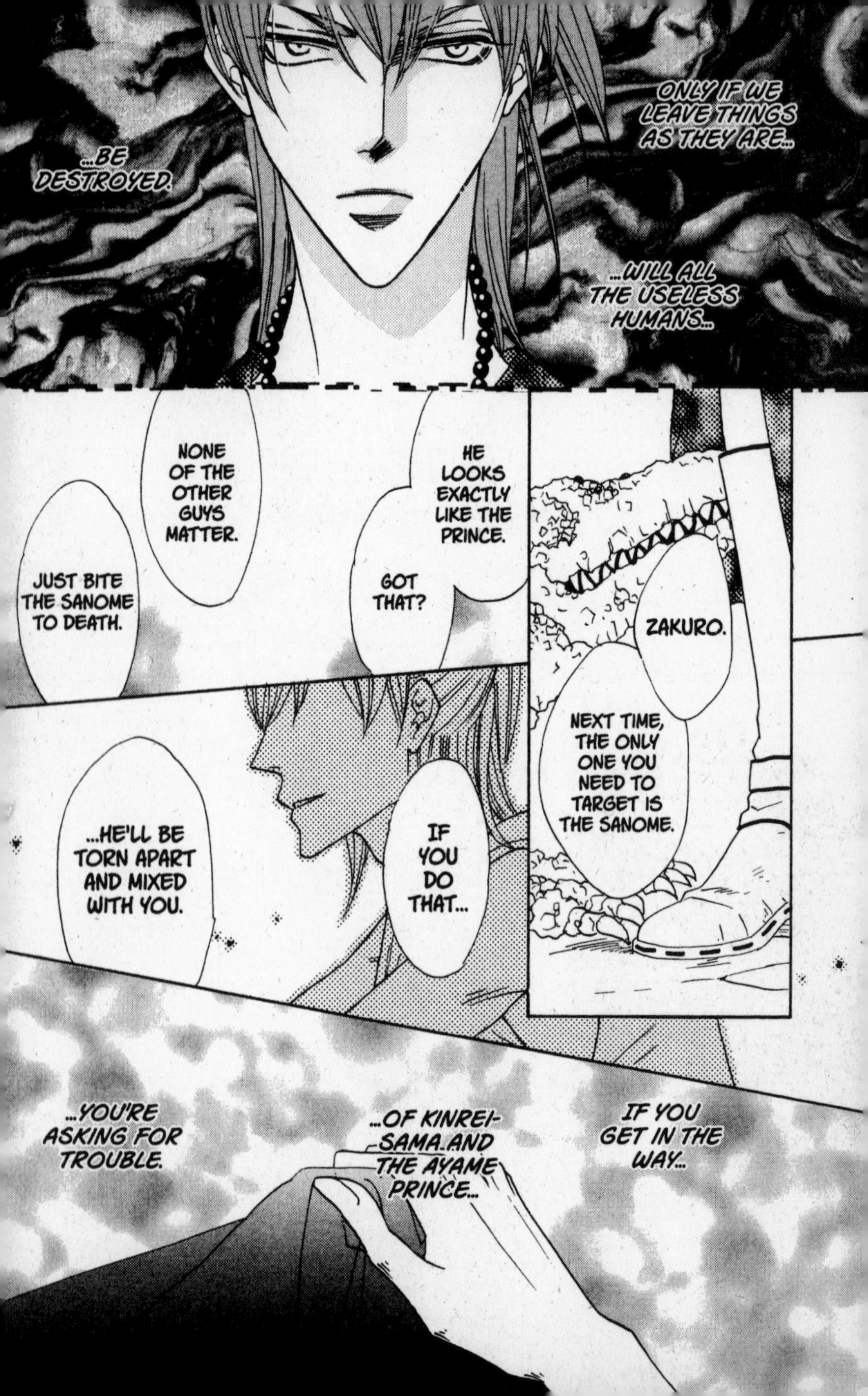
ONLY IF WE LEAVE THINGS AS THEY ARE...
...WILL ALL THE USELESS HUMANS...
...BE DESTROYED.
ZAKURO.
NEXT TIME, THE ONLY ONE YOU NEED TO TARGET IS THE SANOME.
HE LOOKS EXACTLY LIKE THE PRINCE.
GOT THAT?
NONE OF THE OTHER GUYS MATTER.
JUST BITE THE SANOME TO DEATH.
IF YOU DO THAT...
...HE'LL BE TORN APART AND MIXED WITH YOU.
IF YOU GET IN THE WAY...
...OF KINREI-SAMA AND THE AYAME PRINCE...
...YOU'RE ASKING FOR TROUBLE.

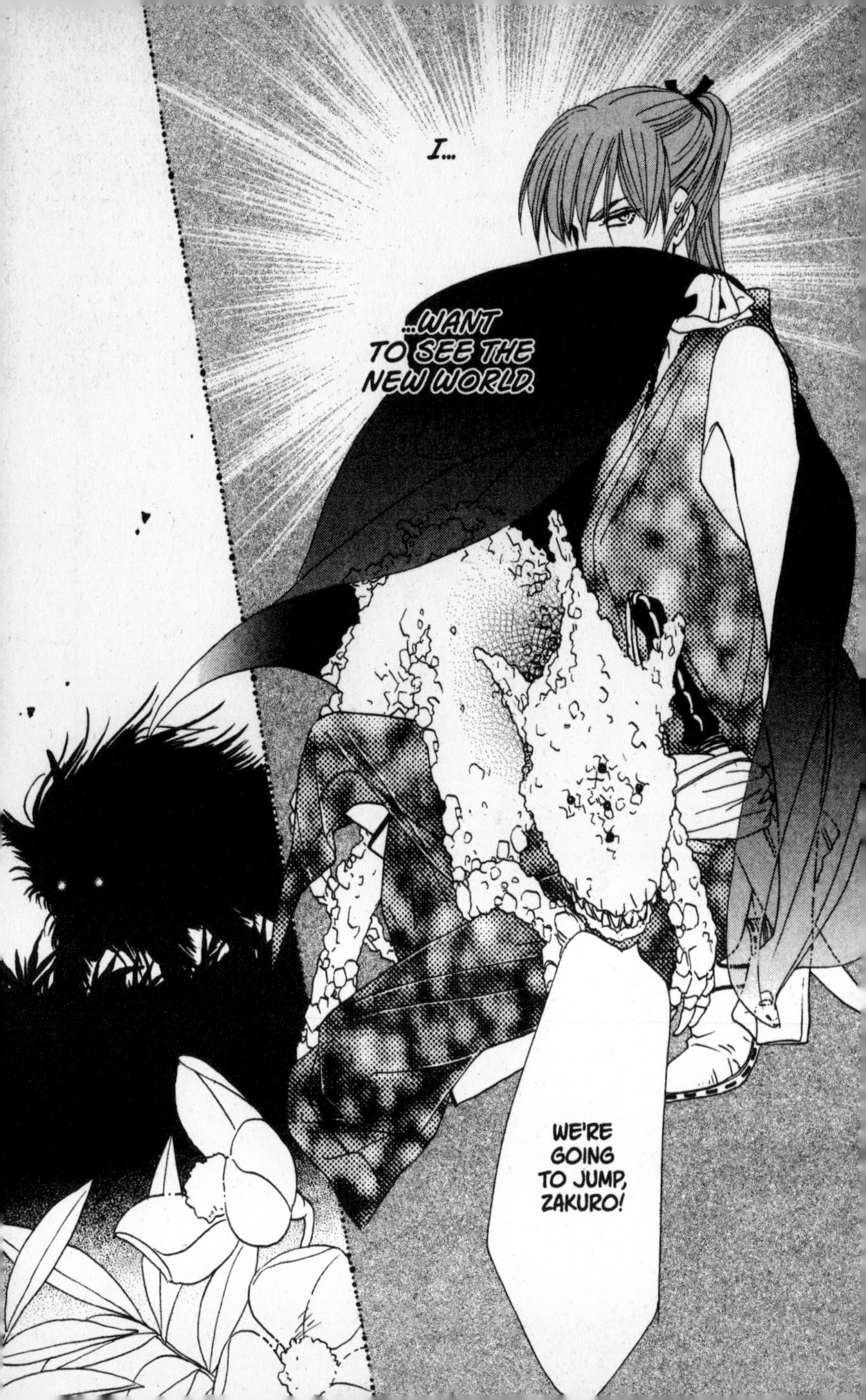
I...
...WANT TO SEE THE NEW WORLD.
WE'RE GOING TO JUMP, ZAKURO!

Stone Wolf

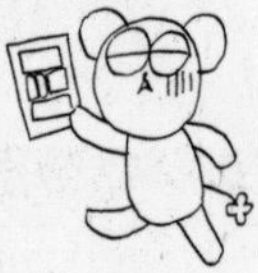

Hello! I am out of time again! Yay!
No, it was because I took it upon myself to draw and color the cover all on my own.
And something that doesn't happen often, I made an illustration for the back as well, and well...

I got in over my head.

(I thought about giving up, but then I wasn't able to pull out once I started.)

But I'm happy that it was drawn, so it's all good.

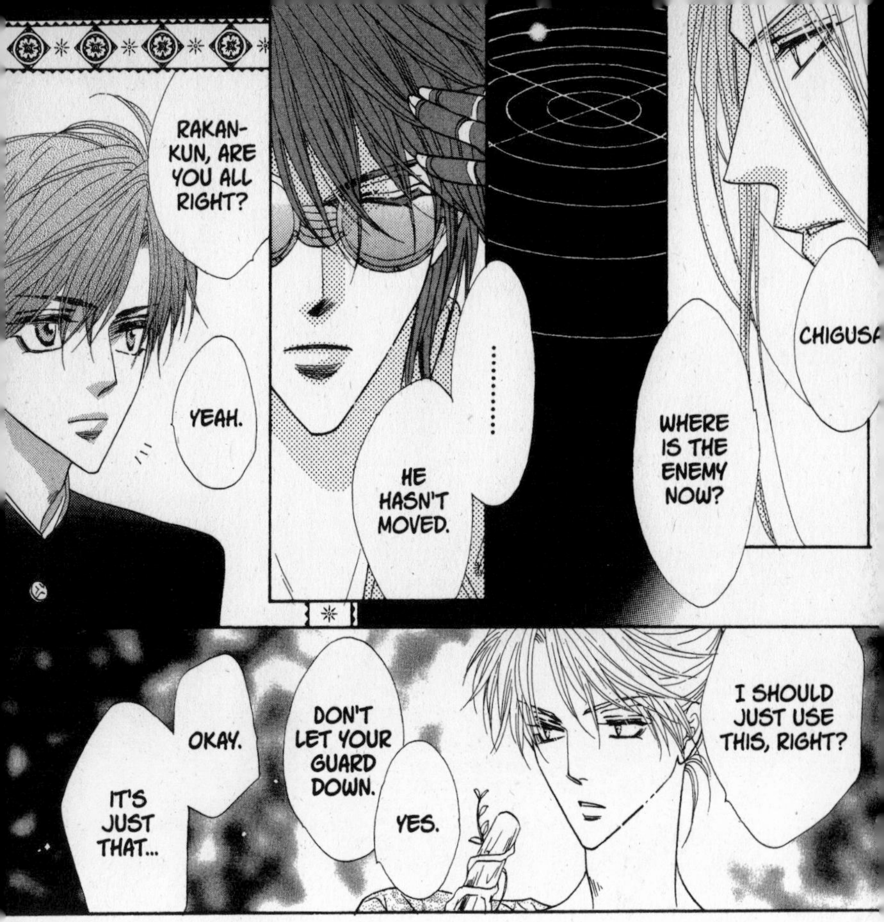
CHIGUSA
WHERE IS THE ENEMY NOW?
......
HE HASN'T MOVED.
RAKAN-KUN, ARE YOU ALL RIGHT?
YEAH.
I SHOULD JUST USE THIS, RIGHT?
DON'T LET YOUR GUARD DOWN.
YES.
OKAY.
IT'S JUST THAT...

ICHI*RACI TALK

WHICH OF YOUR CHARACTERS DO YOU MOST WANT TO BE FRIENDS WITH?

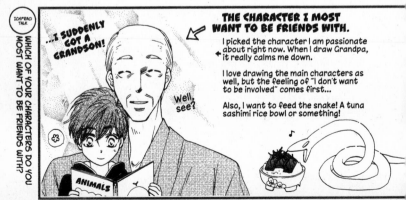

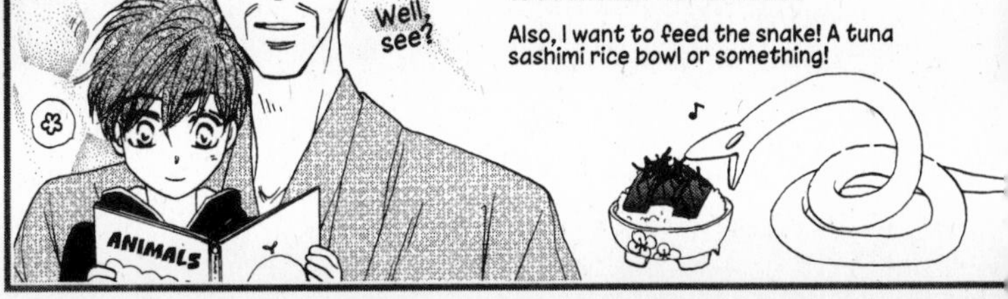
...I SUDDENLY GOT A GRANDSON!
Well, see?
ANIMALS

THE CHARACTER I MOST WANT TO BE FRIENDS WITH.

I picked the character I am passionate about right now. When I draw Grandpa, it really calms me down.

I love drawing the main characters as well, but the feeling of "I don't want to be involved" comes first...

Also, I want to feed the snake! A tuna sashimi rice bowl or something!

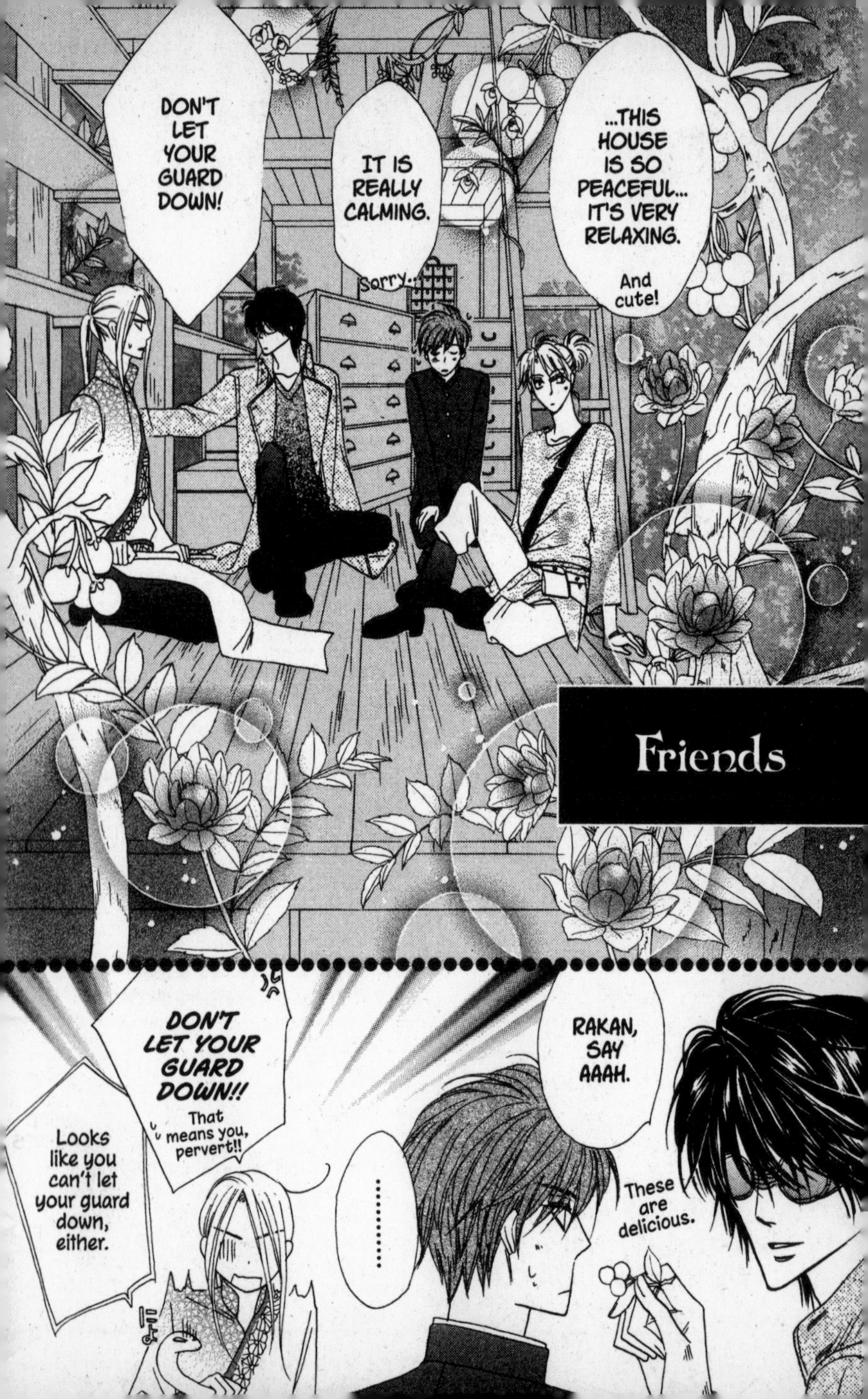
...THIS HOUSE IS SO PEACEFUL... IT'S VERY RELAXING.
And cute!
IT IS REALLY CALMING.
Sorry...
DON'T LET YOUR GUARD DOWN!
Friends
RAKAN, SAY AAAH.
These are delicious.
......
DON'T LET YOUR GUARD DOWN!!
That means you, pervert!!
Looks like you can't let your guard down, either.

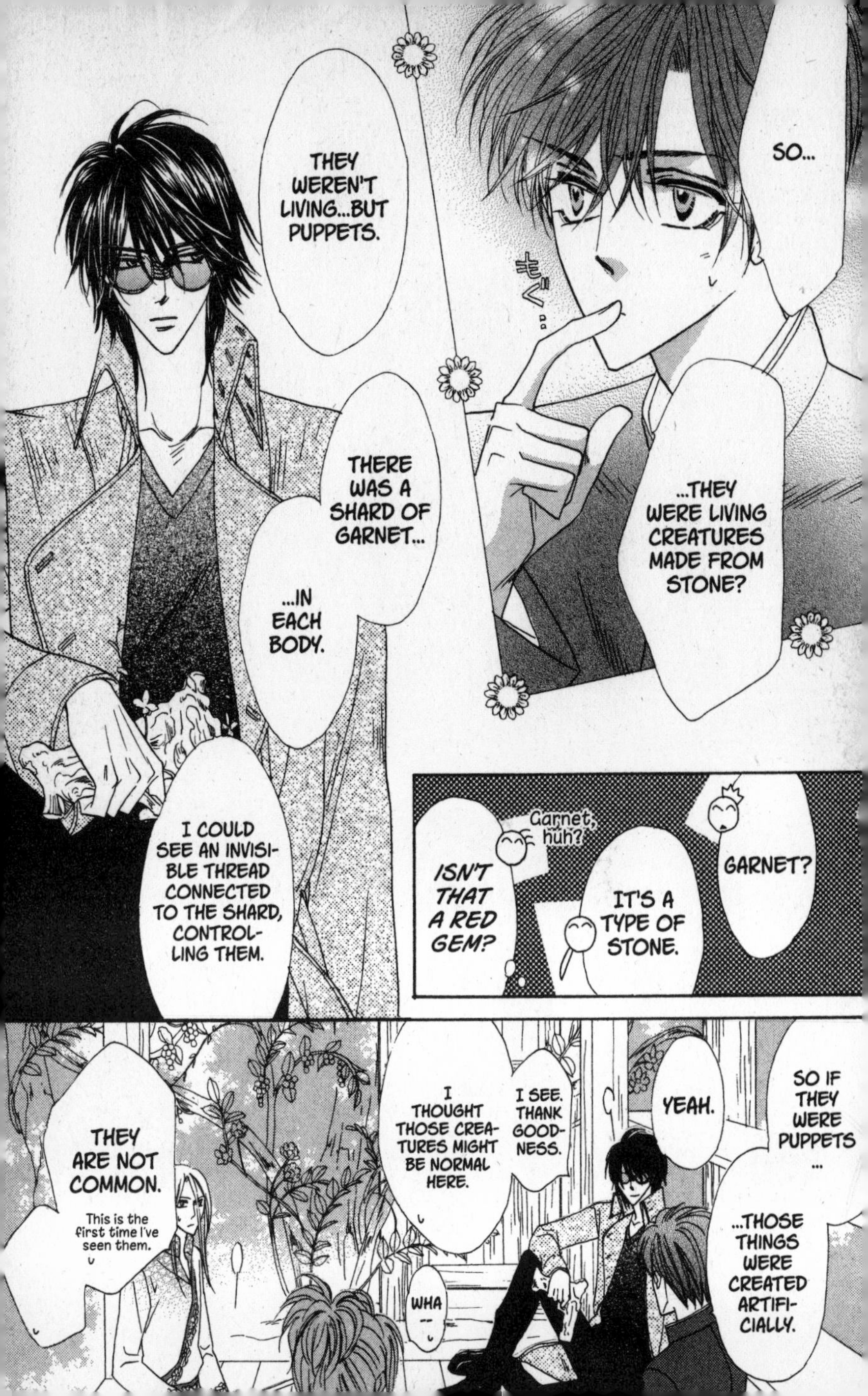
SO...
もぐ…
...THEY WERE LIVING CREATURES MADE FROM STONE?
THEY WEREN'T LIVING...BUT PUPPETS.
THERE WAS A SHARD OF GARNET...
...IN EACH BODY.
I COULD SEE AN INVISIBLE THREAD CONNECTED TO THE SHARD, CONTROLLING THEM.
GARNET?
IT'S A TYPE OF STONE.
Garnet, huh?
ISN'T THAT A RED GEM?
SO IF THEY WERE PUPPETS...
...THOSE THINGS WERE CREATED ARTIFICIALLY.
YEAH.
I SEE. THANK GOODNESS.
I THOUGHT THOSE CREATURES MIGHT BE NORMAL HERE.
WHA--
THEY ARE NOT COMMON.
This is the first time I've seen them.

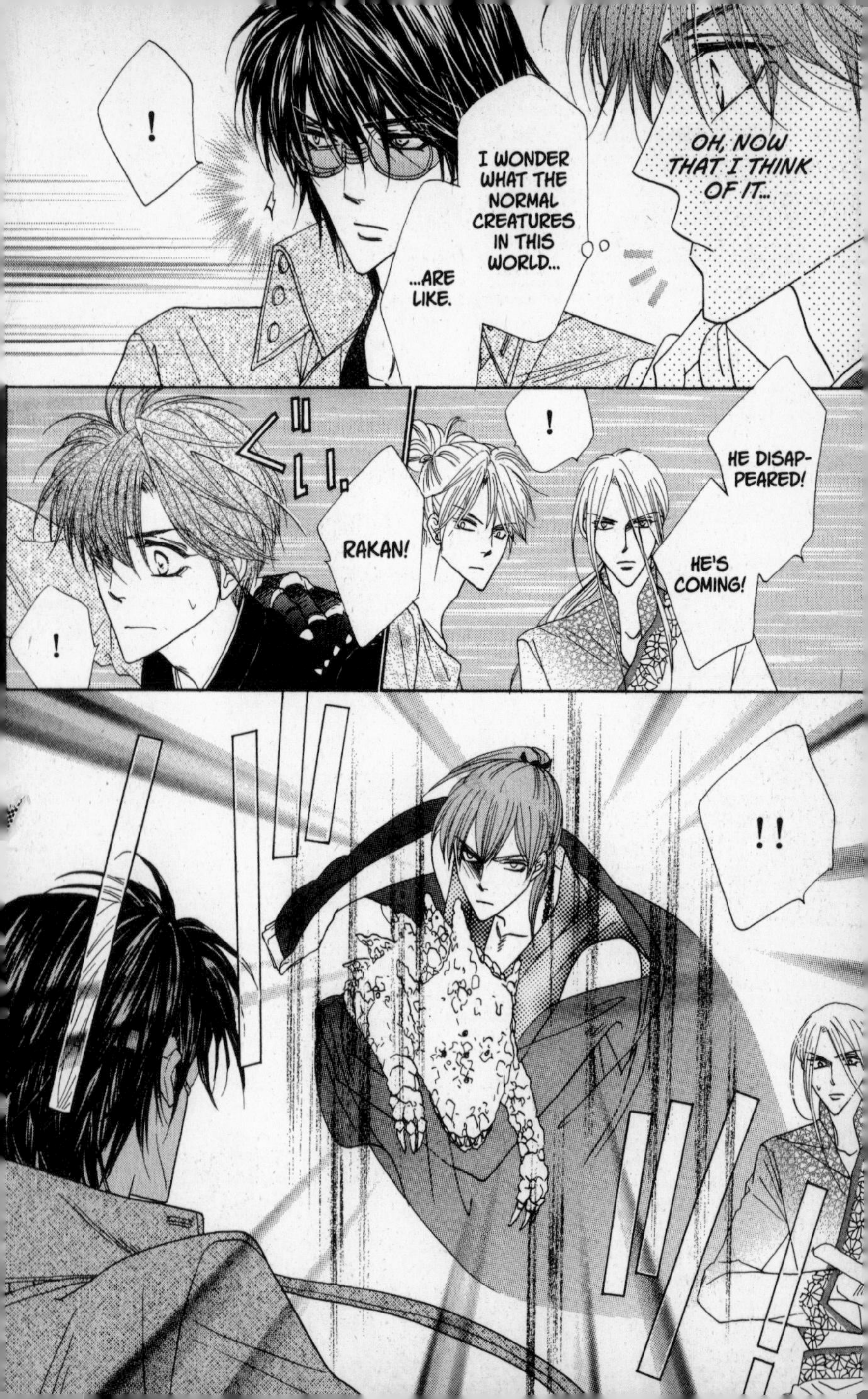
OH, NOW THAT I THINK OF IT...
I WONDER WHAT THE NORMAL CREATURES IN THIS WORLD...
...ARE LIKE.
!
HE DISAP-PEARED!
!
HE'S COMING!
RAKAN!
!
!!

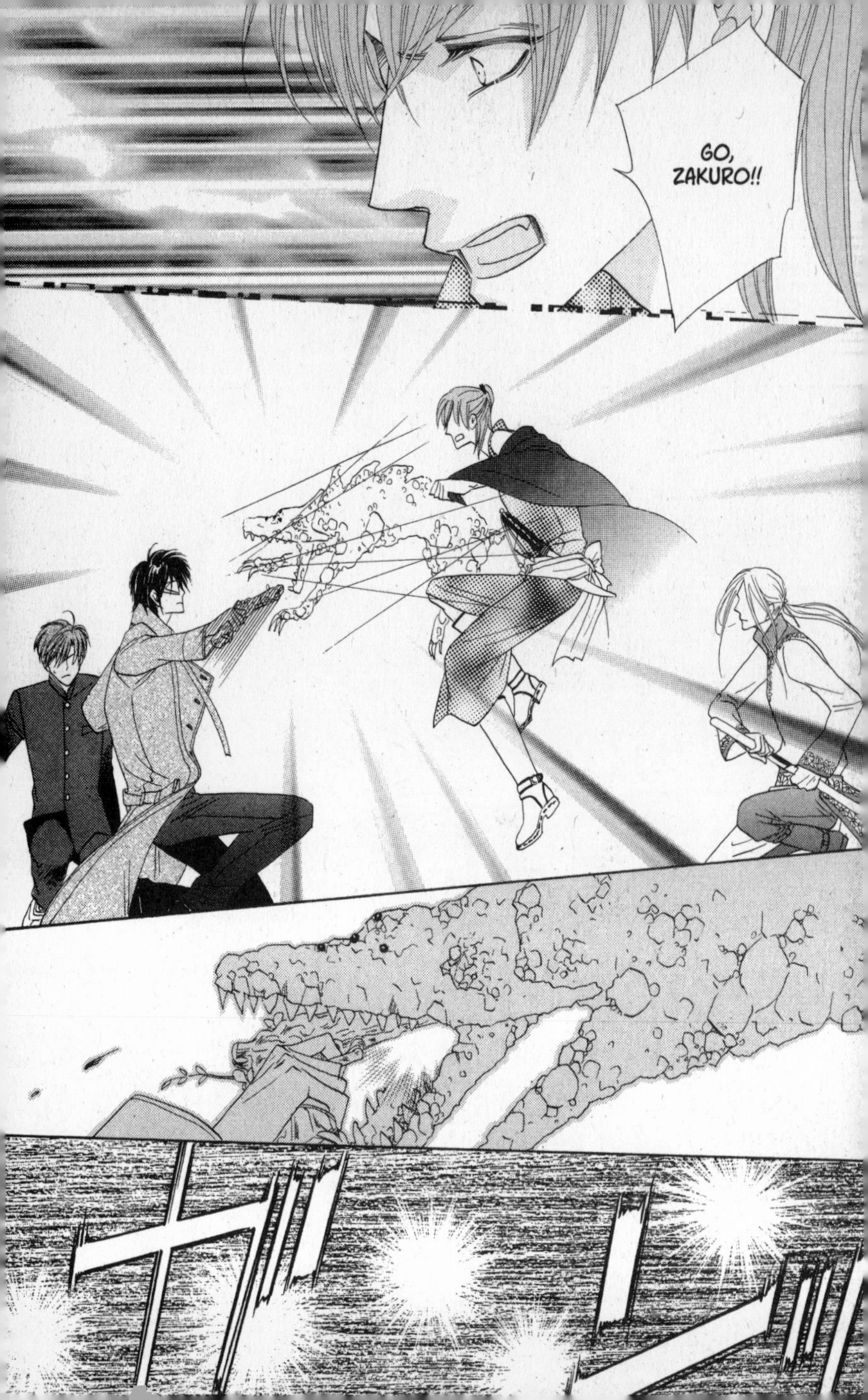
GO, ZAKURO!!

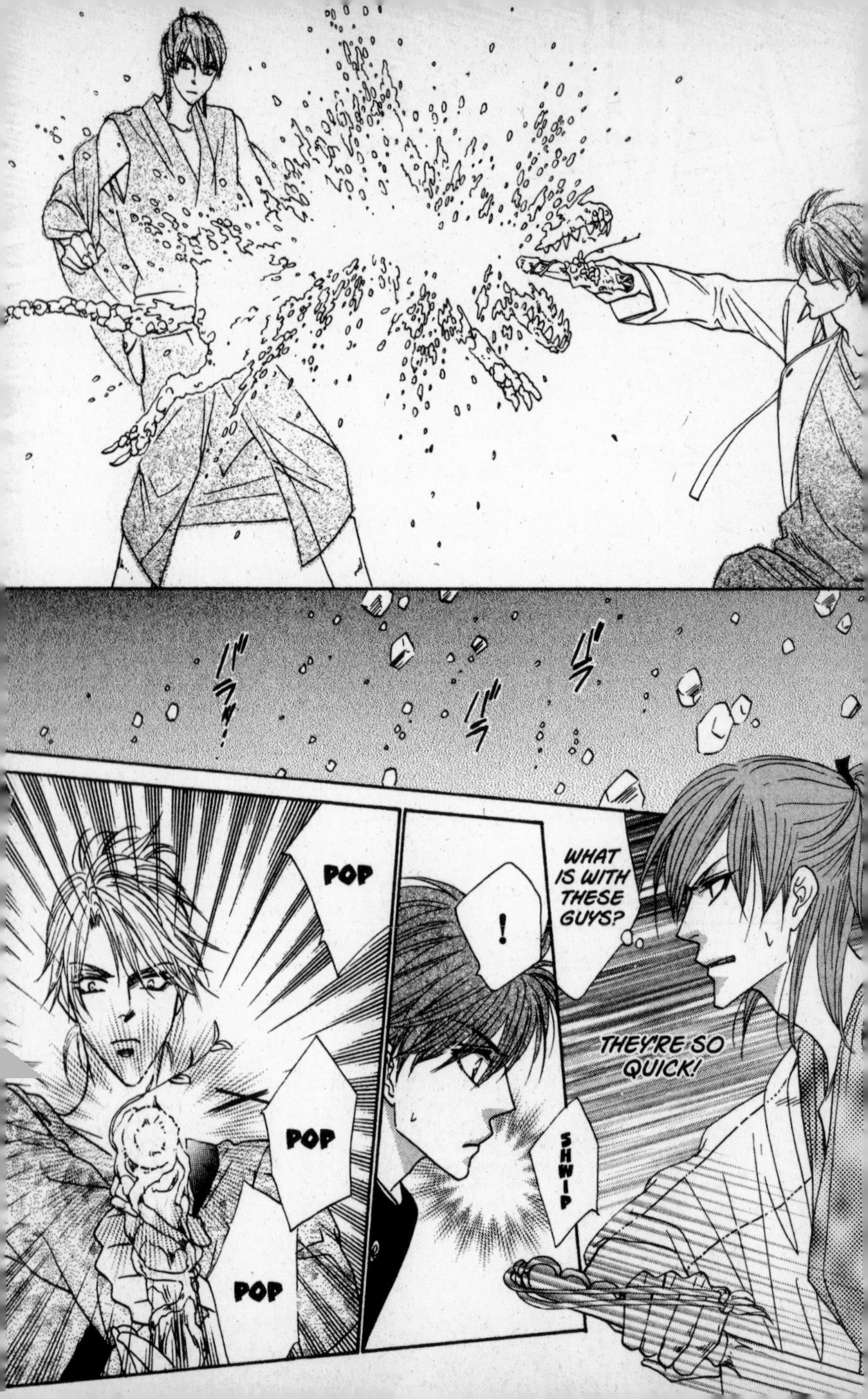
WHAT IS WITH THESE GUYS?
THEY'RE SO QUICK!
!
SHWIP
POP
POP
POP

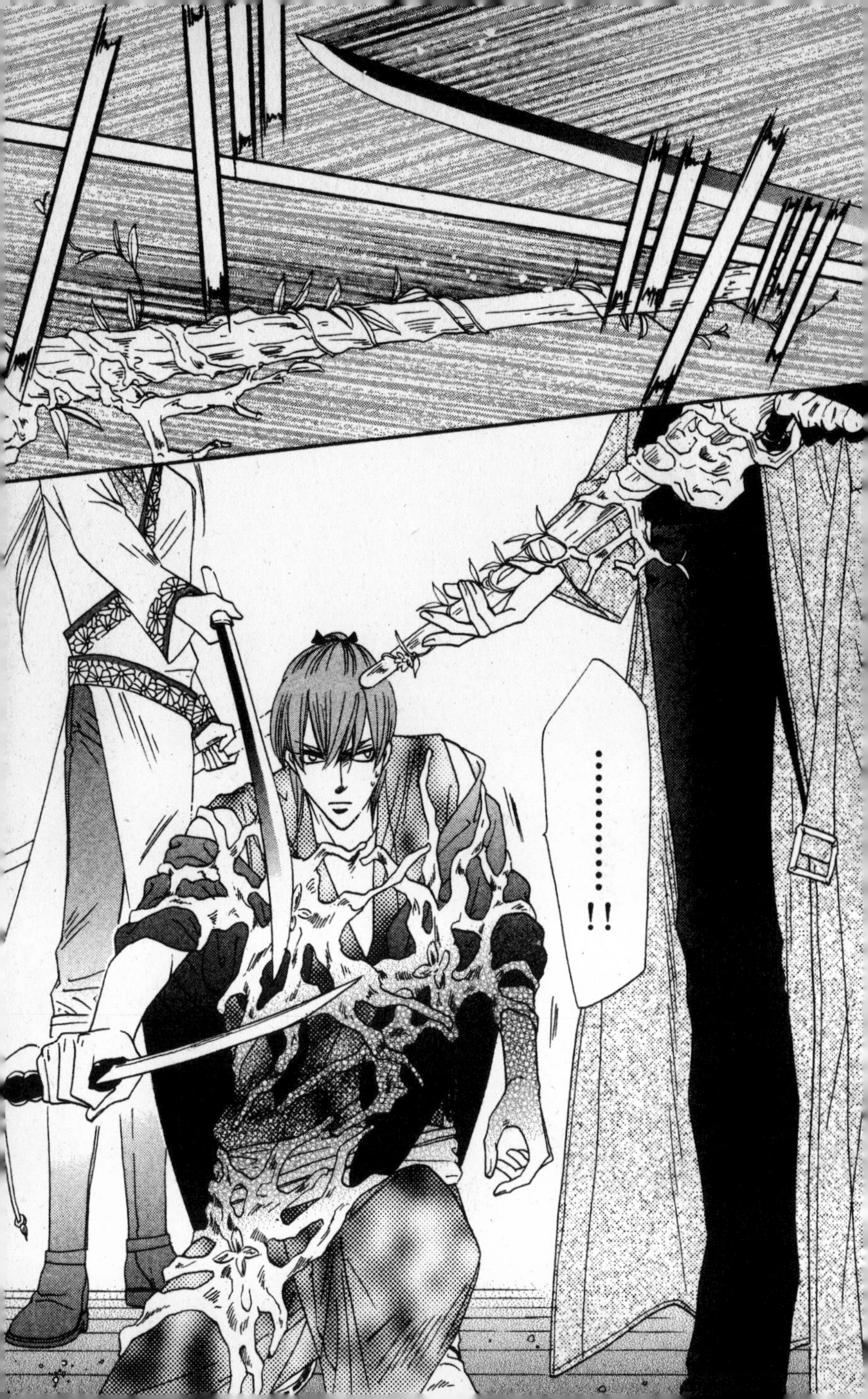
...........!!

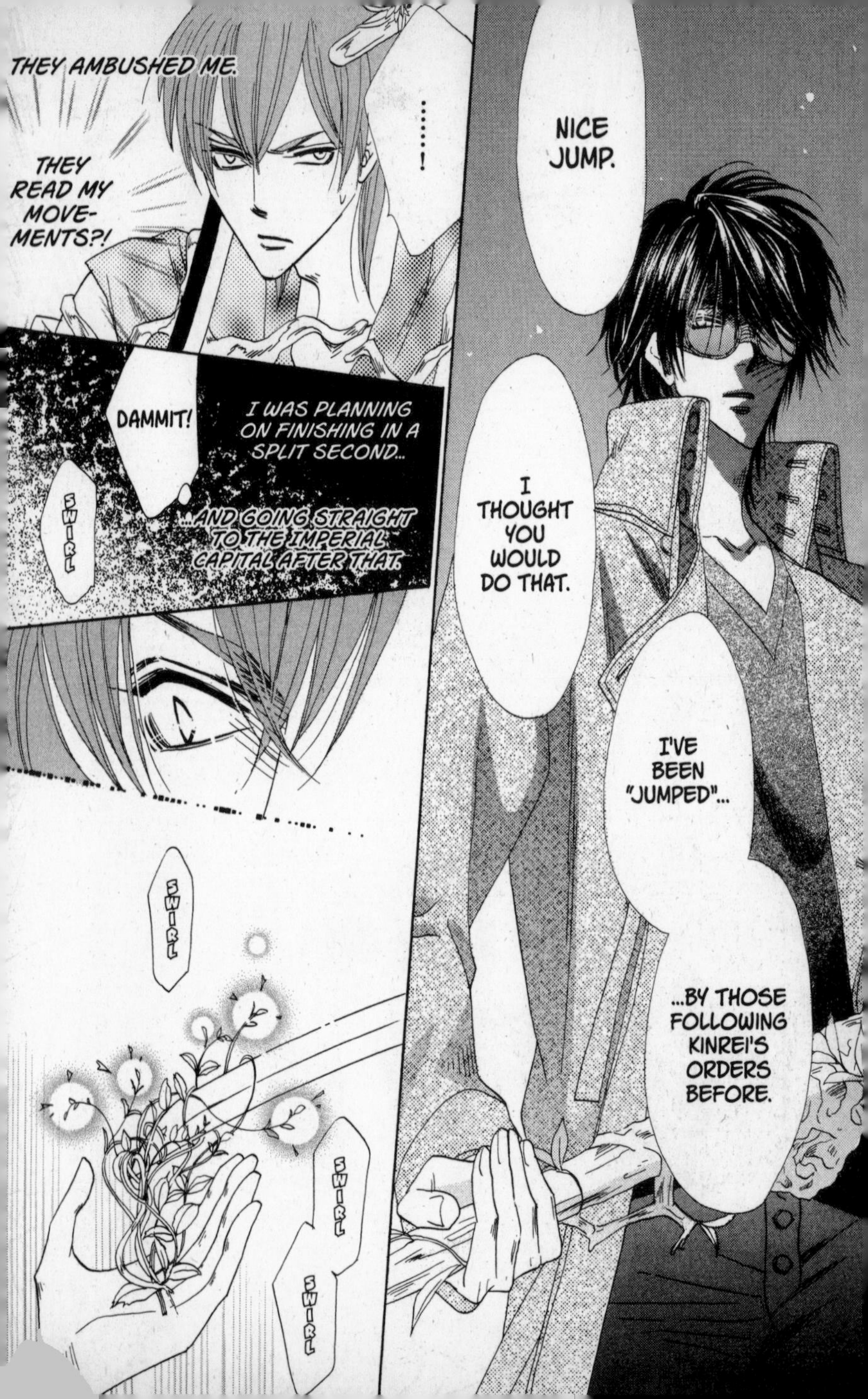
NICE JUMP.
I THOUGHT YOU WOULD DO THAT.
I'VE BEEN "JUMPED"...
...BY THOSE FOLLOWING KINREI'S ORDERS BEFORE.
......!
THEY AMBUSHED ME.
THEY READ MY MOVE-MENTS?!
I WAS PLANNING ON FINISHING IN A SPLIT SECOND...
DAMMIT!
...AND GOING STRAIGHT TO THE IMPERIAL CAPITAL AFTER THAT.
SWIRL
SWIRL
SWIRL
SWIRL

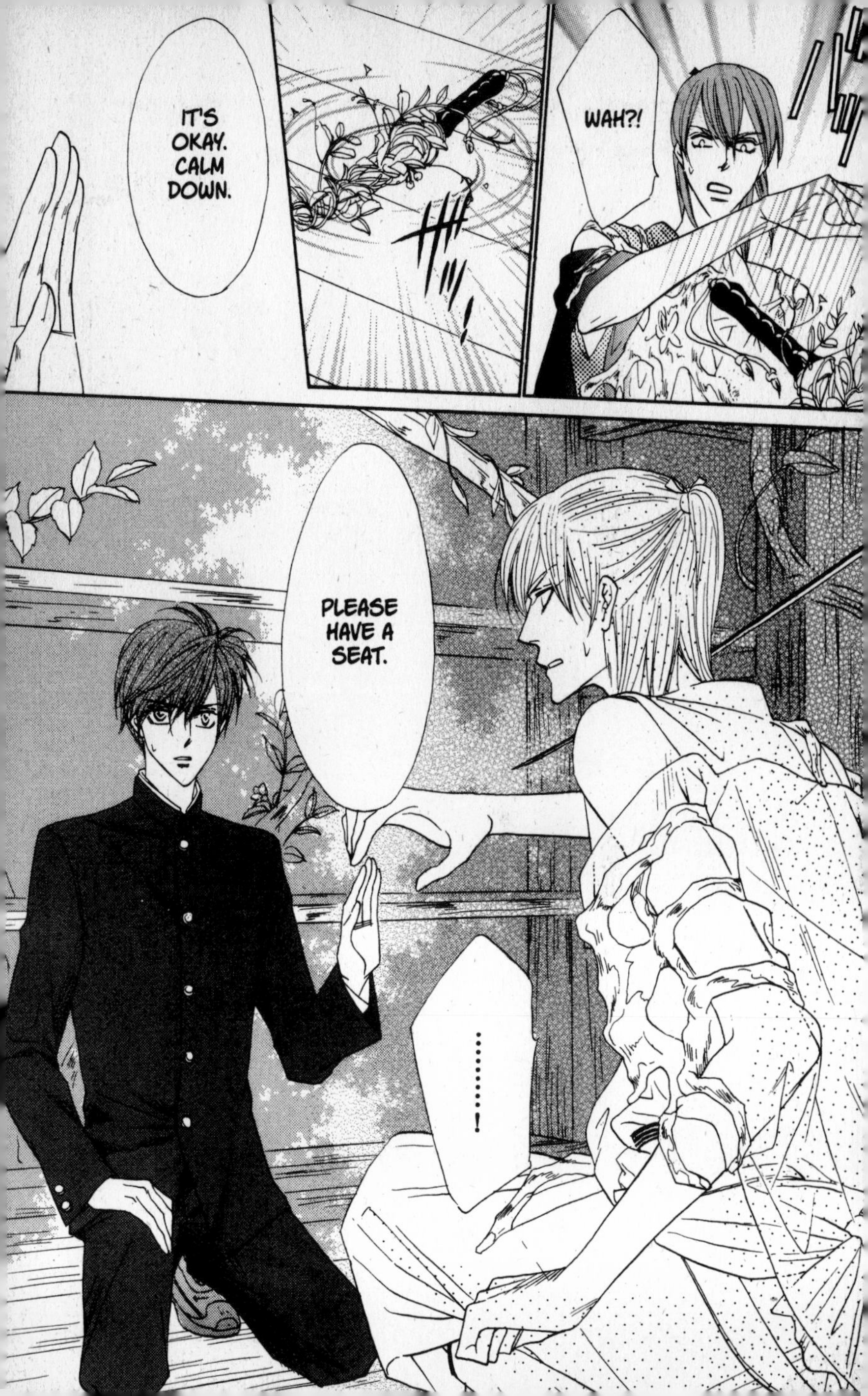
WAH?!
IT'S OKAY. CALM DOWN.
PLEASE HAVE A SEAT.
.......!

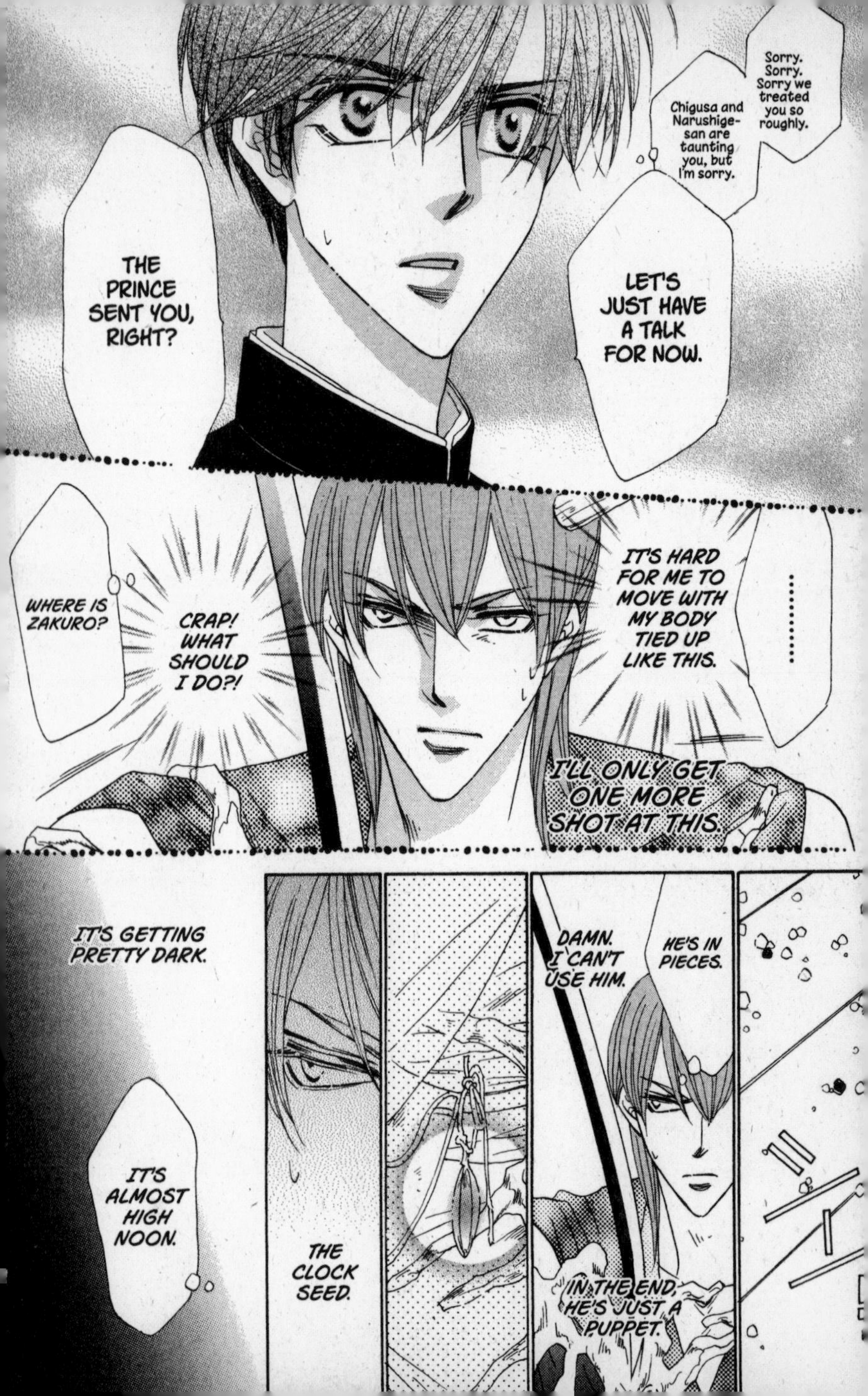
Sorry. Sorry. Sorry we treated you so roughly.
Chigusa and Narushige-san are taunting you, but I'm sorry.
LET'S JUST HAVE A TALK FOR NOW.
THE PRINCE SENT YOU, RIGHT?
......
IT'S HARD FOR ME TO MOVE WITH MY BODY TIED UP LIKE THIS.
I'LL ONLY GET ONE MORE SHOT AT THIS.
CRAP! WHAT SHOULD I DO?!
WHERE IS ZAKURO?
HE'S IN PIECES.
DAMN. I CAN'T USE HIM.
IN THE END, HE'S JUST A PUPPET.
THE CLOCK SEED.
IT'S GETTING PRETTY DARK.
IT'S ALMOST HIGH NOON.

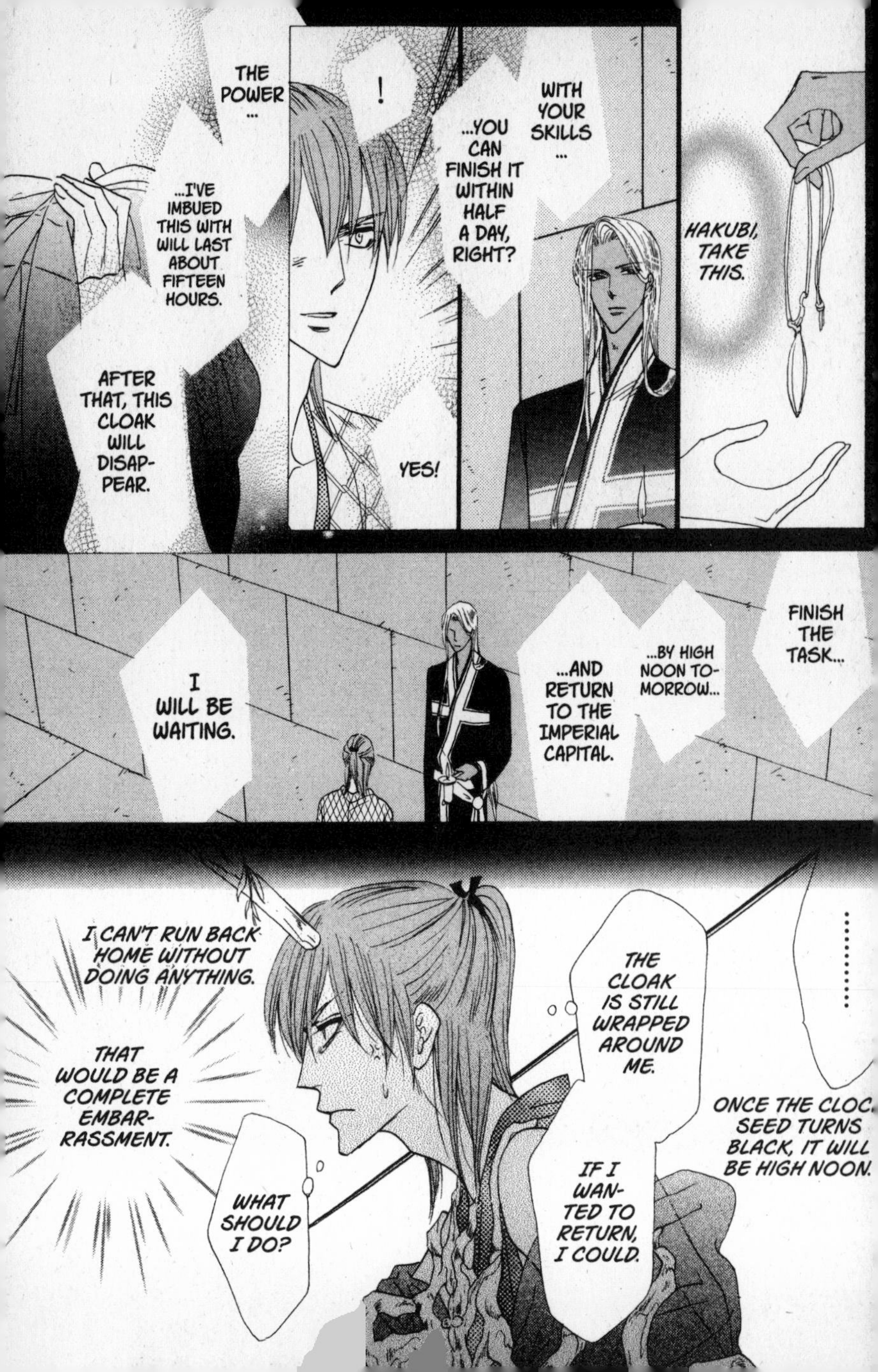
HAKUBI, TAKE THIS.
WITH YOUR SKILLS...
...YOU CAN FINISH IT WITHIN HALF A DAY, RIGHT?
!
YES!
THE POWER...
...I'VE IMBUED THIS WITH WILL LAST ABOUT FIFTEEN HOURS.
AFTER THAT, THIS CLOAK WILL DISAPPEAR.
FINISH THE TASK...
...BY HIGH NOON TOMORROW...
...AND RETURN TO THE IMPERIAL CAPITAL.
I WILL BE WAITING.
....
ONCE THE CLOC SEED TURNS BLACK, IT WILL BE HIGH NOON.
THE CLOAK IS STILL WRAPPED AROUND ME.
IF I WANTED TO RETURN, I COULD.
I CAN'T RUN BACK HOME WITHOUT DOING ANYTHING.
THAT WOULD BE A COMPLETE EMBARRASSMENT.
WHAT SHOULD I DO?

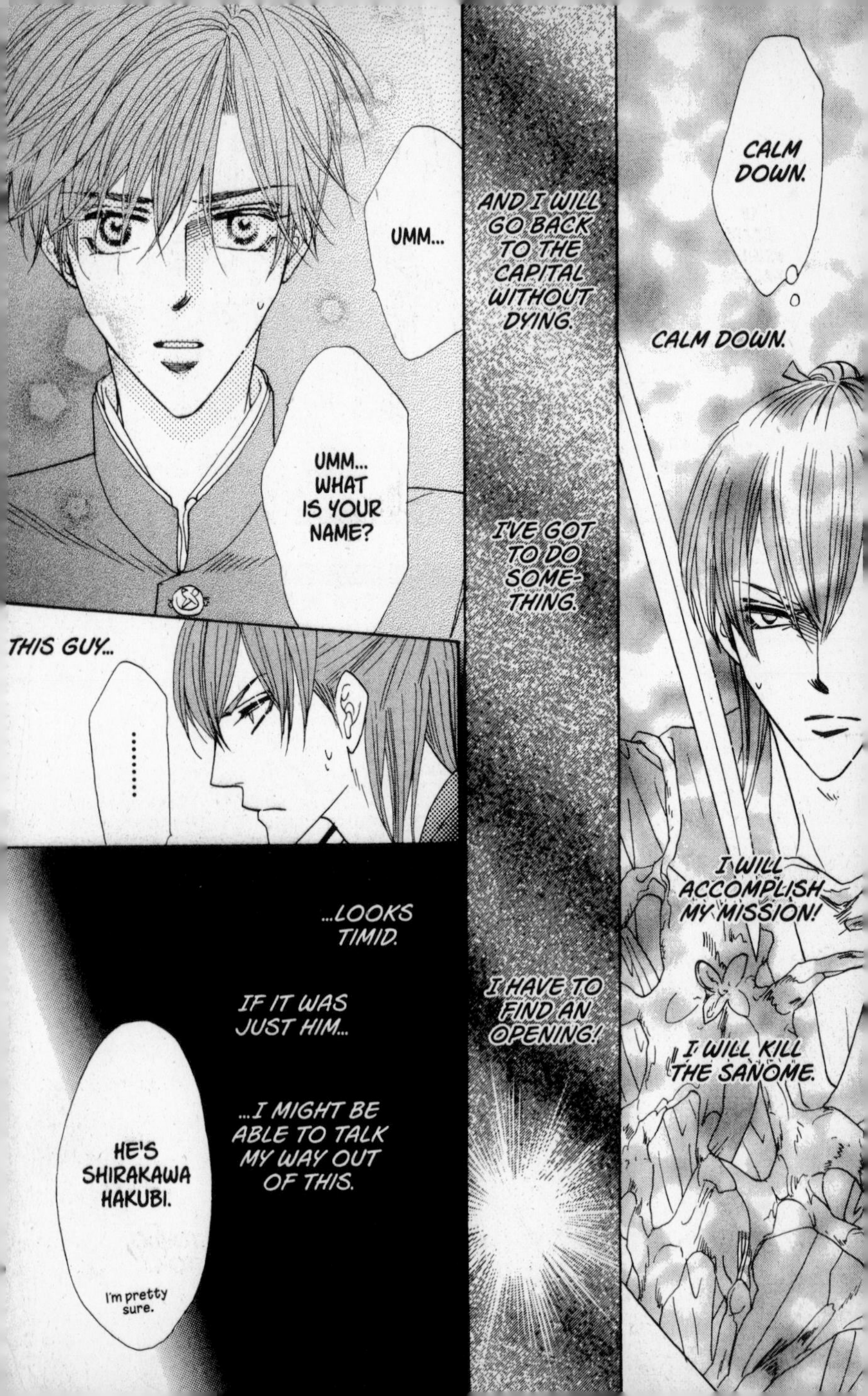
CALM DOWN.
CALM DOWN.
I WILL ACCOMPLISH MY MISSION!
I WILL KILL THE SANOME.
AND I WILL GO BACK TO THE CAPITAL WITHOUT DYING.
I'VE GOT TO DO SOME-THING.
I HAVE TO FIND AN OPENING!
UMM...
UMM... WHAT IS YOUR NAME?
THIS GUY...
......
...LOOKS TIMID.
IF IT WAS JUST HIM...
...I MIGHT BE ABLE TO TALK MY WAY OUT OF THIS.
HE'S SHIRAKAWA HAKUBI.
I'm pretty sure.

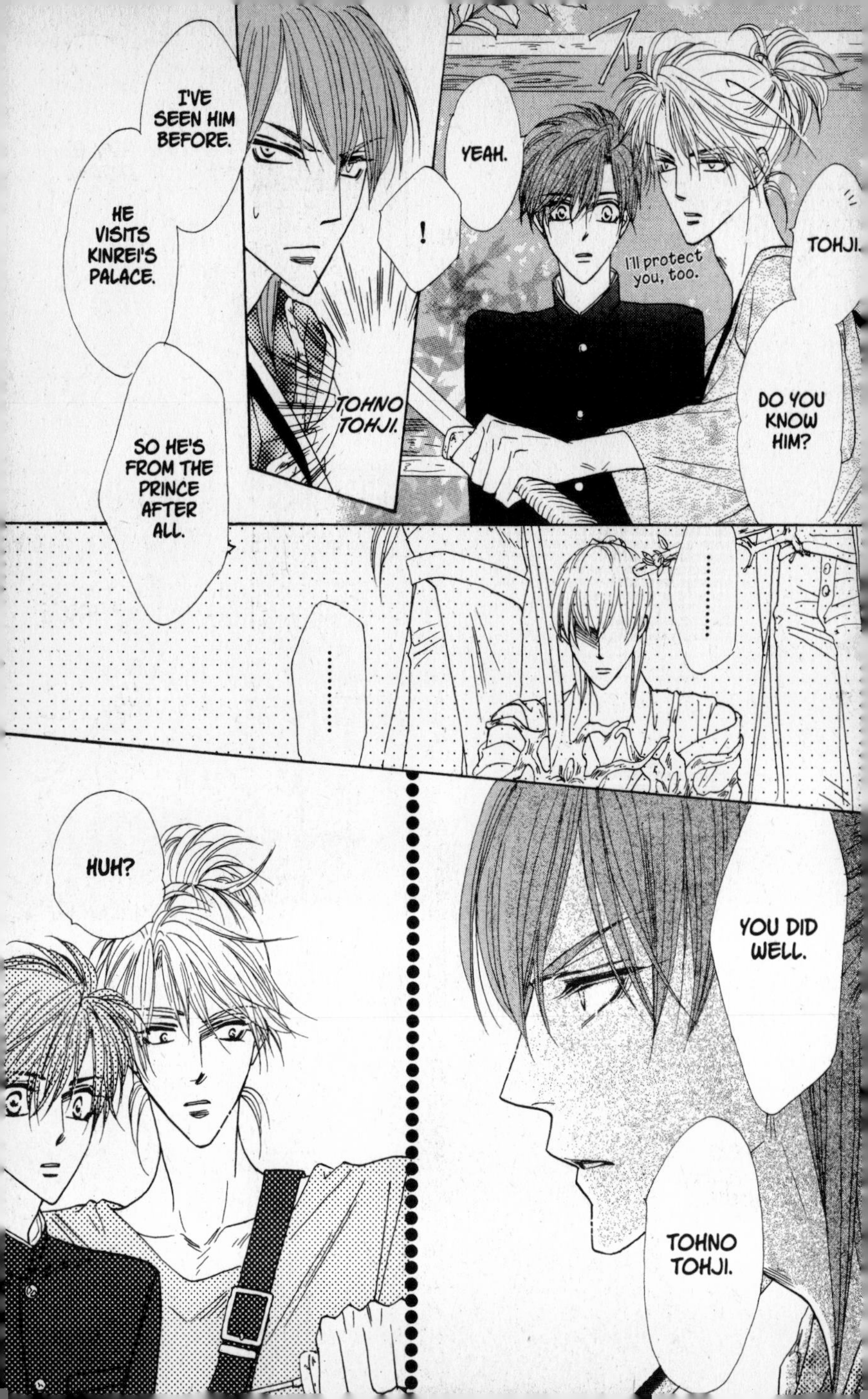
TOHJI.
I'll protect you, too.
DO YOU KNOW HIM?
YEAH.
!
TOHNO TOHJI.
I'VE SEEN HIM BEFORE.
HE VISITS KINREI'S PALACE.
SO HE'S FROM THE PRINCE AFTER ALL.
......
......
YOU DID WELL.
TOHNO TOHJI.
HUH?

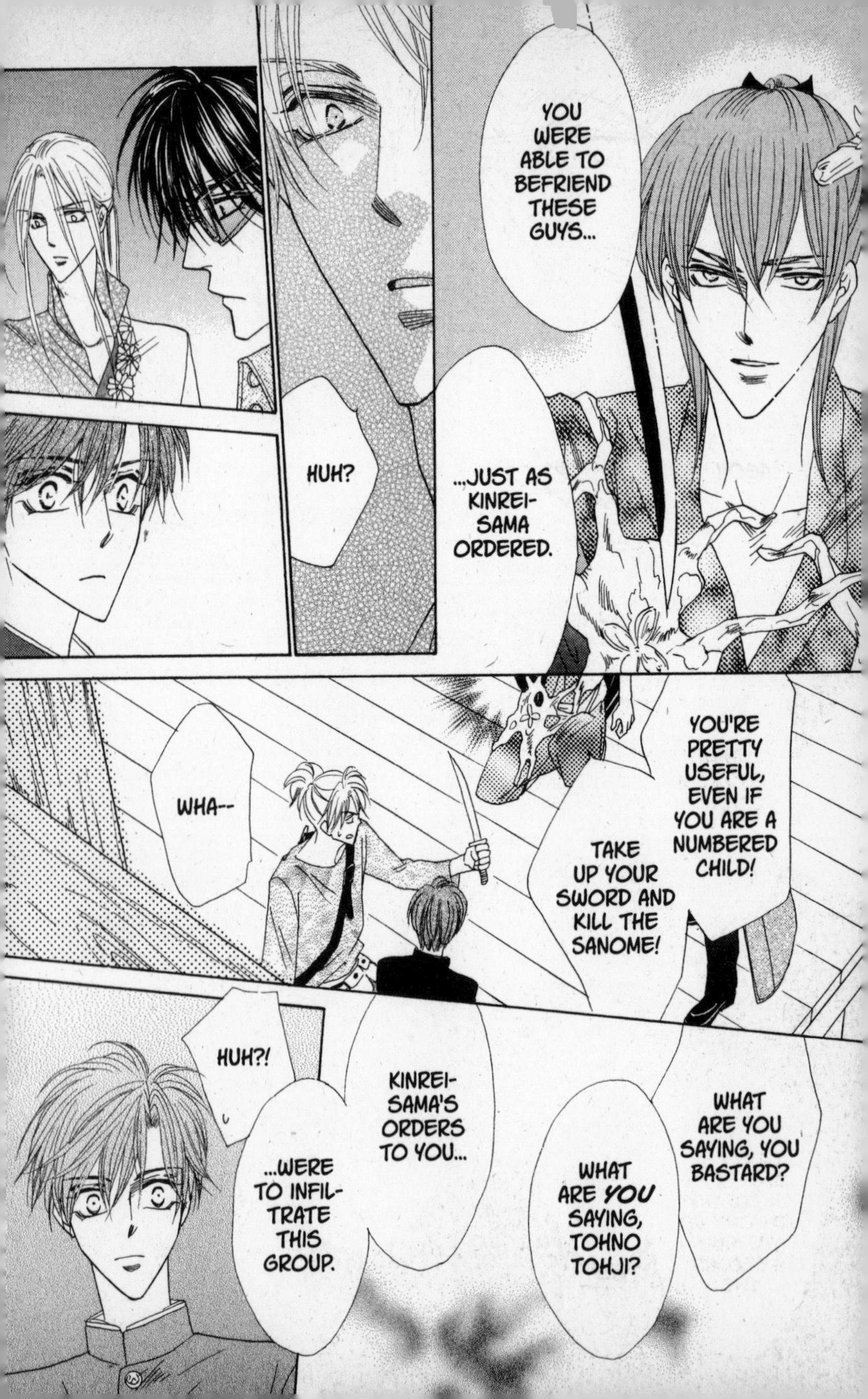
YOU WERE ABLE TO BEFRIEND THESE GUYS...
...JUST AS KINREI-SAMA ORDERED.
HUH?
YOU'RE PRETTY USEFUL, EVEN IF YOU ARE A NUMBERED CHILD!
TAKE UP YOUR SWORD AND KILL THE SANOME!
WHA--
WHAT ARE YOU SAYING, YOU BASTARD?
WHAT ARE *YOU* SAYING, TOHNO TOHJI?
KINREI-SAMA'S ORDERS TO YOU...
...WERE TO INFILTRATE THIS GROUP.
HUH?!

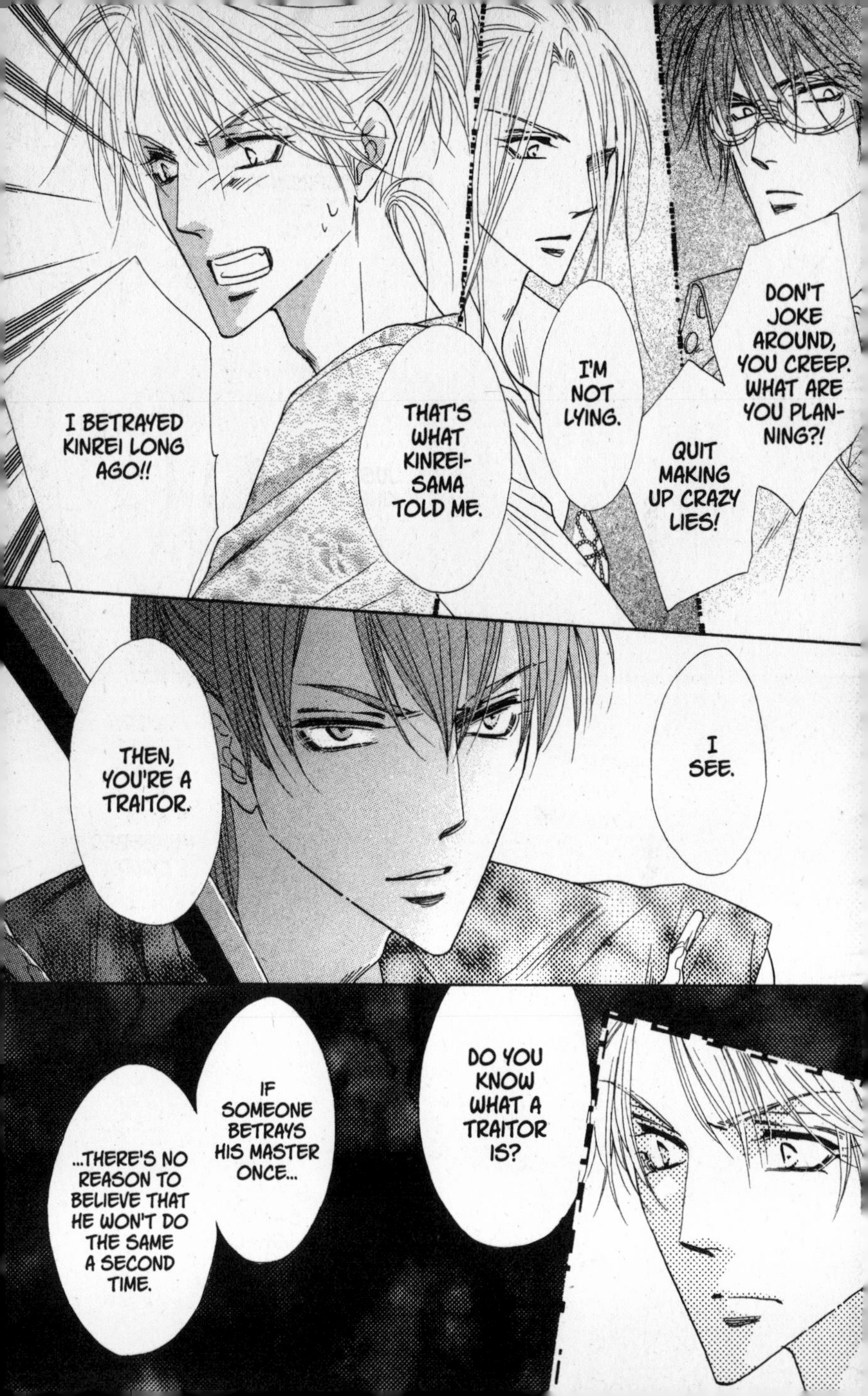
DON'T JOKE AROUND, YOU CREEP. WHAT ARE YOU PLAN-NING?!
QUIT MAKING UP CRAZY LIES!
I'M NOT LYING.
THAT'S WHAT KINREI-SAMA TOLD ME.
I BETRAYED KINREI LONG AGO!!
I SEE.
THEN, YOU'RE A TRAITOR.
DO YOU KNOW WHAT A TRAITOR IS?
IF SOMEONE BETRAYS HIS MASTER ONCE...
...THERE'S NO REASON TO BELIEVE THAT HE WON'T DO THE SAME A SECOND TIME.

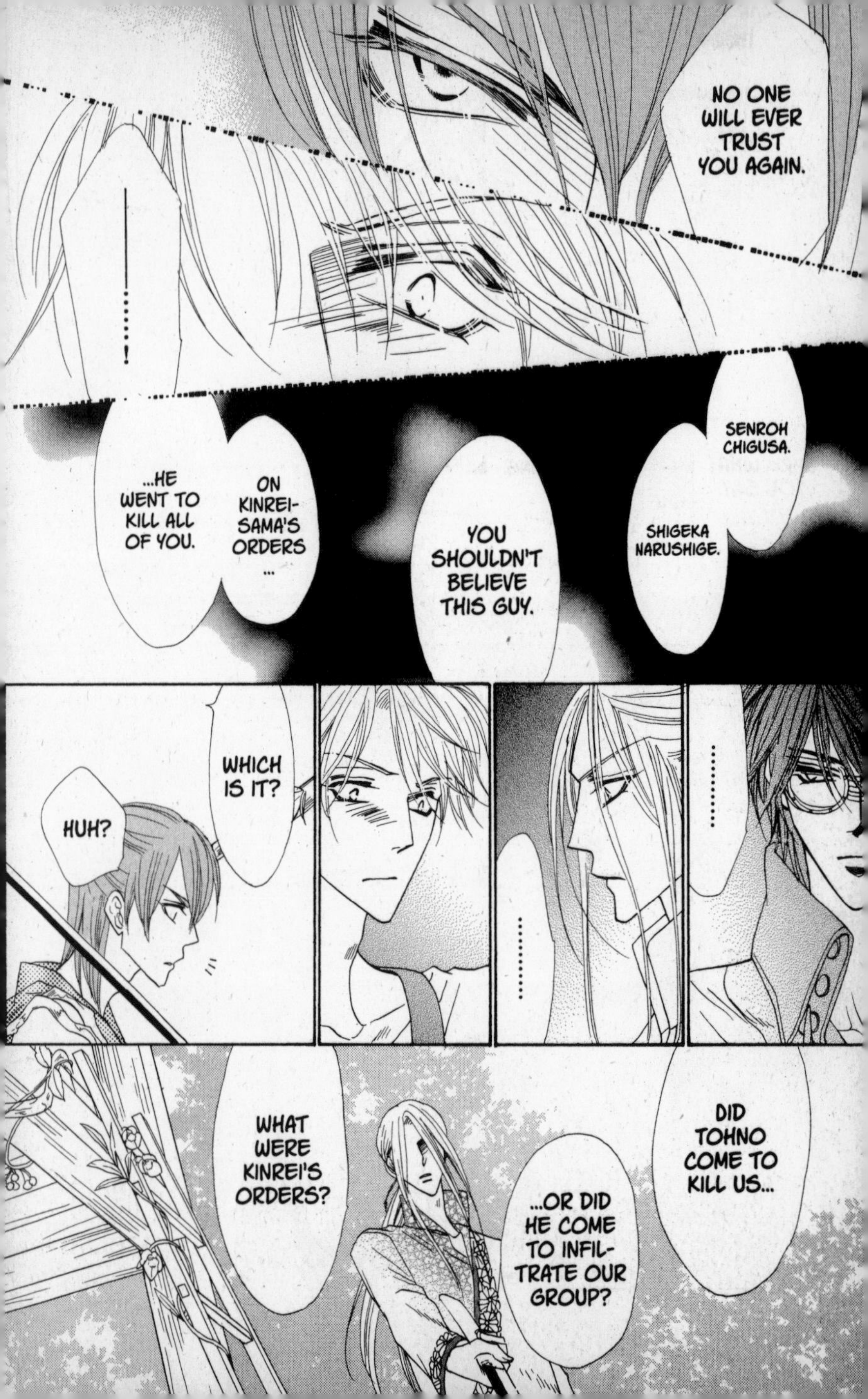
NO ONE WILL EVER TRUST YOU AGAIN.
......!
SENROH CHIGUSA.
SHIGEKA NARUSHIGE.
YOU SHOULDN'T BELIEVE THIS GUY.
ON KINREI-SAMA'S ORDERS ...
...HE WENT TO KILL ALL OF YOU.
......
......
WHICH IS IT?
HUH?
DID TOHNO COME TO KILL US...
...OR DID HE COME TO INFILTRATE OUR GROUP?
WHAT WERE KINREI'S ORDERS?

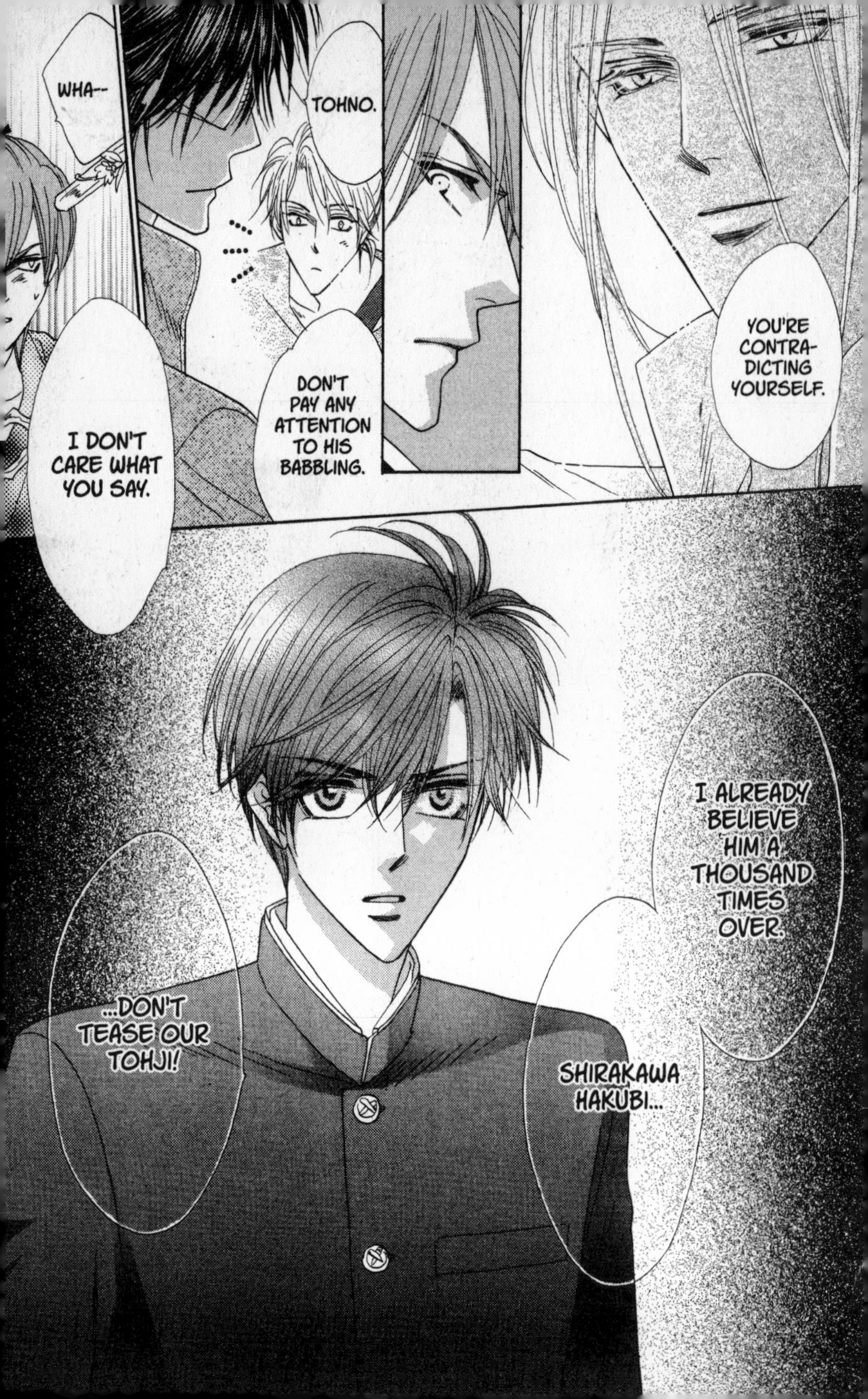

YOU'RE CONTRADICTING YOURSELF.
TOHNO.
WHA--
...
DON'T PAY ANY ATTENTION TO HIS BABBLING.
I DON'T CARE WHAT YOU SAY.
I ALREADY BELIEVE HIM A THOUSAND TIMES OVER.
SHIRAKAWA HAKUBI...
...DON'T TEASE OUR TOHJI!

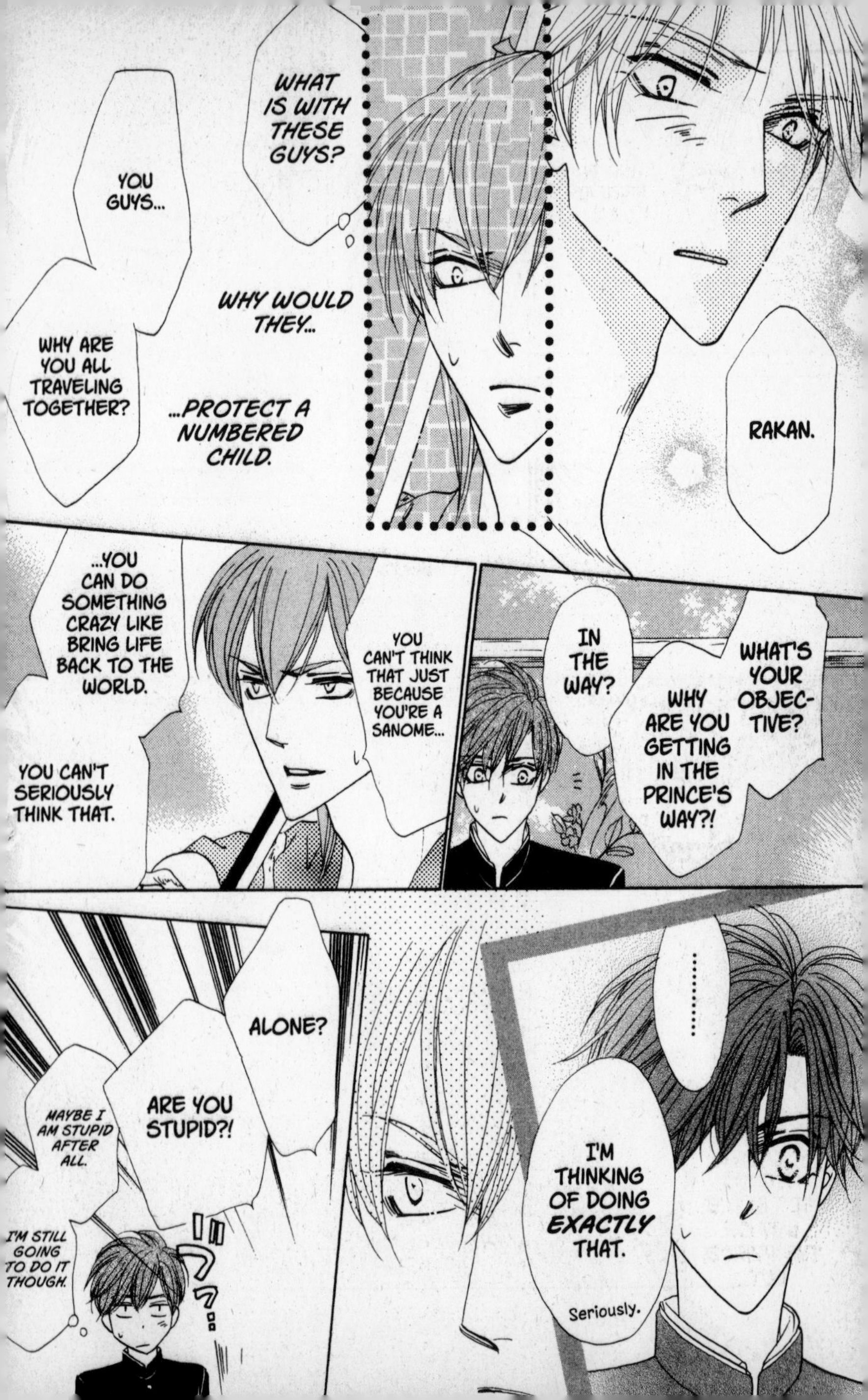
RAKAN.
WHAT IS WITH THESE GUYS?
WHY WOULD THEY...
...PROTECT A NUMBERED CHILD.
YOU GUYS...
WHY ARE YOU ALL TRAVELING TOGETHER?
WHAT'S YOUR OBJECTIVE?
IN THE WAY?
WHY ARE YOU GETTING IN THE PRINCE'S WAY?!
YOU CAN'T THINK THAT JUST BECAUSE YOU'RE A SANOME...
...YOU CAN DO SOMETHING CRAZY LIKE BRING LIFE BACK TO THE WORLD.
YOU CAN'T SERIOUSLY THINK THAT.
......
I'M THINKING OF DOING EXACTLY THAT.
Seriously.
ALONE?
ARE YOU STUPID?!
MAYBE I AM STUPID AFTER ALL.
I'M STILL GOING TO DO IT THOUGH.

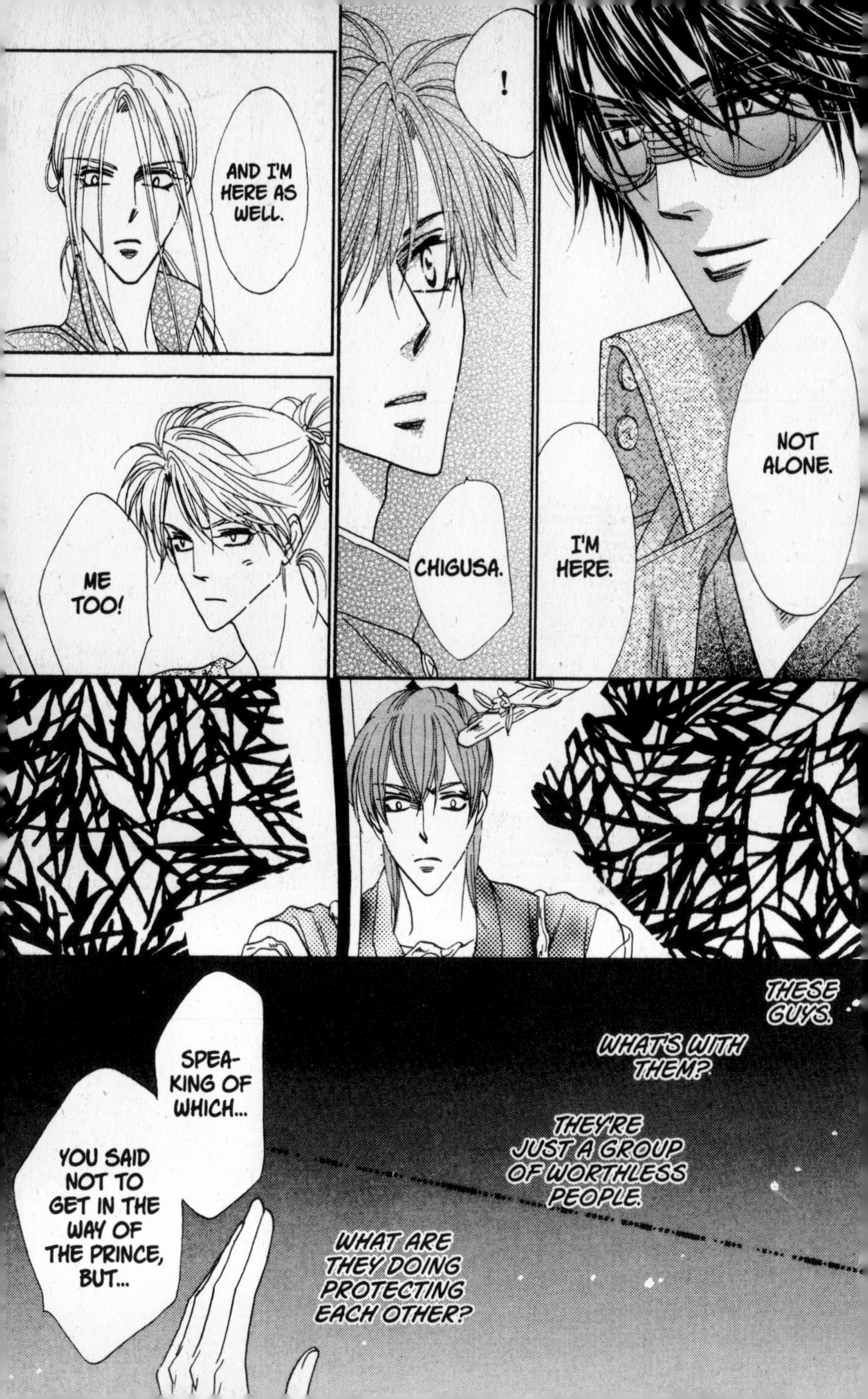
NOT ALONE.
I'M HERE.
!
CHIGUSA.
AND I'M HERE AS WELL.
ME TOO!
THESE GUYS.
WHAT'S WITH THEM?
THEY'RE JUST A GROUP OF WORTHLESS PEOPLE.
WHAT ARE THEY DOING PROTECTING EACH OTHER?
SPEA- KING OF WHICH...
YOU SAID NOT TO GET IN THE WAY OF THE PRINCE, BUT...

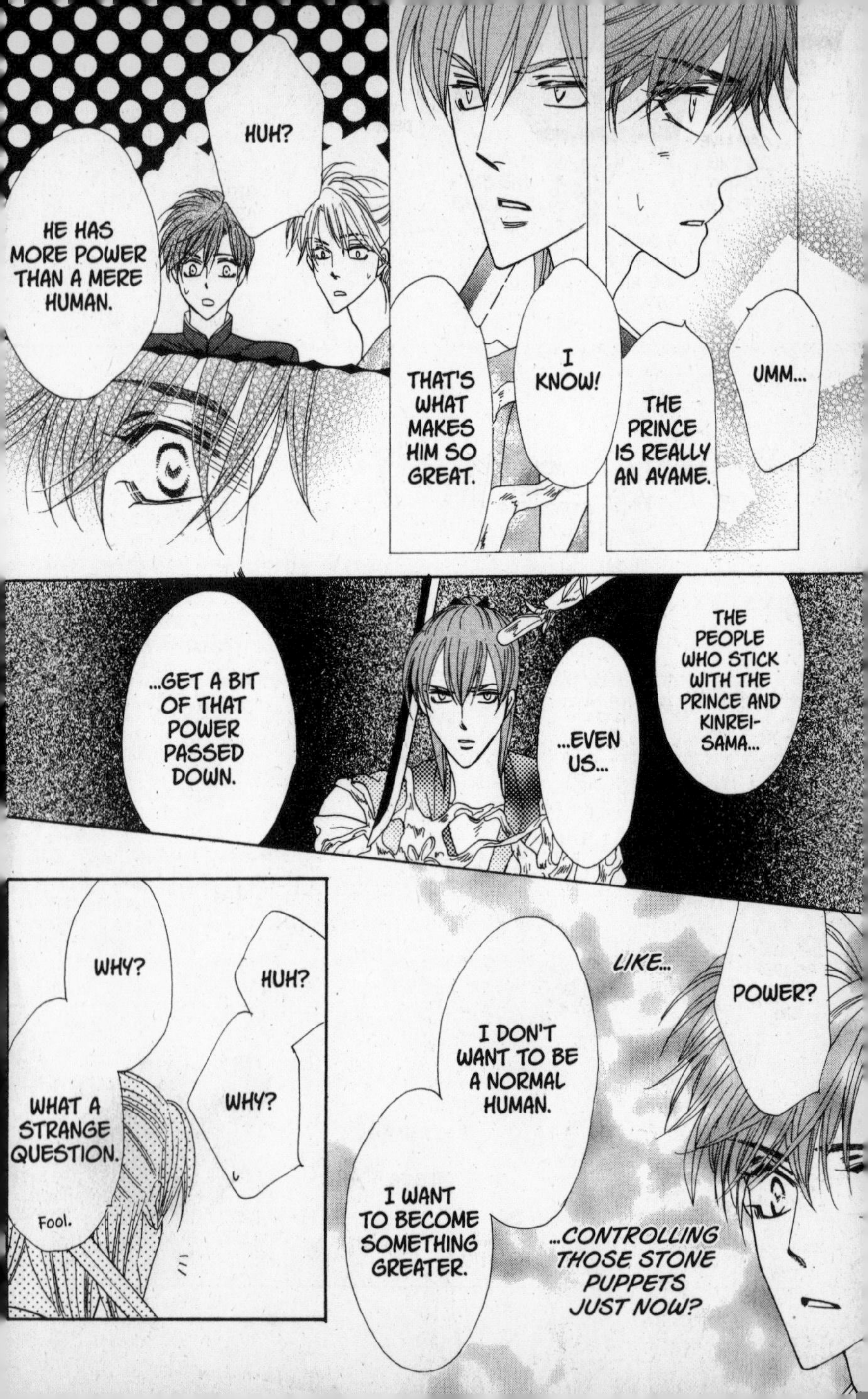
UMM...
THE PRINCE IS REALLY AN AYAME.
I KNOW!
THAT'S WHAT MAKES HIM SO GREAT.
HUH?
HE HAS MORE POWER THAN A MERE HUMAN.
THE PEOPLE WHO STICK WITH THE PRINCE AND KINREI-SAMA...
...EVEN US...
...GET A BIT OF THAT POWER PASSED DOWN.
POWER?
LIKE...
...CONTROLLING THOSE STONE PUPPETS JUST NOW?
I DON'T WANT TO BE A NORMAL HUMAN.
I WANT TO BECOME SOMETHING GREATER.
HUH?
WHY?
WHY?
WHAT A STRANGE QUESTION.
Fool.

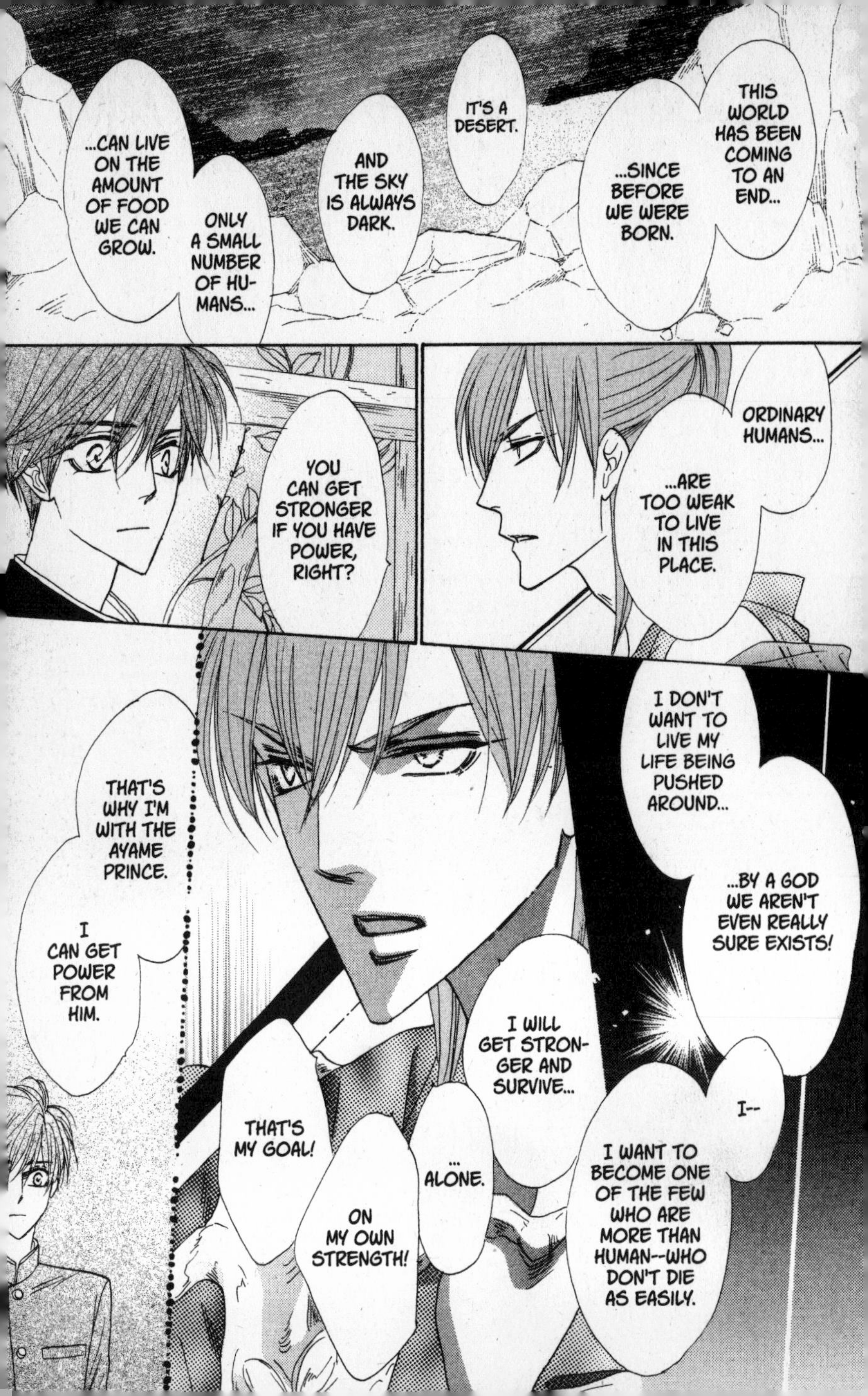
THIS WORLD HAS BEEN COMING TO AN END...
...SINCE BEFORE WE WERE BORN.
IT'S A DESERT.
AND THE SKY IS ALWAYS DARK.
ONLY A SMALL NUMBER OF HU-MANS...
...CAN LIVE ON THE AMOUNT OF FOOD WE CAN GROW.
ORDINARY HUMANS...
...ARE TOO WEAK TO LIVE IN THIS PLACE.
YOU CAN GET STRONGER IF YOU HAVE POWER, RIGHT?
I DON'T WANT TO LIVE MY LIFE BEING PUSHED AROUND...
...BY A GOD WE AREN'T EVEN REALLY SURE EXISTS!
THAT'S WHY I'M WITH THE AYAME PRINCE.
I CAN GET POWER FROM HIM.
I--
I WANT TO BECOME ONE OF THE FEW WHO ARE MORE THAN HUMAN--WHO DON'T DIE AS EASILY.
I WILL GET STRON-GER AND SURVIVE...
...ALONE.
ON MY OWN STRENGTH!
THAT'S MY GOAL!

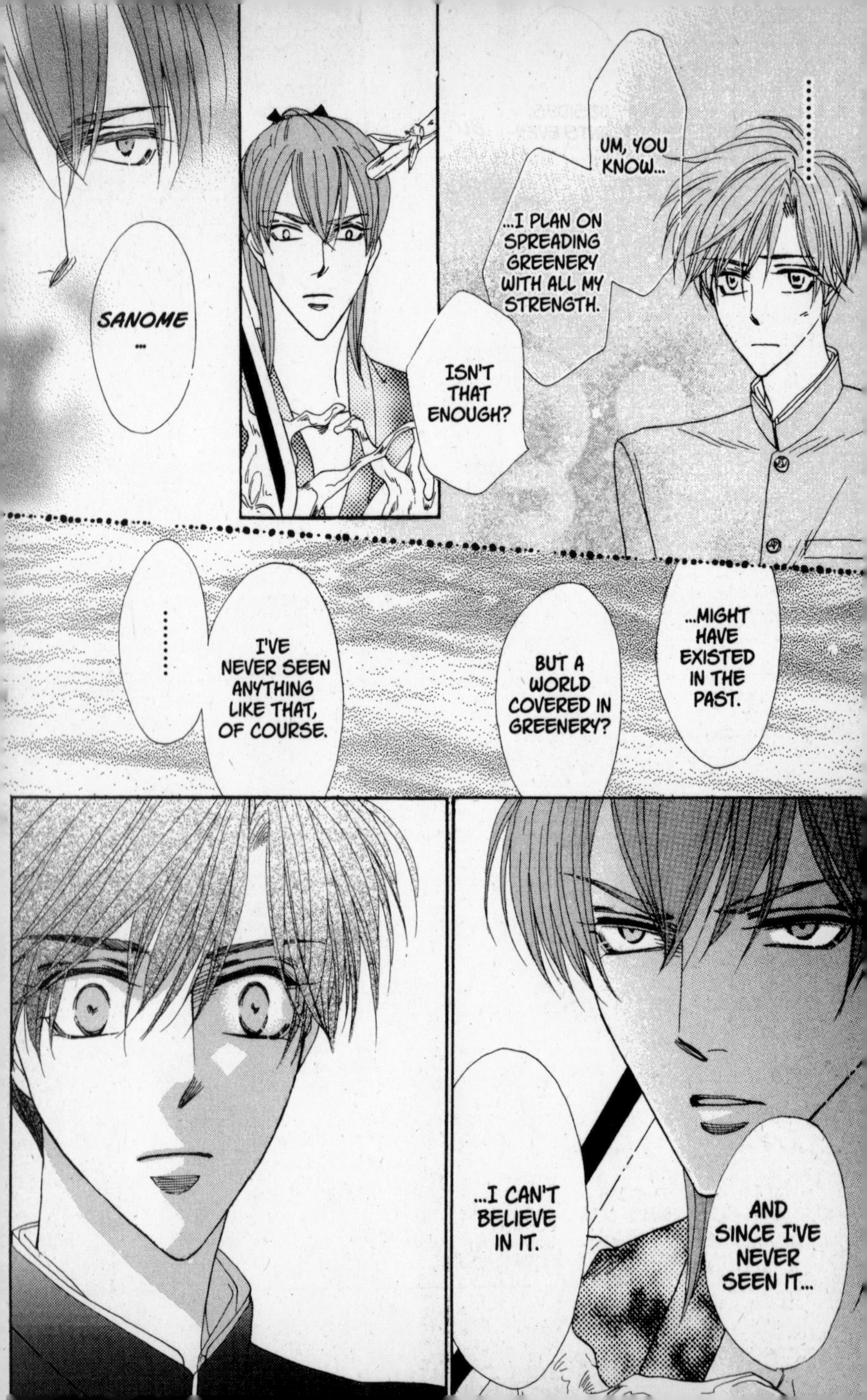
......
UM, YOU KNOW...
...I PLAN ON SPREADING GREENERY WITH ALL MY STRENGTH.
ISN'T THAT ENOUGH?
SANOME ...
...MIGHT HAVE EXISTED IN THE PAST.
BUT A WORLD COVERED IN GREENERY?
I'VE NEVER SEEN ANYTHING LIKE THAT, OF COURSE.
......
AND SINCE I'VE NEVER SEEN IT...
...I CAN'T BELIEVE IN IT.

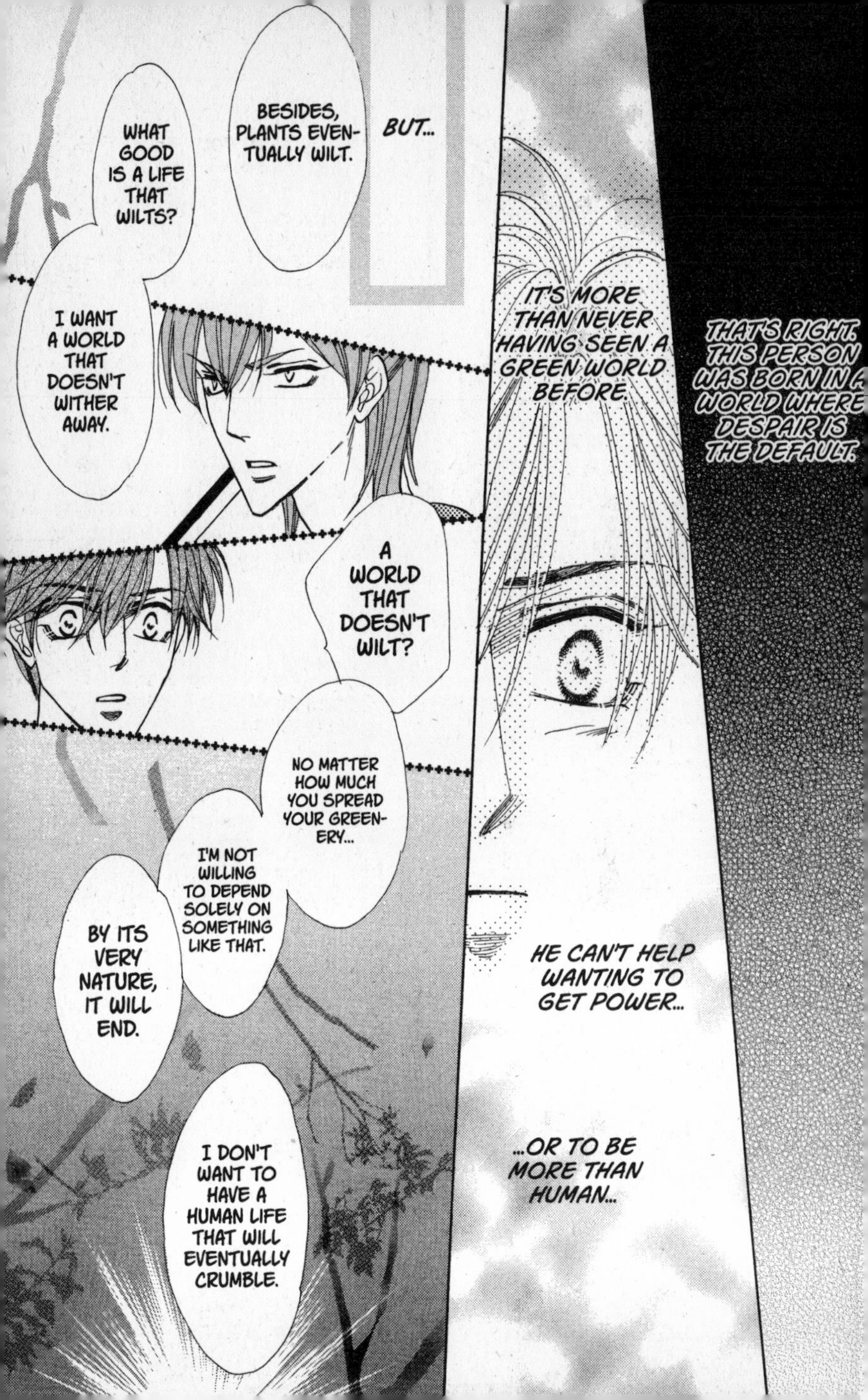
THAT'S RIGHT. THIS PERSON WAS BORN IN A WORLD WHERE DESPAIR IS THE DEFAULT.
IT'S MORE THAN NEVER HAVING SEEN A GREEN WORLD BEFORE.
HE CAN'T HELP WANTING TO GET POWER...
...OR TO BE MORE THAN HUMAN...
BUT...
BESIDES, PLANTS EVEN-TUALLY WILT.
WHAT GOOD IS A LIFE THAT WILTS?
I WANT A WORLD THAT DOESN'T WITHER AWAY.
A WORLD THAT DOESN'T WILT?
NO MATTER HOW MUCH YOU SPREAD YOUR GREEN-ERY...
I'M NOT WILLING TO DEPEND SOLELY ON SOMETHING LIKE THAT.
BY ITS VERY NATURE, IT WILL END.
I DON'T WANT TO HAVE A HUMAN LIFE THAT WILL EVENTUALLY CRUMBLE.

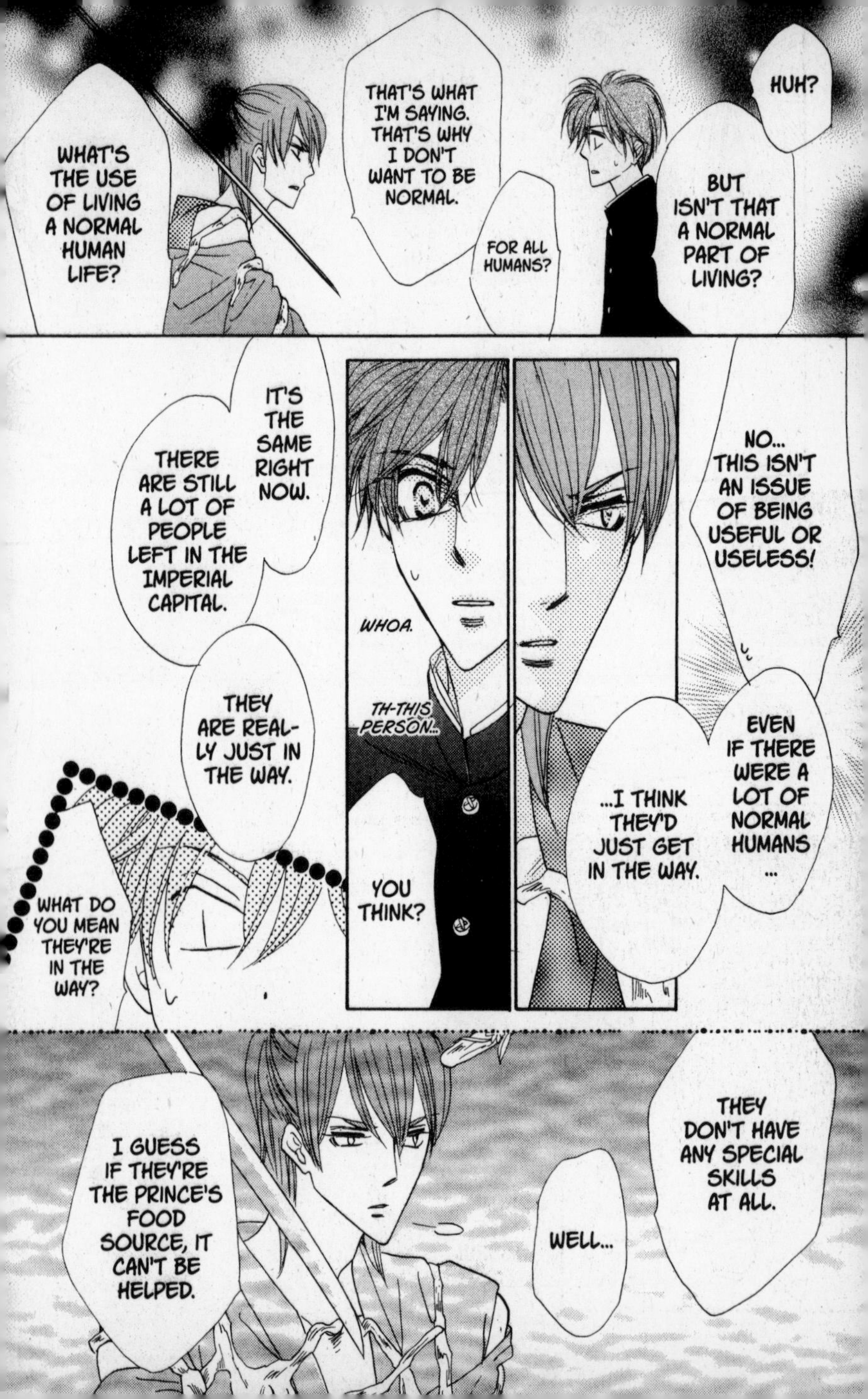
HUH?
BUT ISN'T THAT A NORMAL PART OF LIVING?
FOR ALL HUMANS?
THAT'S WHAT I'M SAYING. THAT'S WHY I DON'T WANT TO BE NORMAL.
WHAT'S THE USE OF LIVING A NORMAL HUMAN LIFE?
NO... THIS ISN'T AN ISSUE OF BEING USEFUL OR USELESS!
EVEN IF THERE WERE A LOT OF NORMAL HUMANS ...
...I THINK THEY'D JUST GET IN THE WAY.
WHOA.
TH-THIS PERSON...
YOU THINK?
IT'S THE SAME RIGHT NOW.
THERE ARE STILL A LOT OF PEOPLE LEFT IN THE IMPERIAL CAPITAL.
THEY ARE REAL-LY JUST IN THE WAY.
WHAT DO YOU MEAN THEY'RE IN THE WAY?
THEY DON'T HAVE ANY SPECIAL SKILLS AT ALL.
WELL...
I GUESS IF THEY'RE THE PRINCE'S FOOD SOURCE, IT CAN'T BE HELPED.

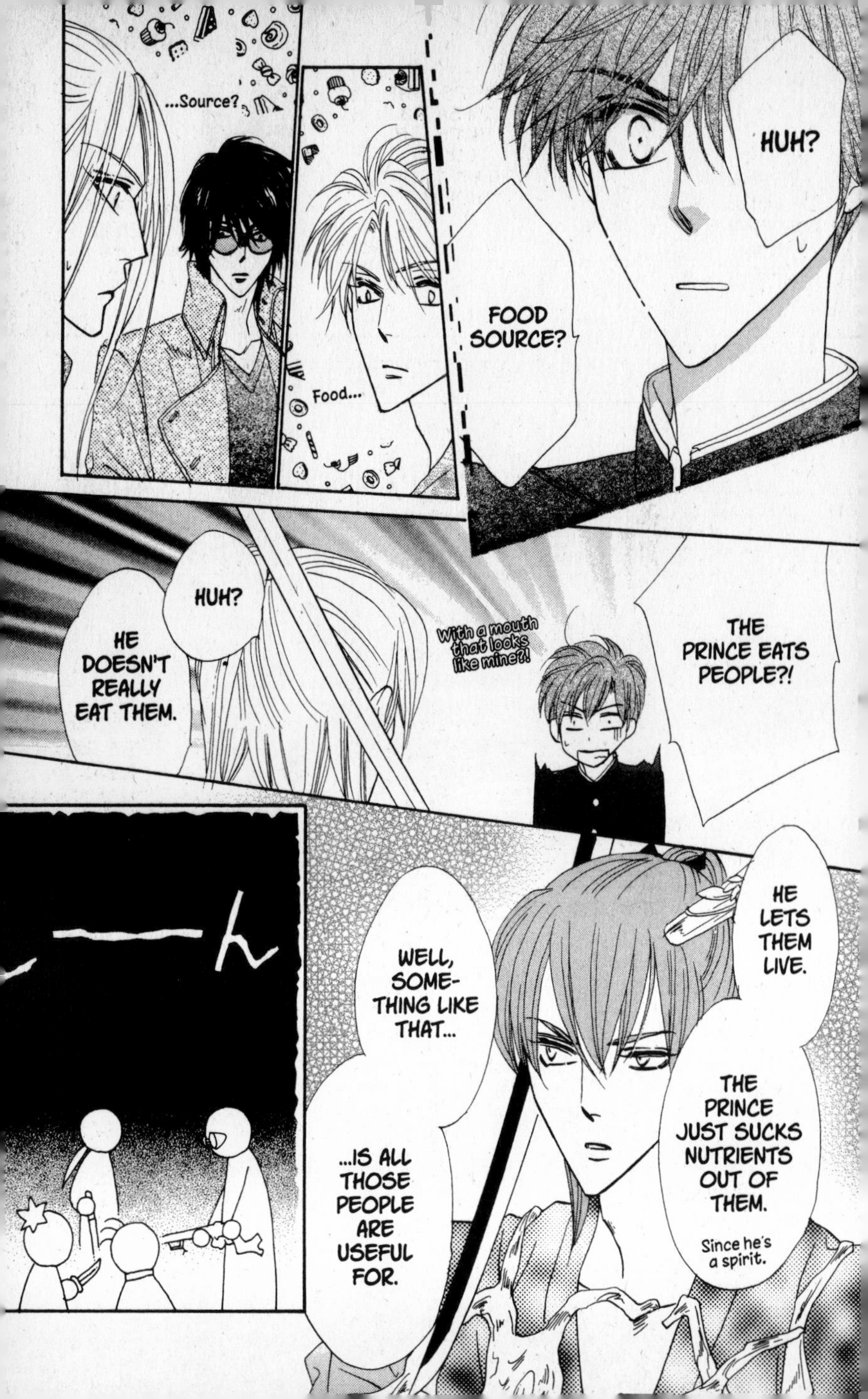
HUH?
FOOD SOURCE?
Food...
...Source?
THE PRINCE EATS PEOPLE?!
With a mouth that looks like mine?!
HUH?
HE DOESN'T REALLY EAT THEM.
HE LETS THEM LIVE.
THE PRINCE JUST SUCKS NUTRIENTS OUT OF THEM.
Since he's a spirit.
WELL, SOME-THING LIKE THAT...
...IS ALL THOSE PEOPLE ARE USEFUL FOR.

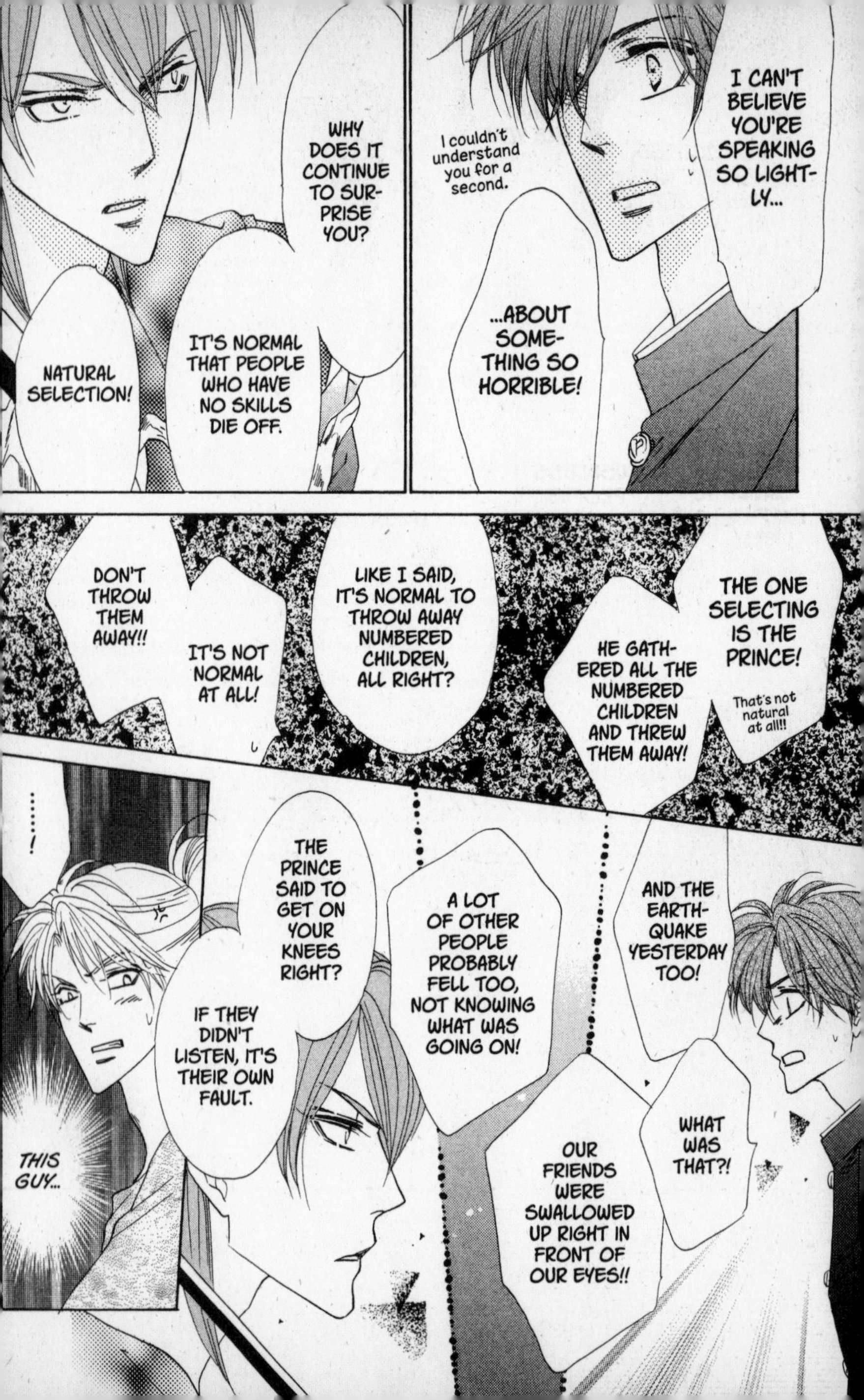
I CAN'T BELIEVE YOU'RE SPEAKING SO LIGHT-LY...
I couldn't understand you for a second.
...ABOUT SOME-THING SO HORRIBLE!
WHY DOES IT CONTINUE TO SUR-PRISE YOU?
IT'S NORMAL THAT PEOPLE WHO HAVE NO SKILLS DIE OFF.
NATURAL SELECTION!
THE ONE SELECTING IS THE PRINCE!
That's not natural at all!!
HE GATH-ERED ALL THE NUMBERED CHILDREN AND THREW THEM AWAY!
LIKE I SAID, IT'S NORMAL TO THROW AWAY NUMBERED CHILDREN, ALL RIGHT?
IT'S NOT NORMAL AT ALL!
DON'T THROW THEM AWAY!!
AND THE EARTH-QUAKE YESTERDAY TOO!
WHAT WAS THAT?!
OUR FRIENDS WERE SWALLOWED UP RIGHT IN FRONT OF OUR EYES!!
A LOT OF OTHER PEOPLE PROBABLY FELL TOO, NOT KNOWING WHAT WAS GOING ON!
THE PRINCE SAID TO GET ON YOUR KNEES RIGHT?
IF THEY DIDN'T LISTEN, IT'S THEIR OWN FAULT.
......!
THIS GUY...

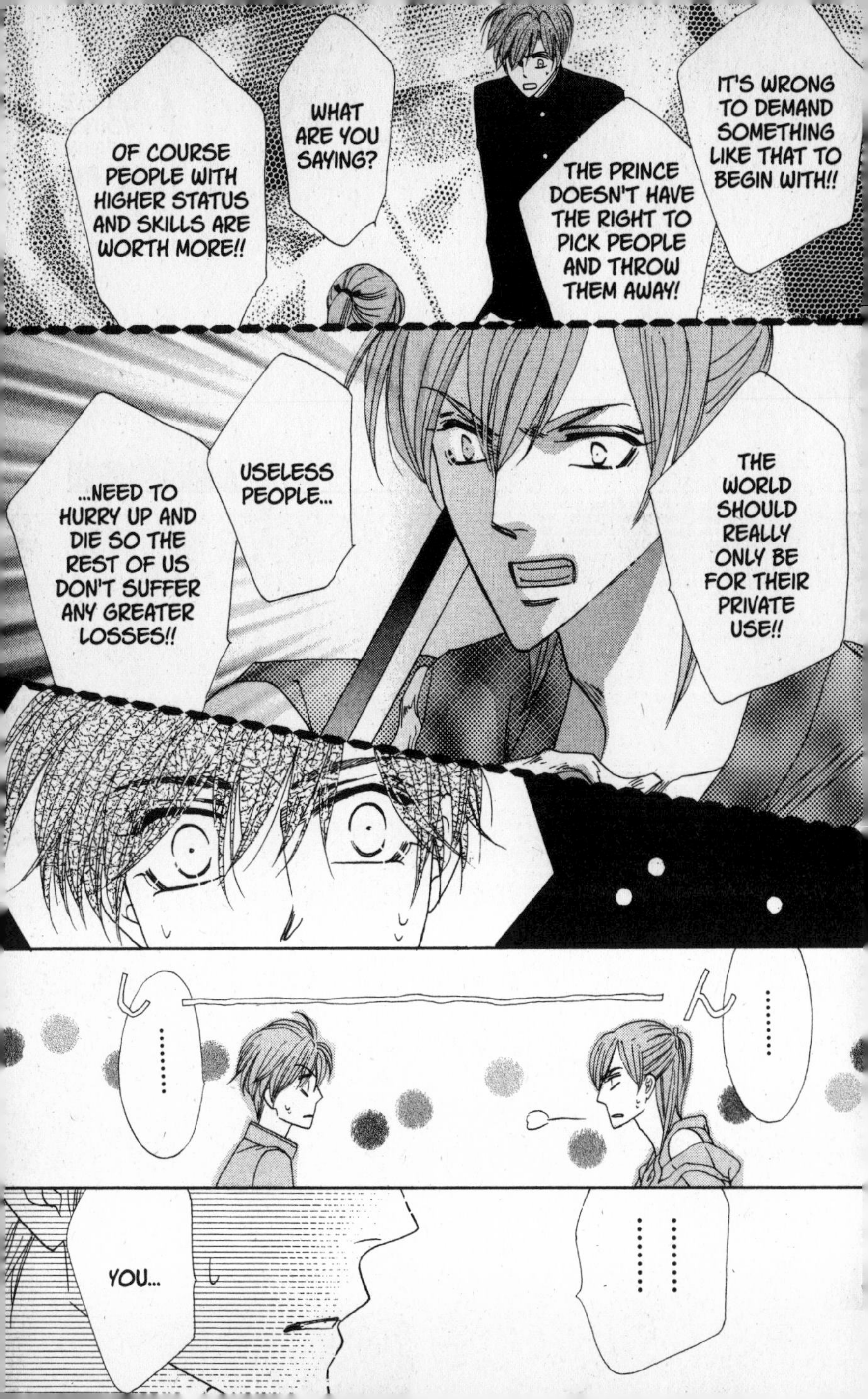
IT'S WRONG TO DEMAND SOMETHING LIKE THAT TO BEGIN WITH!!
THE PRINCE DOESN'T HAVE THE RIGHT TO PICK PEOPLE AND THROW THEM AWAY!
WHAT ARE YOU SAYING?
OF COURSE PEOPLE WITH HIGHER STATUS AND SKILLS ARE WORTH MORE!!
THE WORLD SHOULD REALLY ONLY BE FOR THEIR PRIVATE USE!!
USELESS PEOPLE...
...NEED TO HURRY UP AND DIE SO THE REST OF US DON'T SUFFER ANY GREATER LOSSES!!
......
......
....
YOU...

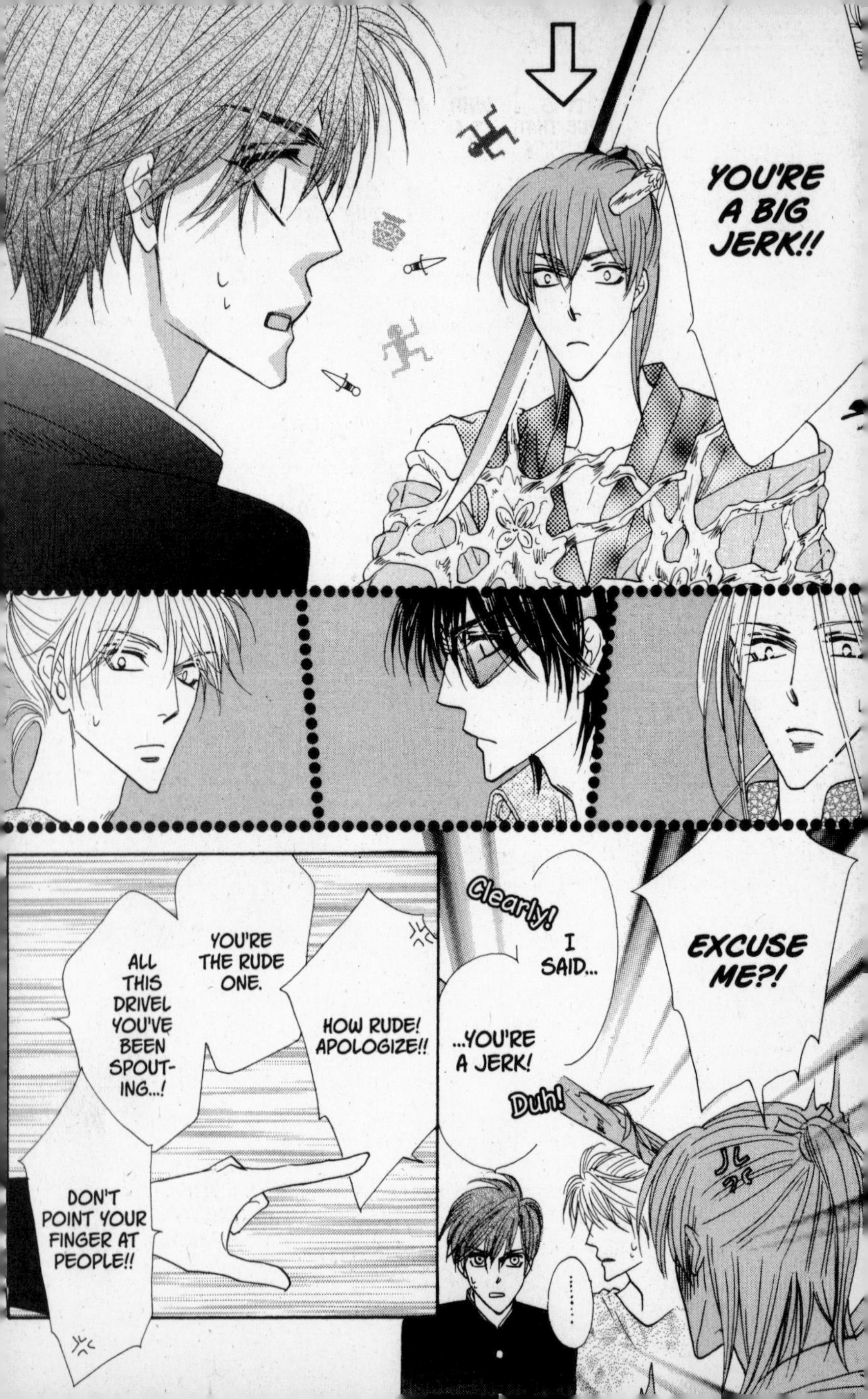
YOU'RE A BIG JERK!!
EXCUSE ME?!
I SAID...
Clearly!
...YOU'RE A JERK!
Duh!
......
HOW RUDE! APOLOGIZE!!
YOU'RE THE RUDE ONE.
ALL THIS DRIVEL YOU'VE BEEN SPOUTING...!
DON'T POINT YOUR FINGER AT PEOPLE!!

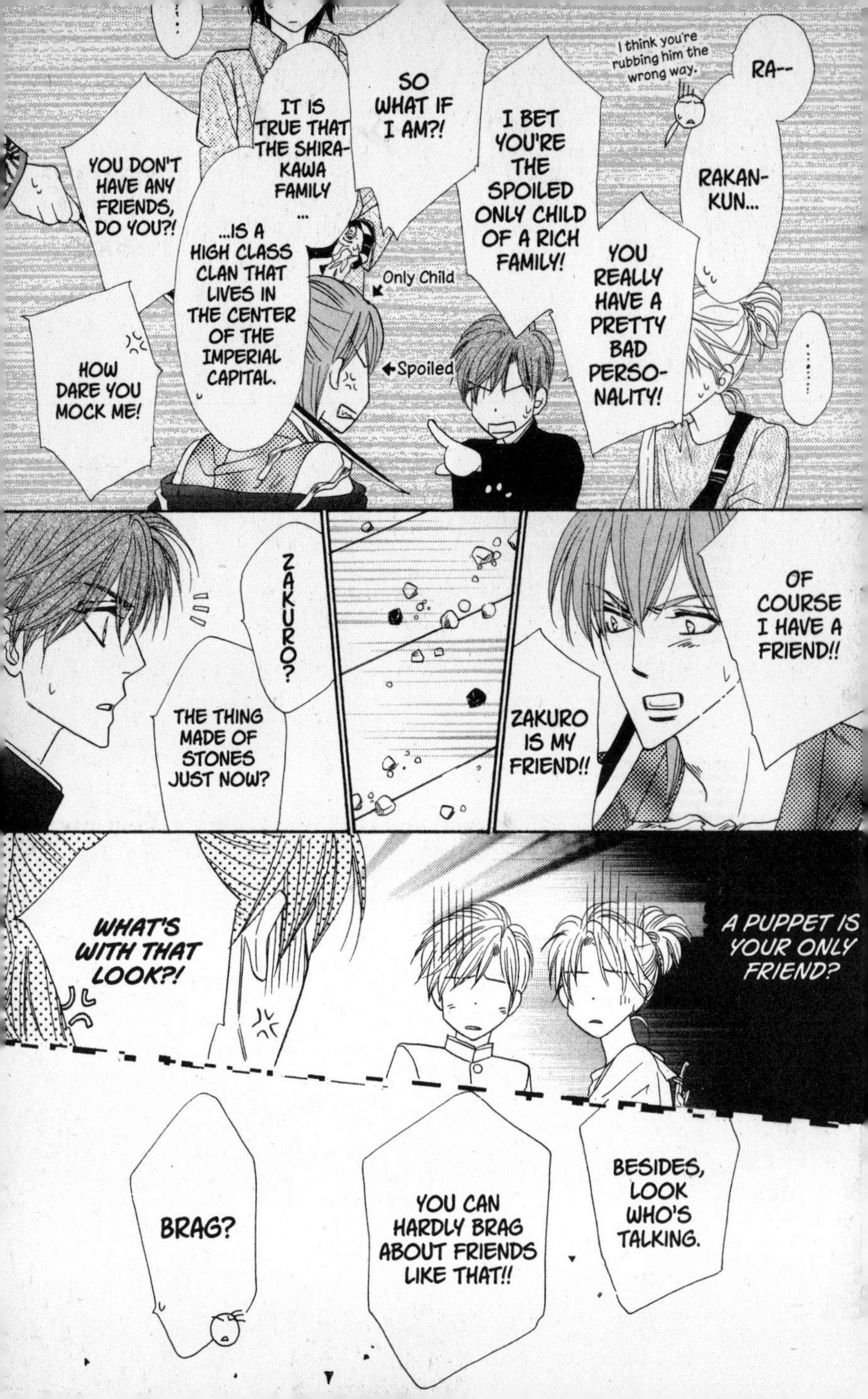
...
RA--
I think you're rubbing him the wrong way.
RAKAN-KUN...
...
I BET YOU'RE THE SPOILED ONLY CHILD OF A RICH FAMILY!
YOU REALLY HAVE A PRETTY BAD PERSONALITY!
SO WHAT IF I AM?!
Only Child
Spoiled
IT IS TRUE THAT THE SHIRAKAWA FAMILY ...
...IS A HIGH CLASS CLAN THAT LIVES IN THE CENTER OF THE IMPERIAL CAPITAL.
YOU DON'T HAVE ANY FRIENDS, DO YOU?!
HOW DARE YOU MOCK ME!
OF COURSE I HAVE A FRIEND!!
ZAKURO IS MY FRIEND!!
ZAKURO?
THE THING MADE OF STONES JUST NOW?
A PUPPET IS YOUR ONLY FRIEND?
WHAT'S WITH THAT LOOK?!
BESIDES, LOOK WHO'S TALKING.
YOU CAN HARDLY BRAG ABOUT FRIENDS LIKE THAT!!
BRAG?

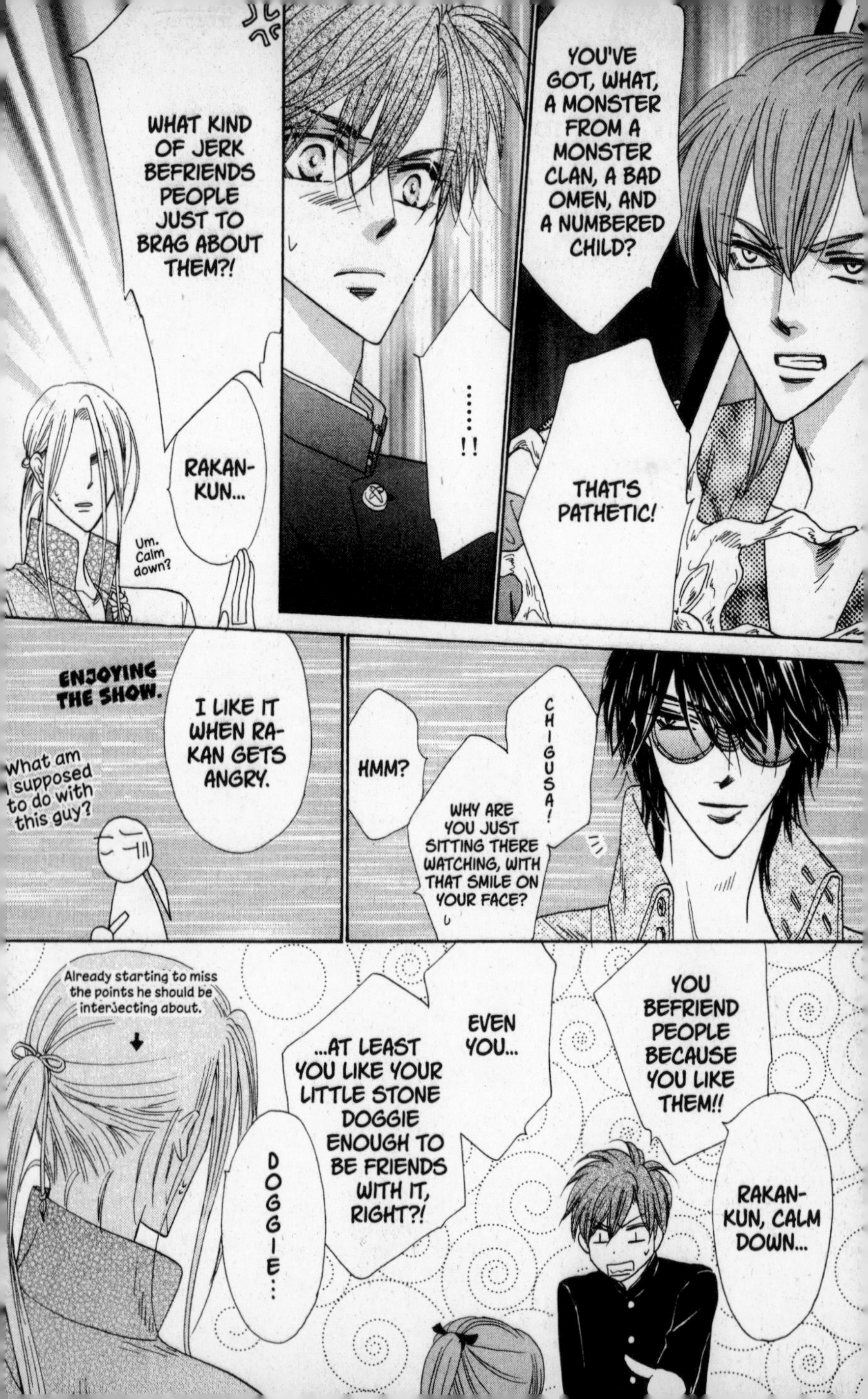
YOU'VE GOT, WHAT, A MONSTER FROM A MONSTER CLAN, A BAD OMEN, AND A NUMBERED CHILD?
THAT'S PATHETIC!
......!!
WHAT KIND OF JERK BEFRIENDS PEOPLE JUST TO BRAG ABOUT THEM?!
RAKAN-KUN...
Um. Calm down?
CHIGUSA!
WHY ARE YOU JUST SITTING THERE WATCHING, WITH THAT SMILE ON YOUR FACE?
HMM?
I LIKE IT WHEN RA-KAN GETS ANGRY.
ENJOYING THE SHOW.
What am supposed to do with this guy?
YOU BEFRIEND PEOPLE BECAUSE YOU LIKE THEM!!
RAKAN-KUN, CALM DOWN...
EVEN YOU...
...AT LEAST YOU LIKE YOUR LITTLE STONE DOGGIE ENOUGH TO BE FRIENDS WITH IT, RIGHT?!
DOGGIE...
Already starting to miss the points he should be interjecting about.

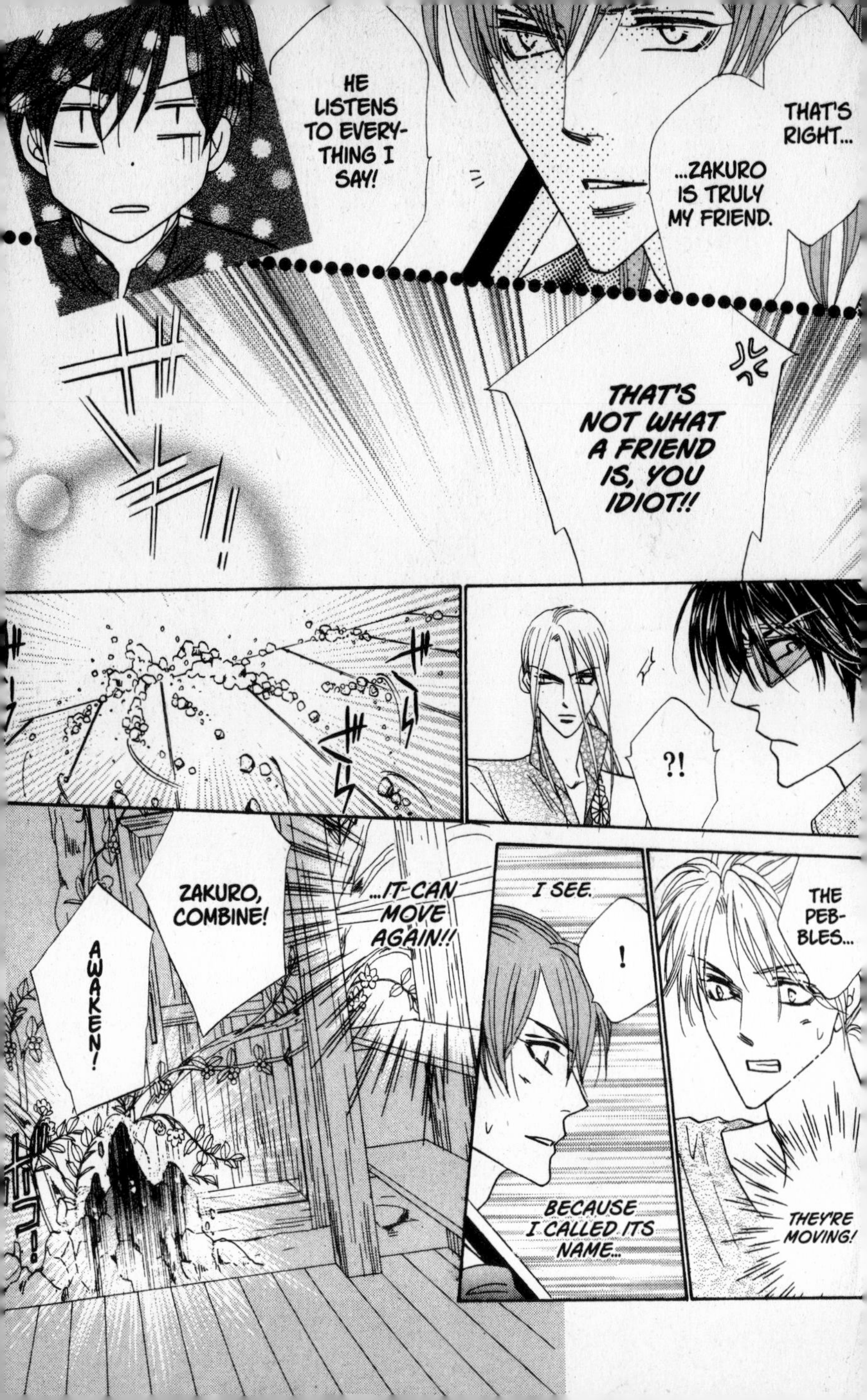
THAT'S RIGHT...
...ZAKURO IS TRULY MY FRIEND.
HE LISTENS TO EVERY-THING I SAY!
THAT'S NOT WHAT A FRIEND IS, YOU IDIOT!!
?!
THE PEB-BLES...
THEY'RE MOVING!
I SEE.
!
BECAUSE I CALLED ITS NAME...
...IT CAN MOVE AGAIN!!
ZAKURO, COMBINE!
AWAKEN!

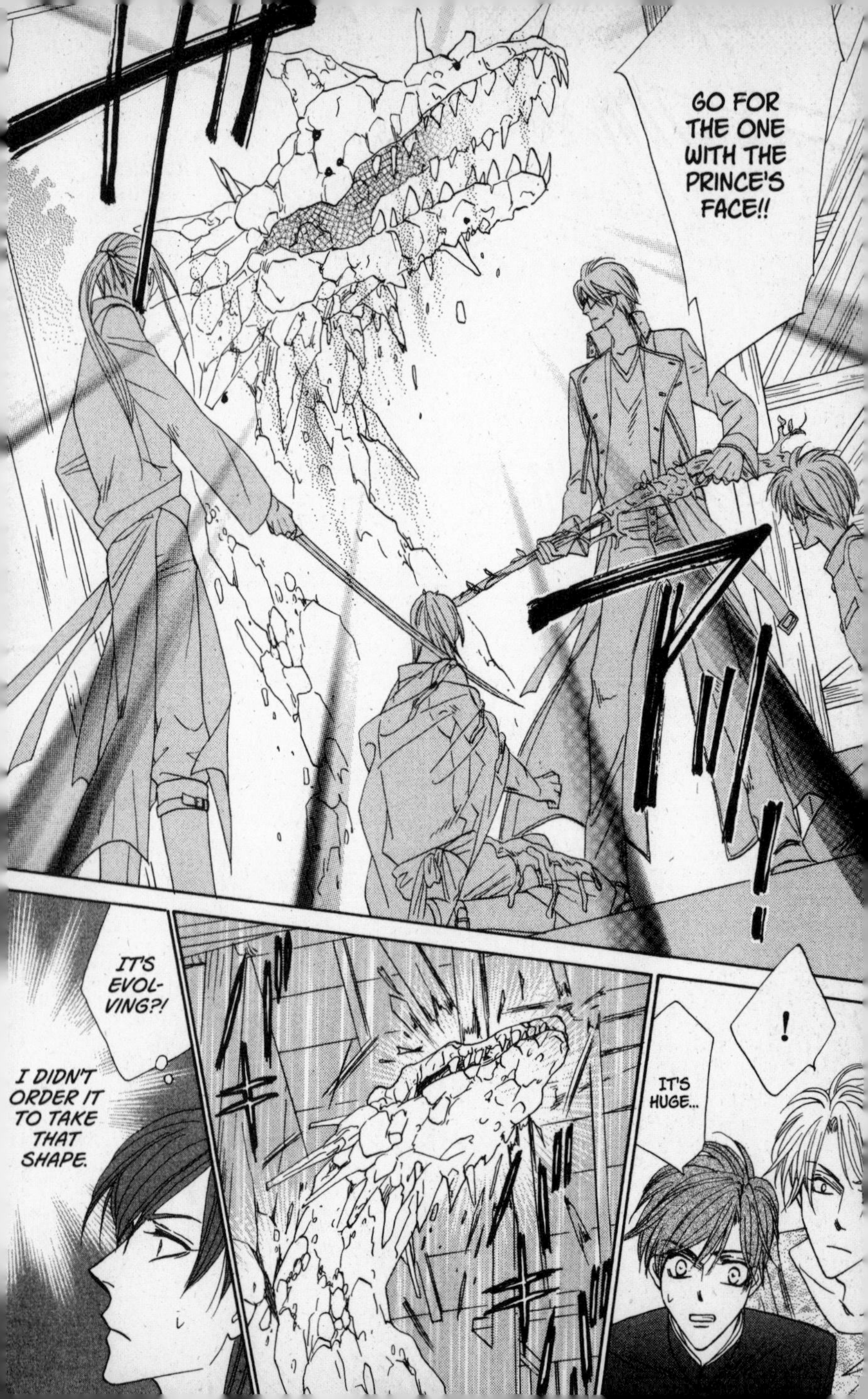
GO FOR THE ONE WITH THE PRINCE'S FACE!!
!
IT'S HUGE...
IT'S EVOLVING?!
I DIDN'T ORDER IT TO TAKE THAT SHAPE.

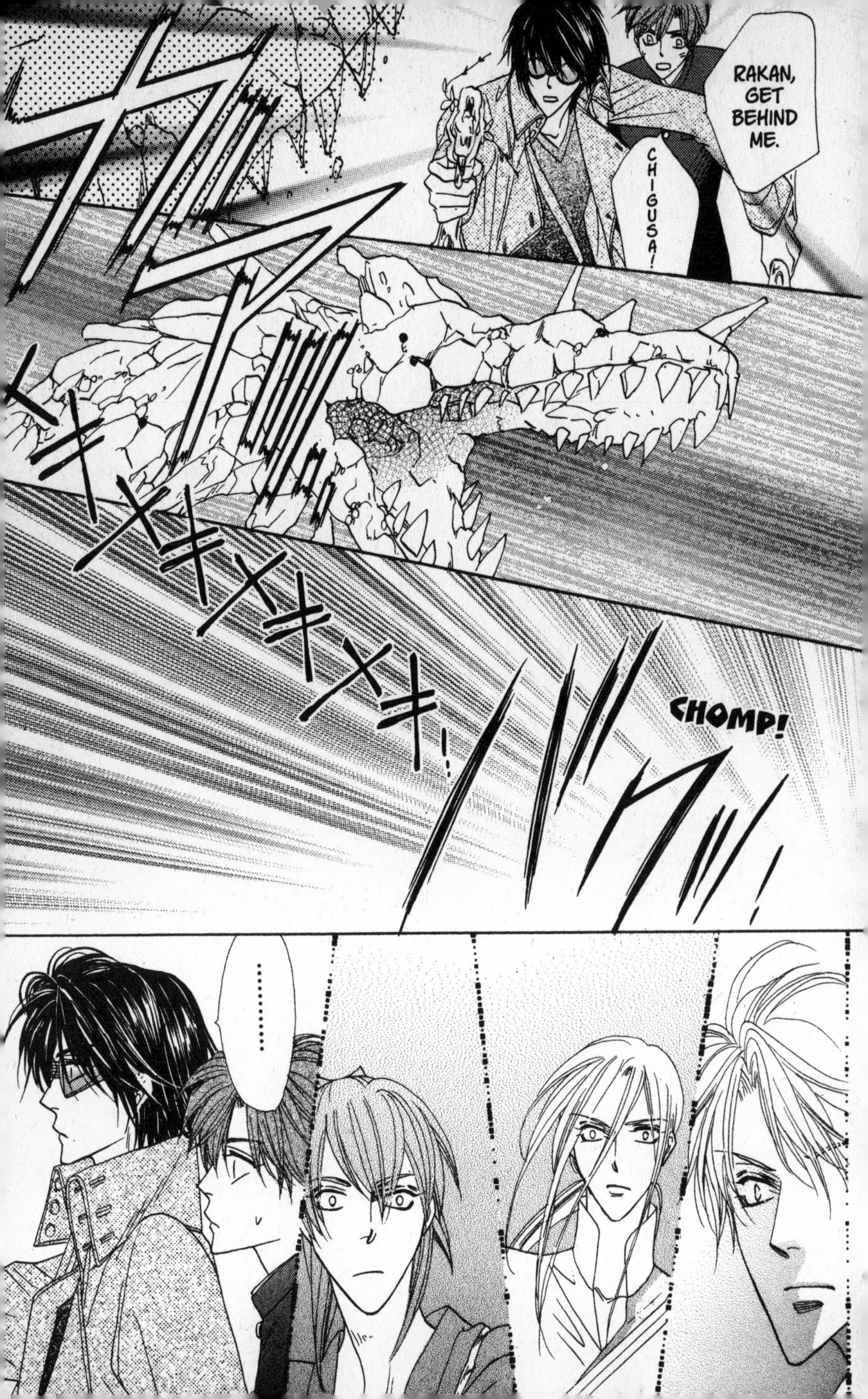
RAKAN, GET BEHIND ME.
CHIGUSA!
CHOMP!
...

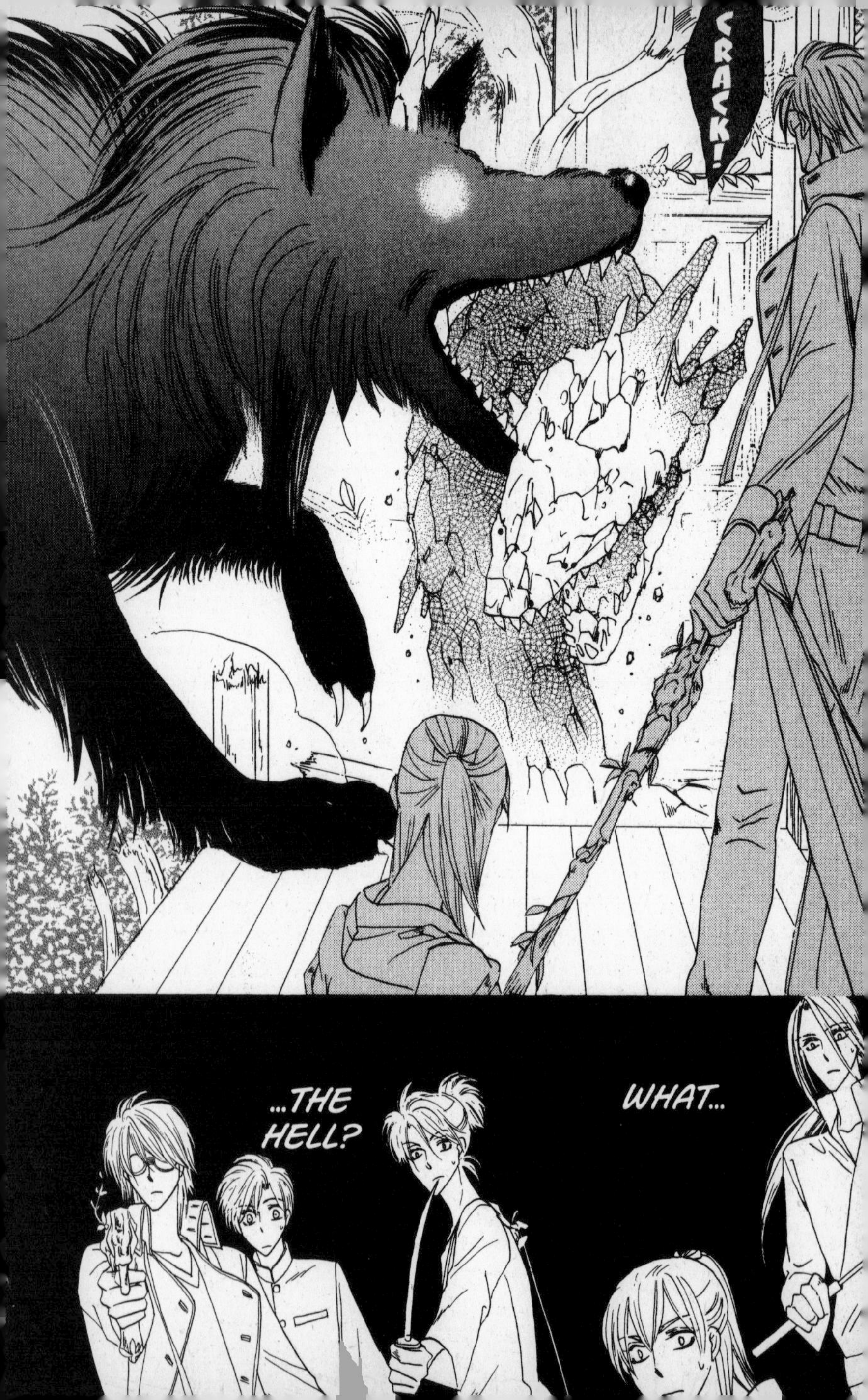
CRACK!
WHAT...
...THE HELL?

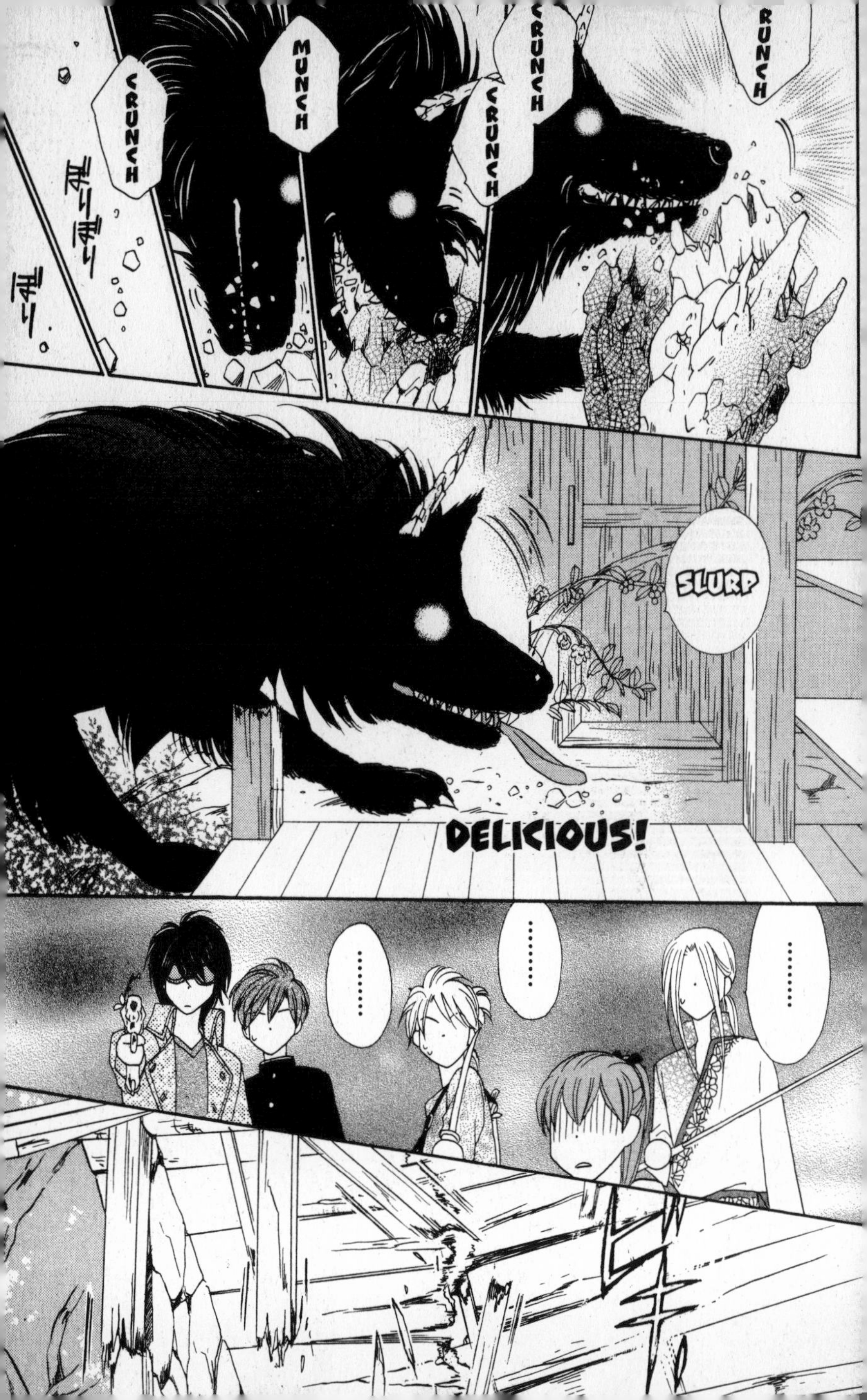
RUNCH
CRUNCH
CRUNCH
MUNCH
CRUNCH
SLURP
DELICIOUS!
....
....
....

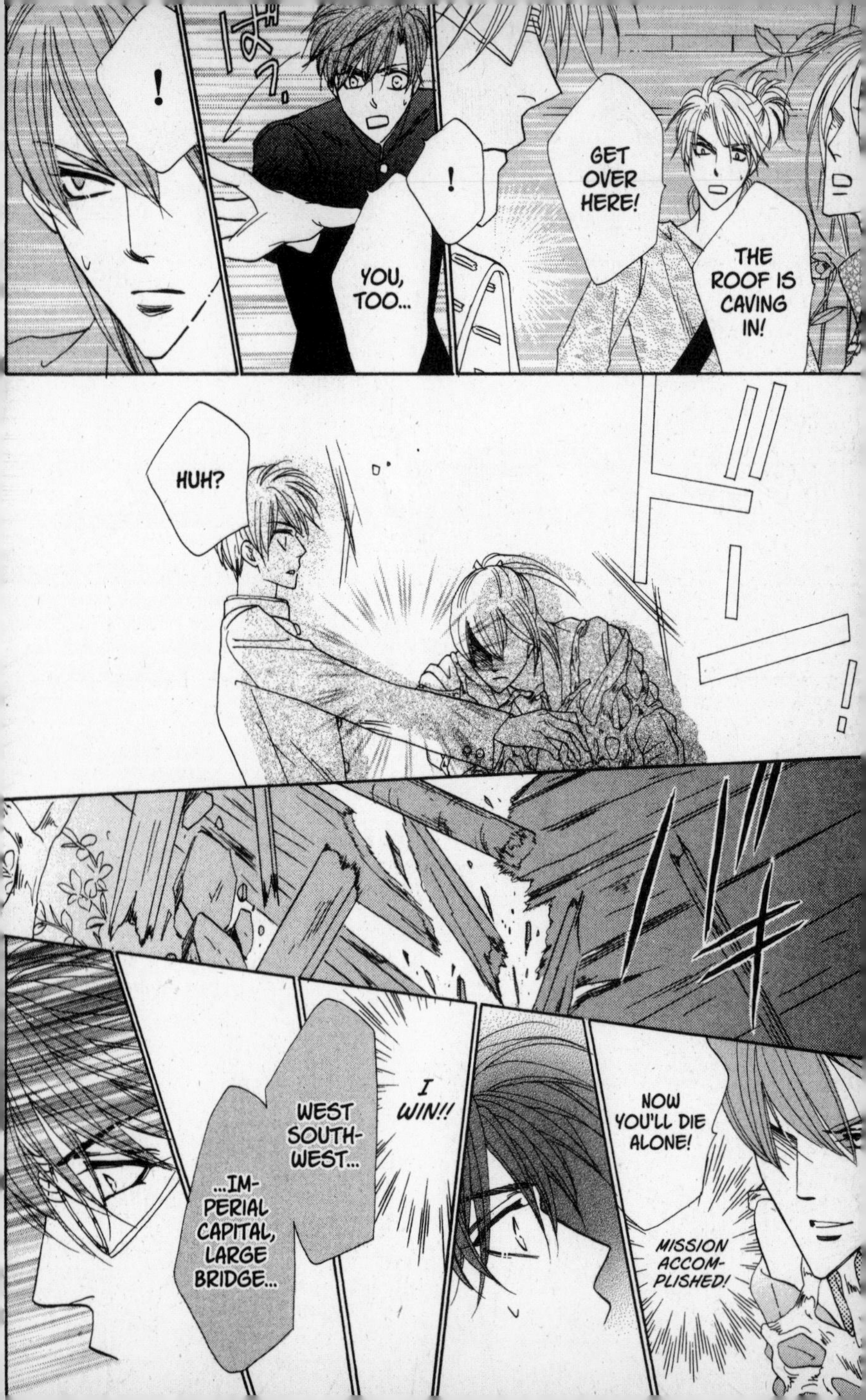
GET OVER HERE!
THE ROOF IS CAVING IN!
!
YOU, TOO...
!
HUH?
NOW YOU'LL DIE ALONE!
MISSION ACCOM-PLISHED!
I WIN!!
WEST SOUTH-WEST...
...IM-PERIAL CAPITAL, LARGE BRIDGE...

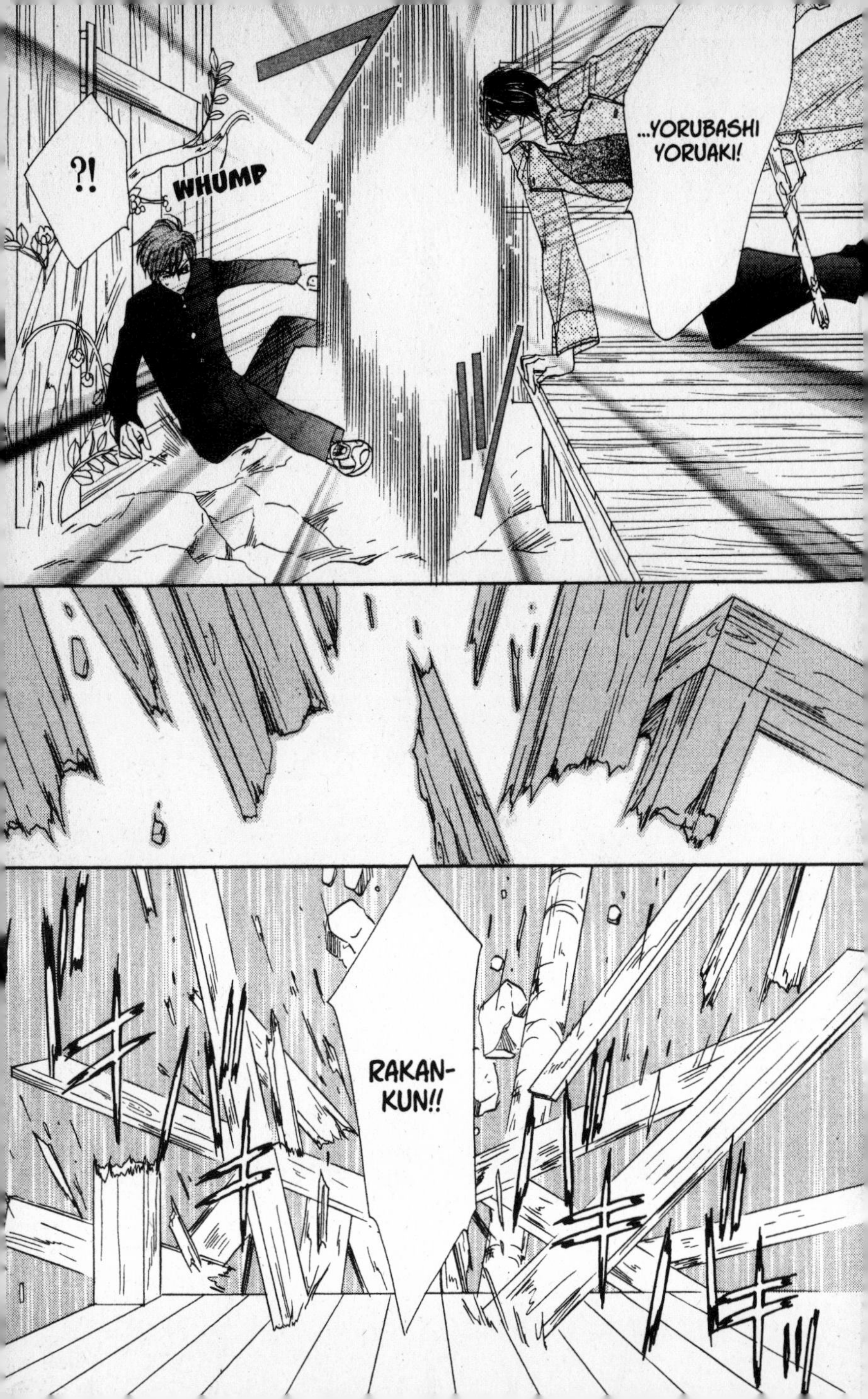
...YORUBASHI YORUAKI!
WHUMP
?!
RAKAN-KUN!!

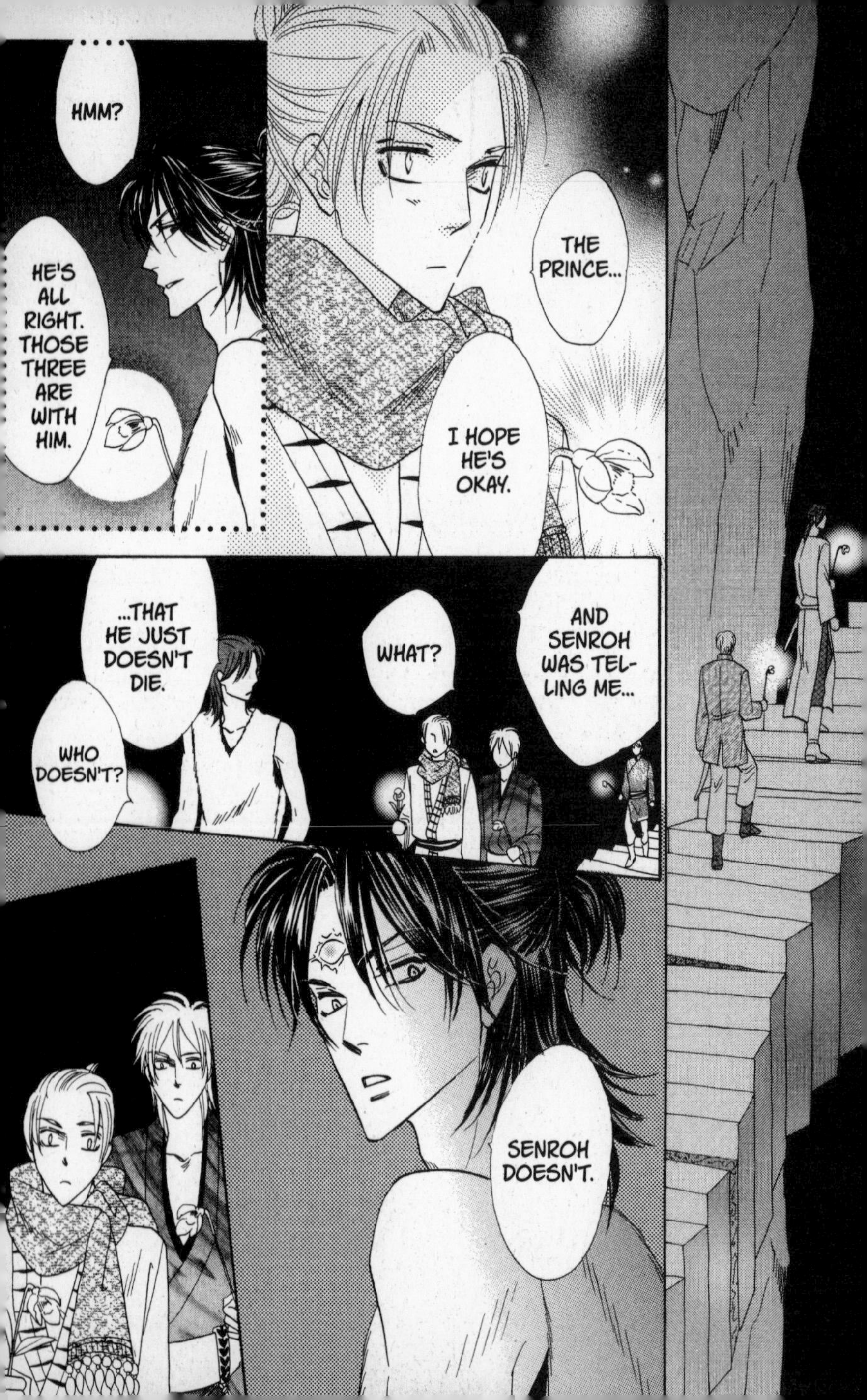

THE PRINCE...
I HOPE HE'S OKAY.
HMM?
HE'S ALL RIGHT. THOSE THREE ARE WITH HIM.
AND SENROH WAS TEL-LING ME...
WHAT?
...THAT HE JUST DOESN'T DIE.
WHO DOESN'T?
SENROH DOESN'T.

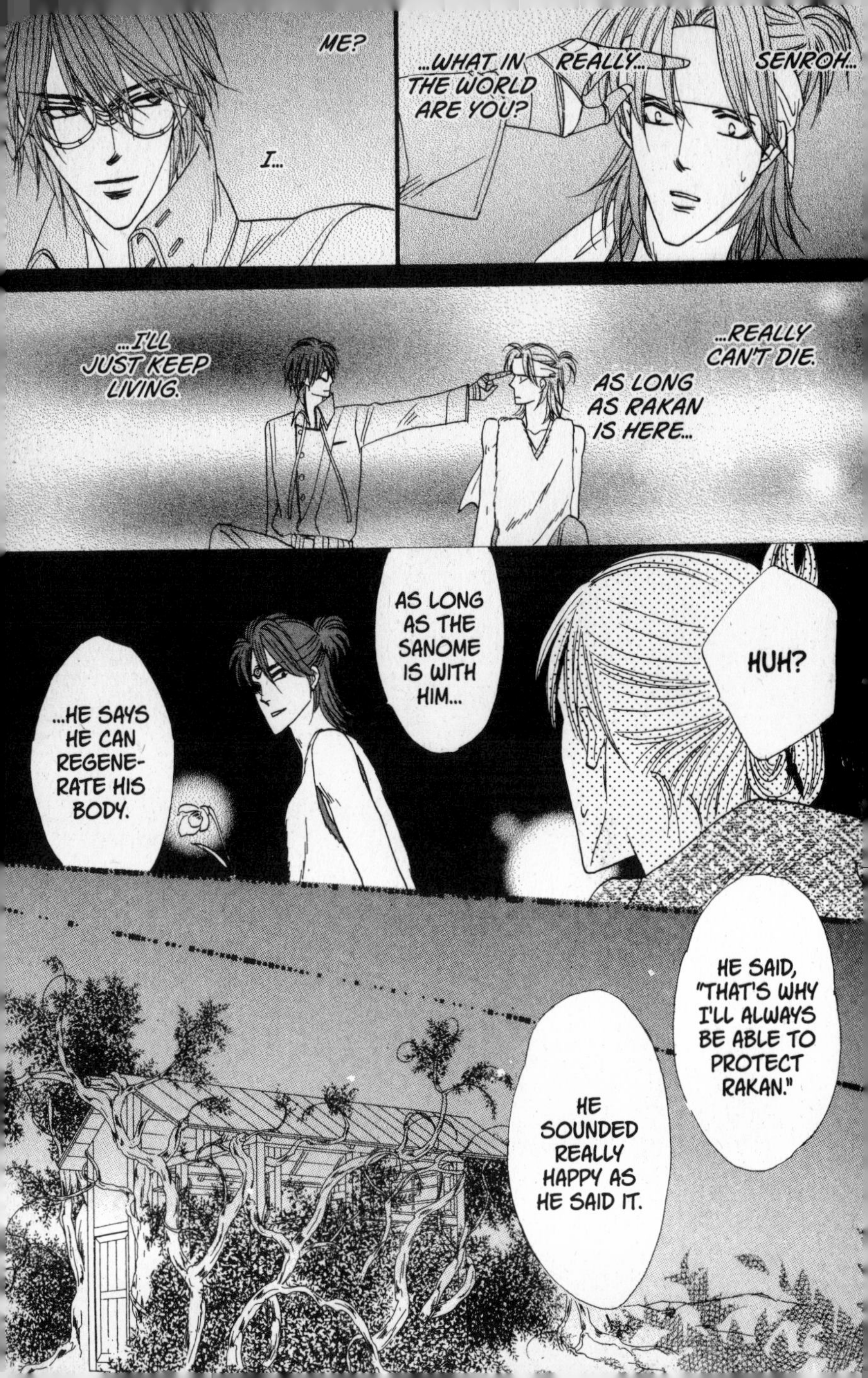
SENROH...
REALLY...
...WHAT IN THE WORLD ARE YOU?
ME?
I...
...REALLY CAN'T DIE.
AS LONG AS RAKAN IS HERE...
...I'LL JUST KEEP LIVING.
HUH?
AS LONG AS THE SANOME IS WITH HIM...
...HE SAYS HE CAN REGENERATE HIS BODY.
HE SAID, "THAT'S WHY I'LL ALWAYS BE ABLE TO PROTECT RAKAN."
HE SOUNDED REALLY HAPPY AS HE SAID IT.

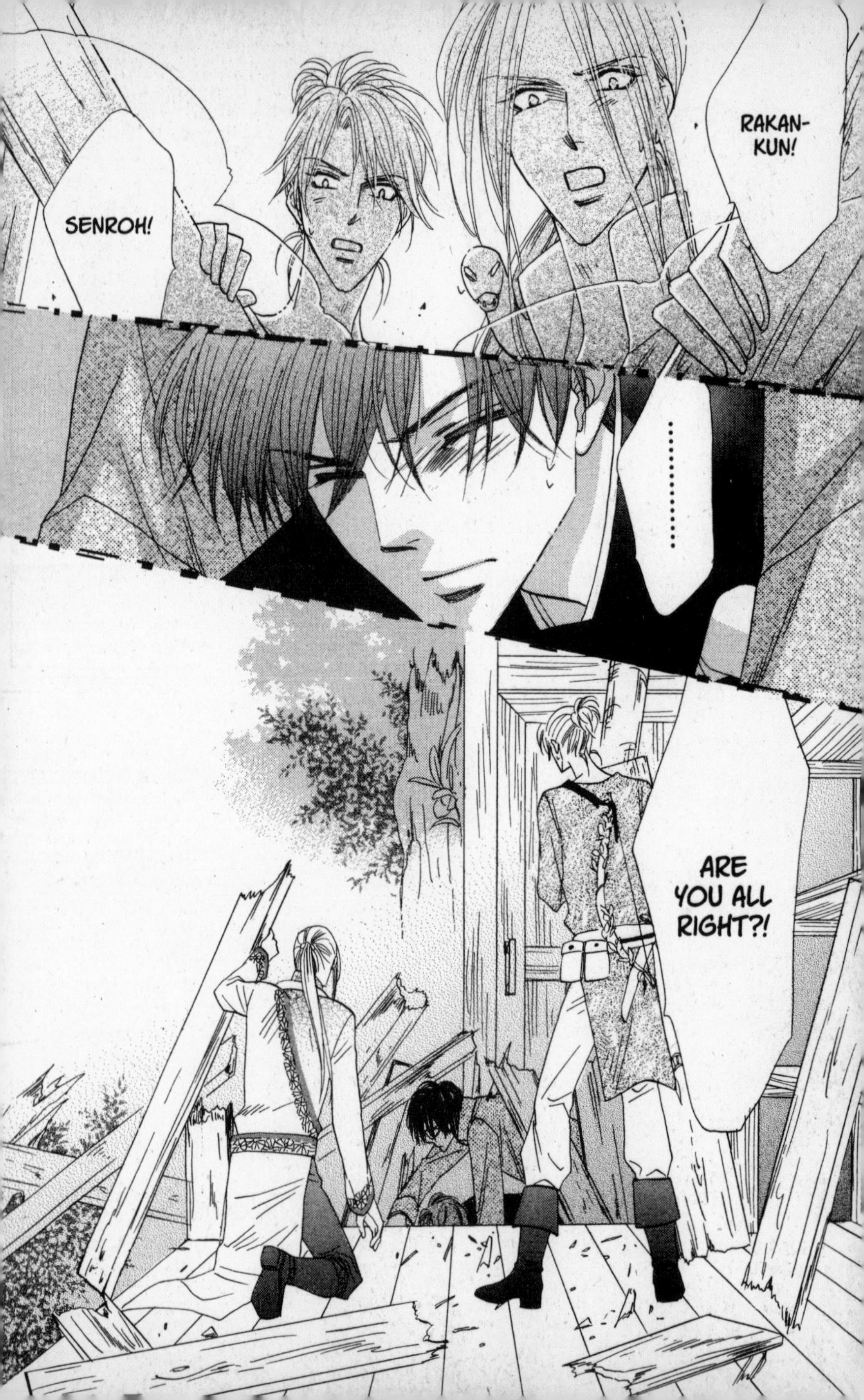
RAKAN-KUN!
SENROH!
......
ARE YOU ALL RIGHT?!

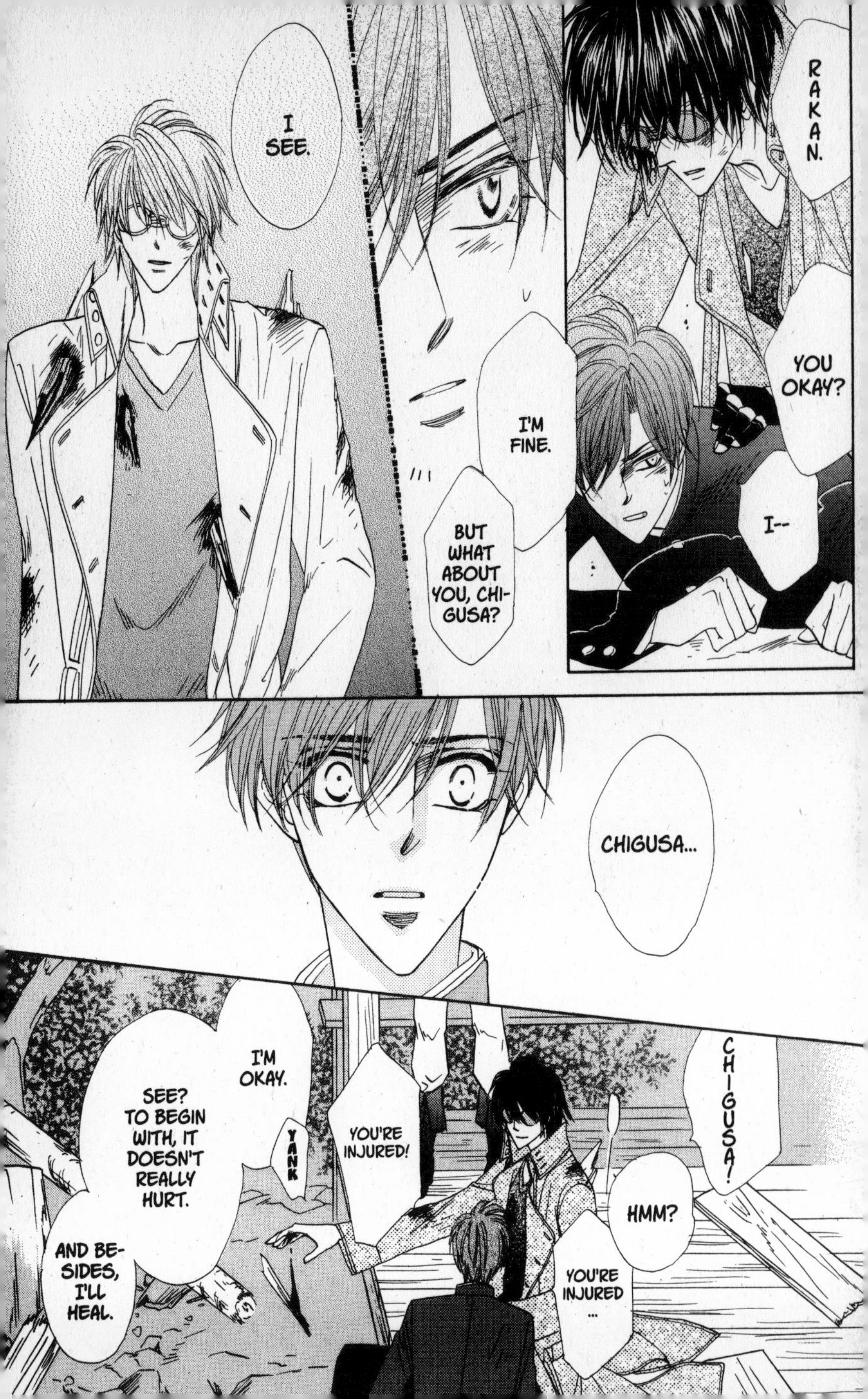
RAKAN.
YOU OKAY?
I--
I'M FINE.
BUT WHAT ABOUT YOU, CHIGUSA?
I SEE.
CHIGUSA...
CHIGUSA!
HMM?
YOU'RE INJURED...
YOU'RE INJURED!
YANK
I'M OKAY.
SEE? TO BEGIN WITH, IT DOESN'T REALLY HURT.
AND BESIDES, I'LL HEAL.

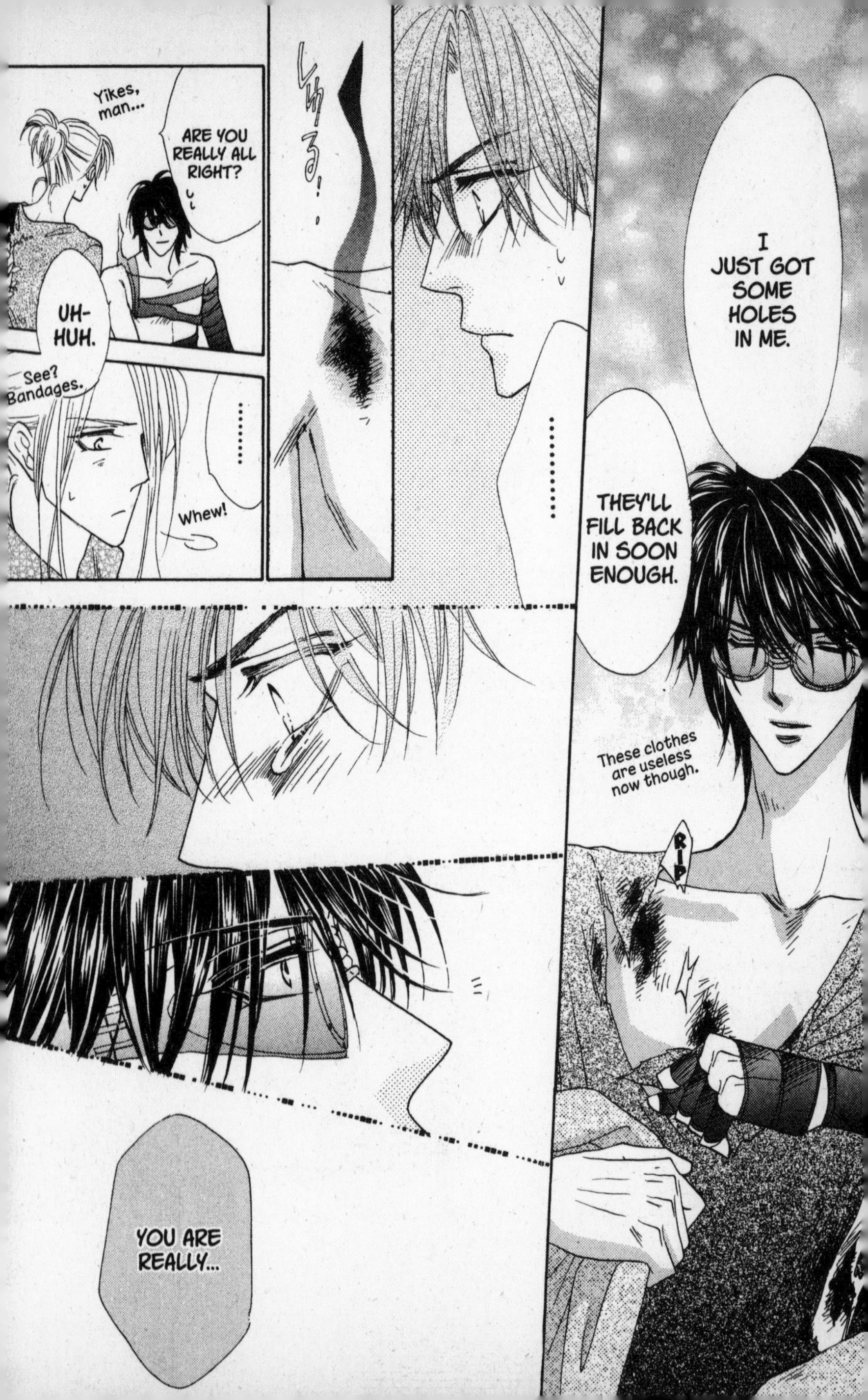
I JUST GOT SOME HOLES IN ME.
THEY'LL FILL BACK IN SOON ENOUGH.
These clothes are useless now though.
RIP
......
しゅる!!
Yikes, man...
ARE YOU REALLY ALL RIGHT?
UH-HUH.
See? Bandages.
......
Whew!
YOU ARE REALLY...

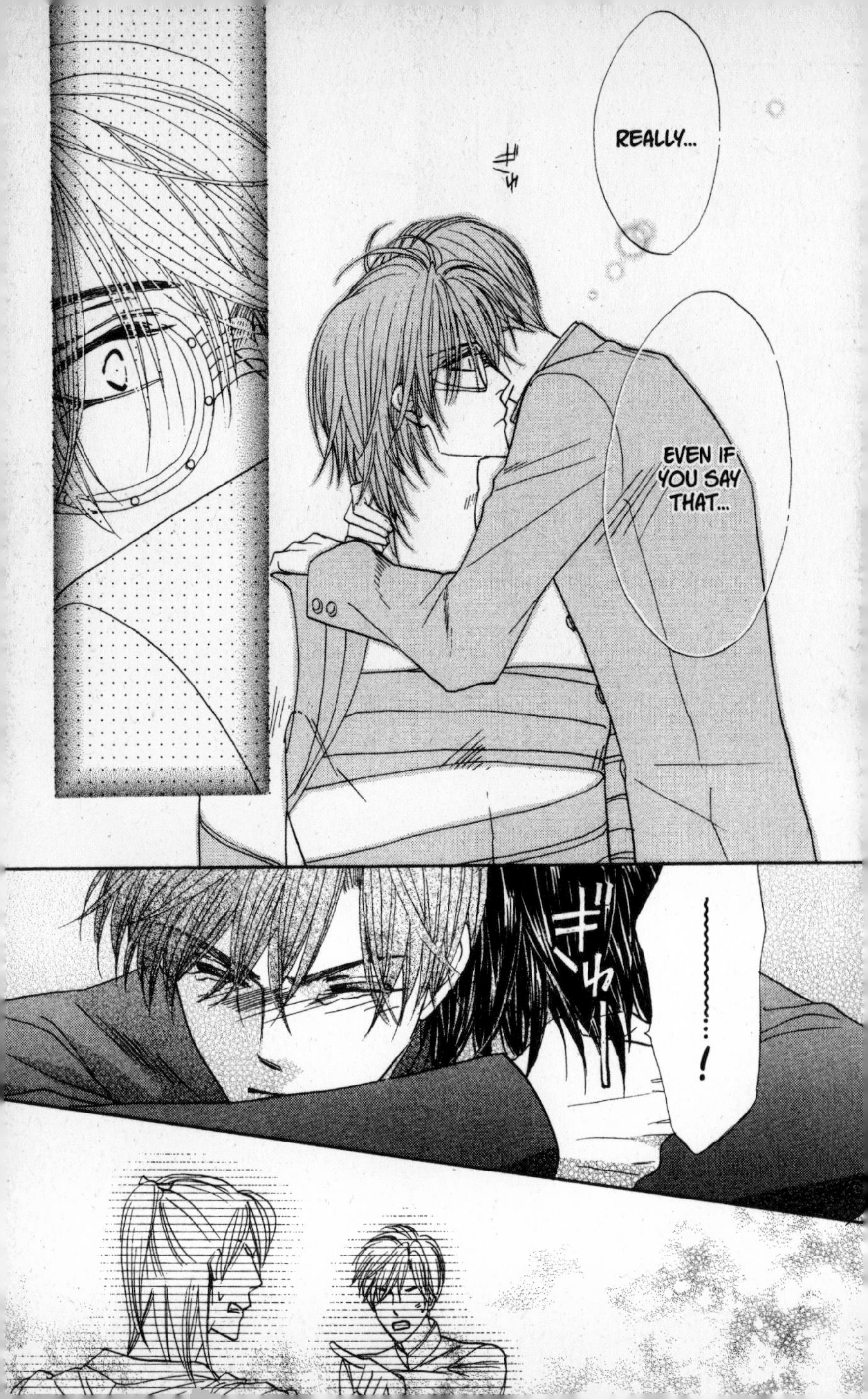
REALLY...
EVEN IF YOU SAY THAT...
ぎゅ
......!
ぎゅー

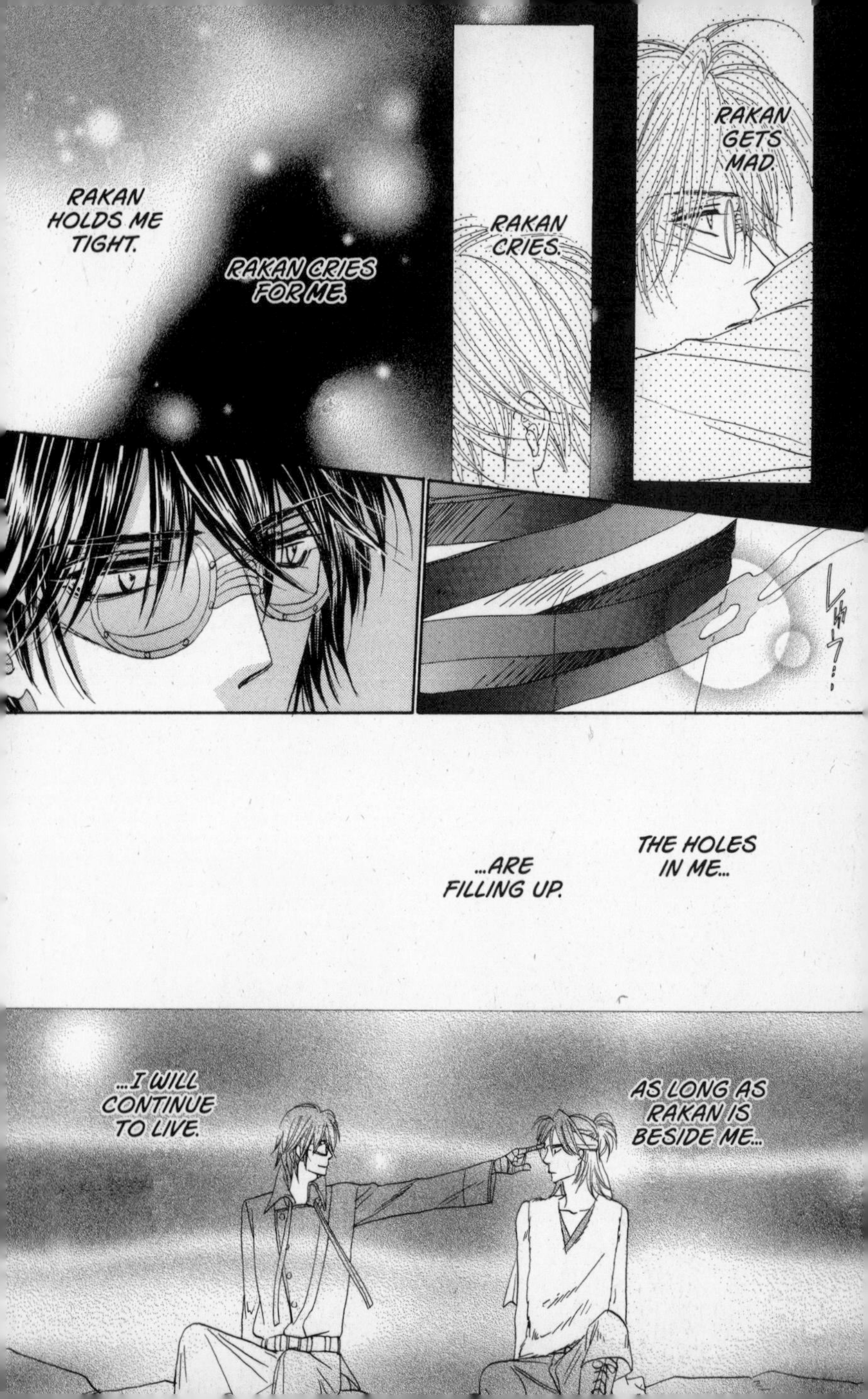
RAKAN GETS MAD.
RAKAN CRIES.
RAKAN HOLDS ME TIGHT.
RAKAN CRIES FOR ME.
THE HOLES IN ME...
...ARE FILLING UP.
AS LONG AS RAKAN IS BESIDE ME...
...I WILL CONTINUE TO LIVE.

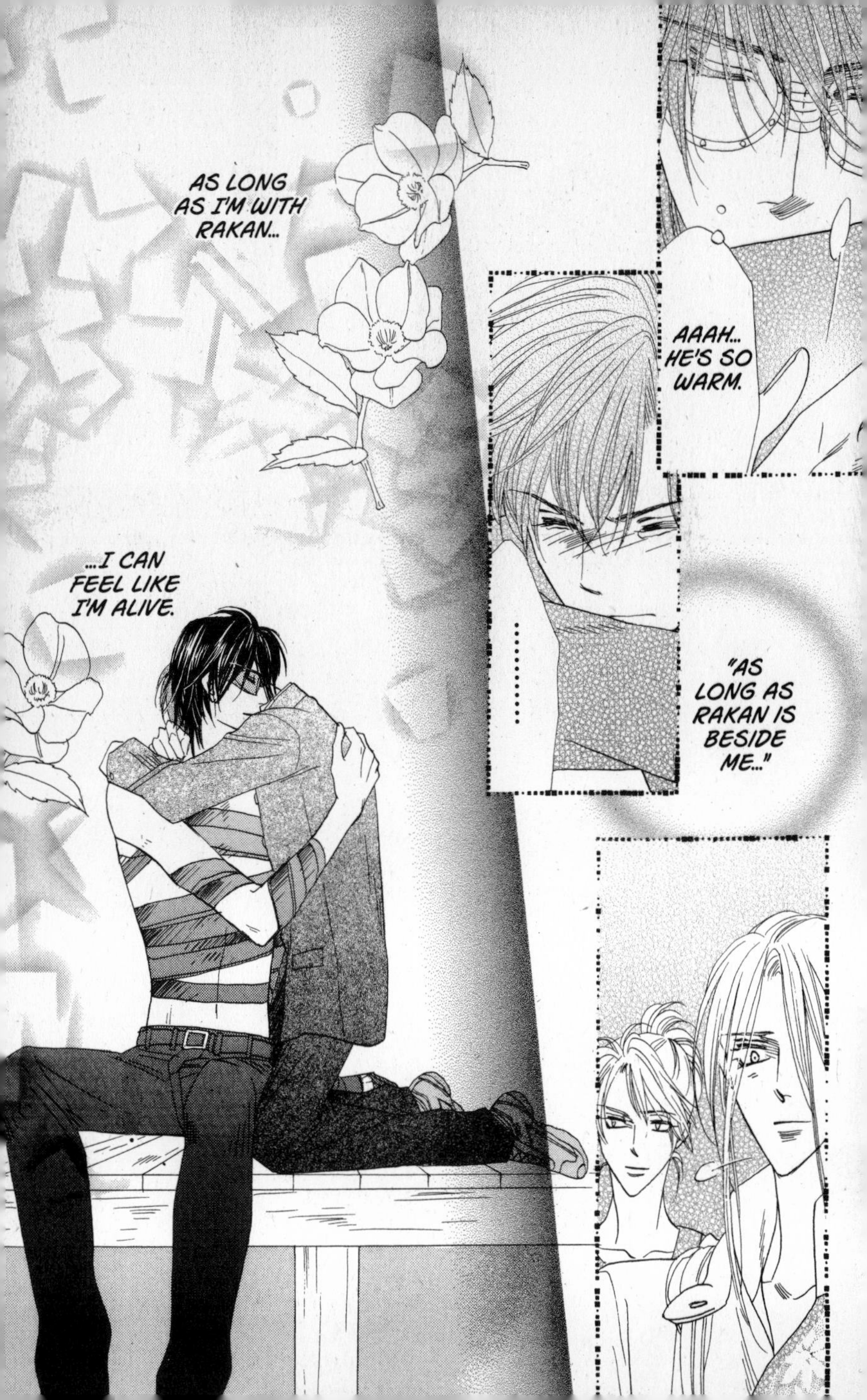
AAAH... HE'S SO WARM.
"AS LONG AS RAKAN IS BESIDE ME..."
AS LONG AS I'M WITH RAKAN...
...I CAN FEEL LIKE I'M ALIVE.

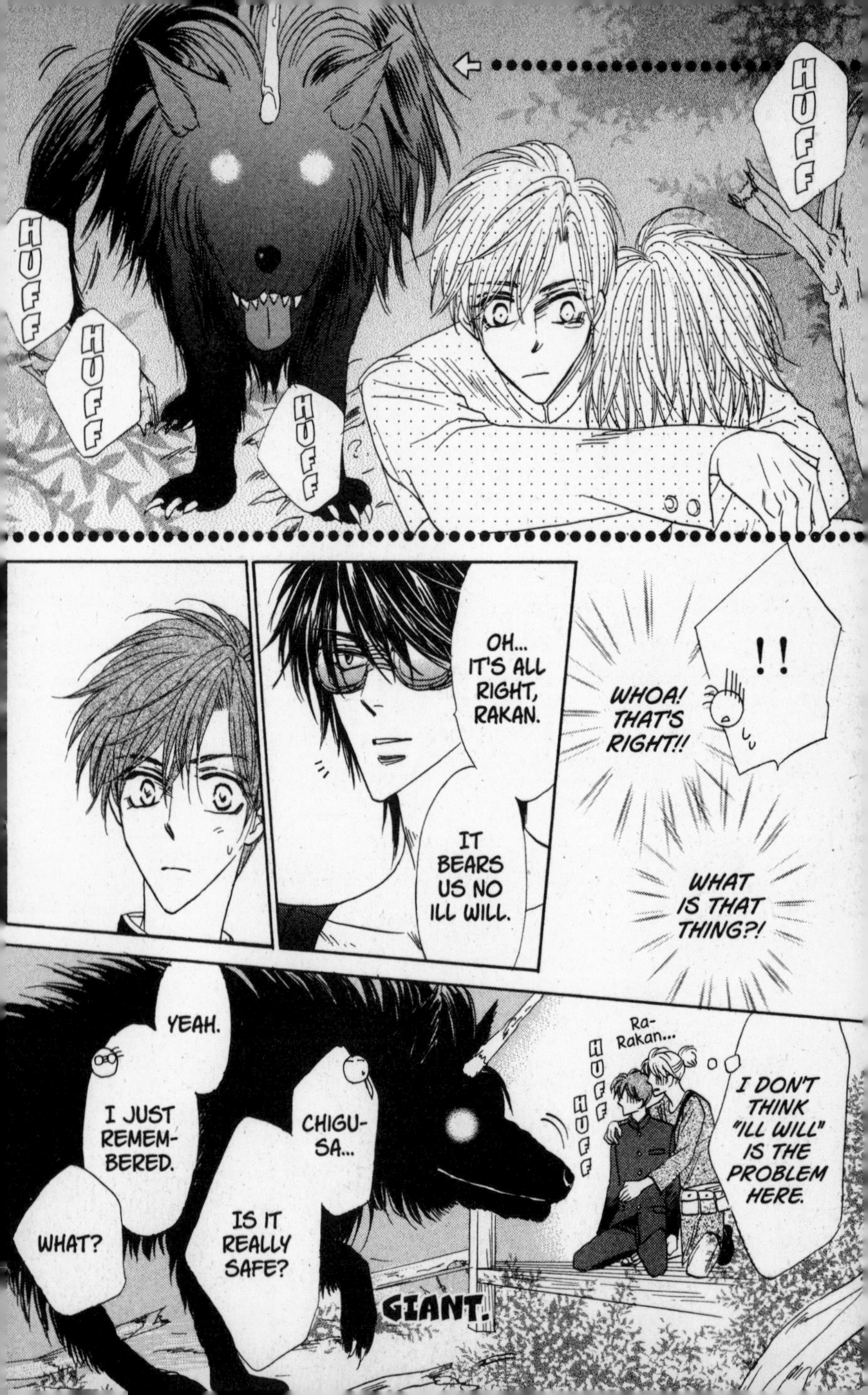
HUFF
HUFF
HUFF
HUFF
!!
WHOA! THAT'S RIGHT!!
WHAT IS THAT THING?!
OH... IT'S ALL RIGHT, RAKAN.
IT BEARS US NO ILL WILL.
I DON'T THINK "ILL WILL" IS THE PROBLEM HERE.
Ra-Rakan...
HUFF
HUFF
CHIGU-SA...
IS IT REALLY SAFE?
YEAH.
I JUST REMEM-BERED.
WHAT?
GIANT.

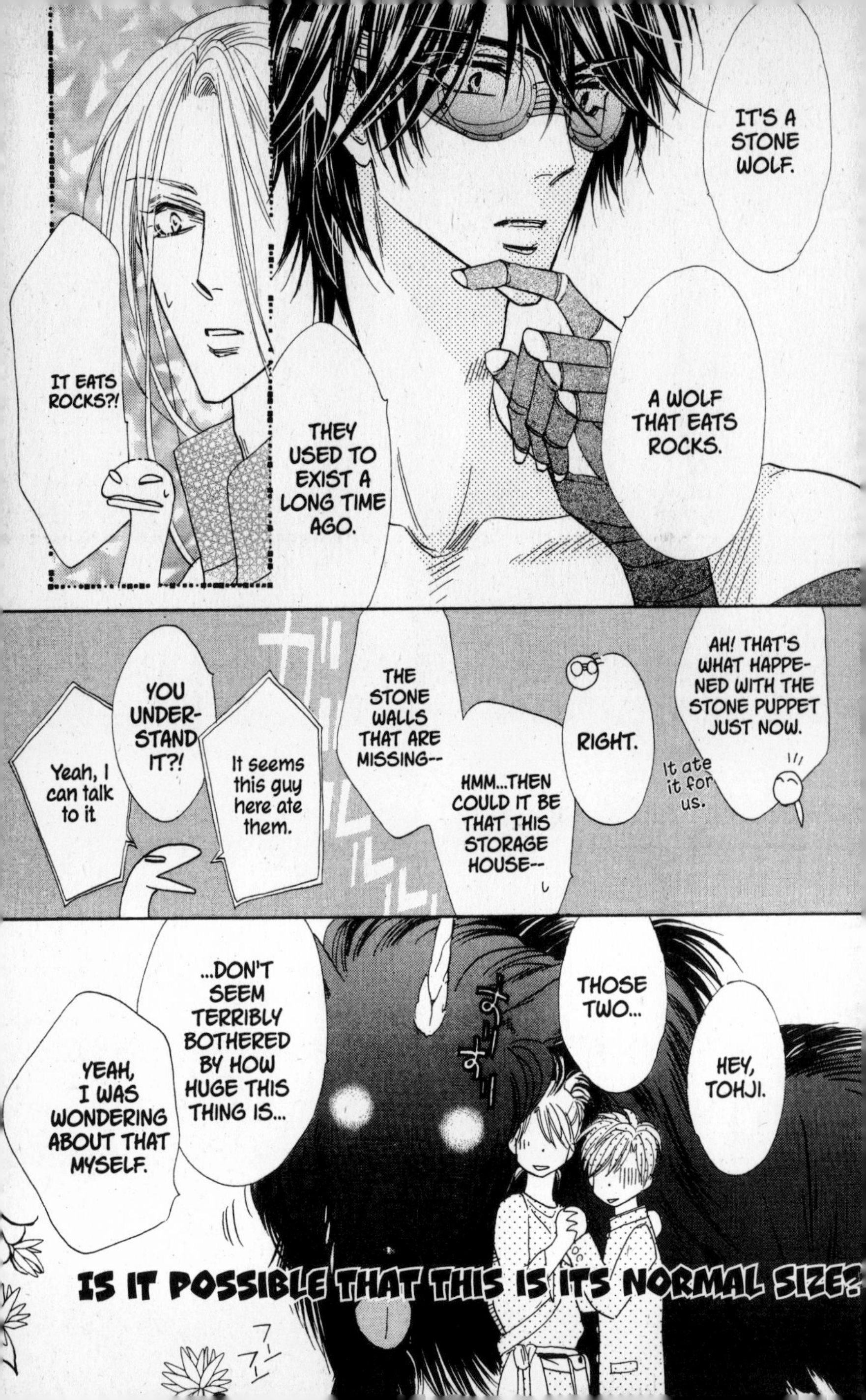
IT'S A STONE WOLF.
A WOLF THAT EATS ROCKS.
THEY USED TO EXIST A LONG TIME AGO.
IT EATS ROCKS?!
AH! THAT'S WHAT HAPPENED WITH THE STONE PUPPET JUST NOW.
It ate it for us.
RIGHT.
THE STONE WALLS THAT ARE MISSING--
HMM...THEN COULD IT BE THAT THIS STORAGE HOUSE--
It seems this guy here ate them.
YOU UNDERSTAND IT?!
Yeah, I can talk to it
HEY, TOHJI.
THOSE TWO...
...DON'T SEEM TERRIBLY BOTHERED BY HOW HUGE THIS THING IS...
YEAH, I WAS WONDERING ABOUT THAT MYSELF.
IS IT POSSIBLE THAT THIS IS ITS NORMAL SIZE?

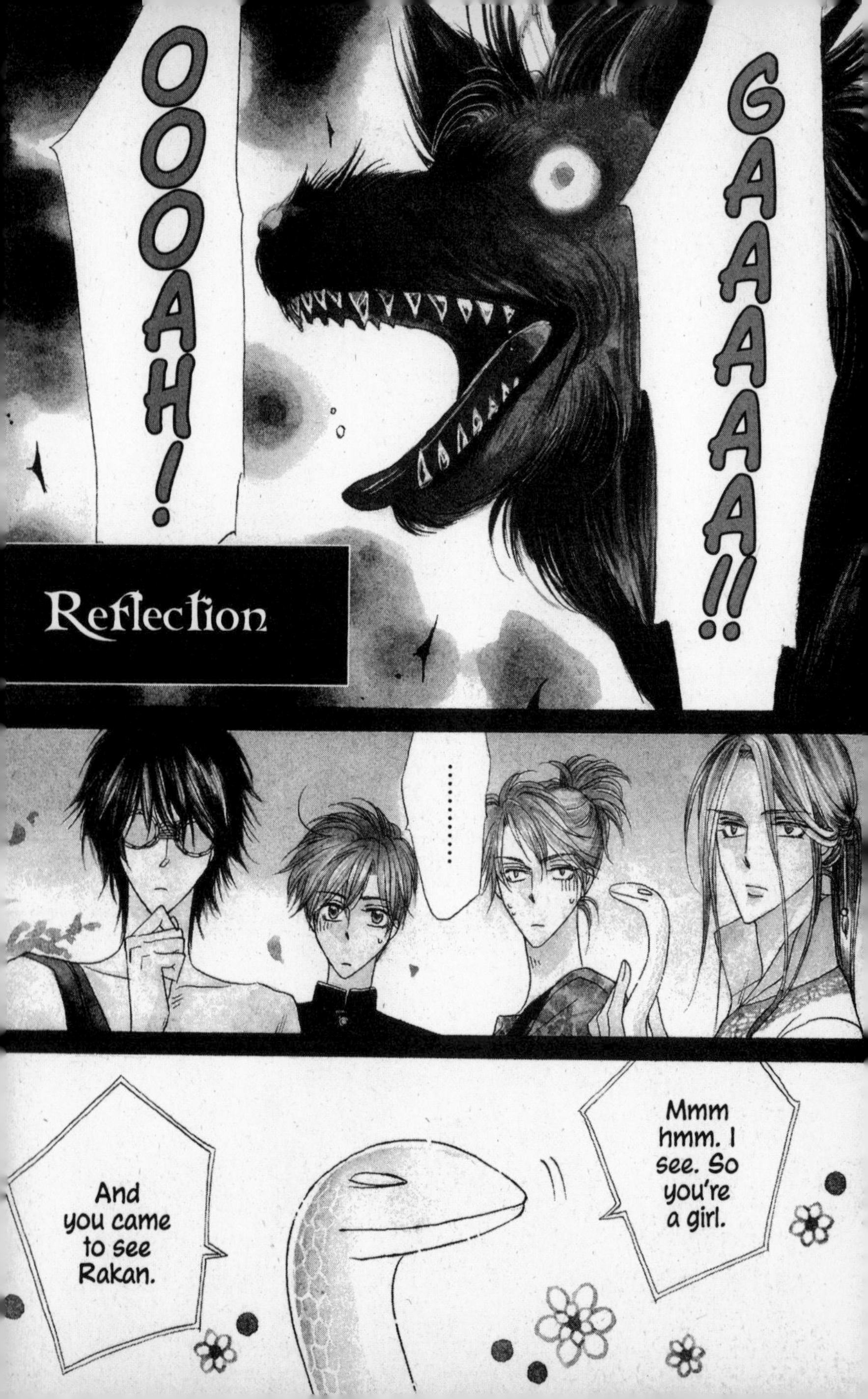
GAAAAAA!!
OOOAH!
Reflection
......
Mmm hmm. I see. So you're a girl.
And you came to see Rakan.

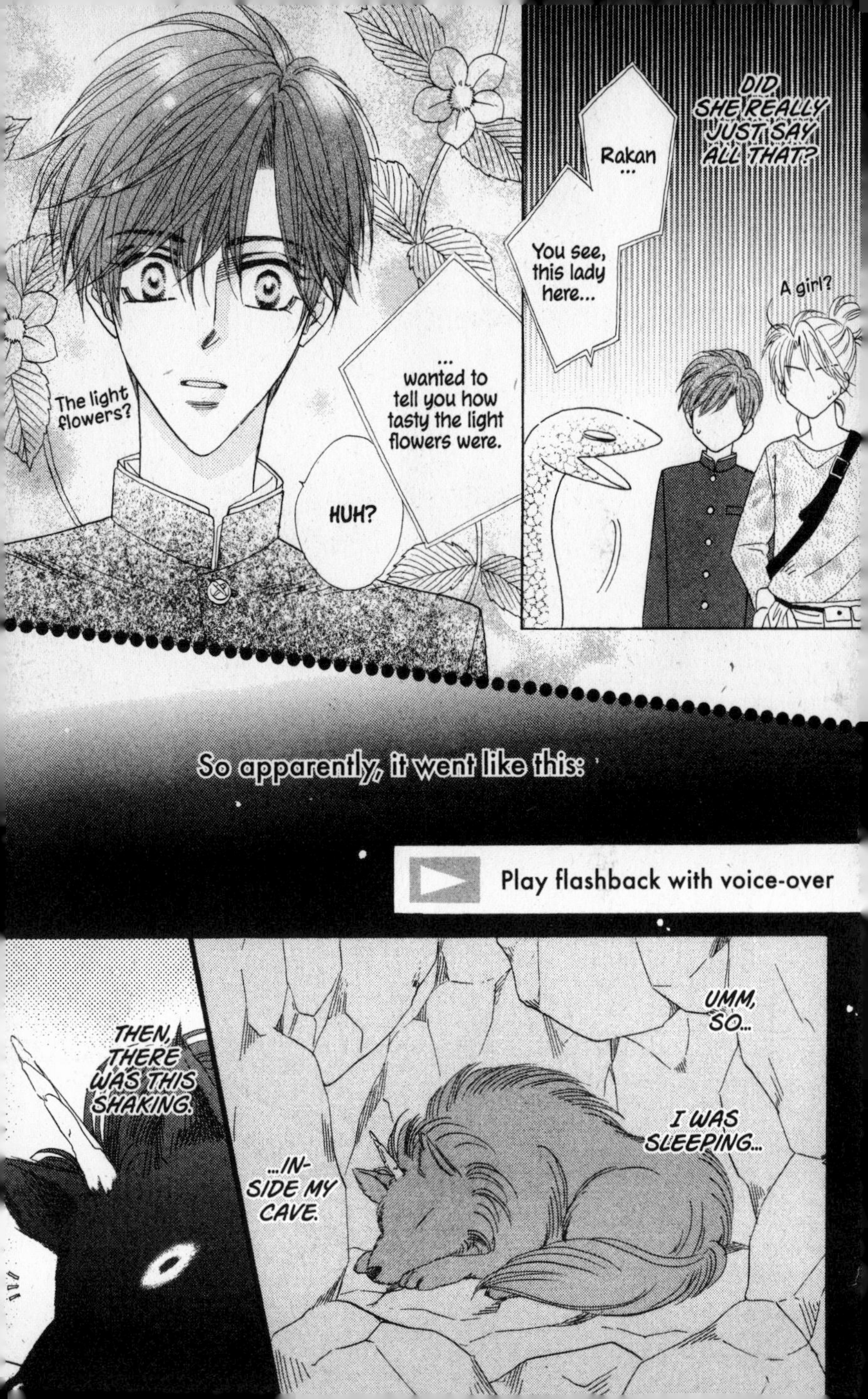
DID SHE REALLY JUST SAY ALL THAT?
Rakan...
You see, this lady here...
A girl?
... wanted to tell you how tasty the light flowers were.
HUH?
The light flowers?
So apparently, it went like this:
Play flashback with voice-over
UMM, SO...
I WAS SLEEPING...
...IN-SIDE MY CAVE.
THEN, THERE WAS THIS SHAKING.

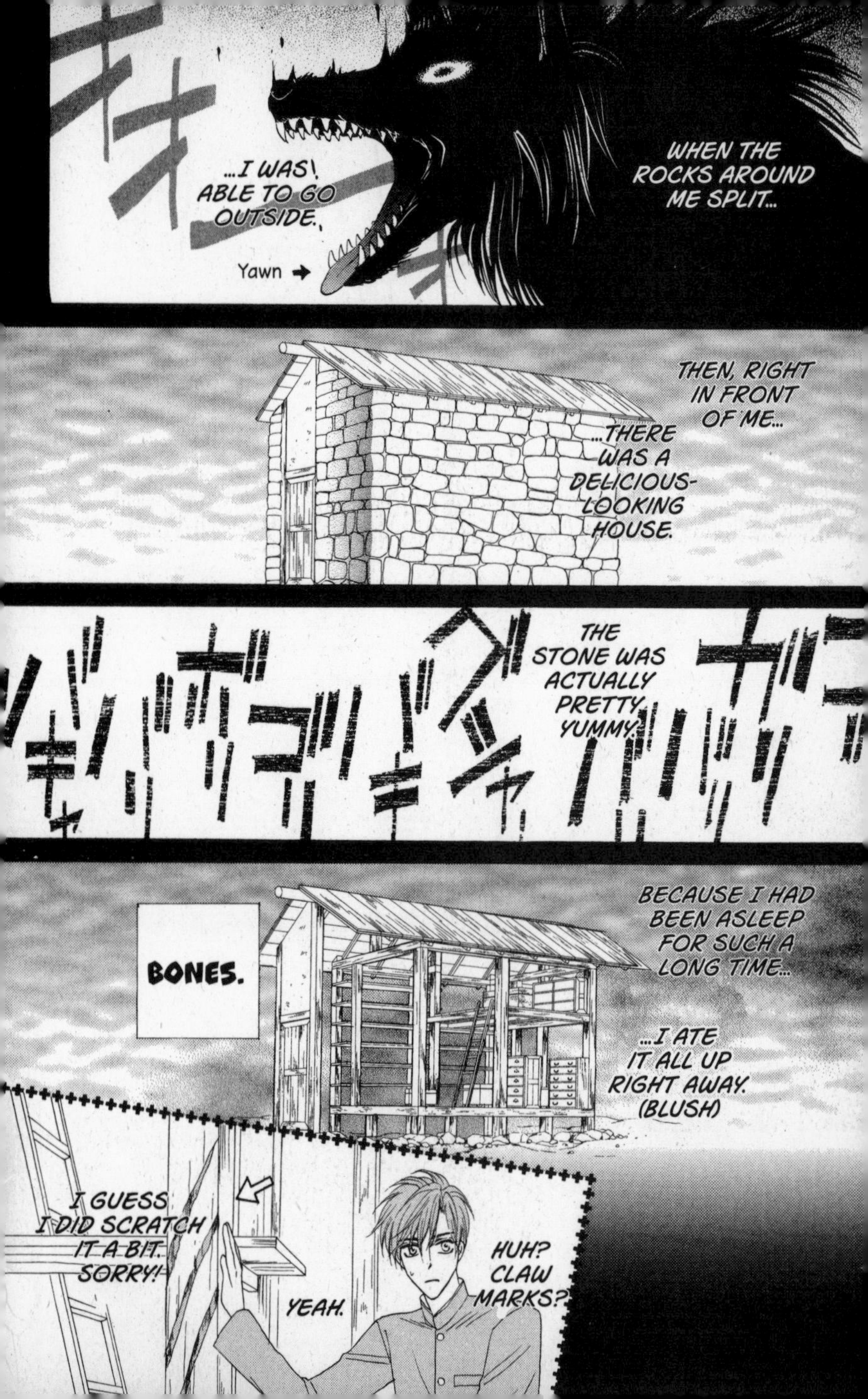
WHEN THE ROCKS AROUND ME SPLIT...
...I WAS ABLE TO GO OUTSIDE.
Yawn
THEN, RIGHT IN FRONT OF ME...
...THERE WAS A DELICIOUS-LOOKING HOUSE.
THE STONE WAS ACTUALLY PRETTY YUMMY.
BECAUSE I HAD BEEN ASLEEP FOR SUCH A LONG TIME...
...I ATE IT ALL UP RIGHT AWAY. (BLUSH)
BONES.
HUH? CLAW MARKS?
YEAH.
I GUESS I DID SCRATCH IT A BIT. SORRY!

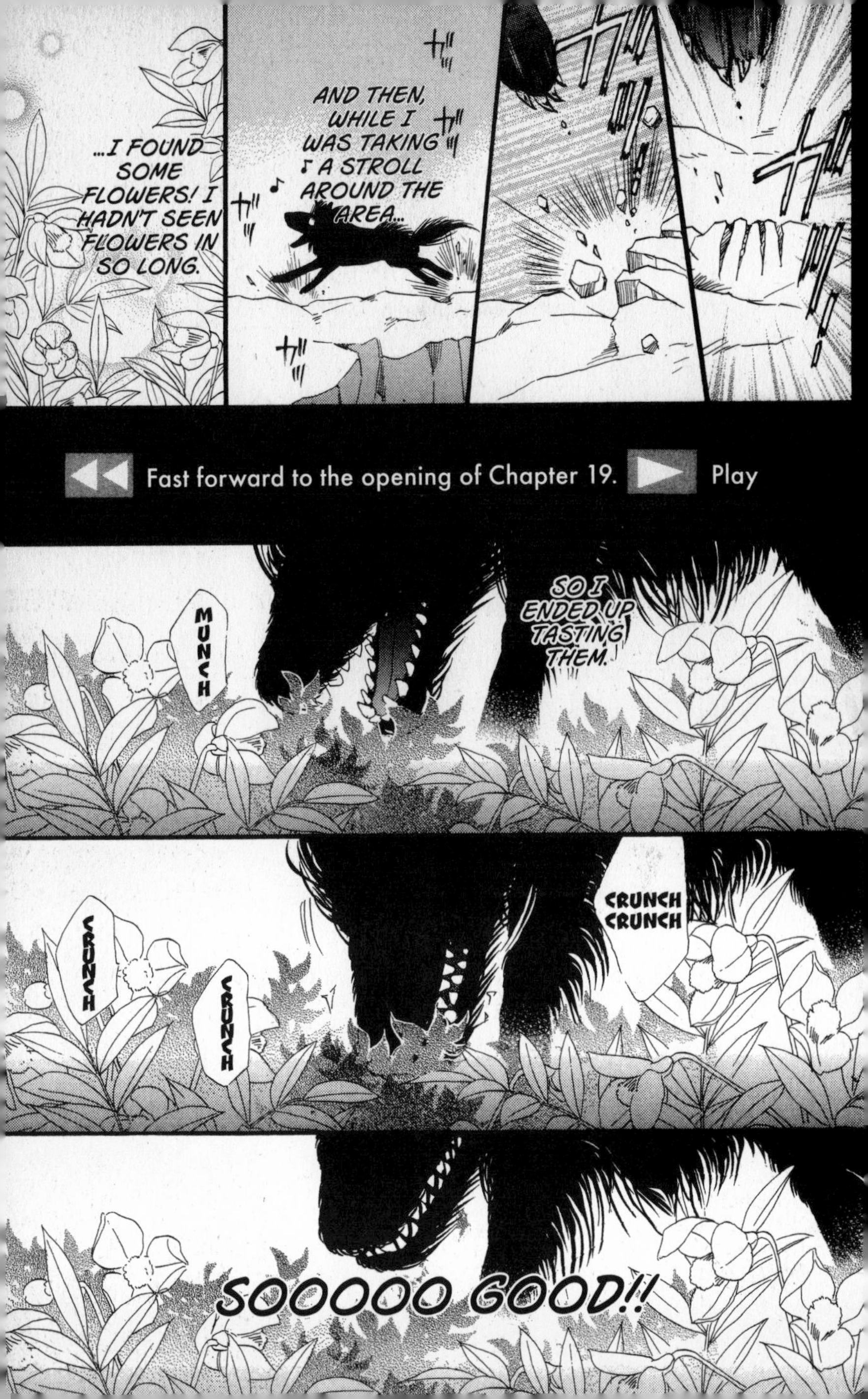
AND THEN, WHILE I WAS TAKING ♪ A STROLL AROUND THE AREA...
...I FOUND SOME FLOWERS! I HADN'T SEEN FLOWERS IN SO LONG.
Fast forward to the opening of Chapter 19.
Play
SO I ENDED UP TASTING THEM.
MUNCH
CRUNCH CRUNCH
CRUNCH
CRUNCH
SOOOOO GOOD!!

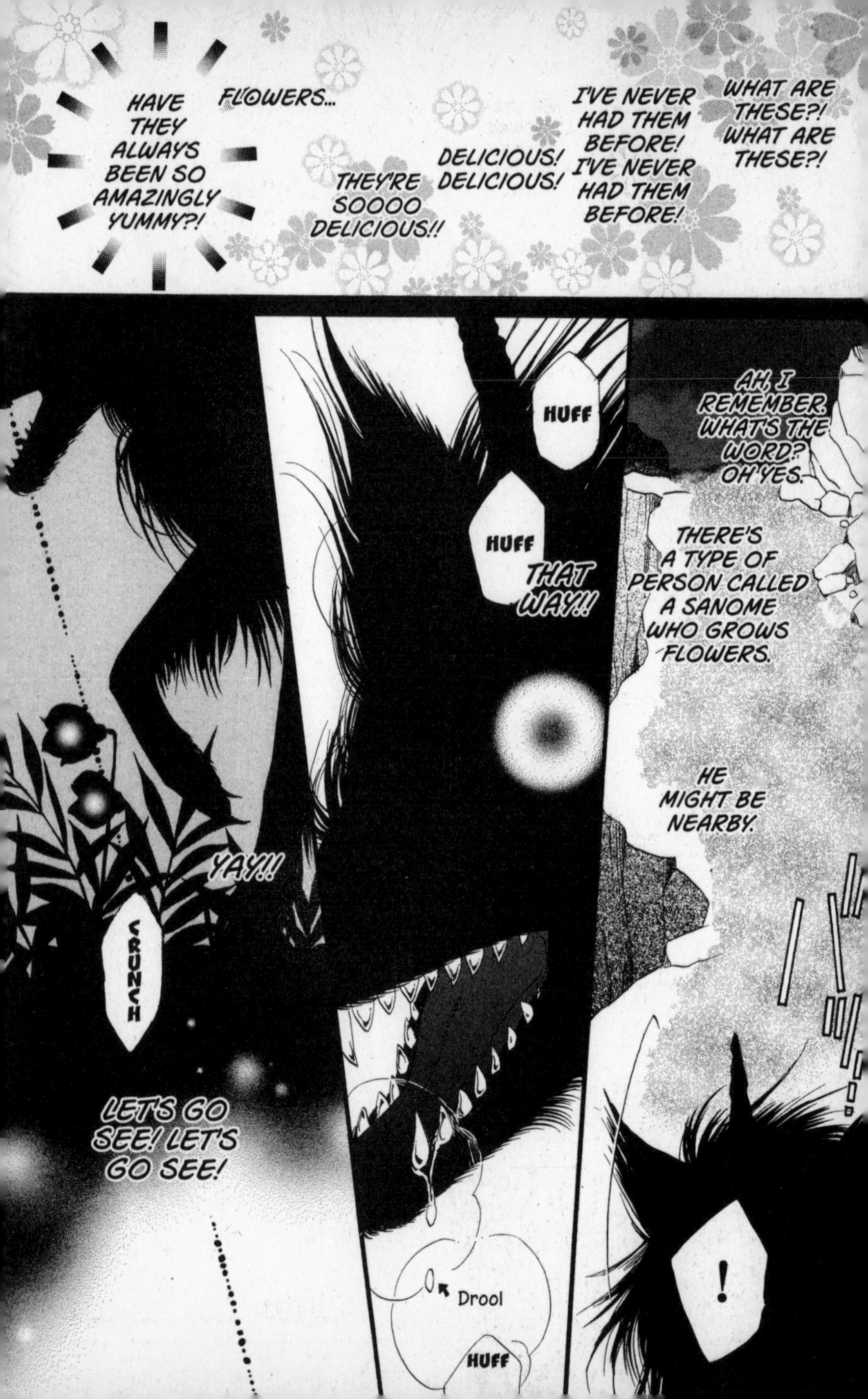
WHAT ARE THESE?! WHAT ARE THESE?!
I'VE NEVER HAD THEM BEFORE! I'VE NEVER HAD THEM BEFORE!
DELICIOUS! DELICIOUS!
THEY'RE SOOOO DELICIOUS!!
FLOWERS...
HAVE THEY ALWAYS BEEN SO AMAZINGLY YUMMY?!
AH, I REMEMBER. WHAT'S THE WORD? OH YES.
THERE'S A TYPE OF PERSON CALLED A SANOME WHO GROWS FLOWERS.
HE MIGHT BE NEARBY.
!
HUFF
HUFF
THAT WAY!!
Drool
HUFF
YAY!!
CRUNCH
LET'S GO SEE! LET'S GO SEE!

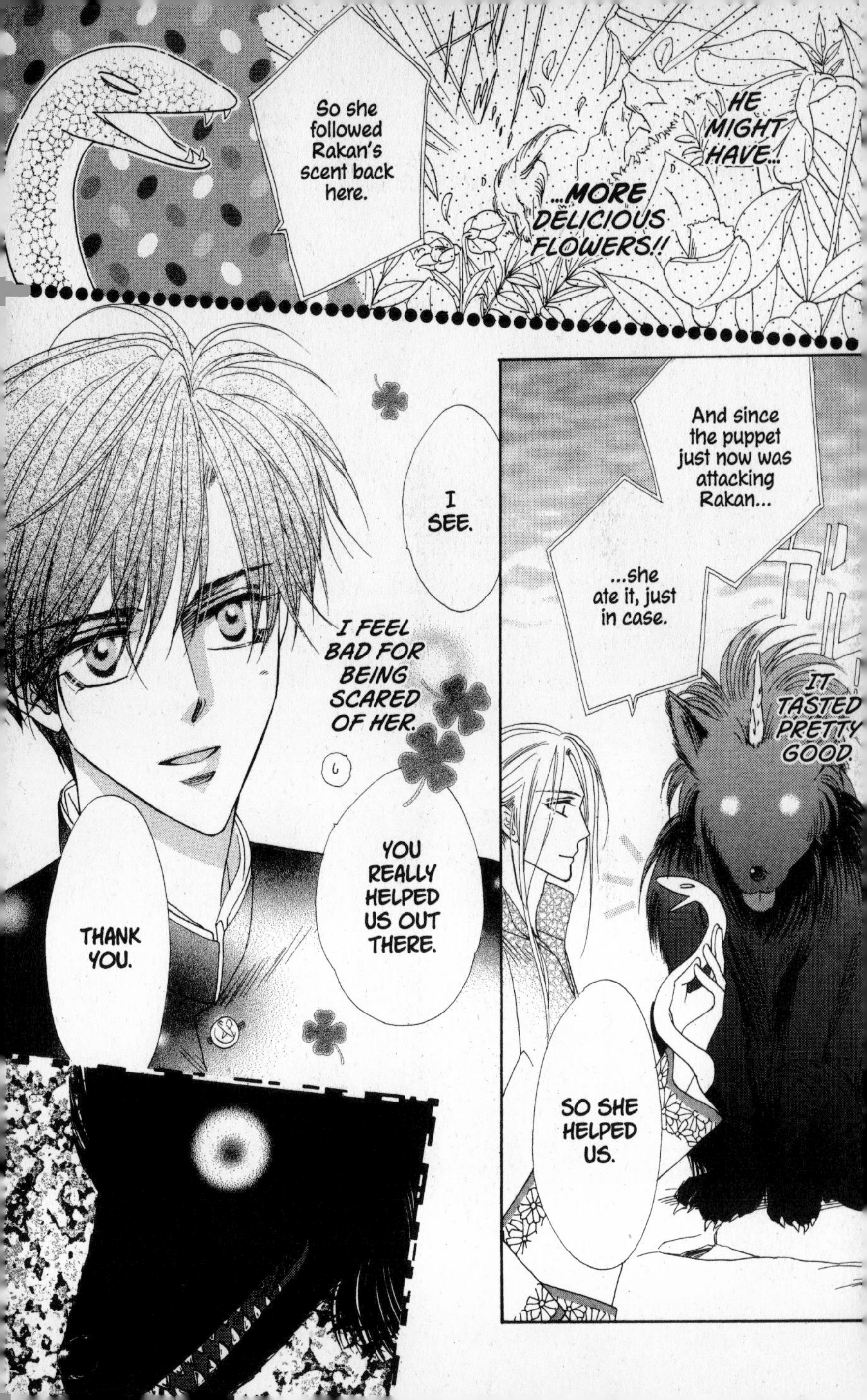
HE MIGHT HAVE...
...MORE DELICIOUS FLOWERS!!
So she followed Rakan's scent back here.
And since the puppet just now was attacking Rakan...
...she ate it, just in case.
IT TASTED PRETTY GOOD.
SO SHE HELPED US.
I SEE.
I FEEL BAD FOR BEING SCARED OF HER.
YOU REALLY HELPED US OUT THERE.
THANK YOU.

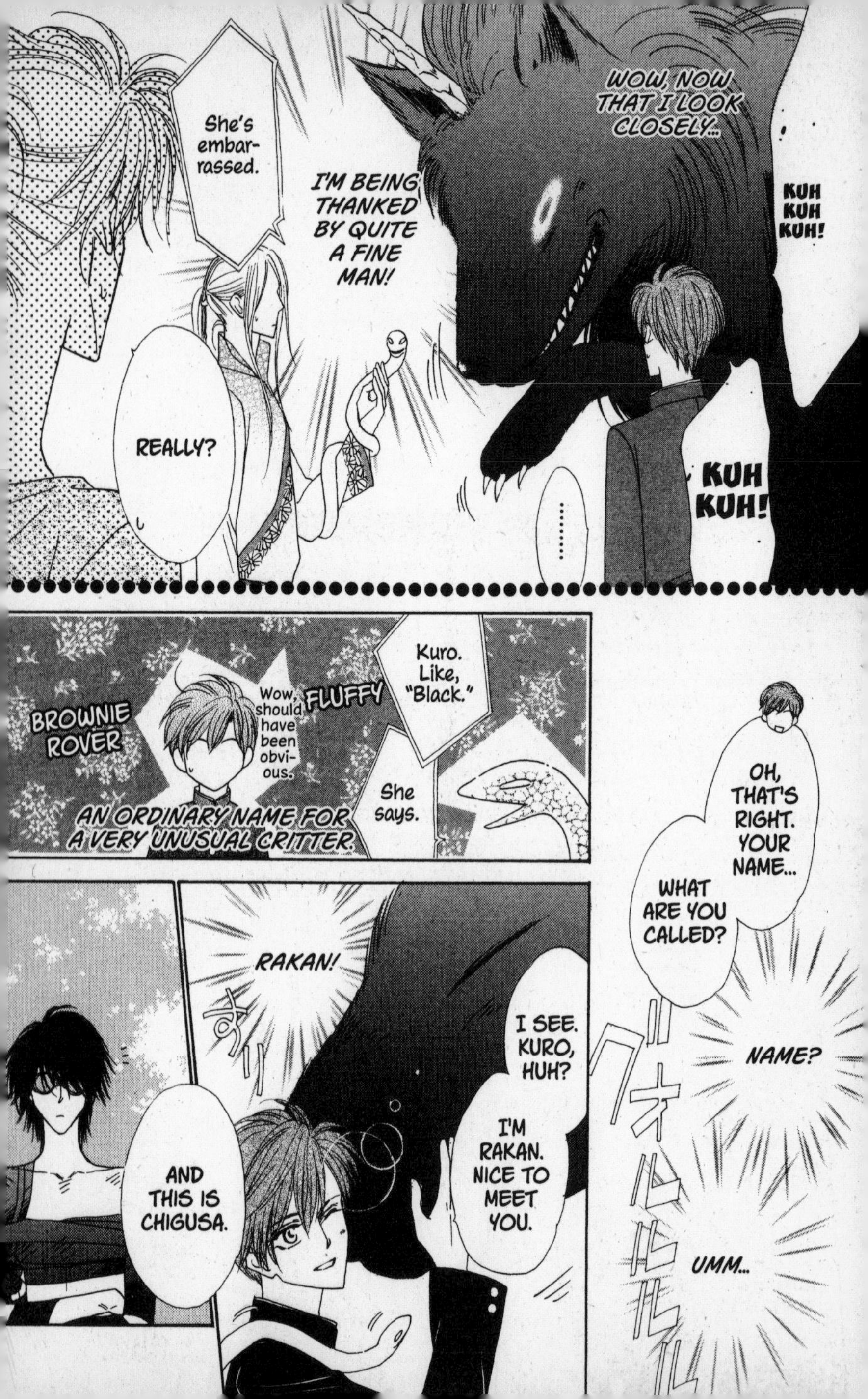
WOW, NOW THAT I LOOK CLOSELY...
KUH KUH KUH!
I'M BEING THANKED BY QUITE A FINE MAN!
She's embarrassed.
KUH KUH!
......
REALLY?
OH, THAT'S RIGHT. YOUR NAME...
WHAT ARE YOU CALLED?
NAME?
UMM...
Kuro. Like, "Black."
She says.
FLUFFY
Wow, should have been obvious.
BROWNIE ROVER
AN ORDINARY NAME FOR A VERY UNUSUAL CRITTER.
RAKAN!
I SEE. KURO, HUH?
I'M RAKAN. NICE TO MEET YOU.
AND THIS IS CHIGUSA.

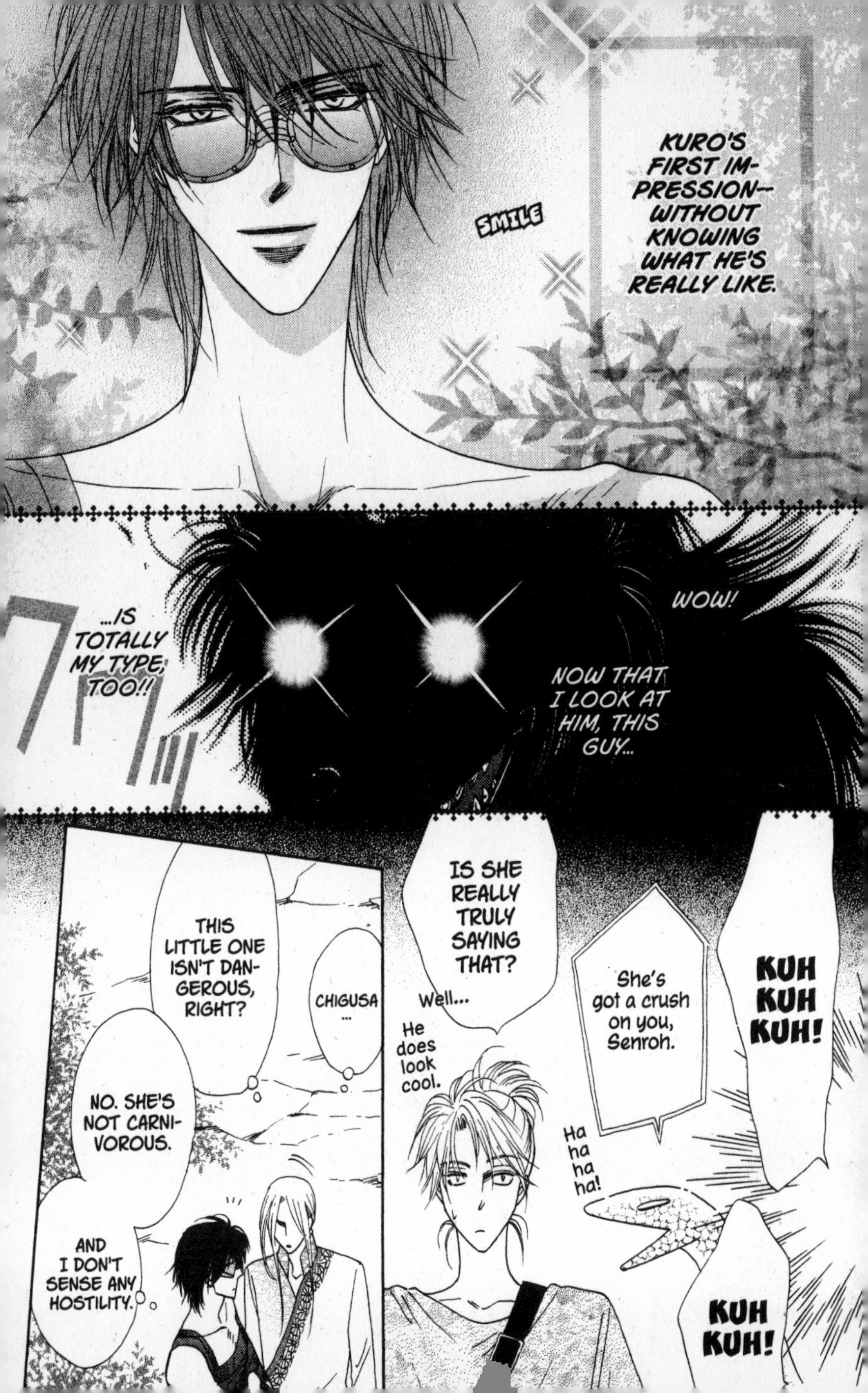
KURO'S FIRST IMPRESSION--WITHOUT KNOWING WHAT HE'S REALLY LIKE.
SMILE
WOW!
NOW THAT I LOOK AT HIM, THIS GUY...
...IS TOTALLY MY TYPE, TOO!!
KUH KUH KUH!
She's got a crush on you, Senroh.
IS SHE REALLY TRULY SAYING THAT?
Well... He does look cool.
Ha ha ha ha!
KUH KUH!
CHIGUSA ...
THIS LITTLE ONE ISN'T DANGEROUS, RIGHT?
NO. SHE'S NOT CARNIVOROUS.
AND I DON'T SENSE ANY HOSTILITY.

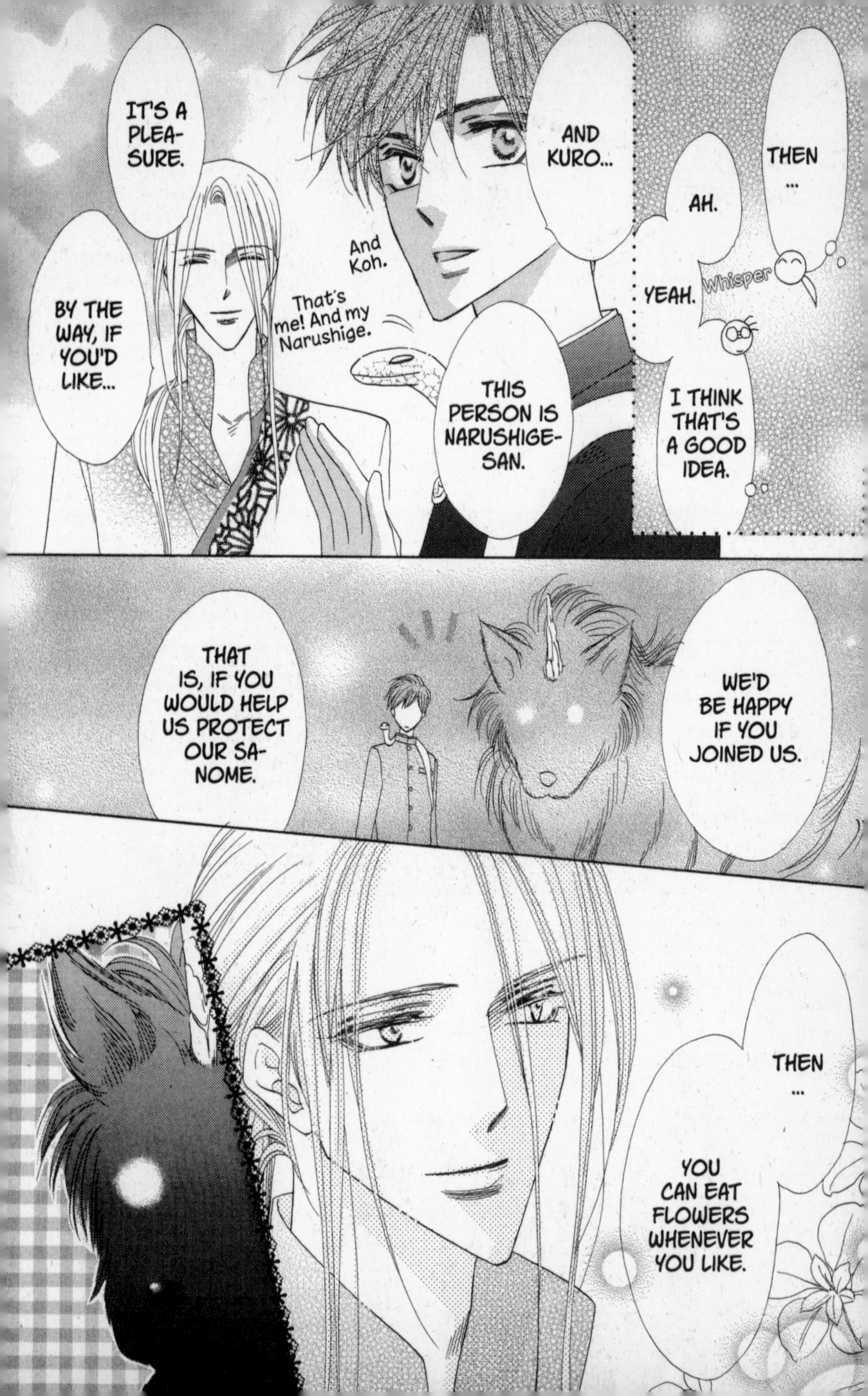
THEN ...
AH.
YEAH.
Whisper
I THINK THAT'S A GOOD IDEA.
AND KURO...
THIS PERSON IS NARUSHIGE-SAN.
And Koh.
That's me! And my Narushige.
IT'S A PLEA-SURE.
BY THE WAY, IF YOU'D LIKE...
WE'D BE HAPPY IF YOU JOINED US.
THAT IS, IF YOU WOULD HELP US PROTECT OUR SA-NOME.
THEN ...
YOU CAN EAT FLOWERS WHENEVER YOU LIKE.

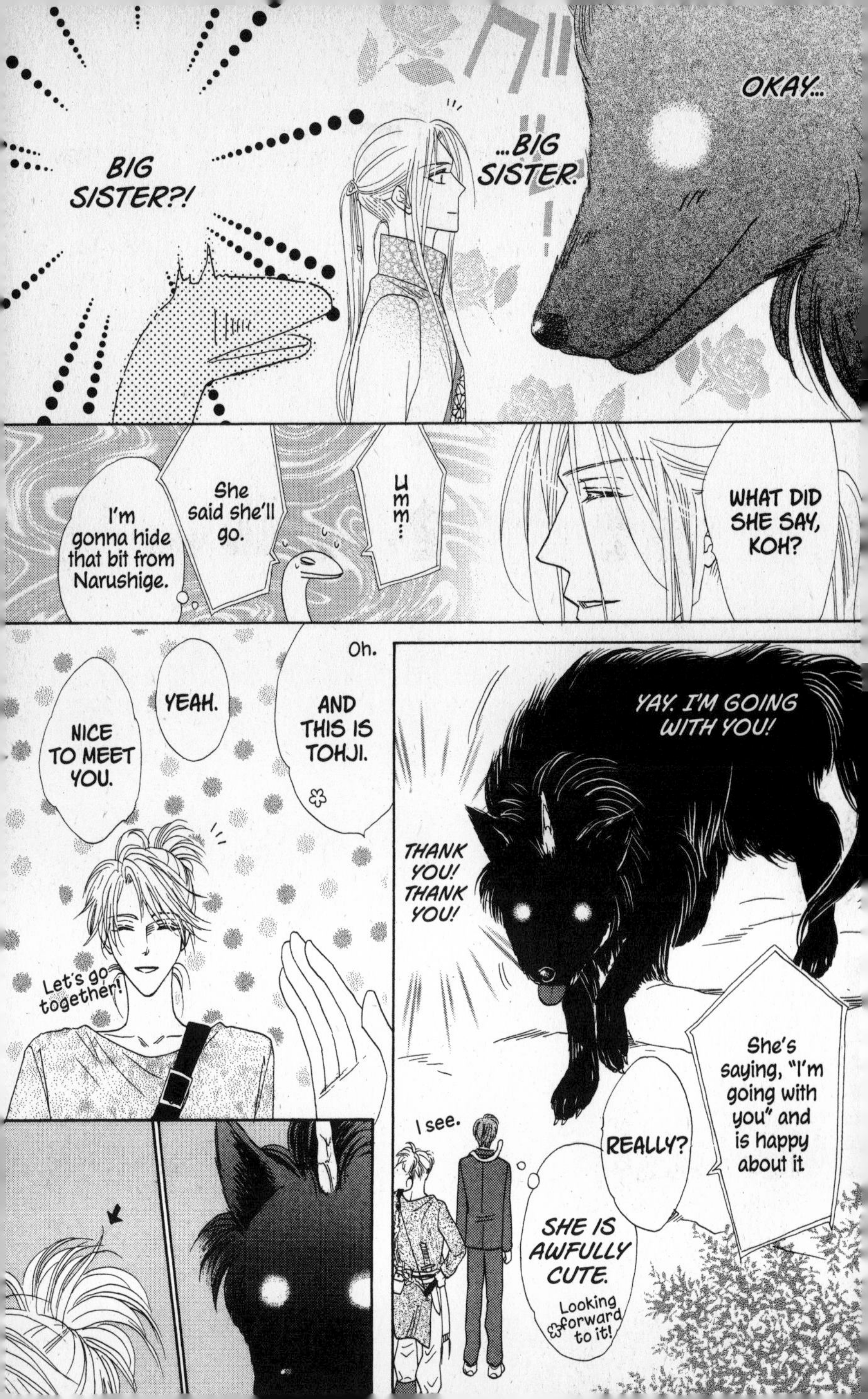
OKAY...
...BIG SISTER.
BIG SISTER?!
WHAT DID SHE SAY, KOH?
Umm...
She said she'll go.
I'm gonna hide that bit from Narushige.
YAY. I'M GOING WITH YOU!
THANK YOU! THANK YOU!
She's saying, "I'm going with you" and is happy about it
REALLY?
I see.
SHE IS AWFULLY CUTE.
Looking forward to it!
Oh.
AND THIS IS TOHJI.
YEAH.
NICE TO MEET YOU.
Let's go together!

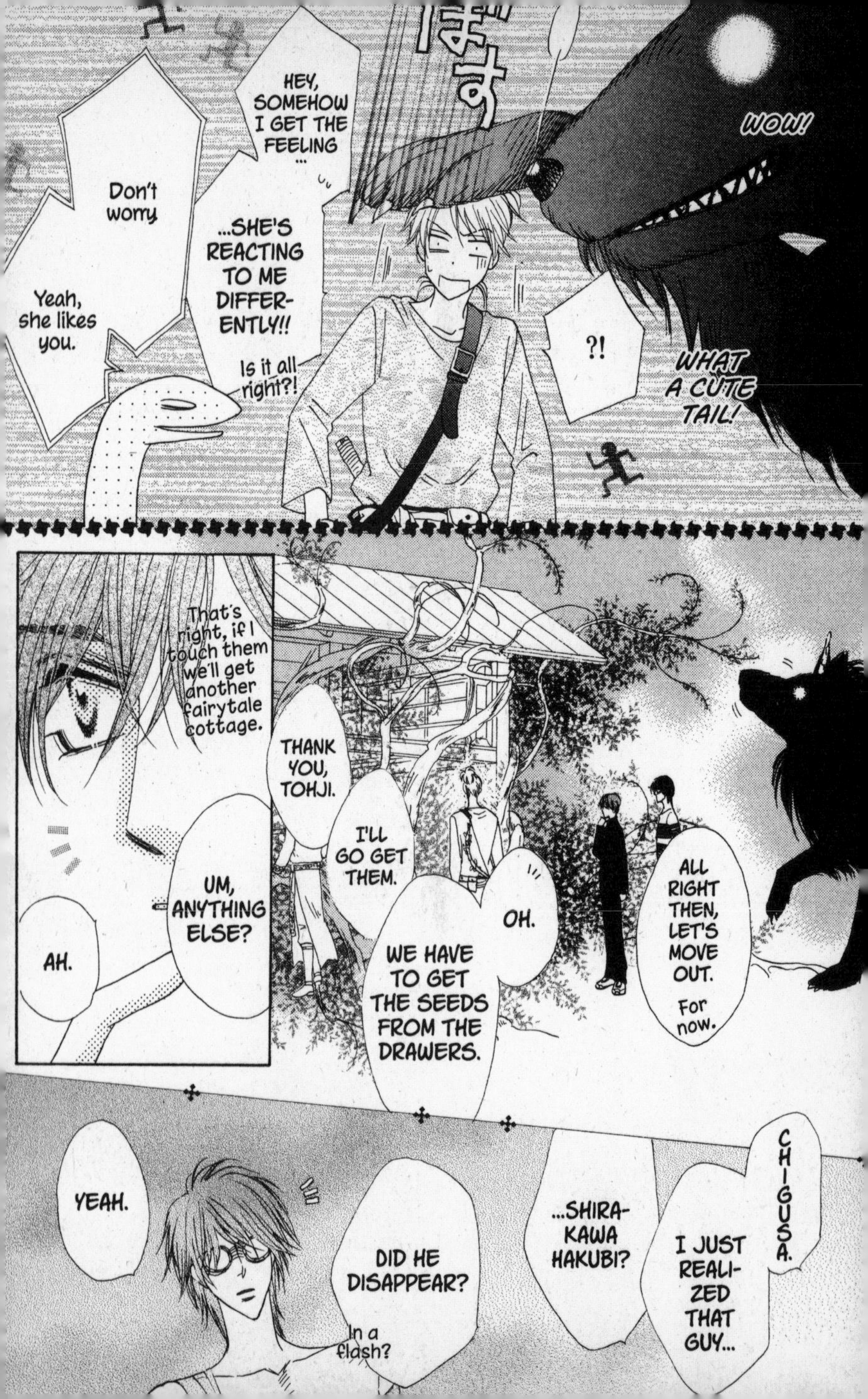
ぼす
WOW!
WHAT A CUTE TAIL!
?!
HEY, SOMEHOW I GET THE FEELING ...
...SHE'S REACTING TO ME DIFFERENTLY!!
Is it all right?!
Don't worry
Yeah, she likes you.
ALL RIGHT THEN, LET'S MOVE OUT.
For now.
OH.
WE HAVE TO GET THE SEEDS FROM THE DRAWERS.
I'LL GO GET THEM.
THANK YOU, TOHJI.
That's right, if I touch them we'll get another fairytale cottage.
UM, ANYTHING ELSE?
AH.
CHIGUSA.
I JUST REALIZED THAT GUY...
...SHIRAKAWA HAKUBI?
DID HE DISAPPEAR?
In a flash?
YEAH.

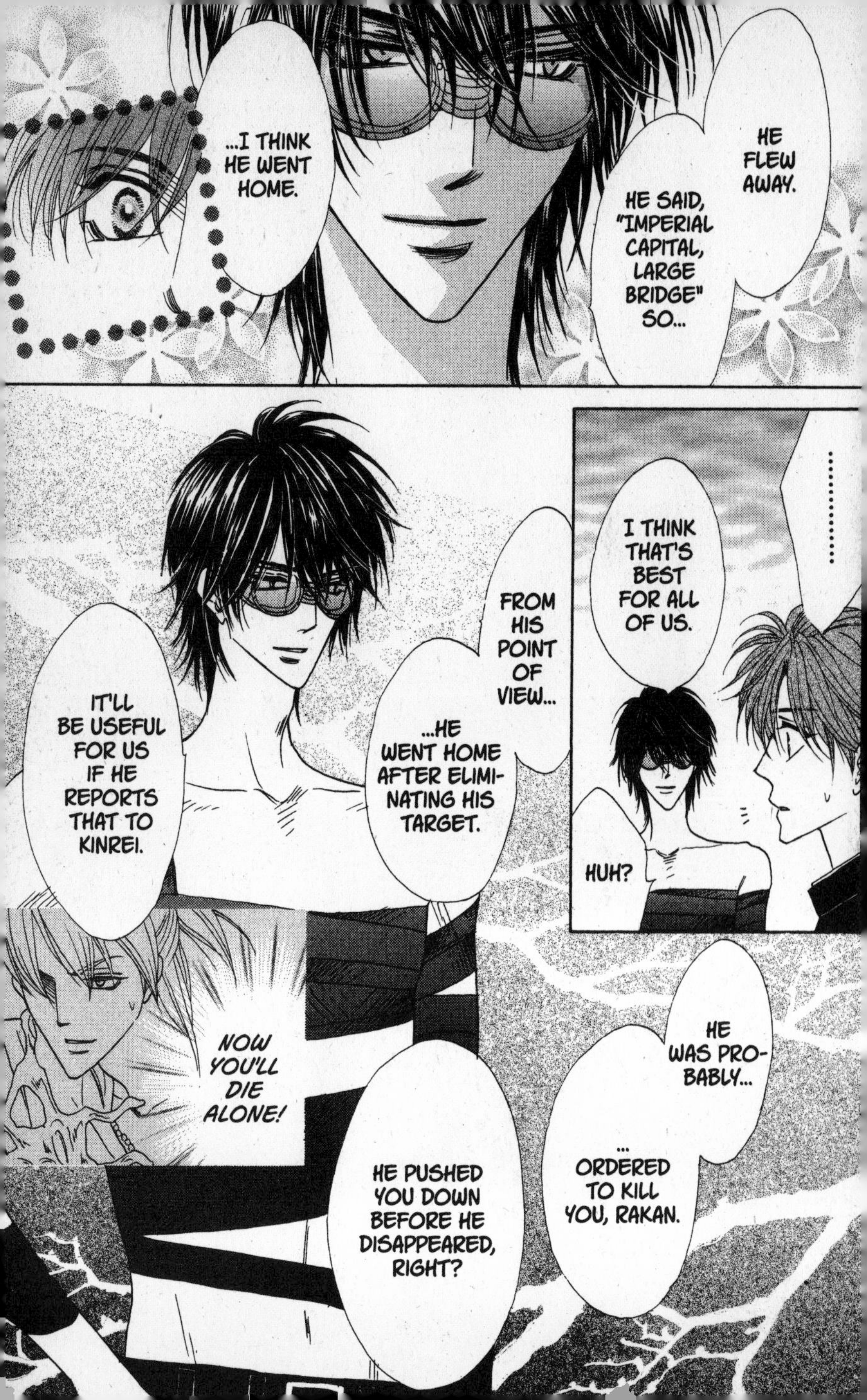
HE FLEW AWAY.
HE SAID, "IMPERIAL CAPITAL, LARGE BRIDGE" SO...
...I THINK HE WENT HOME.
......
I THINK THAT'S BEST FOR ALL OF US.
HUH?
FROM HIS POINT OF VIEW...
...HE WENT HOME AFTER ELIMINATING HIS TARGET.
IT'LL BE USEFUL FOR US IF HE REPORTS THAT TO KINREI.
HE WAS PROBABLY...
...ORDERED TO KILL YOU, RAKAN.
HE PUSHED YOU DOWN BEFORE HE DISAPPEARED, RIGHT?
NOW YOU'LL DIE ALONE!

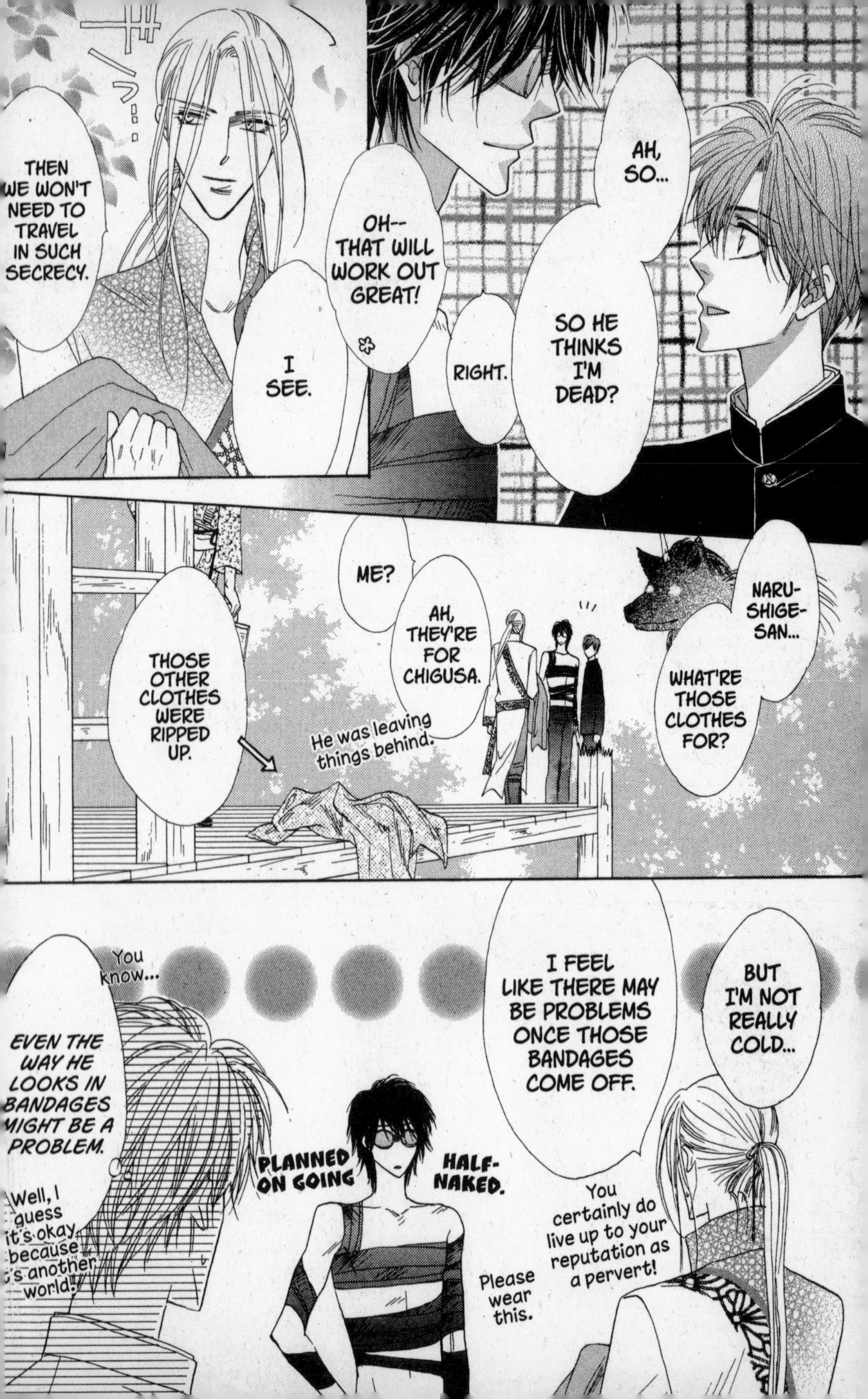

AH, SO...
SO HE THINKS I'M DEAD?
RIGHT.
OH-- THAT WILL WORK OUT GREAT!
I SEE.
THEN WE WON'T NEED TO TRAVEL IN SUCH SECRECY.
NARU-SHIGE-SAN...
WHAT'RE THOSE CLOTHES FOR?
ME?
AH, THEY'RE FOR CHIGUSA.
THOSE OTHER CLOTHES WERE RIPPED UP.
He was leaving things behind.
BUT I'M NOT REALLY COLD...
I FEEL LIKE THERE MAY BE PROBLEMS ONCE THOSE BANDAGES COME OFF.
You certainly do live up to your reputation as a pervert!
Please wear this.
PLANNED ON GOING HALF-NAKED.
You know...
EVEN THE WAY HE LOOKS IN BANDAGES MIGHT BE A PROBLEM.
Well, I guess it's okay because t's another world!

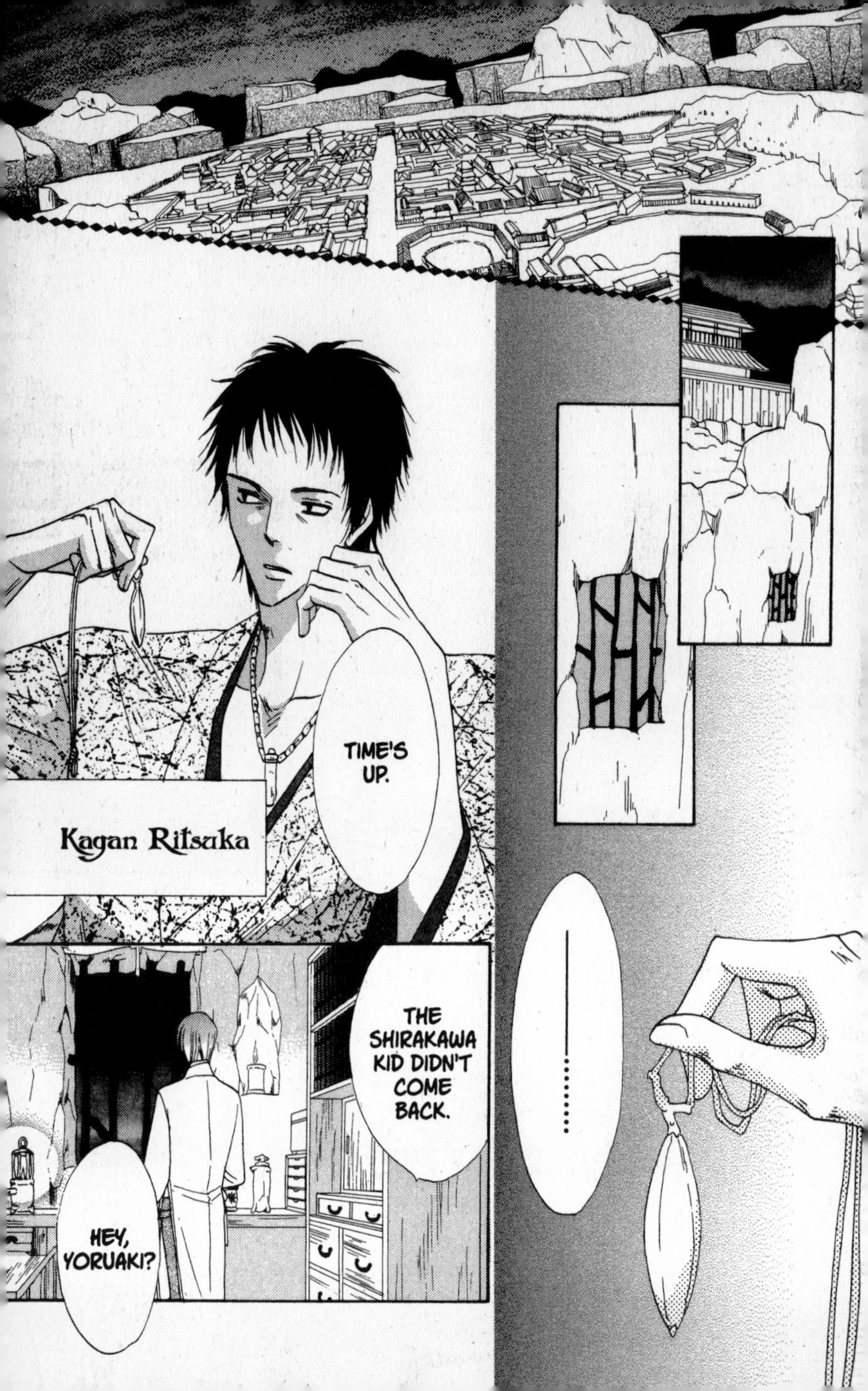
——......
TIME'S UP.
Kagan Ritsuka
THE SHIRAKAWA KID DIDN'T COME BACK.
HEY, YORUAKI?

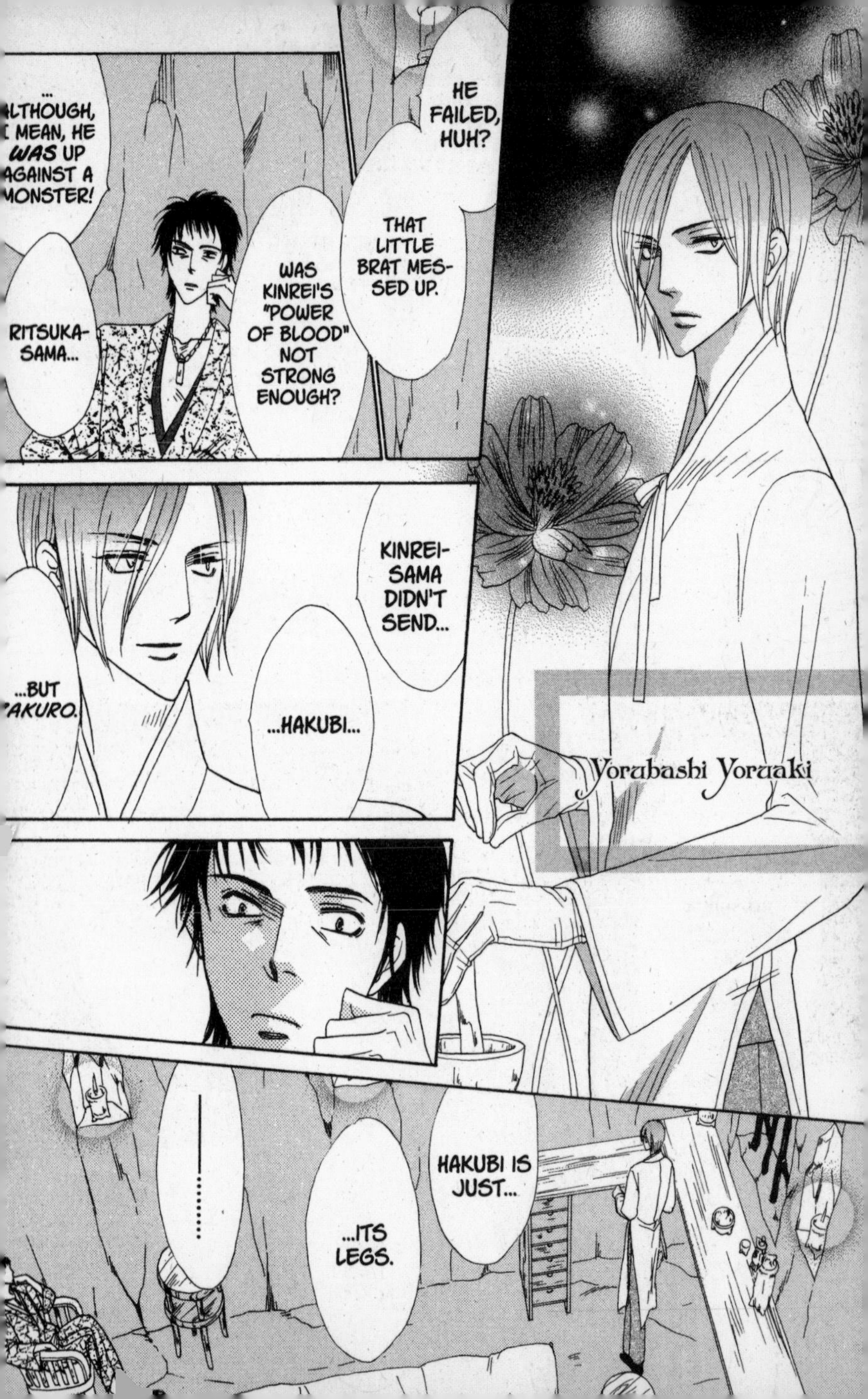
Yorubashi Yoruaki
HE FAILED, HUH?
THAT LITTLE BRAT MES-SED UP.
WAS KINREI'S "POWER OF BLOOD" NOT STRONG ENOUGH?
... LTHOUGH, MEAN, HE WAS UP AGAINST A MONSTER!
RITSUKA-SAMA...
KINREI-SAMA DIDN'T SEND...
...HAKUBI...
...BUT AKURO.
HAKUBI IS JUST...
...ITS LEGS.
......

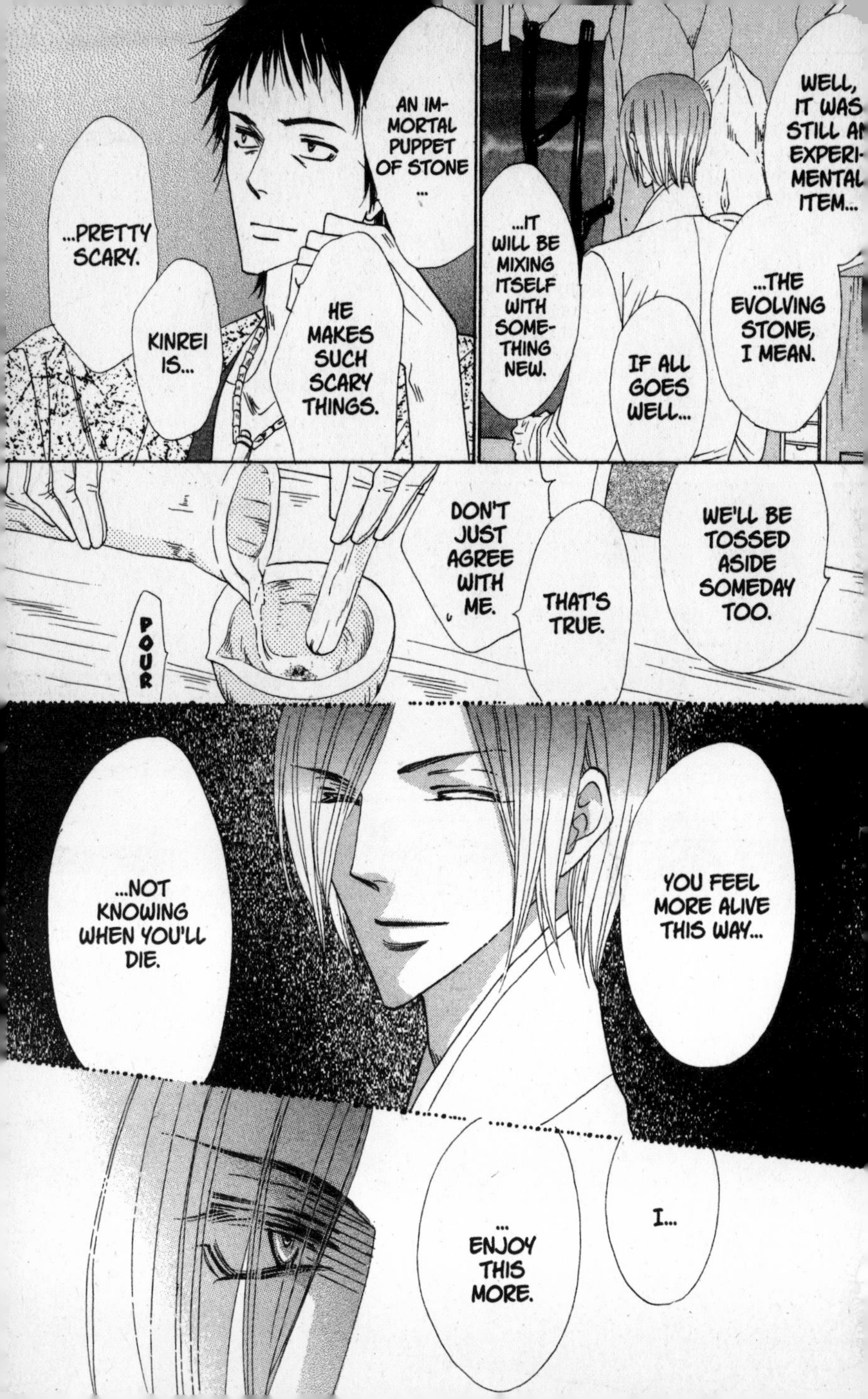
WELL, IT WAS STILL AN EXPERIMENTAL ITEM...
...THE EVOLVING STONE, I MEAN.
IF ALL GOES WELL...
...IT WILL BE MIXING ITSELF WITH SOMETHING NEW.
AN IMMORTAL PUPPET OF STONE...
HE MAKES SUCH SCARY THINGS.
KINREI IS...
...PRETTY SCARY.
WE'LL BE TOSSED ASIDE SOMEDAY TOO.
THAT'S TRUE.
DON'T JUST AGREE WITH ME.
POUR
YOU FEEL MORE ALIVE THIS WAY...
...NOT KNOWING WHEN YOU'LL DIE.
I...
...ENJOY THIS MORE.

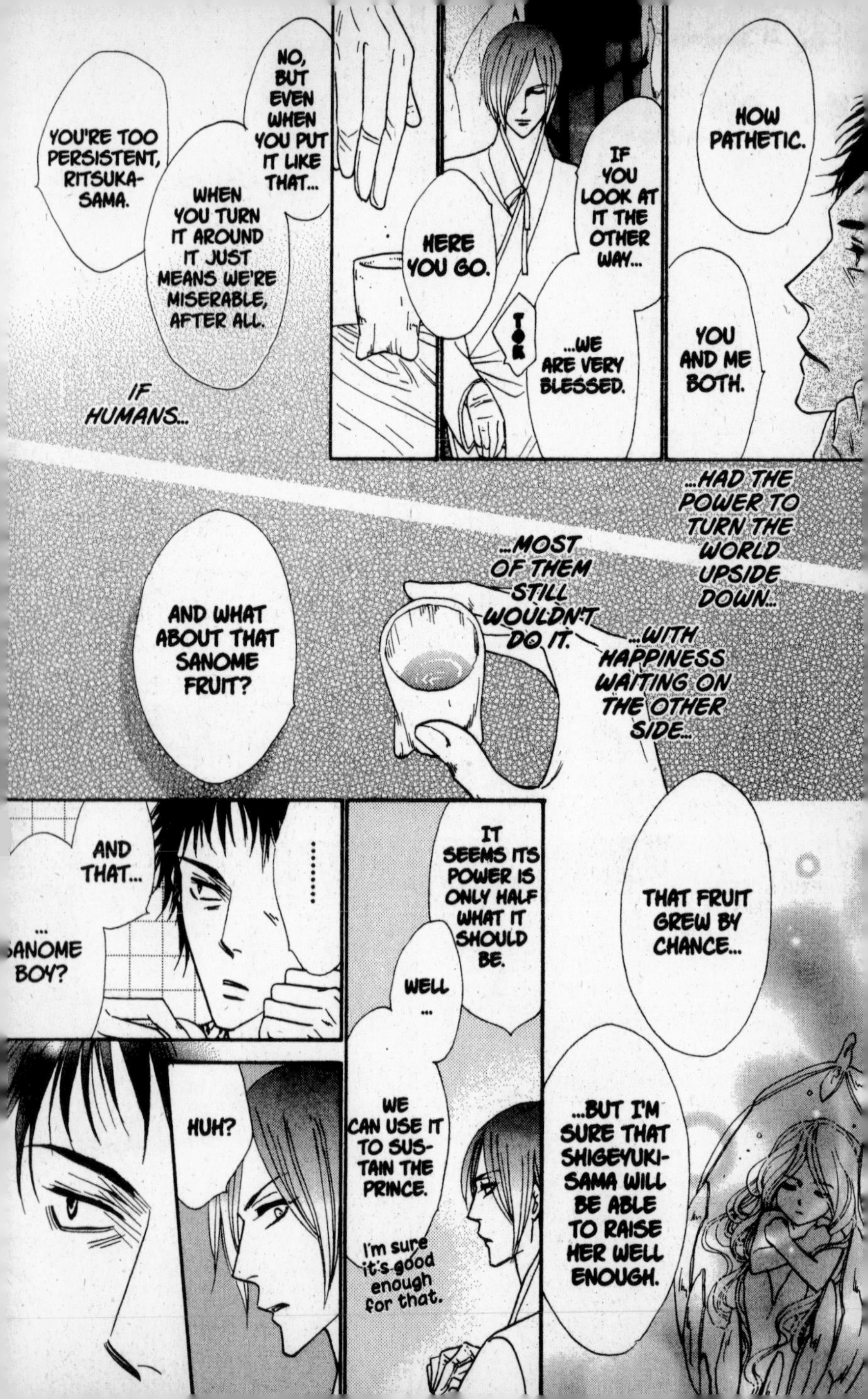
HOW PATHETIC.
YOU AND ME BOTH.
IF YOU LOOK AT IT THE OTHER WAY...
...WE ARE VERY BLESSED.
TOK
HERE YOU GO.
NO, BUT EVEN WHEN YOU PUT IT LIKE THAT...
WHEN YOU TURN IT AROUND IT JUST MEANS WE'RE MISERABLE, AFTER ALL.
YOU'RE TOO PERSISTENT, RITSUKA-SAMA.
IF HUMANS...
...HAD THE POWER TO TURN THE WORLD UPSIDE DOWN...
...WITH HAPPINESS WAITING ON THE OTHER SIDE...
...MOST OF THEM STILL WOULDN'T DO IT.
AND WHAT ABOUT THAT SANOME FRUIT?
THAT FRUIT GREW BY CHANCE...
...BUT I'M SURE THAT SHIGEYUKI-SAMA WILL BE ABLE TO RAISE HER WELL ENOUGH.
IT SEEMS ITS POWER IS ONLY HALF WHAT IT SHOULD BE.
WELL...
WE CAN USE IT TO SUS-TAIN THE PRINCE.
I'm sure it's good enough for that.
AND THAT...
......
...SANOME BOY?
HUH?

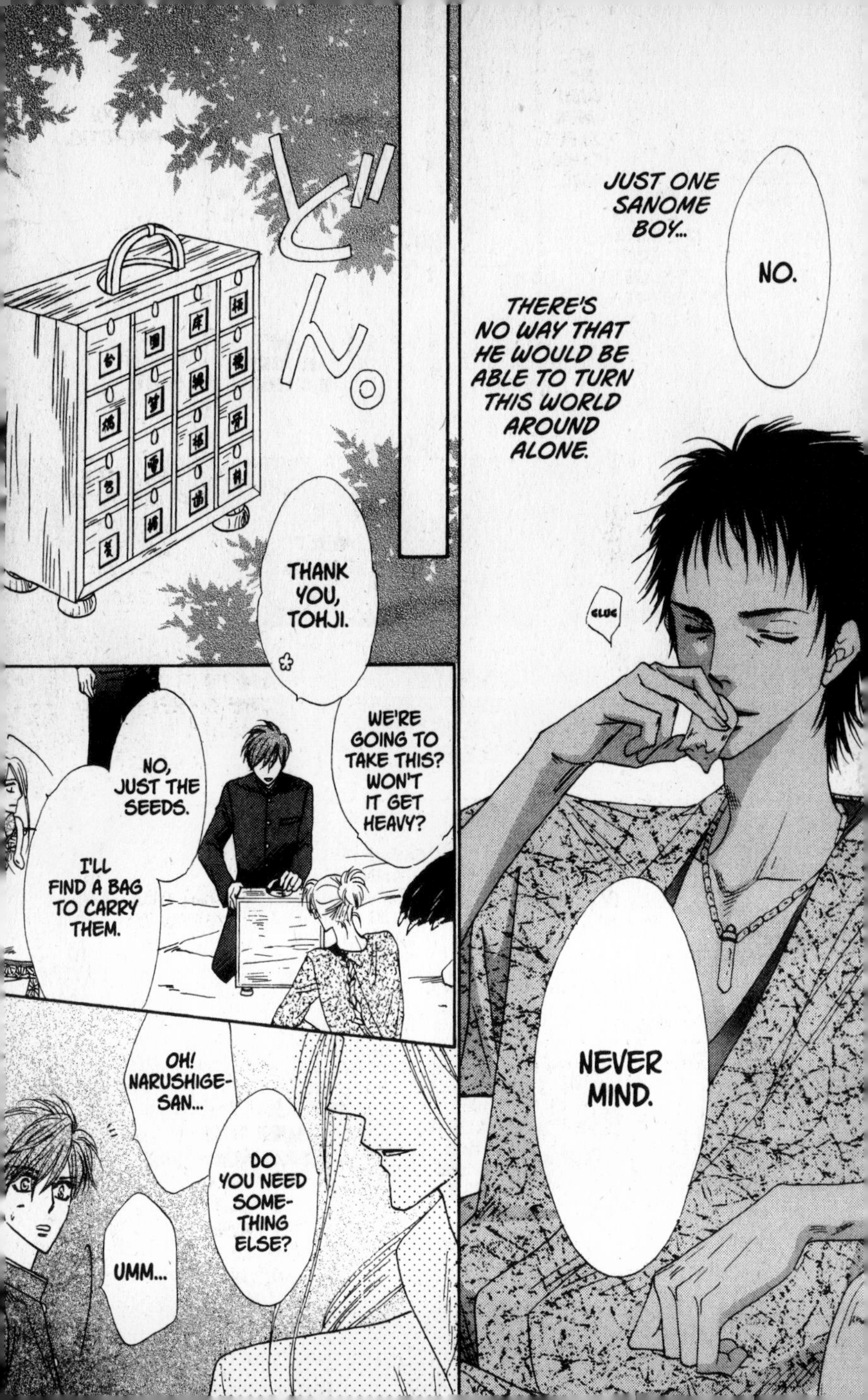
JUST ONE SANOME BOY...
NO.
THERE'S NO WAY THAT HE WOULD BE ABLE TO TURN THIS WORLD AROUND ALONE.
GLUG
NEVER MIND.
どん。
THANK YOU, TOHJI.
WE'RE GOING TO TAKE THIS? WON'T IT GET HEAVY?
NO, JUST THE SEEDS.
I'LL FIND A BAG TO CARRY THEM.
OH! NARUSHIGE-SAN...
DO YOU NEED SOME-THING ELSE?
UMM...

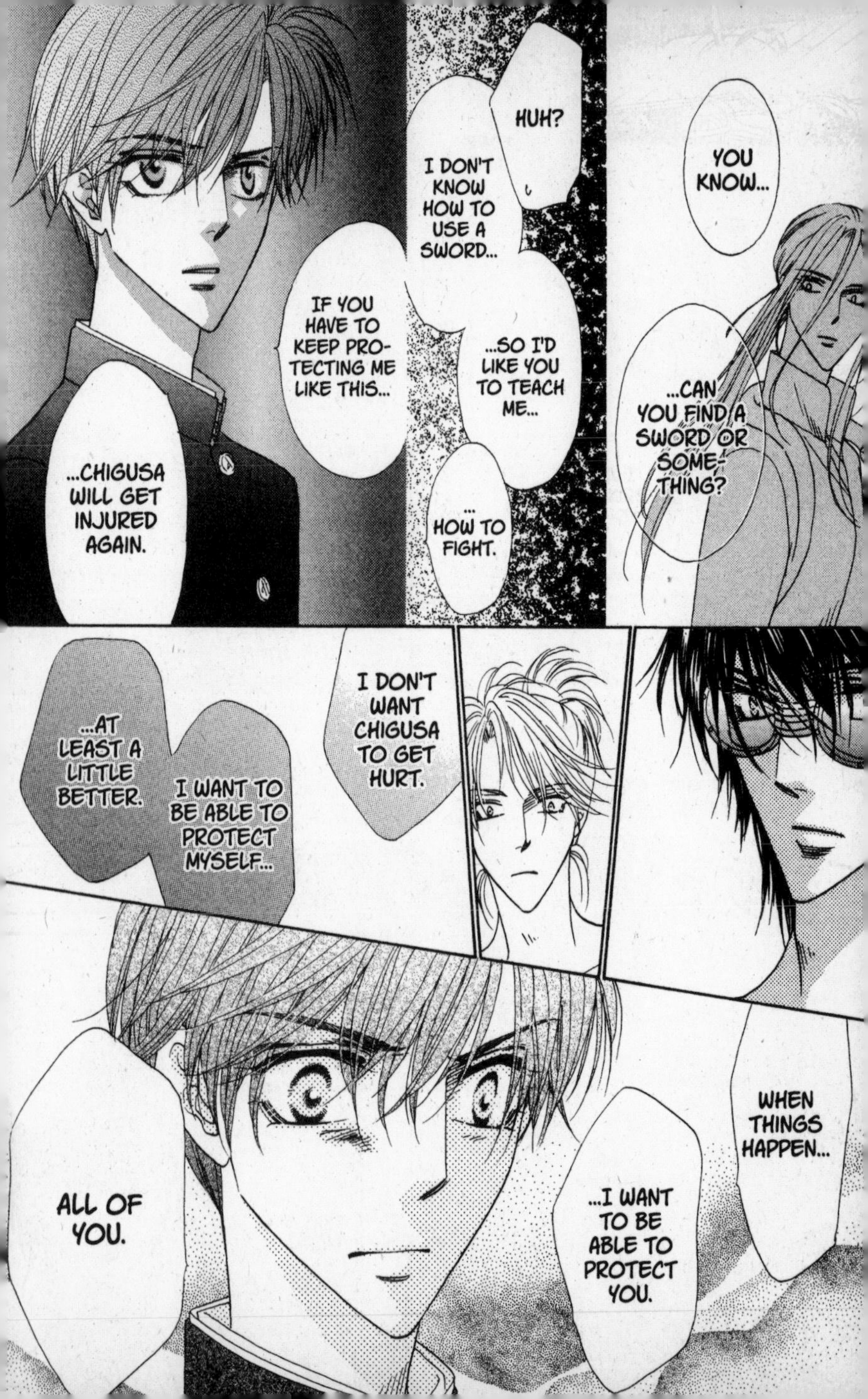
YOU KNOW...
...CAN YOU FIND A SWORD OR SOMETHING?
HUH?
I DON'T KNOW HOW TO USE A SWORD...
...SO I'D LIKE YOU TO TEACH ME...
...HOW TO FIGHT.
IF YOU HAVE TO KEEP PROTECTING ME LIKE THIS...
...CHIGUSA WILL GET INJURED AGAIN.
I DON'T WANT CHIGUSA TO GET HURT.
I WANT TO BE ABLE TO PROTECT MYSELF...
...AT LEAST A LITTLE BETTER.
WHEN THINGS HAPPEN...
...I WANT TO BE ABLE TO PROTECT YOU.
ALL OF YOU.

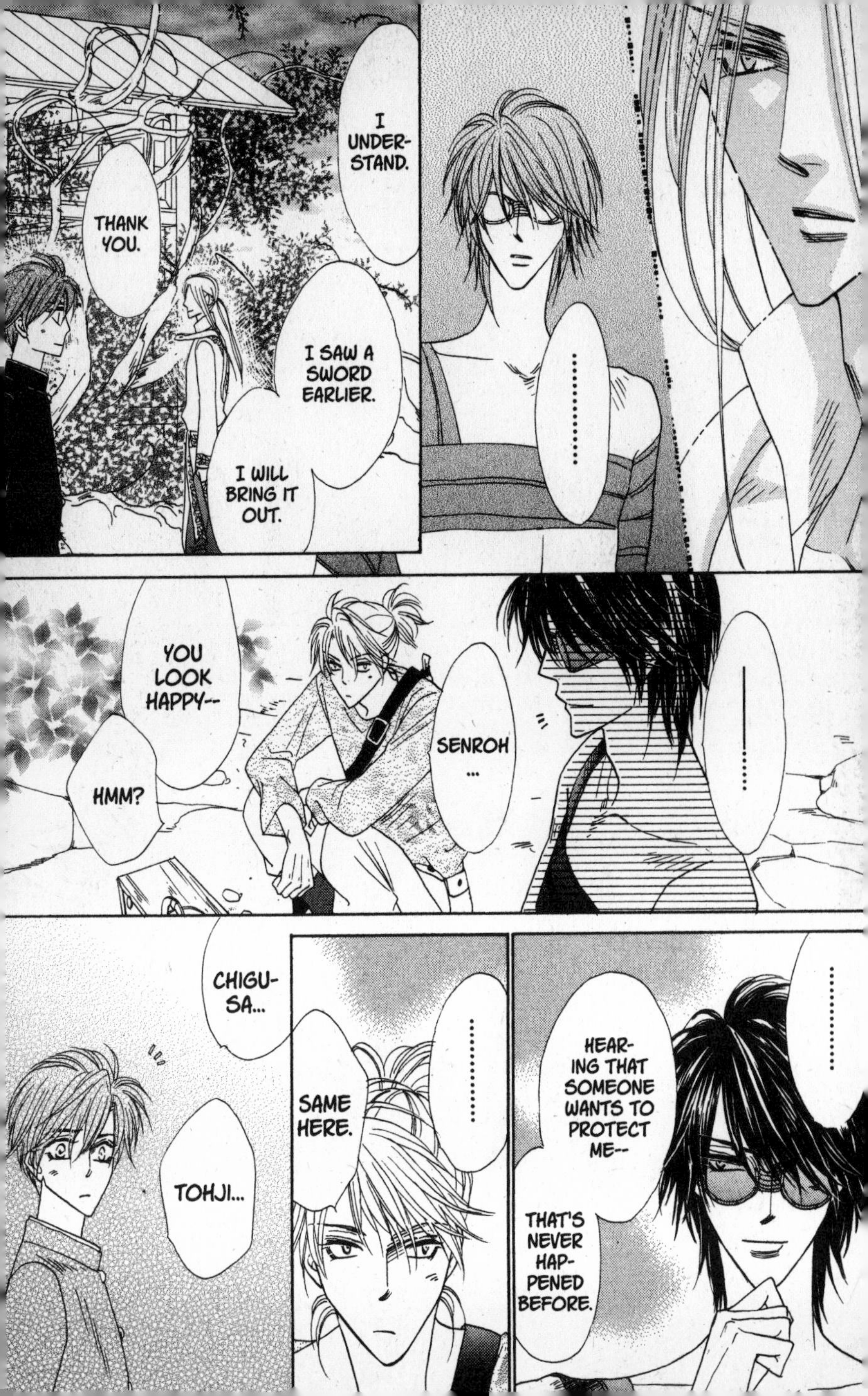

......
I UNDER-STAND.
I SAW A SWORD EARLIER.
I WILL BRING IT OUT.
THANK YOU.
......
SENROH ...
YOU LOOK HAPPY--
HMM?
......
HEAR-ING THAT SOMEONE WANTS TO PROTECT ME--
THAT'S NEVER HAP-PENED BEFORE.
......
SAME HERE.
CHIGU-SA...
TOHJI...

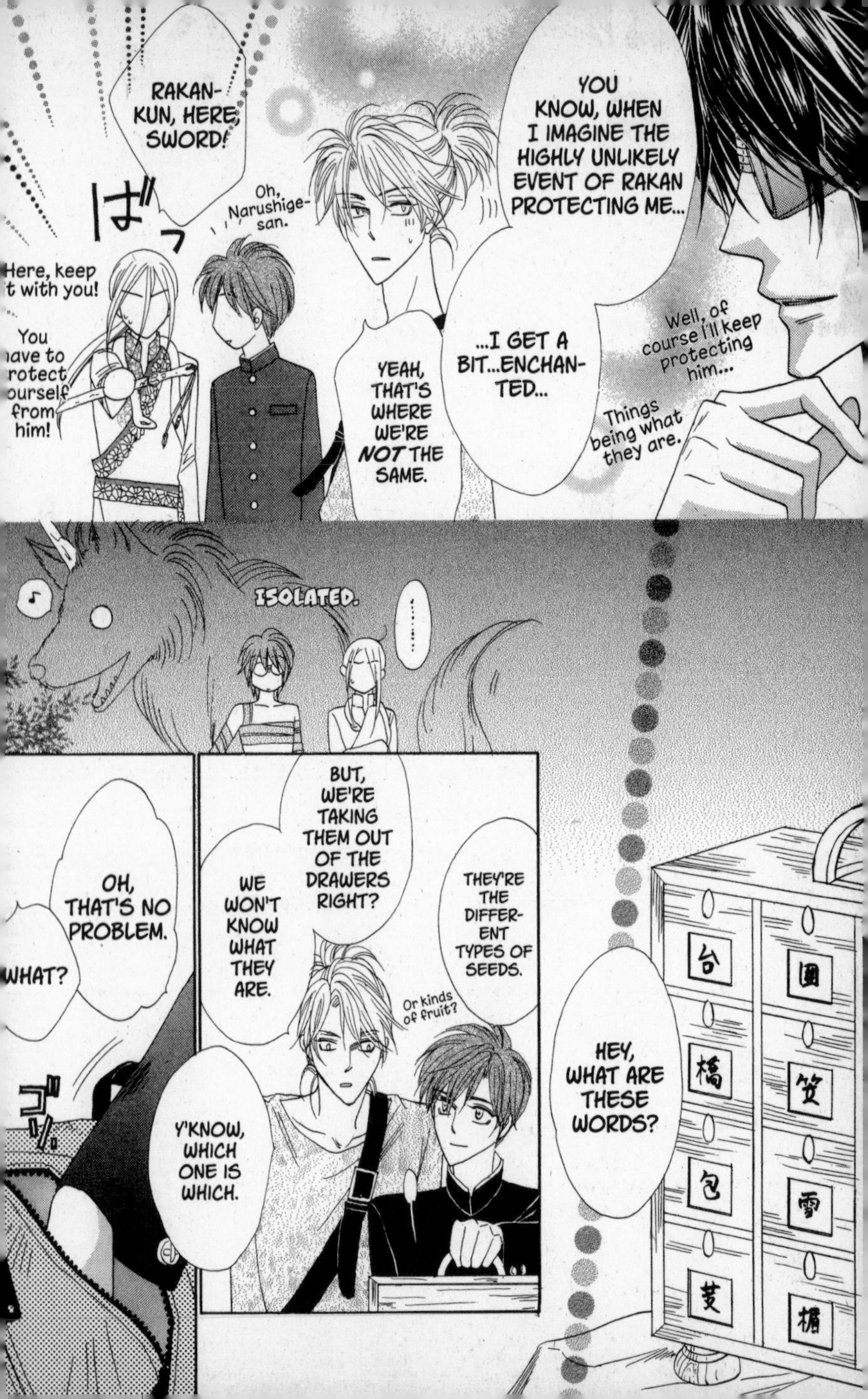
YOU KNOW, WHEN I IMAGINE THE HIGHLY UNLIKELY EVENT OF RAKAN PROTECTING ME...
Well, of course I'll keep protecting him...
Things being what they are.
...I GET A BIT...ENCHANTED...
YEAH, THAT'S WHERE WE'RE NOT THE SAME.
Oh, Narushige-san.
RAKAN-KUN, HERE, SWORD!
ばっ
Here, keep t with you!
You ave to rotect ourself from him!
ISOLATED.
......
HEY, WHAT ARE THESE WORDS?
台
團
橘
笠
包
雪
THEY'RE THE DIFFERENT TYPES OF SEEDS.
Or kinds of fruit?
BUT, WE'RE TAKING THEM OUT OF THE DRAWERS RIGHT?
WE WON'T KNOW WHAT THEY ARE.
Y'KNOW, WHICH ONE IS WHICH.
OH, THAT'S NO PROBLEM.
WHAT?
ゴソ

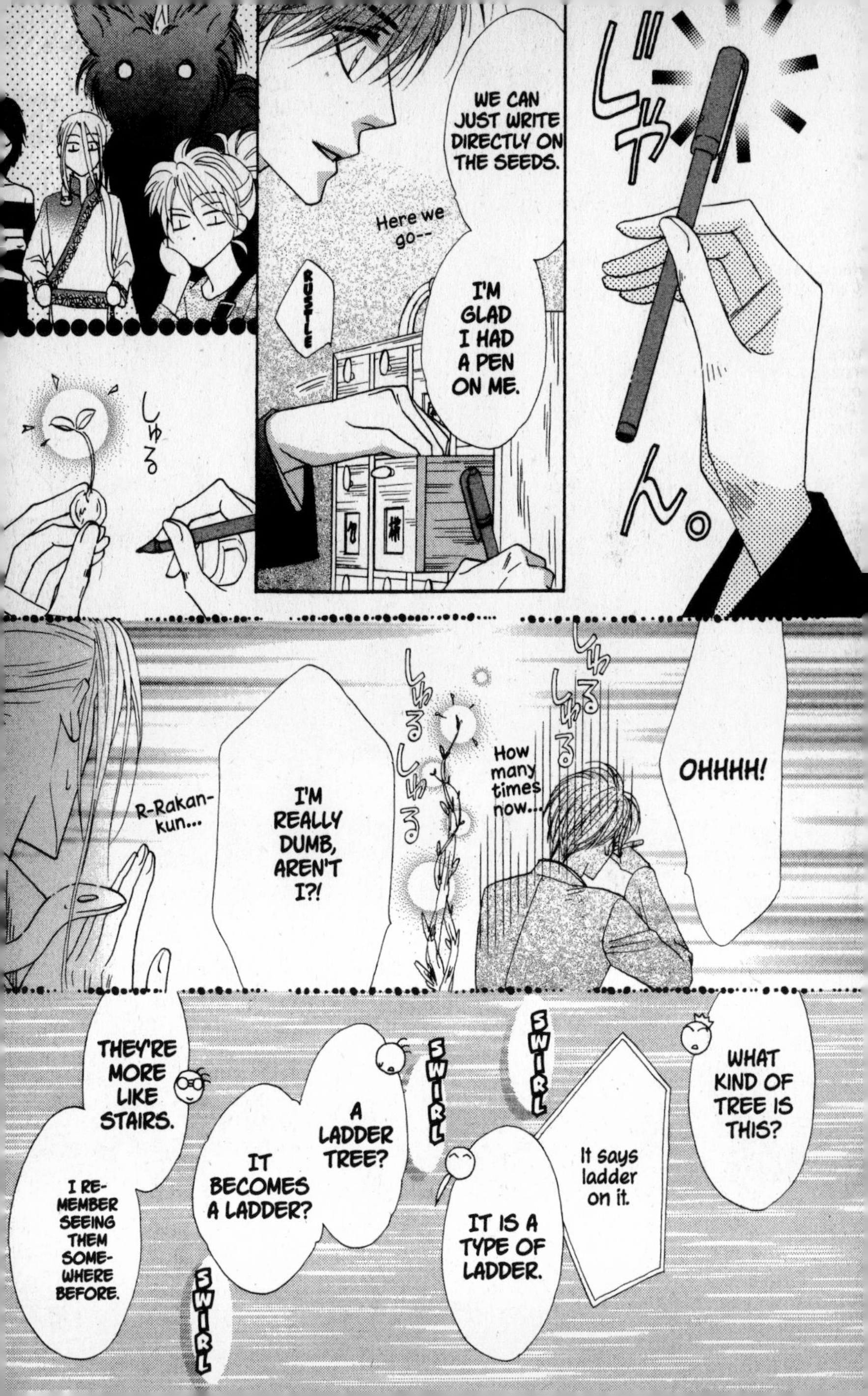
じゃん。
WE CAN JUST WRITE DIRECTLY ON THE SEEDS.
Here we go--
RUSTLE
I'M GLAD I HAD A PEN ON ME.
しゅる
OHHHH!
しゅるしゅる
How many times now...
しゅるしゅる
I'M REALLY DUMB, AREN'T I?!
R-Rakan-kun...
WHAT KIND OF TREE IS THIS?
SWIRL
It says ladder on it.
IT IS A TYPE OF LADDER.
A LADDER TREE?
SWIRL
IT BECOMES A LADDER?
THEY'RE MORE LIKE STAIRS.
I RE-MEMBER SEEING THEM SOME-WHERE BEFORE.
SWIRL

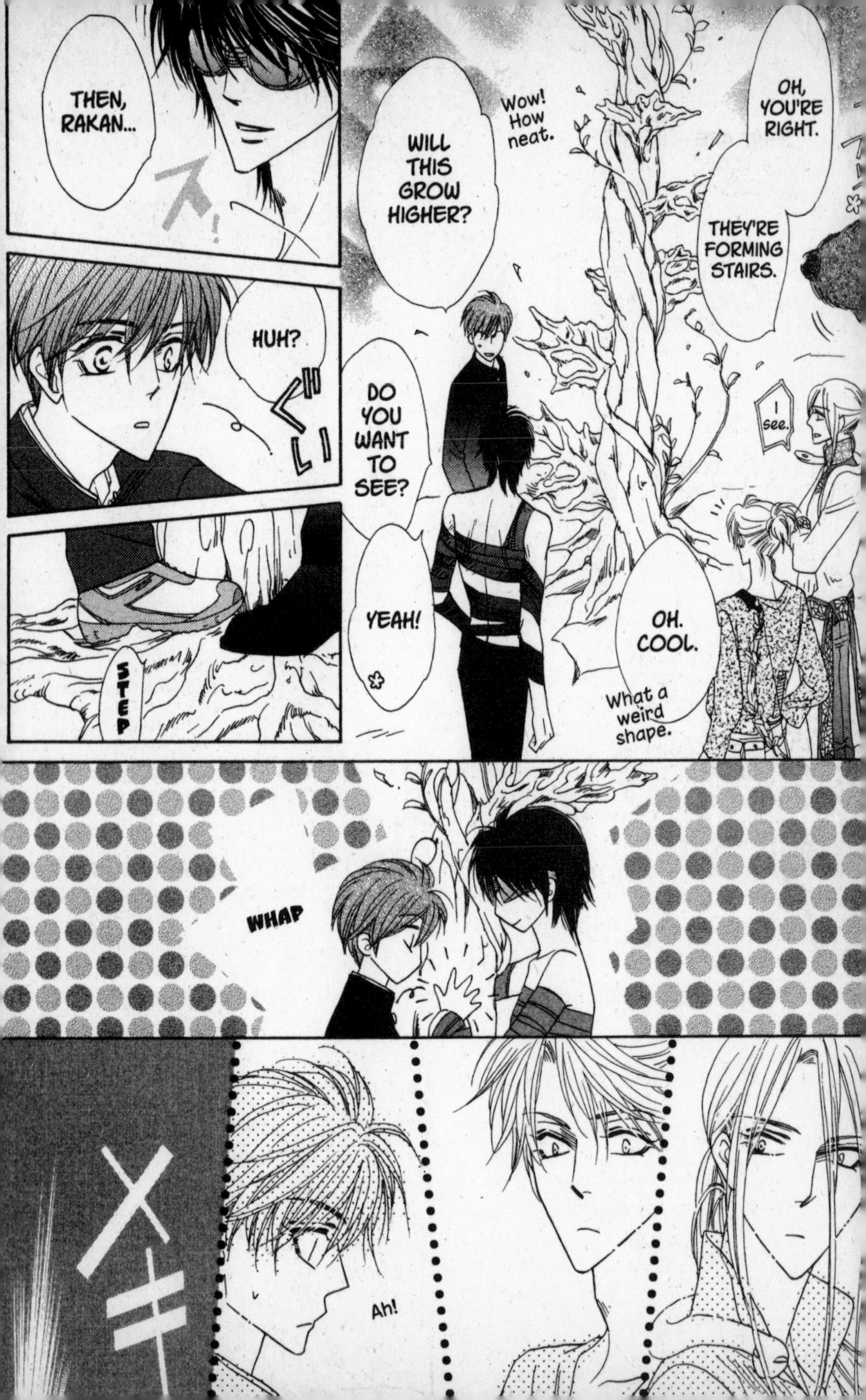
OH, YOU'RE RIGHT.
THEY'RE FORMING STAIRS.
I see.
OH. COOL.
What a weird shape.
Wow! How neat.
WILL THIS GROW HIGHER?
DO YOU WANT TO SEE?
YEAH!
THEN, RAKAN...
HUH?
STEP
WHAP
Ah!

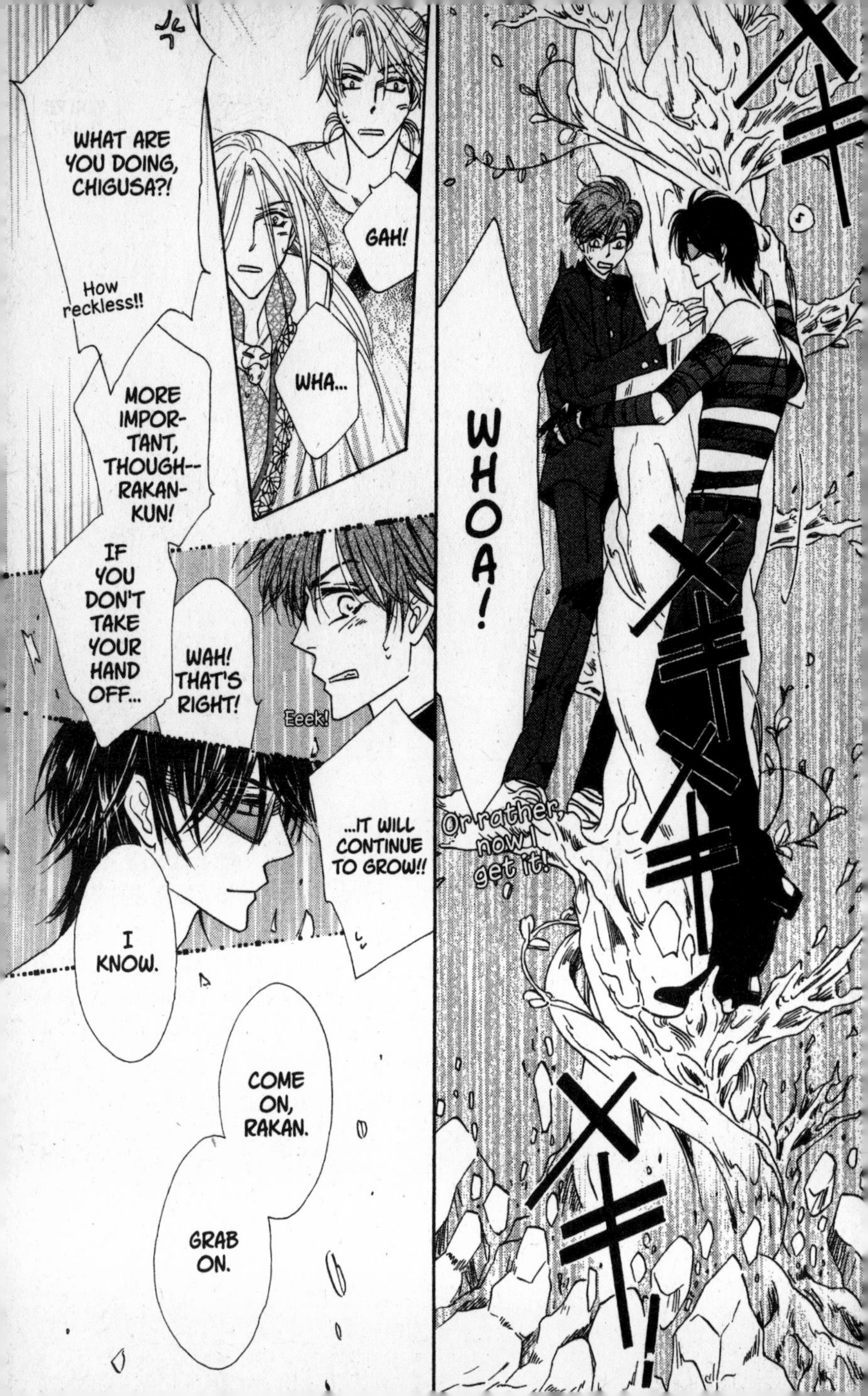
WHOA!
Or rather, now I get it!
GAH!
WHA...
WHAT ARE YOU DOING, CHIGUSA?!
How reckless!!
MORE IMPORTANT, THOUGH--RAKAN-KUN!
IF YOU DON'T TAKE YOUR HAND OFF...
WAH! THAT'S RIGHT!
Eeek!
...IT WILL CONTINUE TO GROW!!
I KNOW.
COME ON, RAKAN.
GRAB ON.

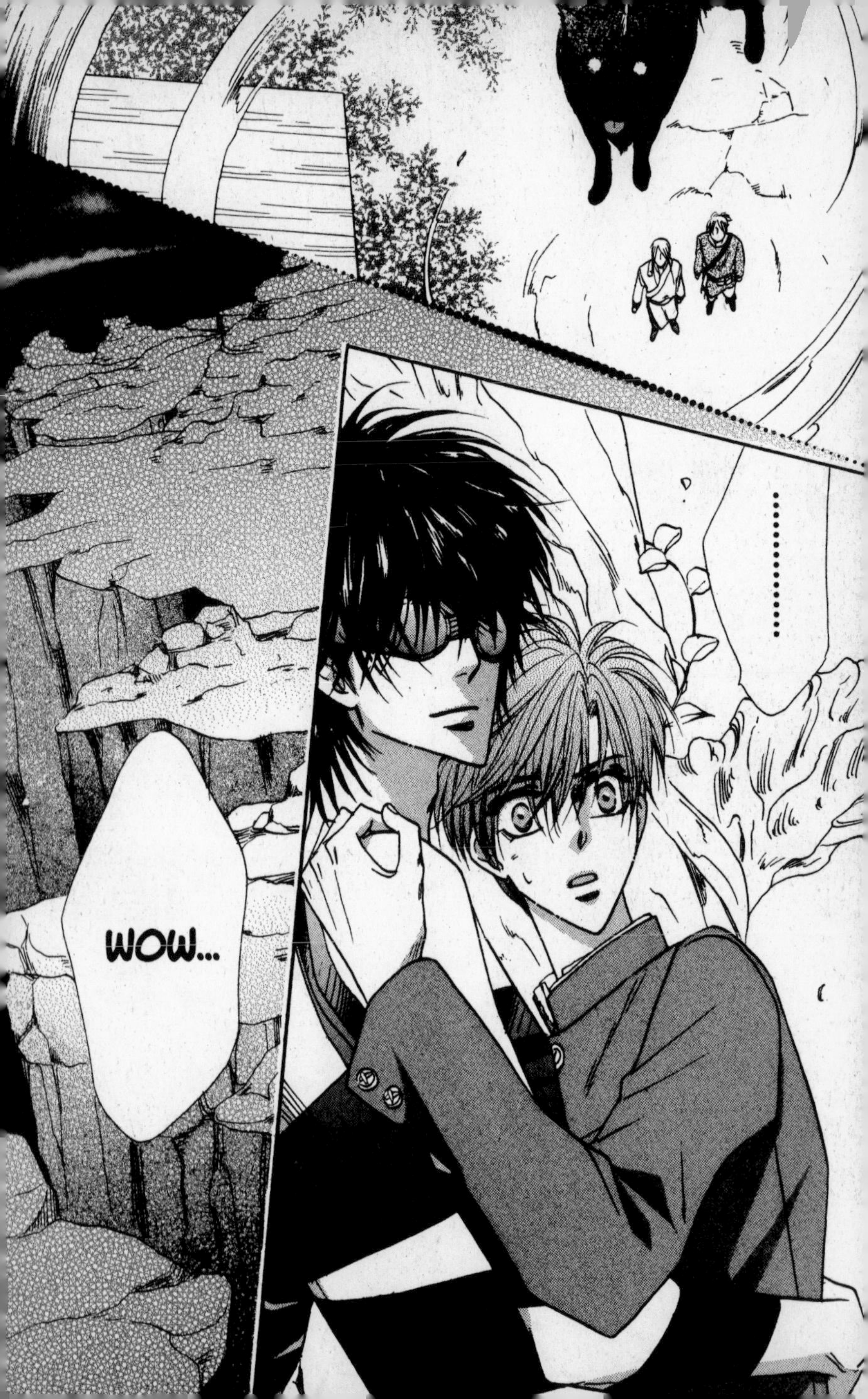

WOW...

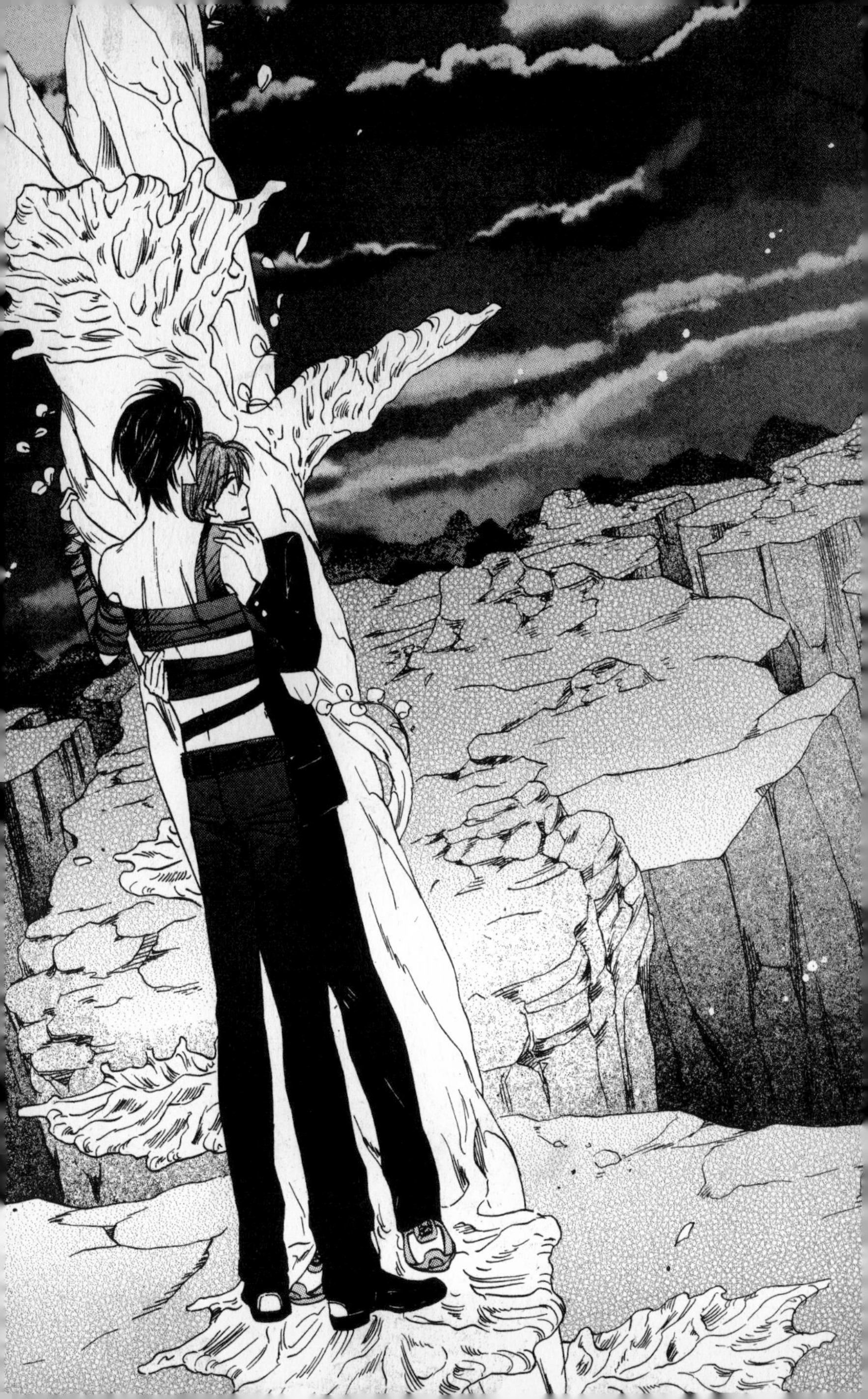

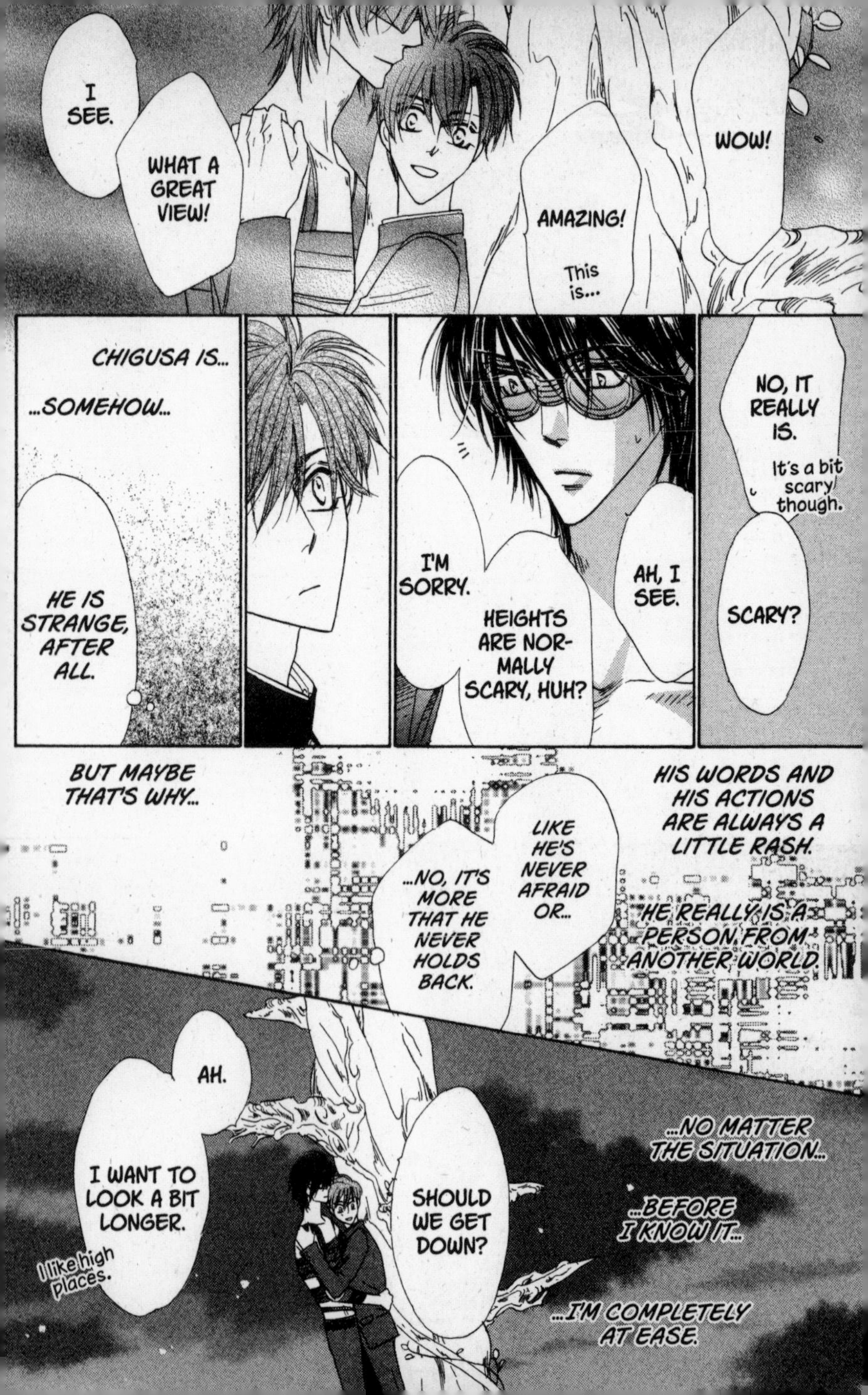
WOW!
AMAZING!
This is...
I SEE.
WHAT A GREAT VIEW!
NO, IT REALLY IS.
It's a bit scary though.
SCARY?
AH, I SEE.
I'M SORRY.
HEIGHTS ARE NOR-MALLY SCARY, HUH?
CHIGUSA IS...
...SOMEHOW...
HE IS STRANGE, AFTER ALL.
HIS WORDS AND HIS ACTIONS ARE ALWAYS A LITTLE RASH.
LIKE HE'S NEVER AFRAID OR...
...NO, IT'S MORE THAT HE NEVER HOLDS BACK.
HE REALLY IS A PERSON FROM ANOTHER WORLD.
BUT MAYBE THAT'S WHY...
...NO MATTER THE SITUATION...
...BEFORE I KNOW IT...
...I'M COMPLETELY AT EASE.
SHOULD WE GET DOWN?
AH.
I WANT TO LOOK A BIT LONGER.
I like high places.

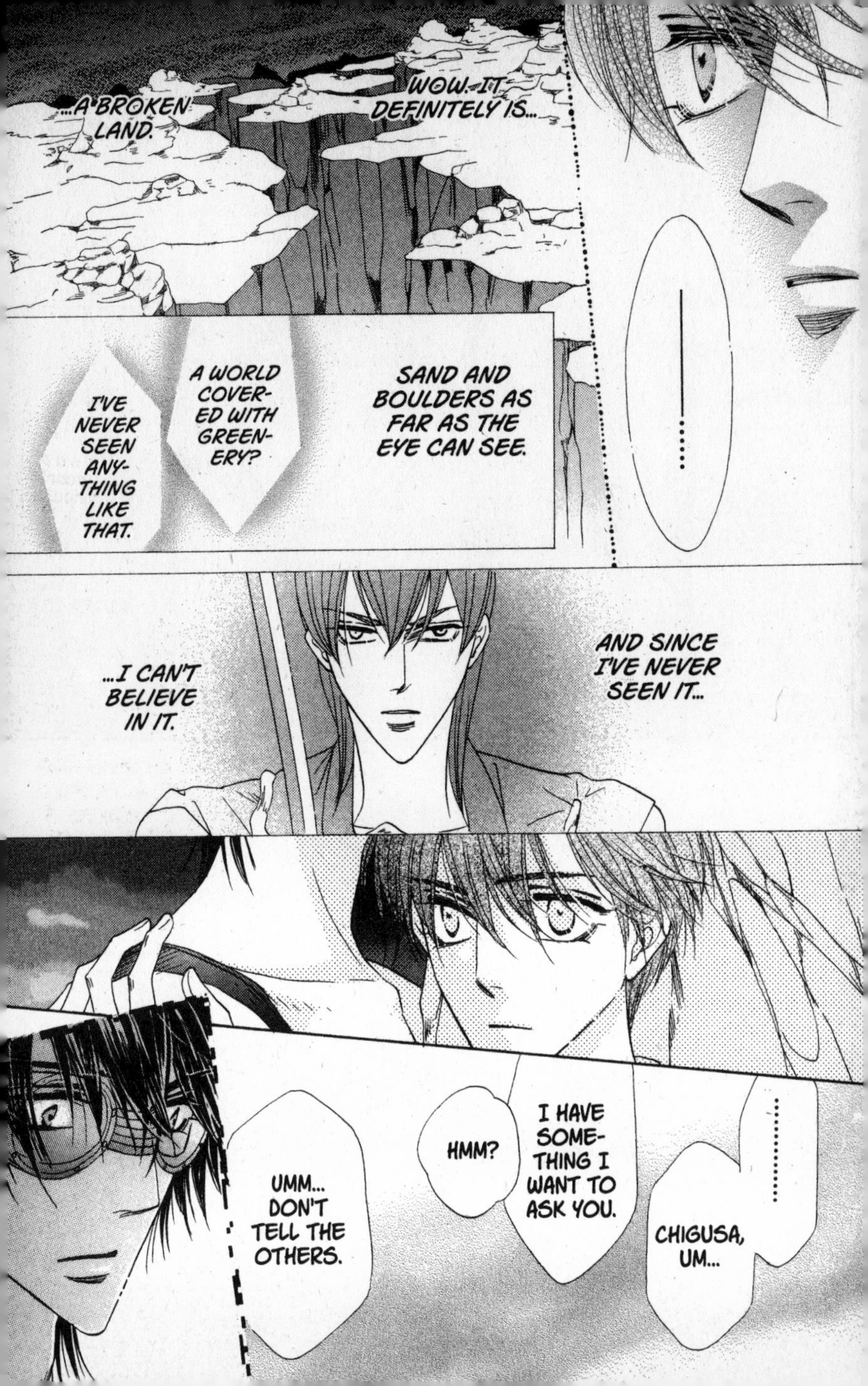
......
WOW. IT DEFINITELY IS...
...A BROKEN LAND.
SAND AND BOULDERS AS FAR AS THE EYE CAN SEE.
A WORLD COVERED WITH GREENERY?
I'VE NEVER SEEN ANYTHING LIKE THAT.
AND SINCE I'VE NEVER SEEN IT...
...I CAN'T BELIEVE IN IT.
......
CHIGUSA, UM...
I HAVE SOMETHING I WANT TO ASK YOU.
HMM?
UMM... DON'T TELL THE OTHERS.

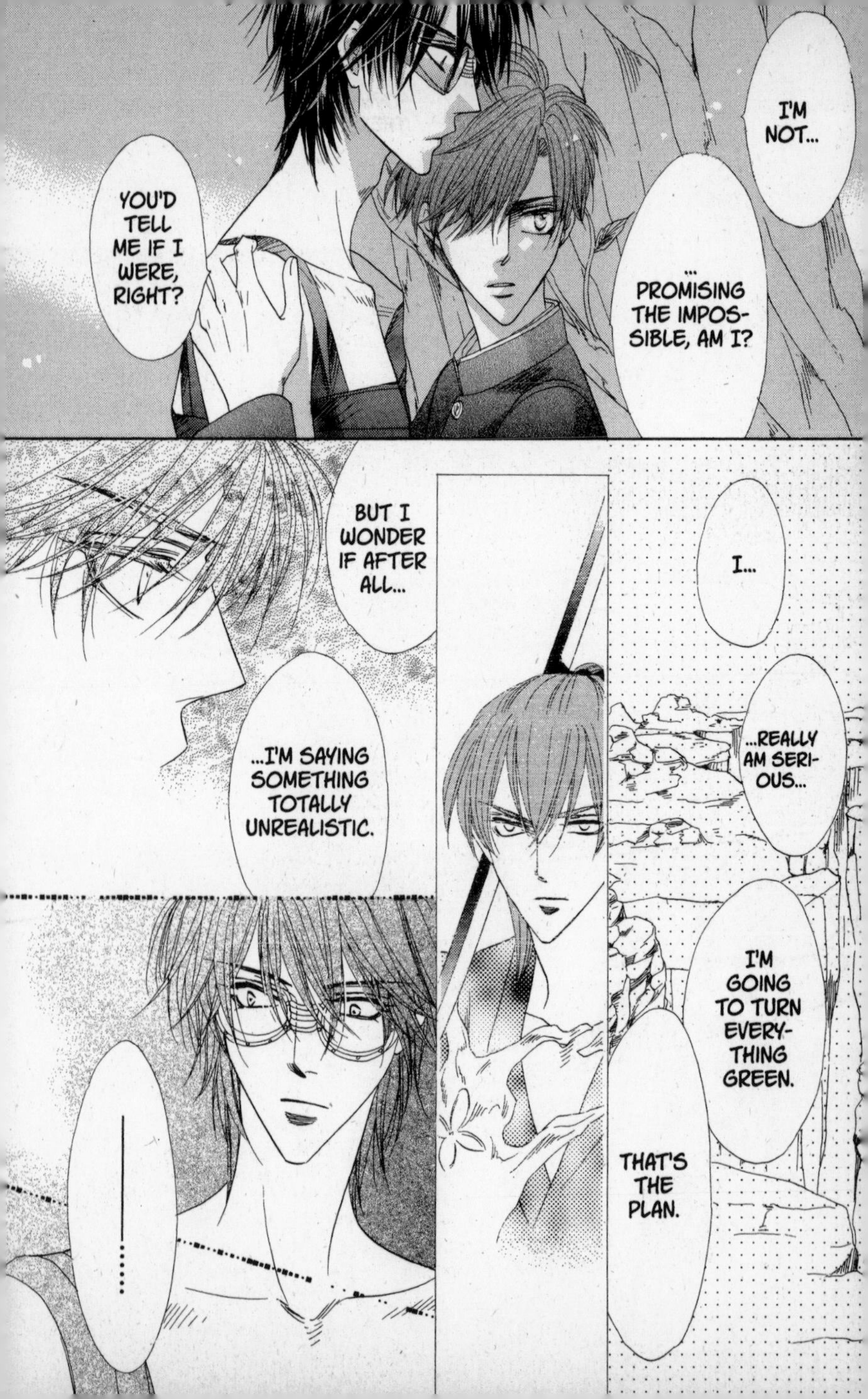
I'M NOT...
...PROMISING THE IMPOSSIBLE, AM I?
YOU'D TELL ME IF I WERE, RIGHT?
I...
...REALLY AM SERIOUS...
I'M GOING TO TURN EVERYTHING GREEN.
THAT'S THE PLAN.
BUT I WONDER IF AFTER ALL...
...I'M SAYING SOMETHING TOTALLY UNREALISTIC.
......

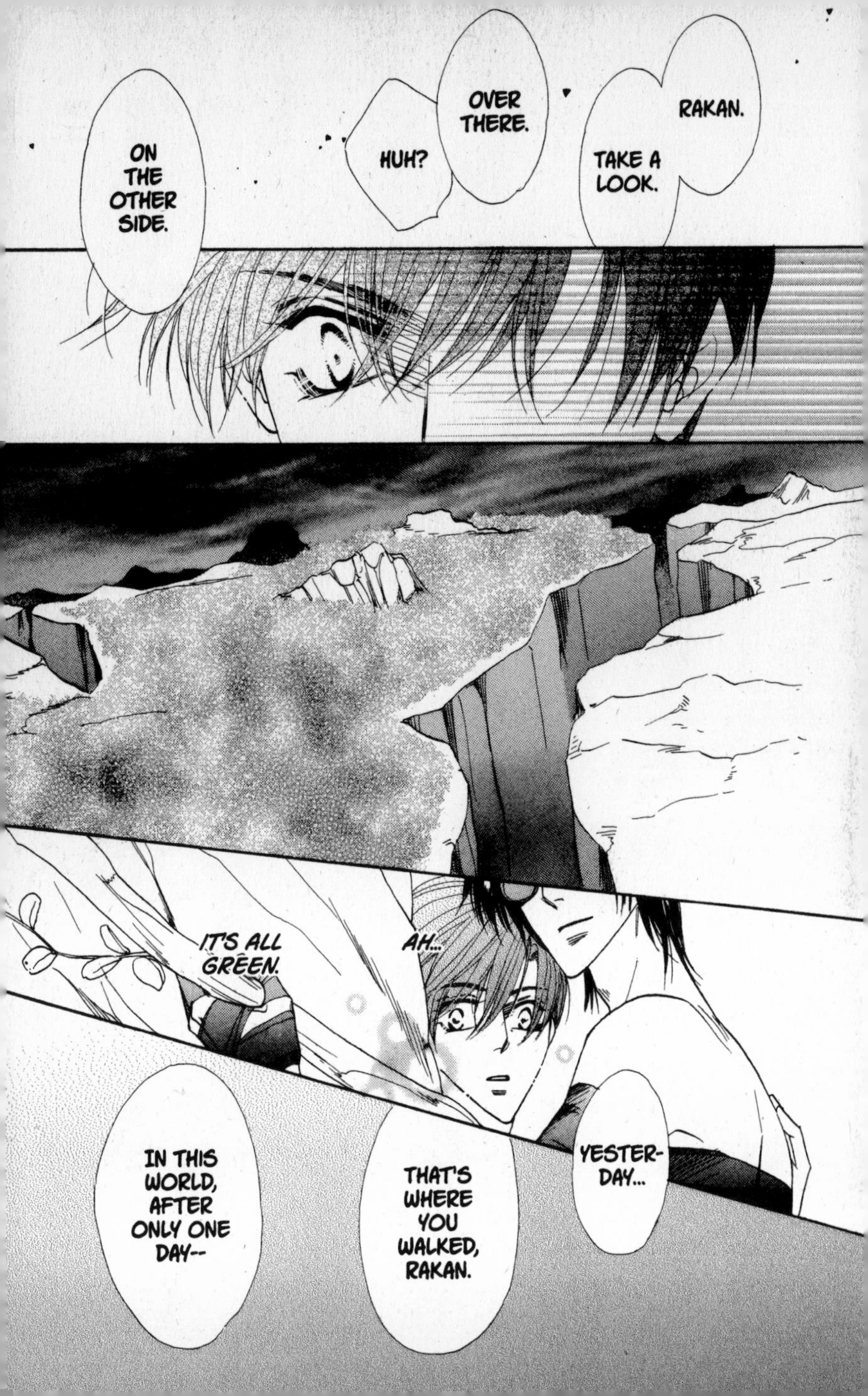
RAKAN.
TAKE A LOOK.
OVER THERE.
HUH?
ON THE OTHER SIDE.
AH...
IT'S ALL GREEN.
YESTER-DAY...
THAT'S WHERE YOU WALKED, RAKAN.
IN THIS WORLD, AFTER ONLY ONE DAY--

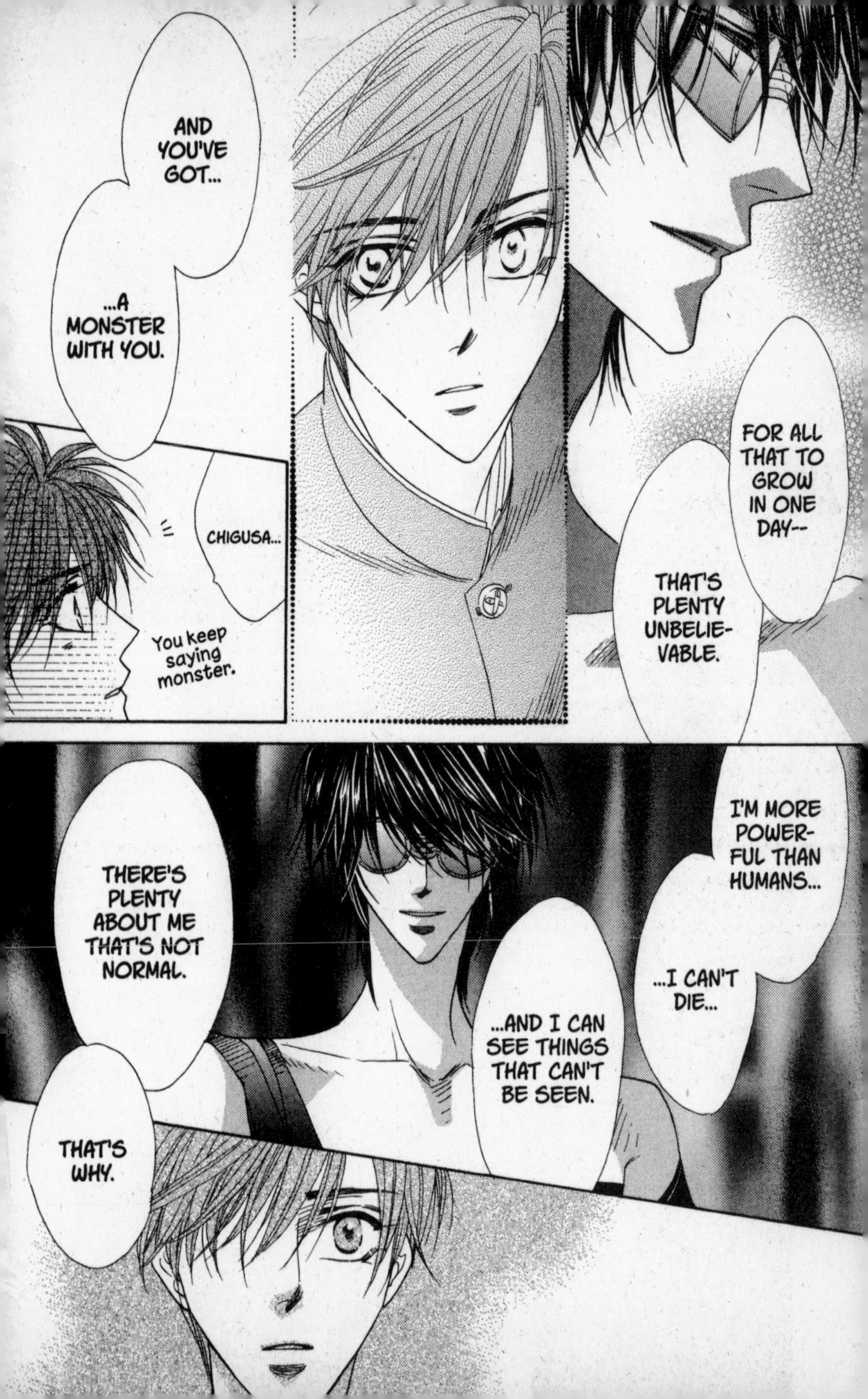
FOR ALL THAT TO GROW IN ONE DAY--
THAT'S PLENTY UNBELIE-VABLE.
AND YOU'VE GOT...
...A MONSTER WITH YOU.
CHIGUSA...
You keep saying monster.
I'M MORE POWER-FUL THAN HUMANS...
...I CAN'T DIE...
...AND I CAN SEE THINGS THAT CAN'T BE SEEN.
THERE'S PLENTY ABOUT ME THAT'S NOT NORMAL.
THAT'S WHY.

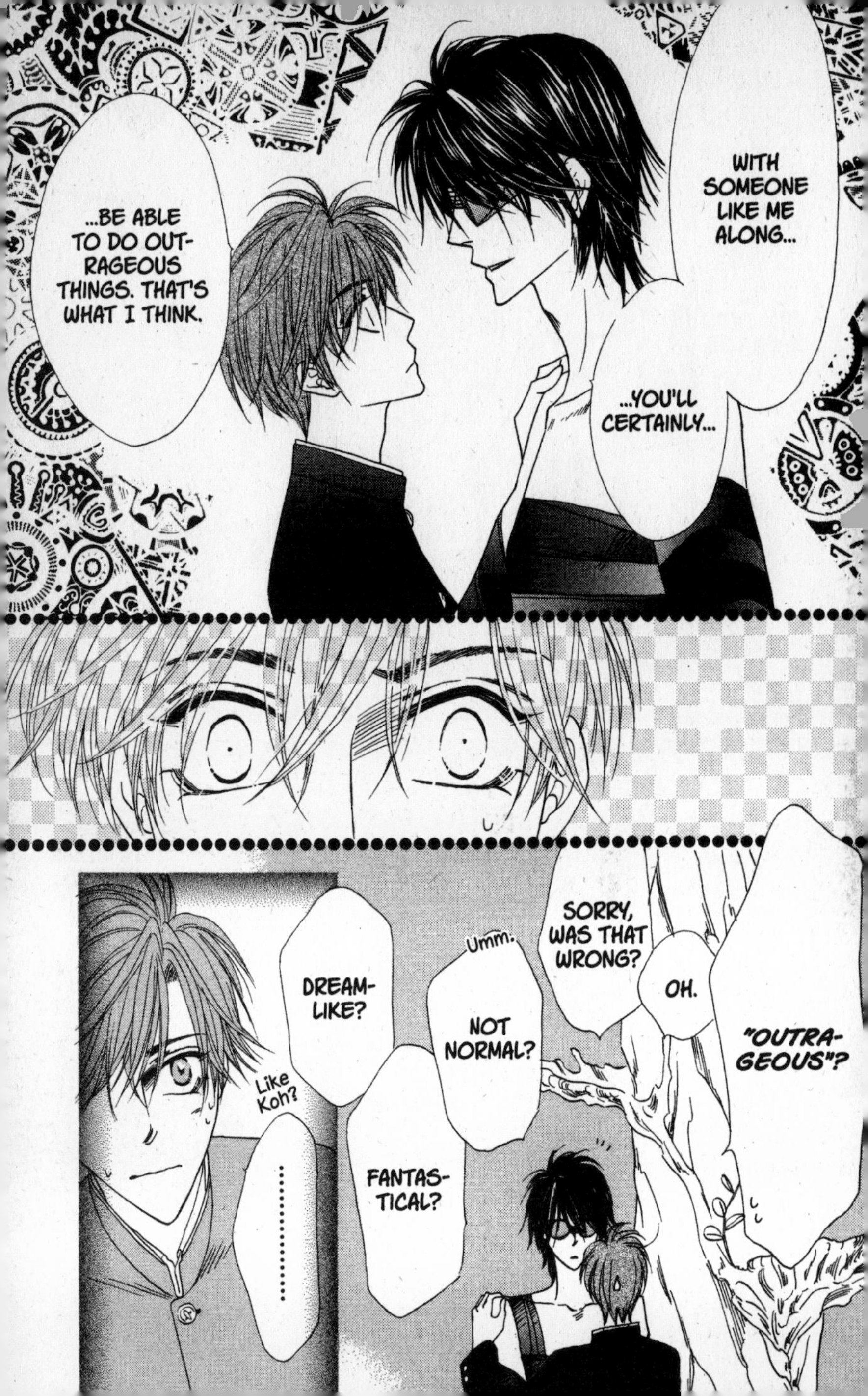
WITH SOMEONE LIKE ME ALONG...
...YOU'LL CERTAINLY...
...BE ABLE TO DO OUT-RAGEOUS THINGS. THAT'S WHAT I THINK.
"OUTRA-GEOUS"?
OH.
SORRY, WAS THAT WRONG?
Umm.
NOT NORMAL?
FANTAS-TICAL?
DREAM-LIKE?
Like Koh?
......

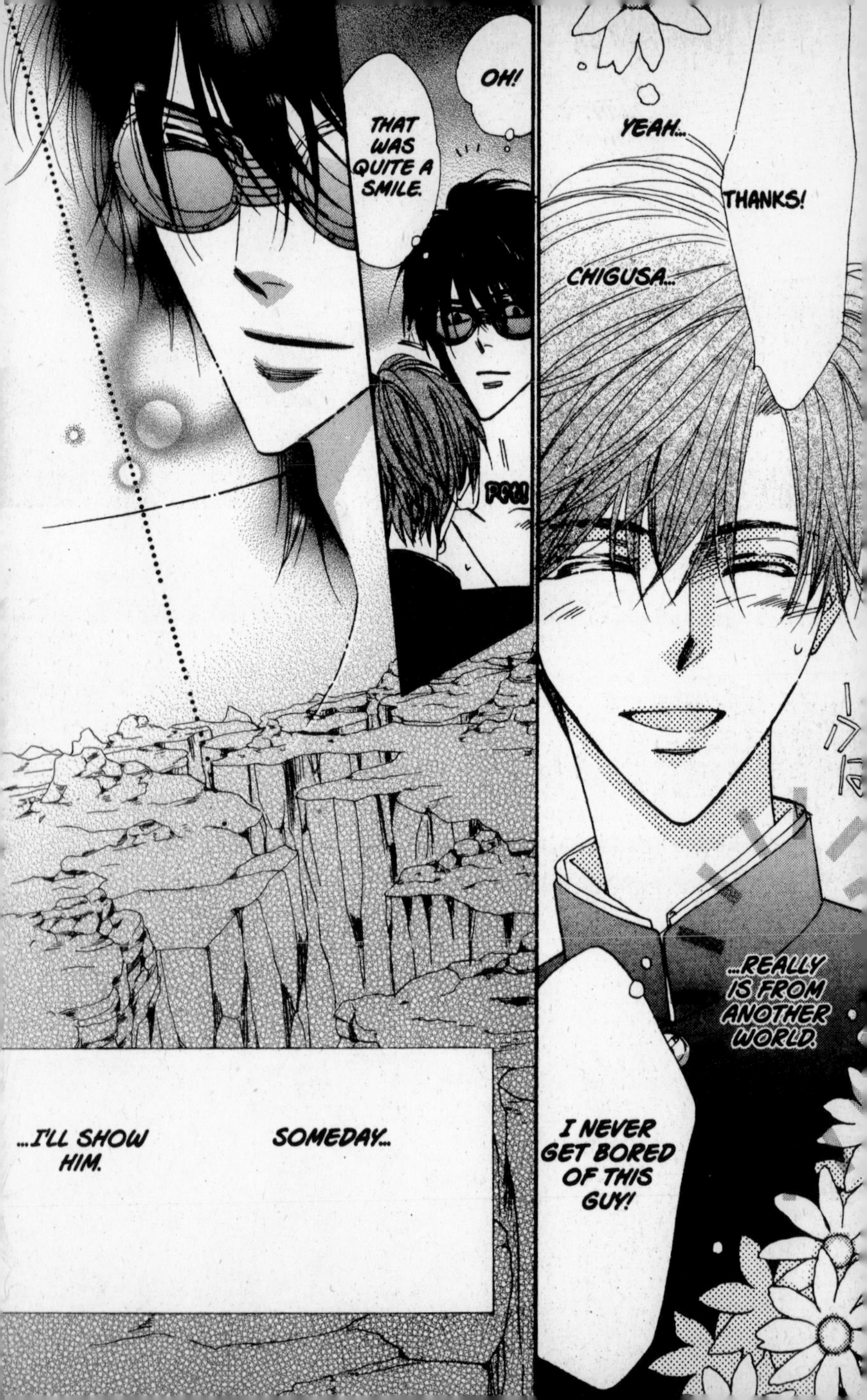
YEAH...
THANKS!
CHIGUSA...
...REALLY IS FROM ANOTHER WORLD.
I NEVER GET BORED OF THIS GUY!
OH!
THAT WAS QUITE A SMILE.
POW
SOMEDAY...
...I'LL SHOW HIM.

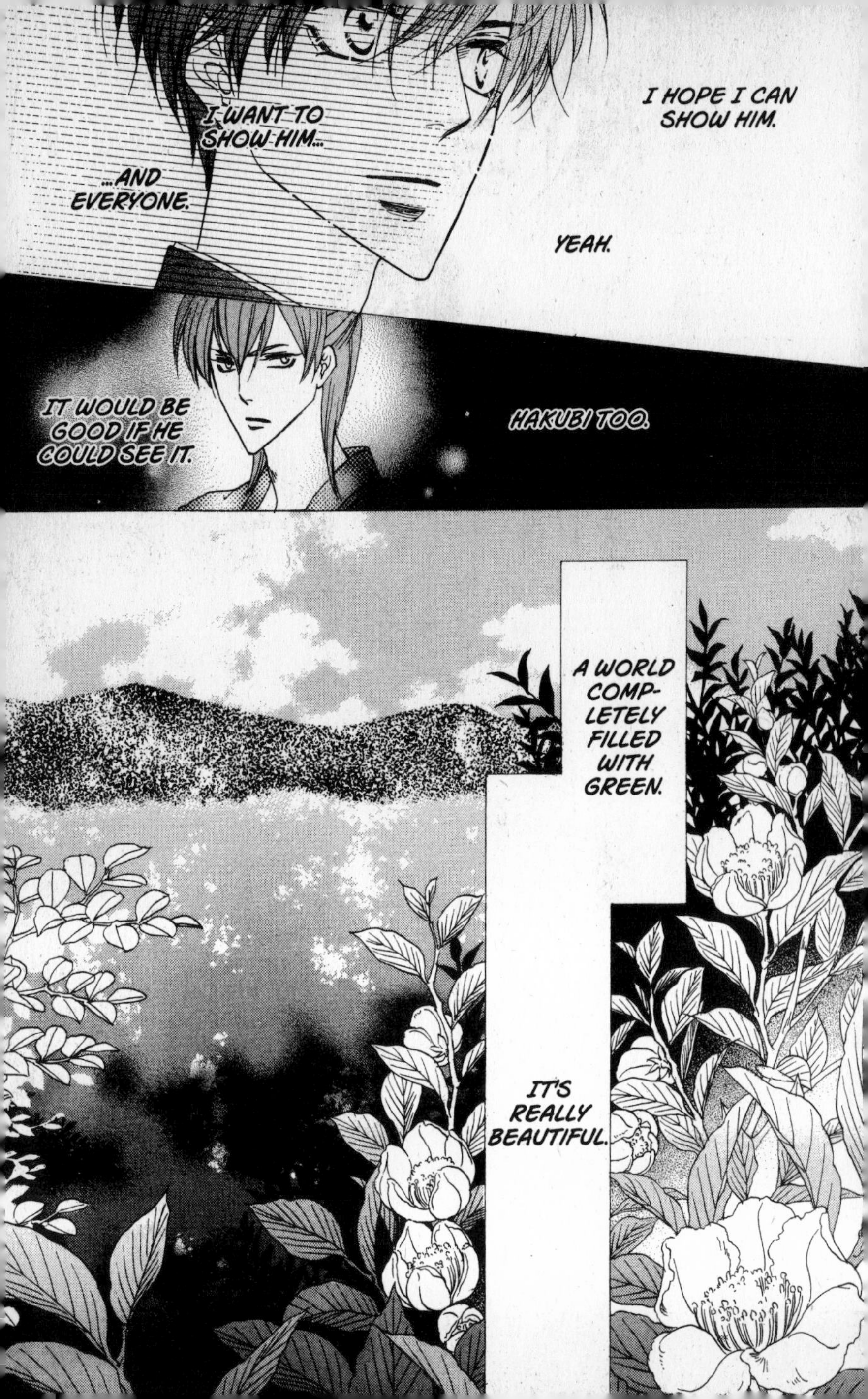
I HOPE I CAN SHOW HIM.
I WANT TO SHOW HIM...
...AND EVERYONE.
YEAH.
HAKUBI TOO.
IT WOULD BE GOOD IF HE COULD SEE IT.
A WORLD COMP-LETELY FILLED WITH GREEN.
IT'S REALLY BEAUTIFUL.

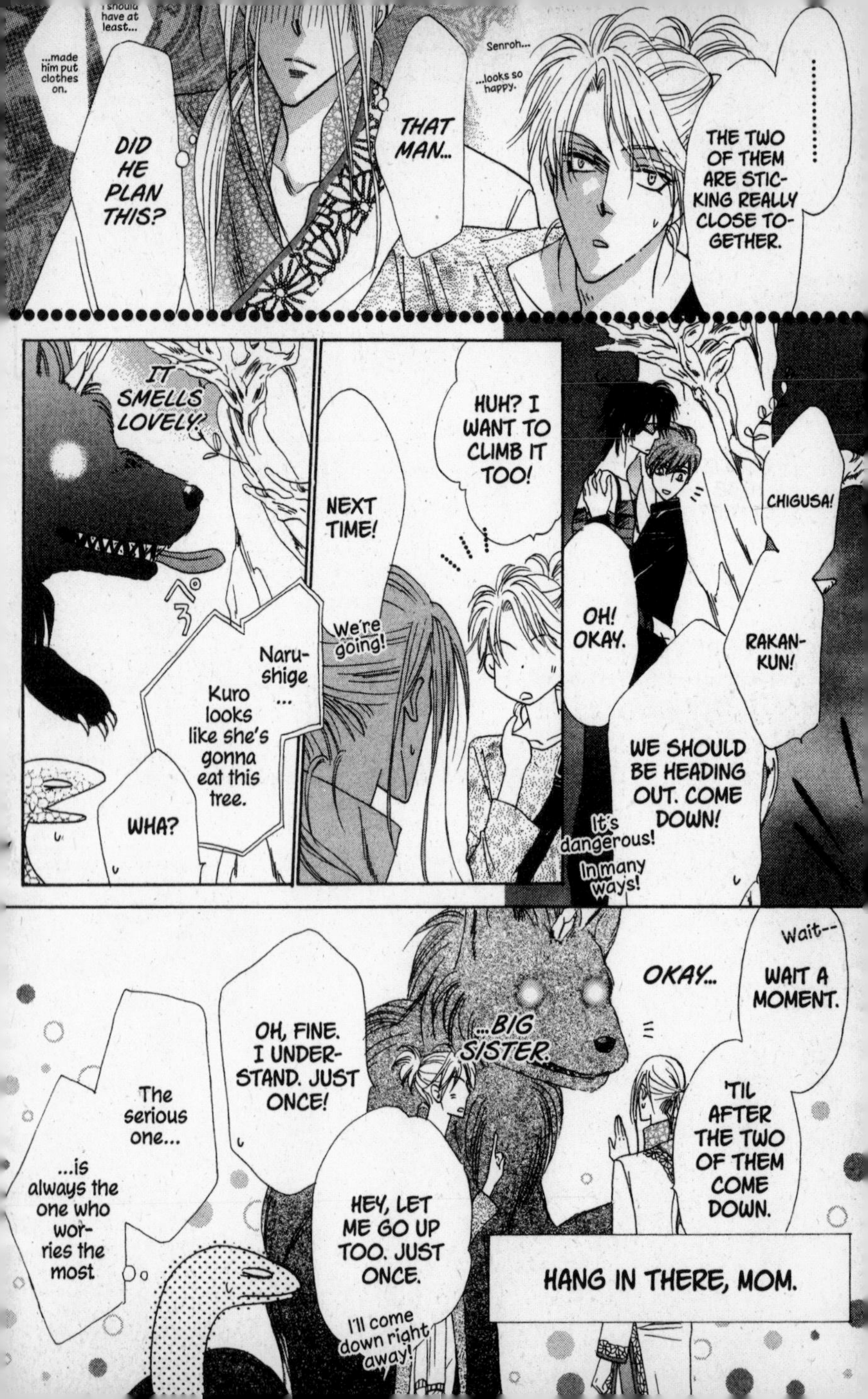
……
THE TWO OF THEM ARE STICKING REALLY CLOSE TOGETHER.
Senroh...
...looks so happy.
THAT MAN...
I should have at least...
...made him put clothes on.
DID HE PLAN THIS?
CHIGUSA!
RAKAN-KUN!
OH! OKAY.
WE SHOULD BE HEADING OUT. COME DOWN!
It's dangerous! In many ways!
HUH? I WANT TO CLIMB IT TOO!
NEXT TIME!
We're going!
IT SMELLS LOVELY!
Narushige... Kuro looks like she's gonna eat this tree.
WHA?
Wait--
WAIT A MOMENT.
OKAY...
'TIL AFTER THE TWO OF THEM COME DOWN.
...BIG SISTER.
OH, FINE. I UNDERSTAND. JUST ONCE!
HEY, LET ME GO UP TOO. JUST ONCE.
I'll come down right away!
The serious one...
...is always the one who worries the most
HANG IN THERE, MOM.

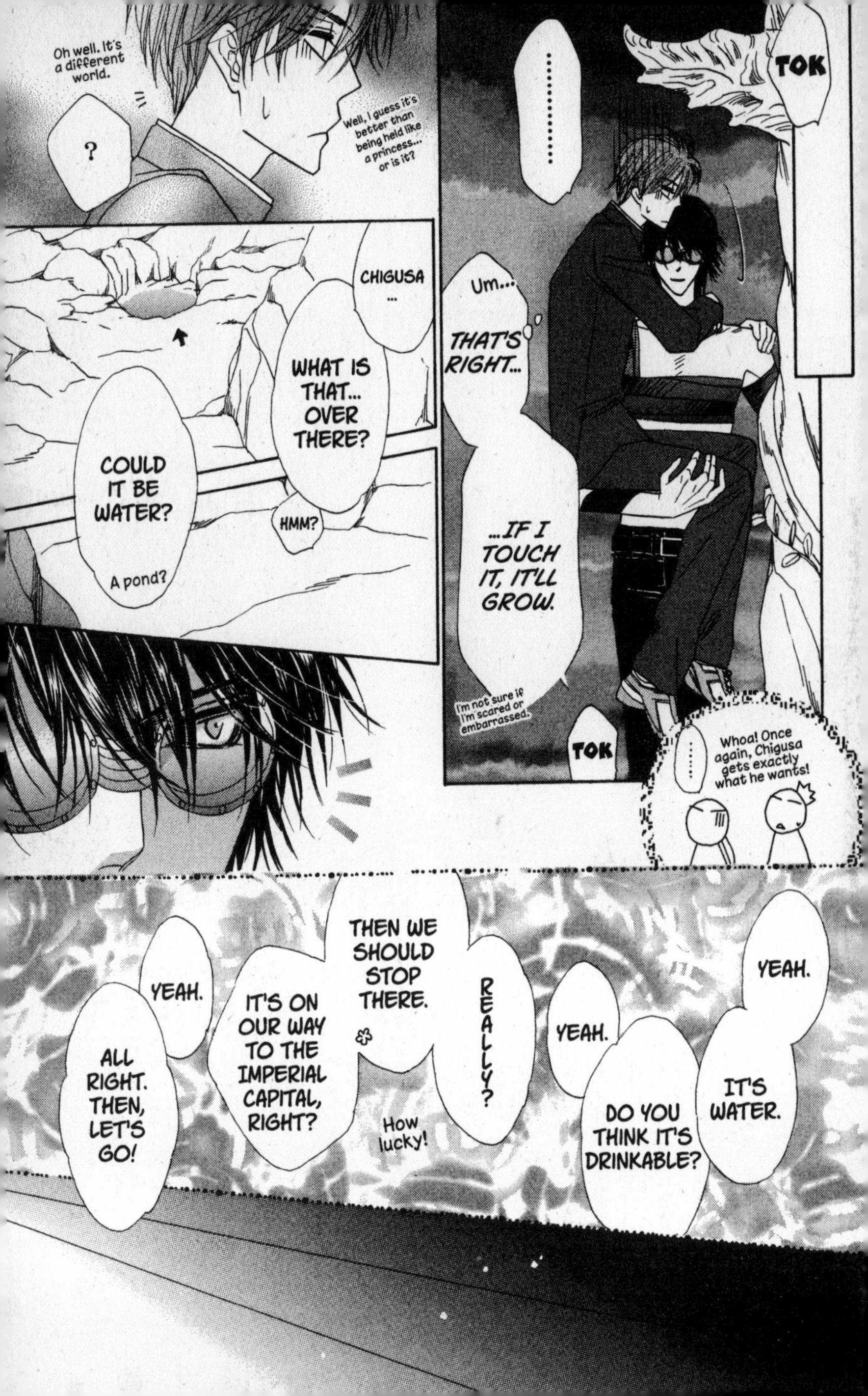
TOK
......
Um...
THAT'S RIGHT...
...IF I TOUCH IT, IT'LL GROW.
I'm not sure if I'm scared or embarrassed.
TOK
Whoa! Once again, Chigusa gets exactly what he wants!
......
Well, I guess it's better than being held like a princess... or is it?
Oh well. It's a different world.
?
CHIGUSA ...
WHAT IS THAT... OVER THERE?
HMM?
COULD IT BE WATER?
A pond?
YEAH.
IT'S WATER.
DO YOU THINK IT'S DRINKABLE?
YEAH.
REALLY?
THEN WE SHOULD STOP THERE.
How lucky!
IT'S ON OUR WAY TO THE IMPERIAL CAPITAL, RIGHT?
YEAH.
ALL RIGHT. THEN, LET'S GO!

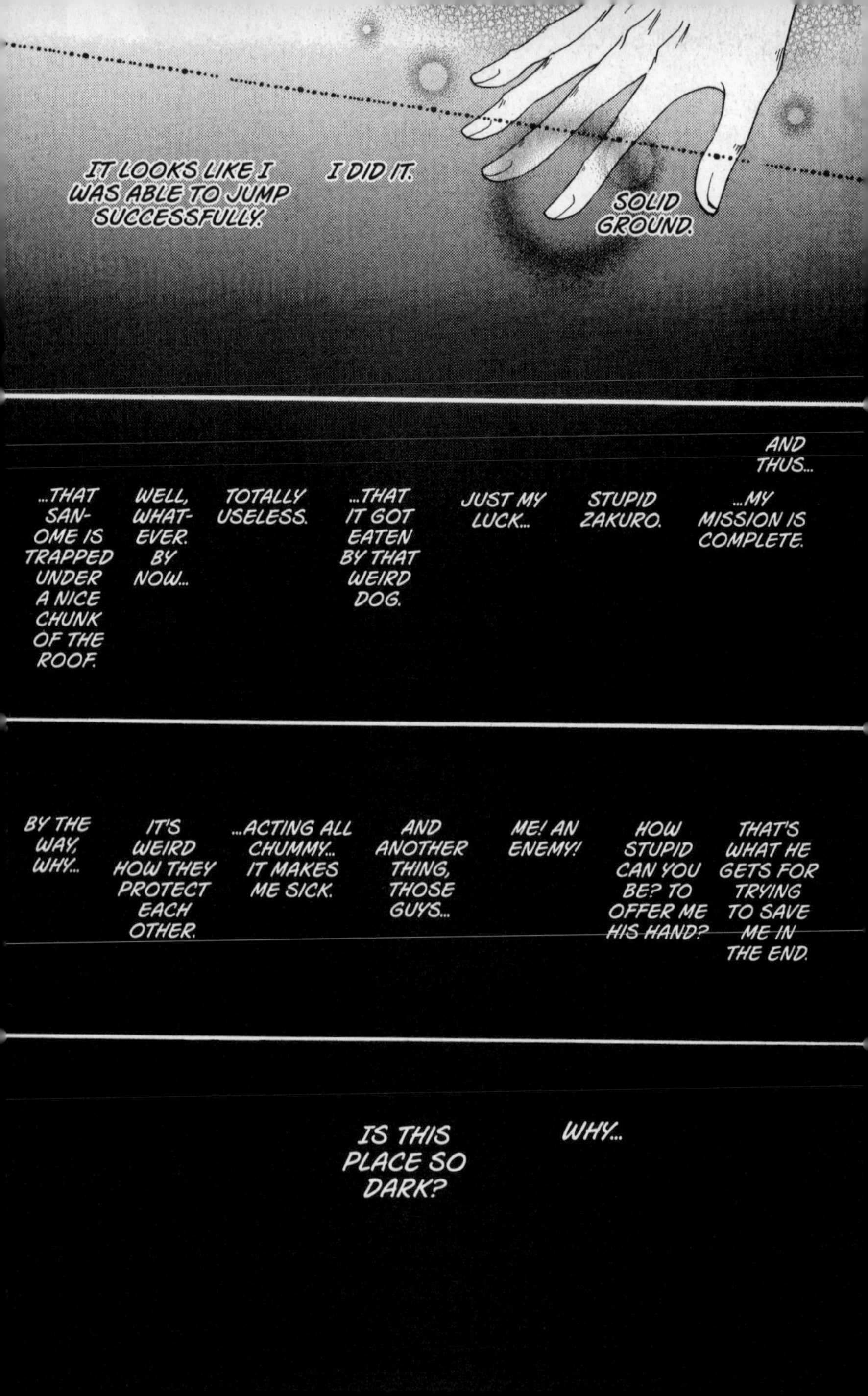
SOLID GROUND.
I DID IT.
IT LOOKS LIKE I WAS ABLE TO JUMP SUCCESSFULLY.
AND THUS...
...MY MISSION IS COMPLETE.
STUPID ZAKURO.
JUST MY LUCK...
...THAT IT GOT EATEN BY THAT WEIRD DOG.
TOTALLY USELESS.
WELL, WHATEVER. BY NOW...
...THAT SANOME IS TRAPPED UNDER A NICE CHUNK OF THE ROOF.
THAT'S WHAT HE GETS FOR TRYING TO SAVE ME IN THE END.
HOW STUPID CAN YOU BE? TO OFFER ME HIS HAND?
ME! AN ENEMY!
AND ANOTHER THING, THOSE GUYS...
...ACTING ALL CHUMMY... IT MAKES ME SICK.
IT'S WEIRD HOW THEY PROTECT EACH OTHER.
BY THE WAY, WHY...
WHY...
IS THIS PLACE SO DARK?

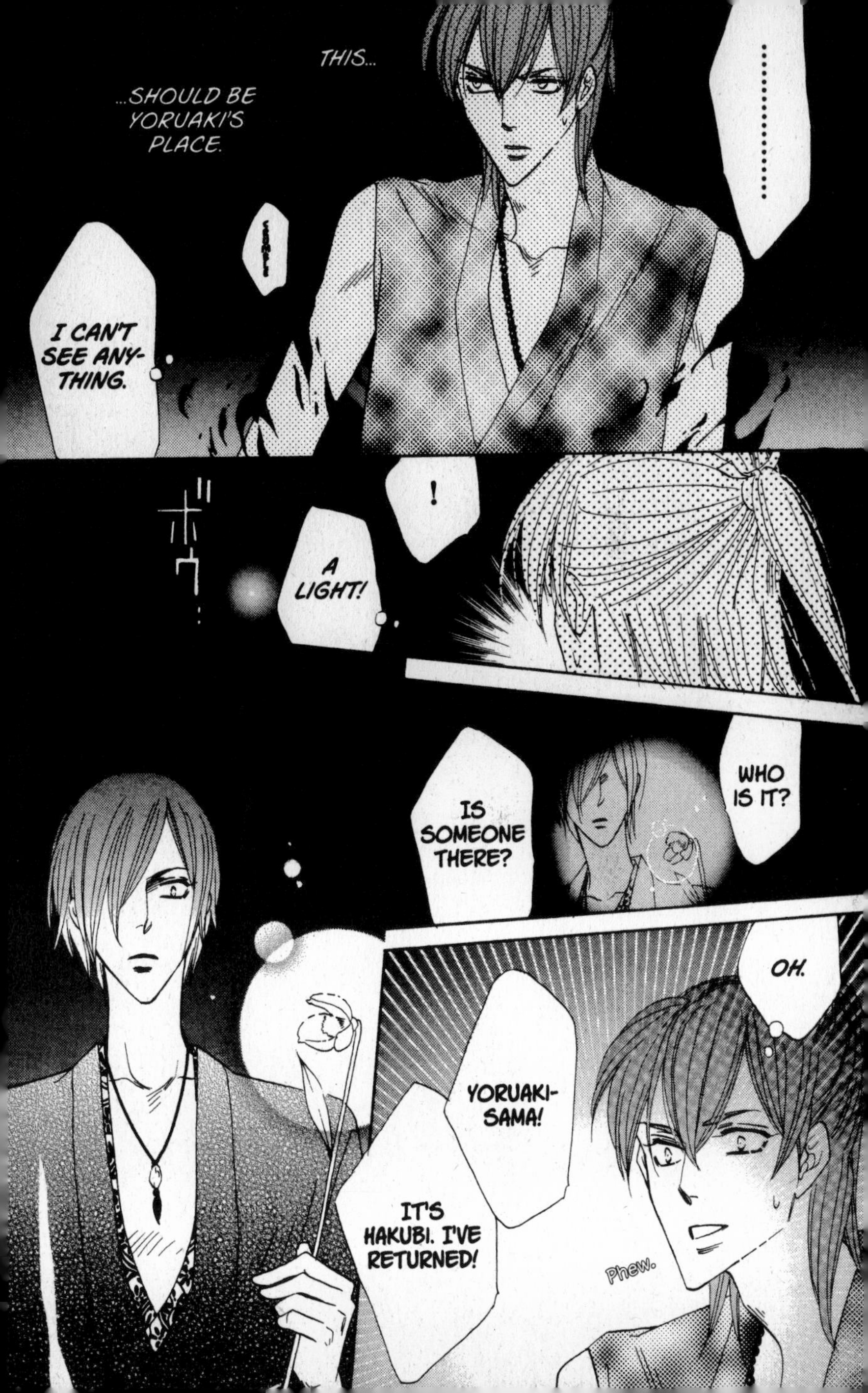
......
THIS...
...SHOULD BE YORUAKI'S PLACE.
I CAN'T SEE ANY-THING.
!
A LIGHT!
ボウ…
WHO IS IT?
IS SOMEONE THERE?
OH.
YORUAKI-SAMA!
IT'S HAKUBI. I'VE RETURNED!
Phew.

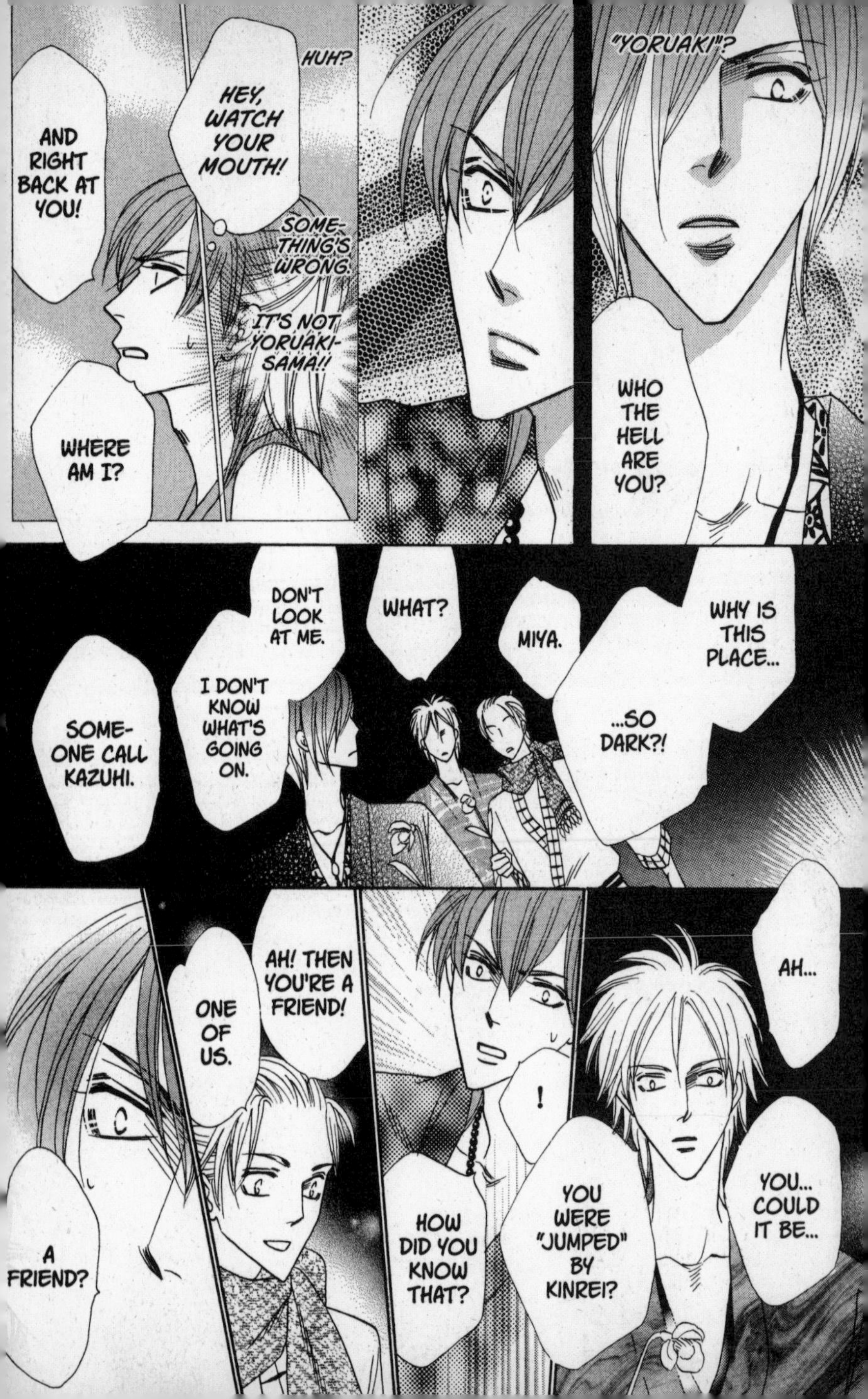
"YORUAKI"?
WHO THE HELL ARE YOU?
HUH?
HEY, WATCH YOUR MOUTH!
SOME-THING'S WRONG.
IT'S NOT YORUAKI-SAMA!!
AND RIGHT BACK AT YOU!
WHERE AM I?
WHY IS THIS PLACE...
...SO DARK?!
MIYA.
WHAT?
DON'T LOOK AT ME.
I DON'T KNOW WHAT'S GOING ON.
SOME-ONE CALL KAZUHI.
AH...
YOU... COULD IT BE...
YOU WERE "JUMPED" BY KINREI?
!
HOW DID YOU KNOW THAT?
AH! THEN YOU'RE A FRIEND!
ONE OF US.
A FRIEND?

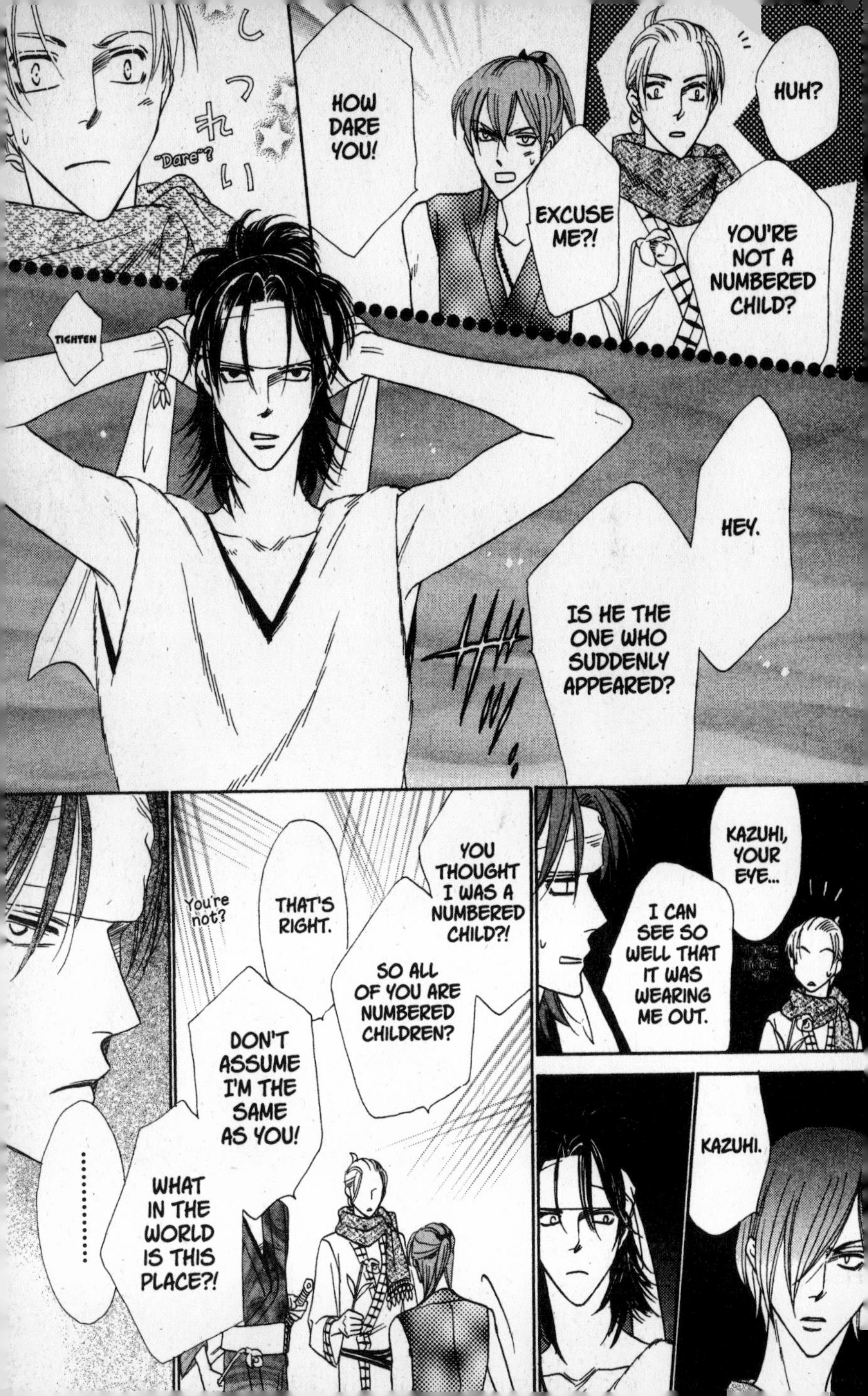
HUH?
YOU'RE NOT A NUMBERED CHILD?
EXCUSE ME?!
HOW DARE YOU!
"Dare"?
HEY.
IS HE THE ONE WHO SUDDENLY APPEARED?
TIGHTEN
KAZUHI, YOUR EYE...
I CAN SEE SO WELL THAT IT WAS WEARING ME OUT.
KAZUHI.
YOU THOUGHT I WAS A NUMBERED CHILD?!
THAT'S RIGHT.
You're not?
SO ALL OF YOU ARE NUMBERED CHILDREN?
DON'T ASSUME I'M THE SAME AS YOU!
WHAT IN THE WORLD IS THIS PLACE?!
....

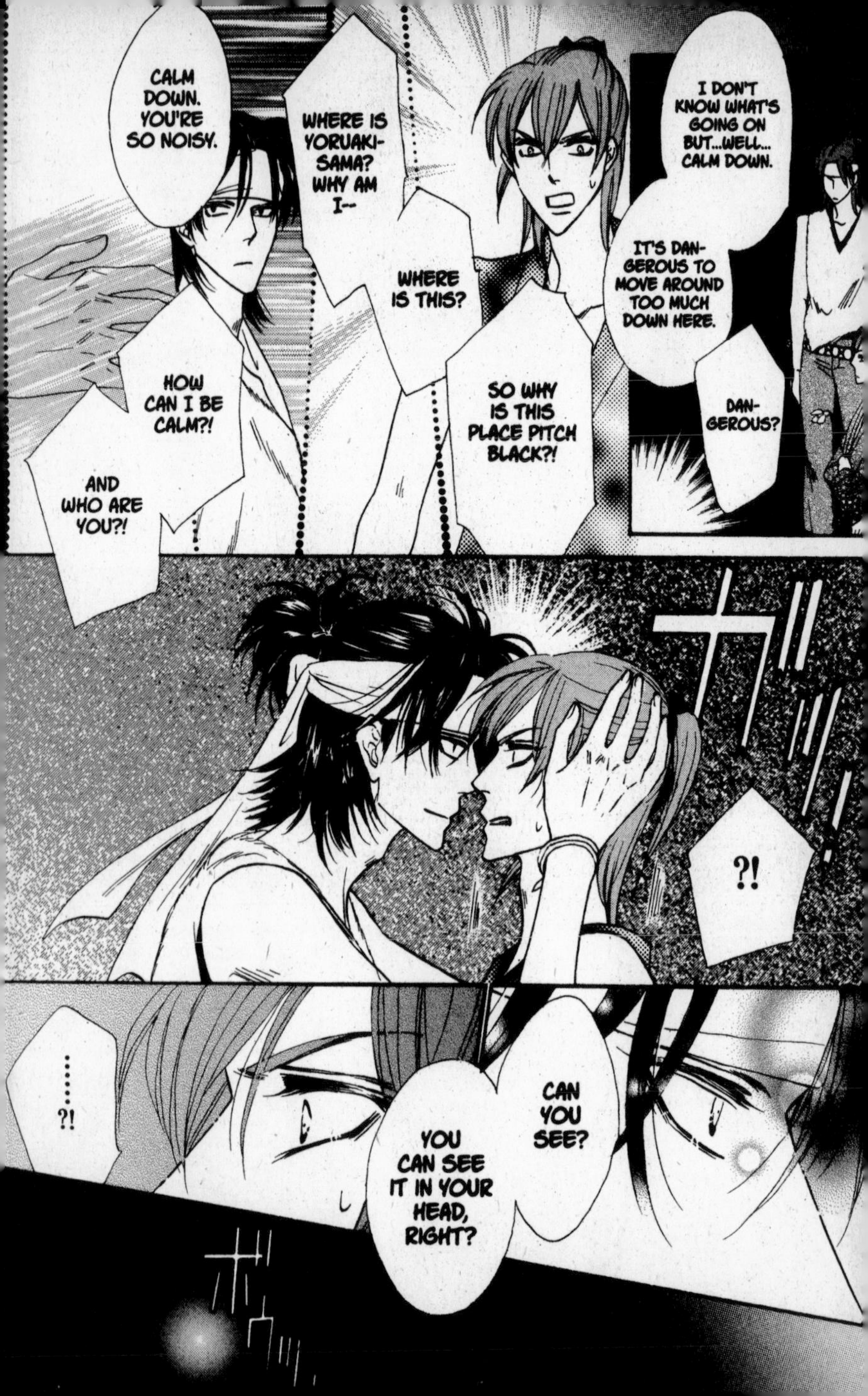

I DON'T KNOW WHAT'S GOING ON BUT...WELL... CALM DOWN.
IT'S DANGEROUS TO MOVE AROUND TOO MUCH DOWN HERE.
DANGEROUS?
WHERE IS YORUAKI-SAMA? WHY AM I--
WHERE IS THIS?
SO WHY IS THIS PLACE PITCH BLACK?!
CALM DOWN. YOU'RE SO NOISY.
HOW CAN I BE CALM?!
AND WHO ARE YOU?!
?!
CAN YOU SEE?
YOU CAN SEE IT IN YOUR HEAD, RIGHT?
......?!

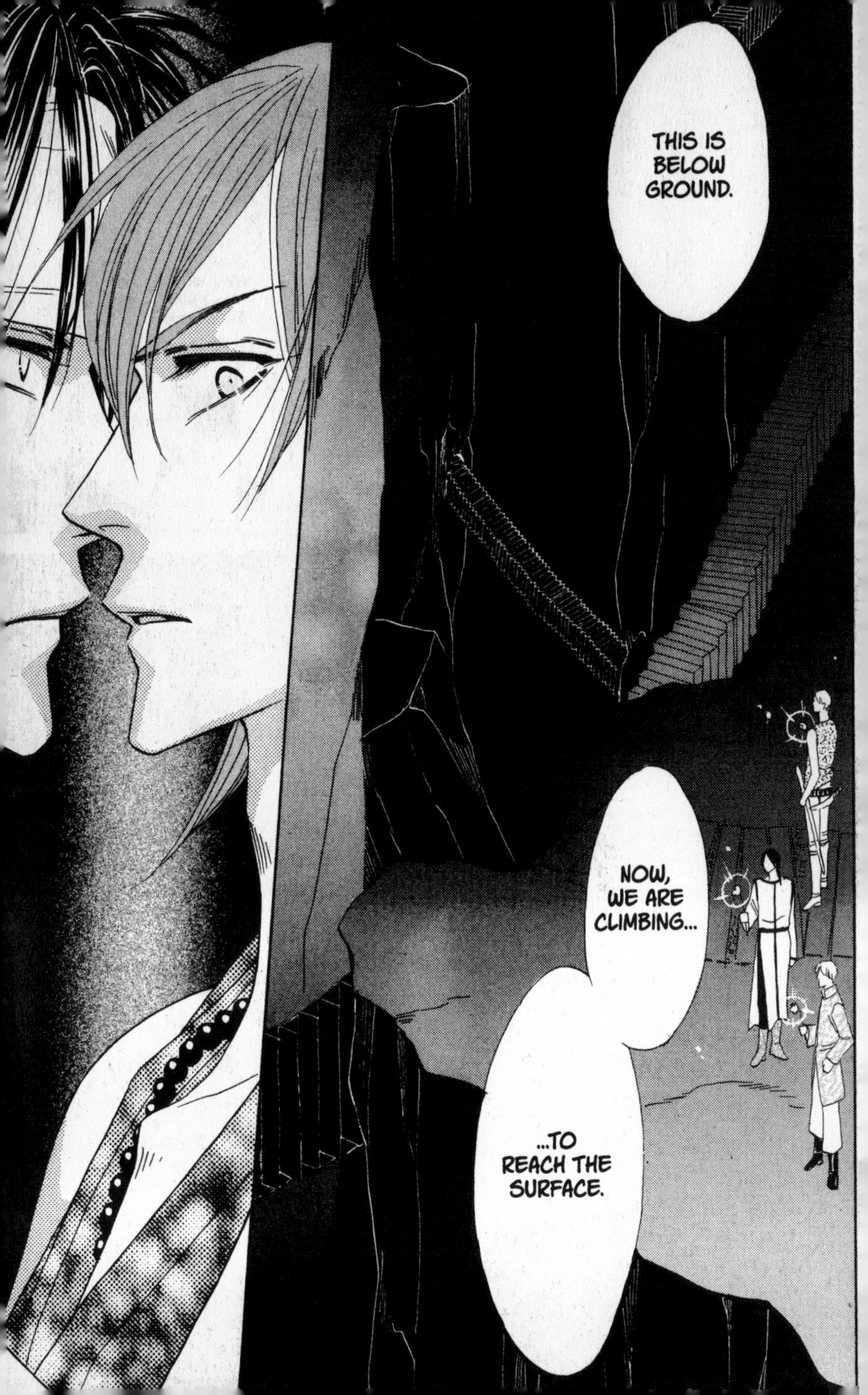
THIS IS BELOW GROUND.
NOW, WE ARE CLIMBING...
...TO REACH THE SURFACE.

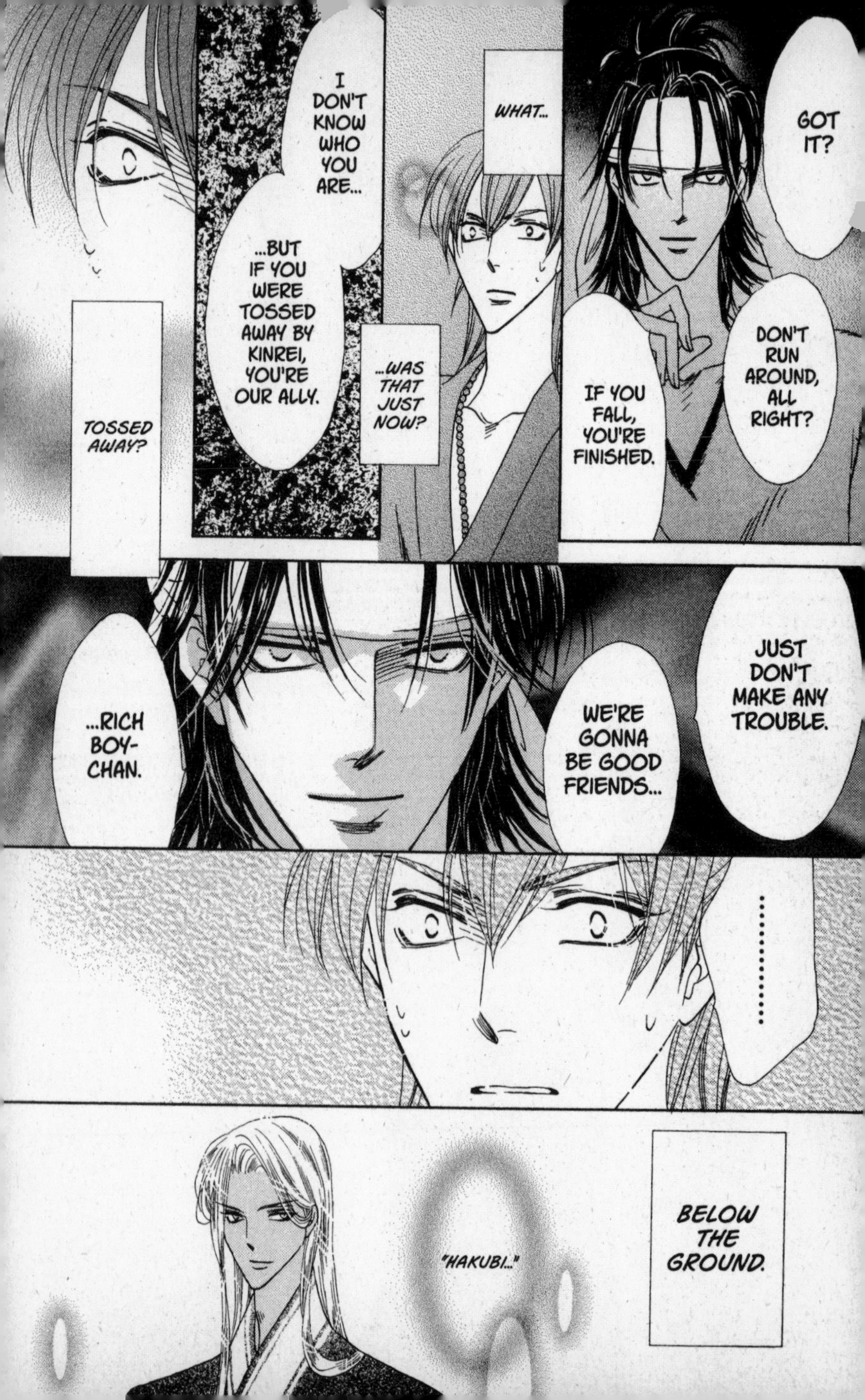
GOT IT?
DON'T RUN AROUND, ALL RIGHT?
IF YOU FALL, YOU'RE FINISHED.
WHAT...
...WAS THAT JUST NOW?
I DON'T KNOW WHO YOU ARE...
...BUT IF YOU WERE TOSSED AWAY BY KINREI, YOU'RE OUR ALLY.
TOSSED AWAY?
JUST DON'T MAKE ANY TROUBLE.
WE'RE GONNA BE GOOD FRIENDS...
...RICH BOY-CHAN.
......
BELOW THE GROUND.
"HAKUBI..."

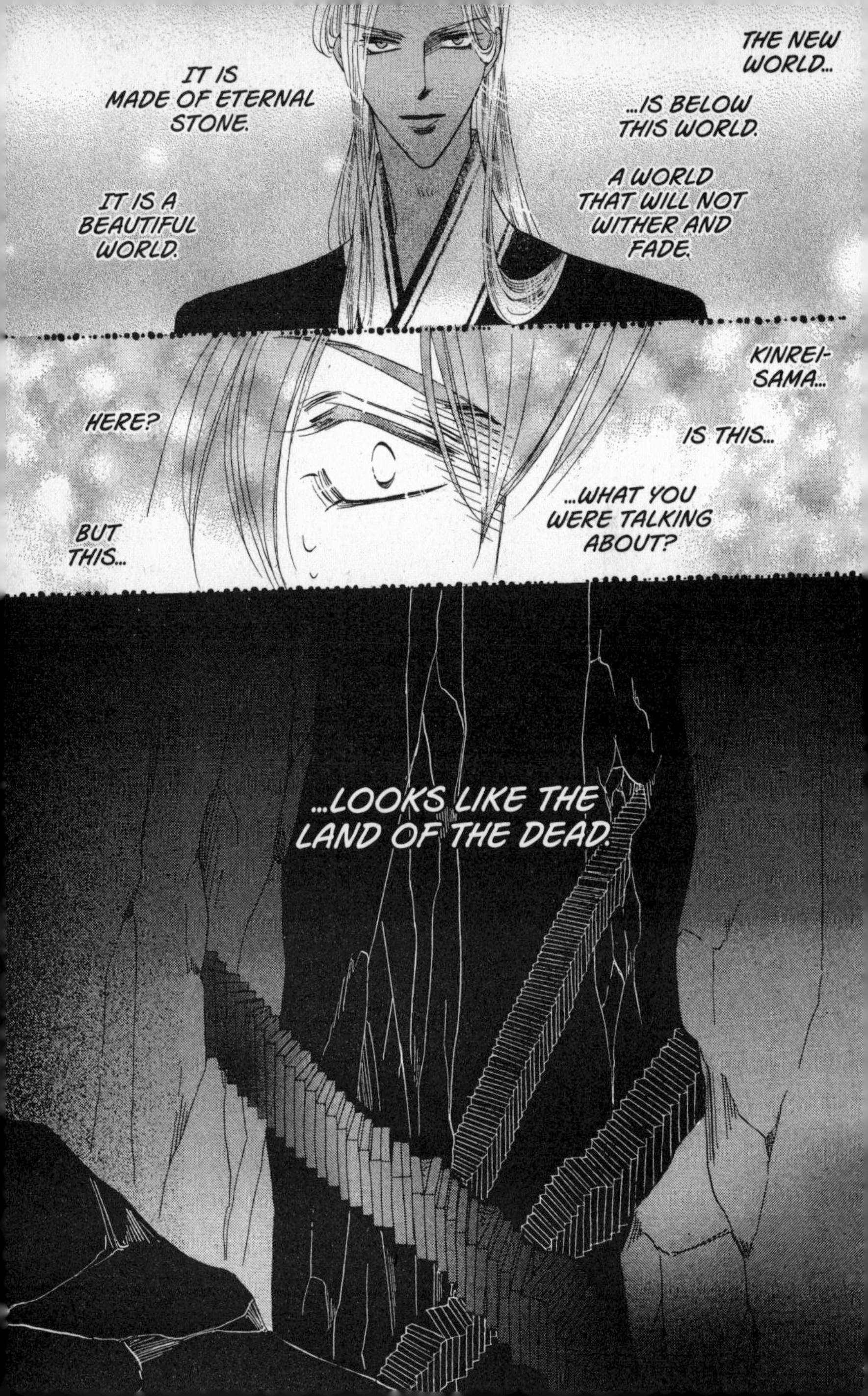
THE NEW WORLD...
...IS BELOW THIS WORLD.
A WORLD THAT WILL NOT WITHER AND FADE.
IT IS MADE OF ETERNAL STONE.
IT IS A BEAUTIFUL WORLD.
KINREI-SAMA...
IS THIS...
...WHAT YOU WERE TALKING ABOUT?
HERE?
BUT THIS...
...LOOKS LIKE THE LAND OF THE DEAD.

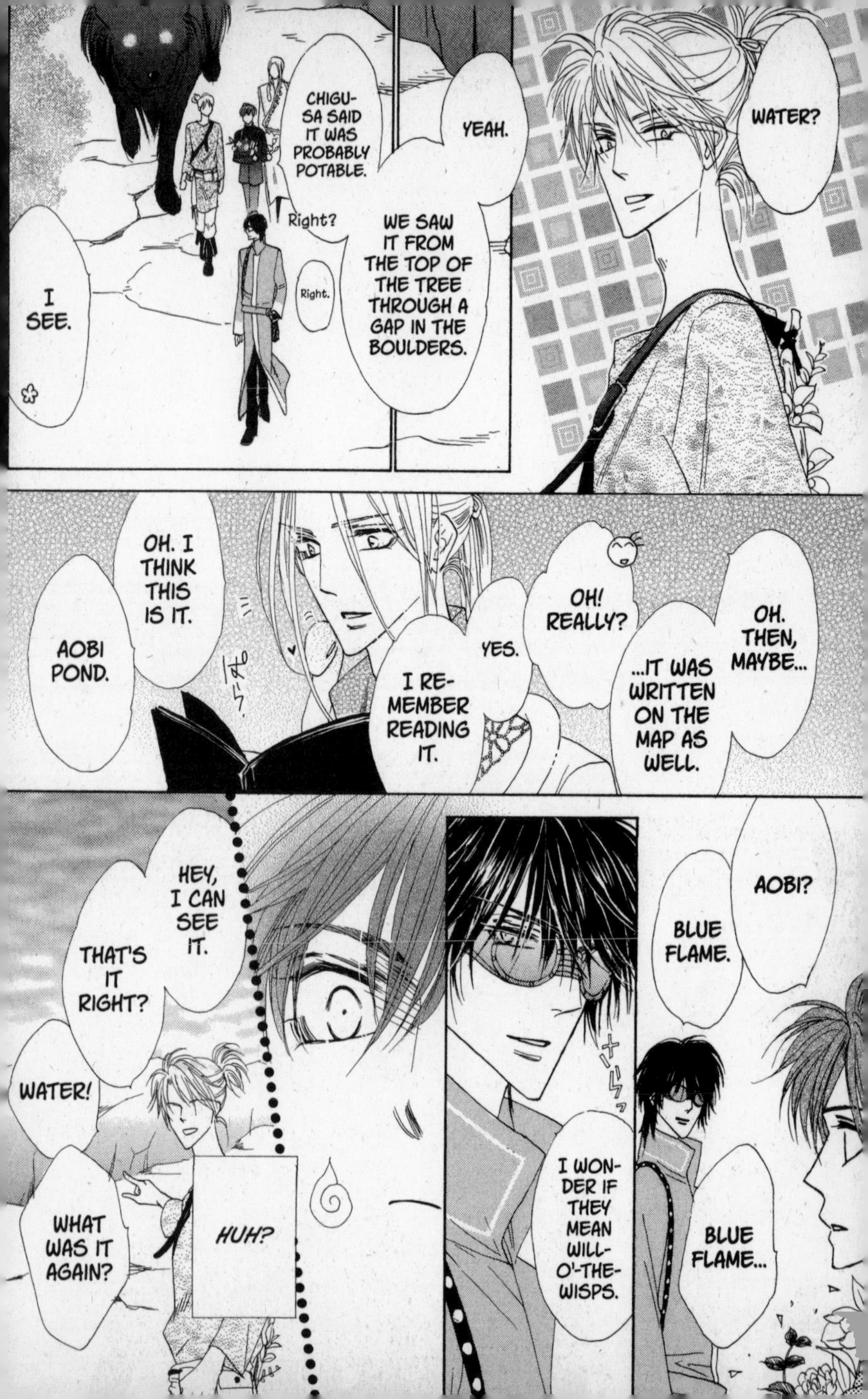
WATER?
YEAH.
CHIGUSA SAID IT WAS PROBABLY POTABLE.
WE SAW IT FROM THE TOP OF THE TREE THROUGH A GAP IN THE BOULDERS.
Right?
Right.
I SEE.
OH. THEN, MAYBE...
...IT WAS WRITTEN ON THE MAP AS WELL.
OH! REALLY?
YES.
I REMEMBER READING IT.
OH. I THINK THIS IS IT.
AOBI POND.
AOBI?
BLUE FLAME.
BLUE FLAME...
I WONDER IF THEY MEAN WILL-O'-THE-WISPS.
HEY, I CAN SEE IT.
THAT'S IT RIGHT?
WATER!
WHAT WAS IT AGAIN?
HUH?

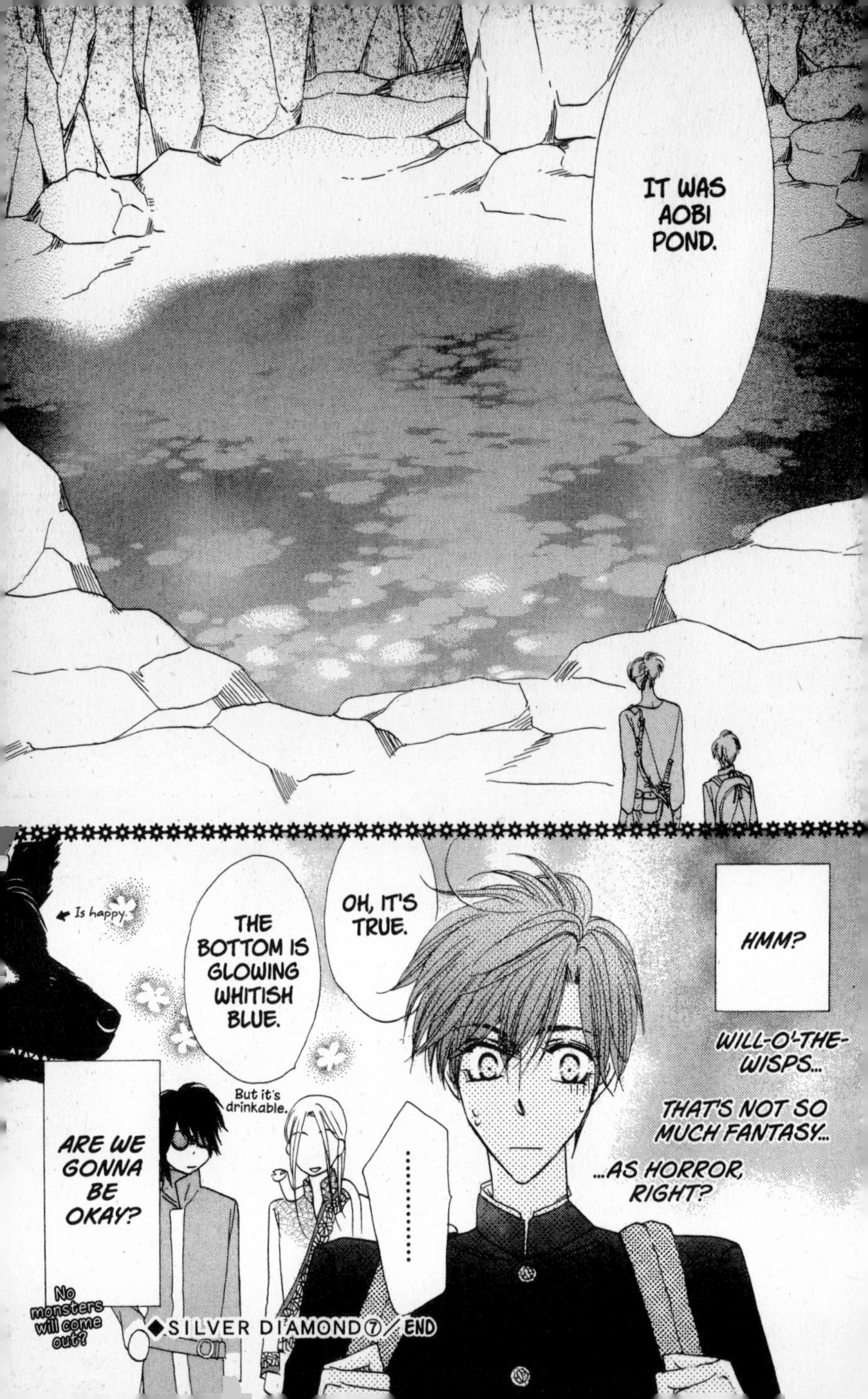
IT WAS AOBI POND.
HMM?
OH, IT'S TRUE.
THE BOTTOM IS GLOWING WHITISH BLUE.
Is happy.
WILL-O'-THE-WISPS...
THAT'S NOT SO MUCH FANTASY...
...AS HORROR, RIGHT?
......
But it's drinkable.
ARE WE GONNA BE OKAY?
No monsters will come out?
◆SILVER DIAMOND⑦/END

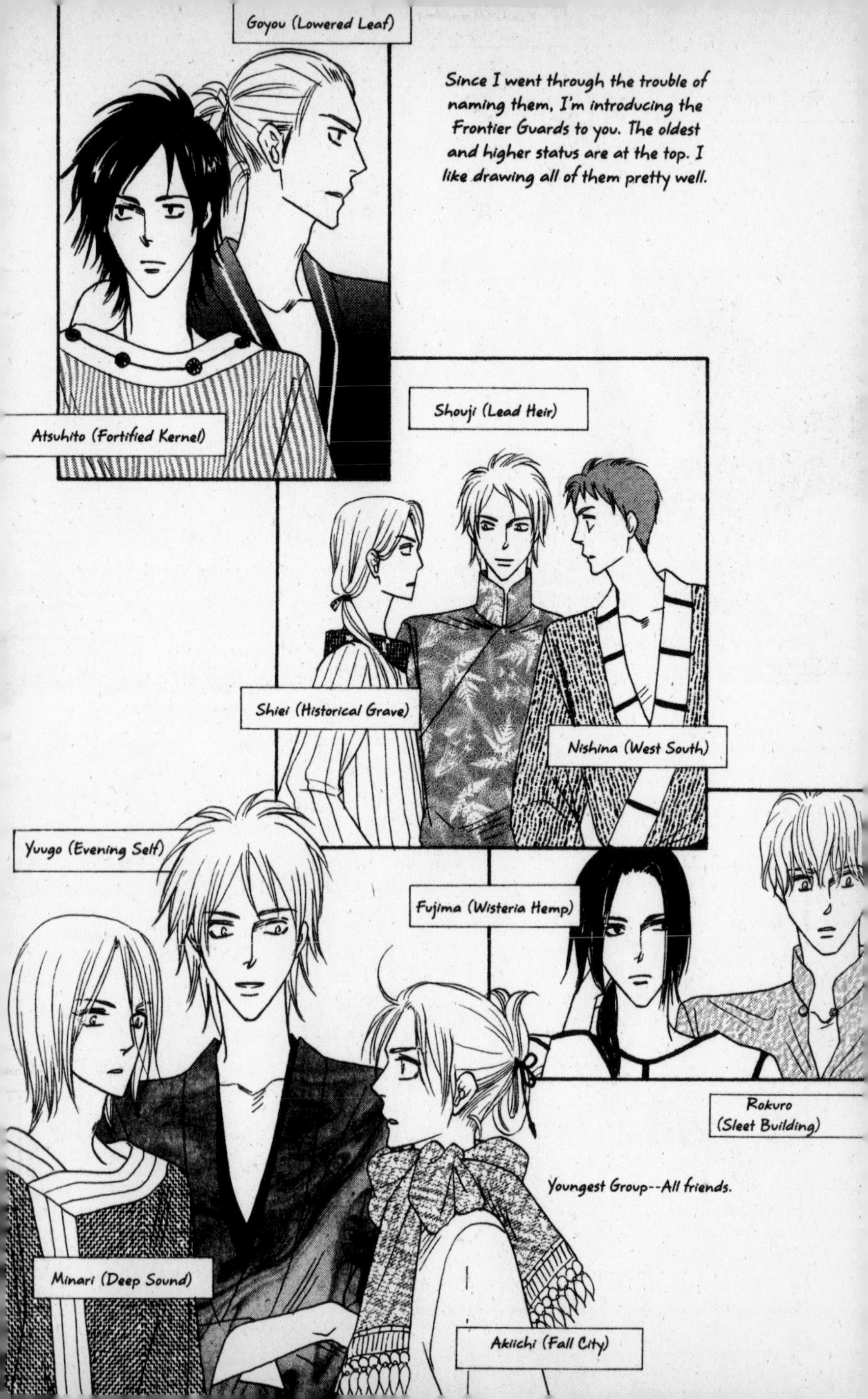
Since I went through the trouble of naming them, I'm introducing the Frontier Guards to you. The oldest and higher status are at the top. I like drawing all of them pretty well.
Goyou (Lowered Leaf)
Atsuhito (Fortified Kernel)
Shouji (Lead Heir)
Nishina (West South)
Shiei (Historical Grave)
Rokuro (Sleet Building)
Fujima (Wisteria Hemp)
Yuugo (Evening Self)
Youngest Group--All friends.
Akiichi (Fall City)
Minari (Deep Sound)

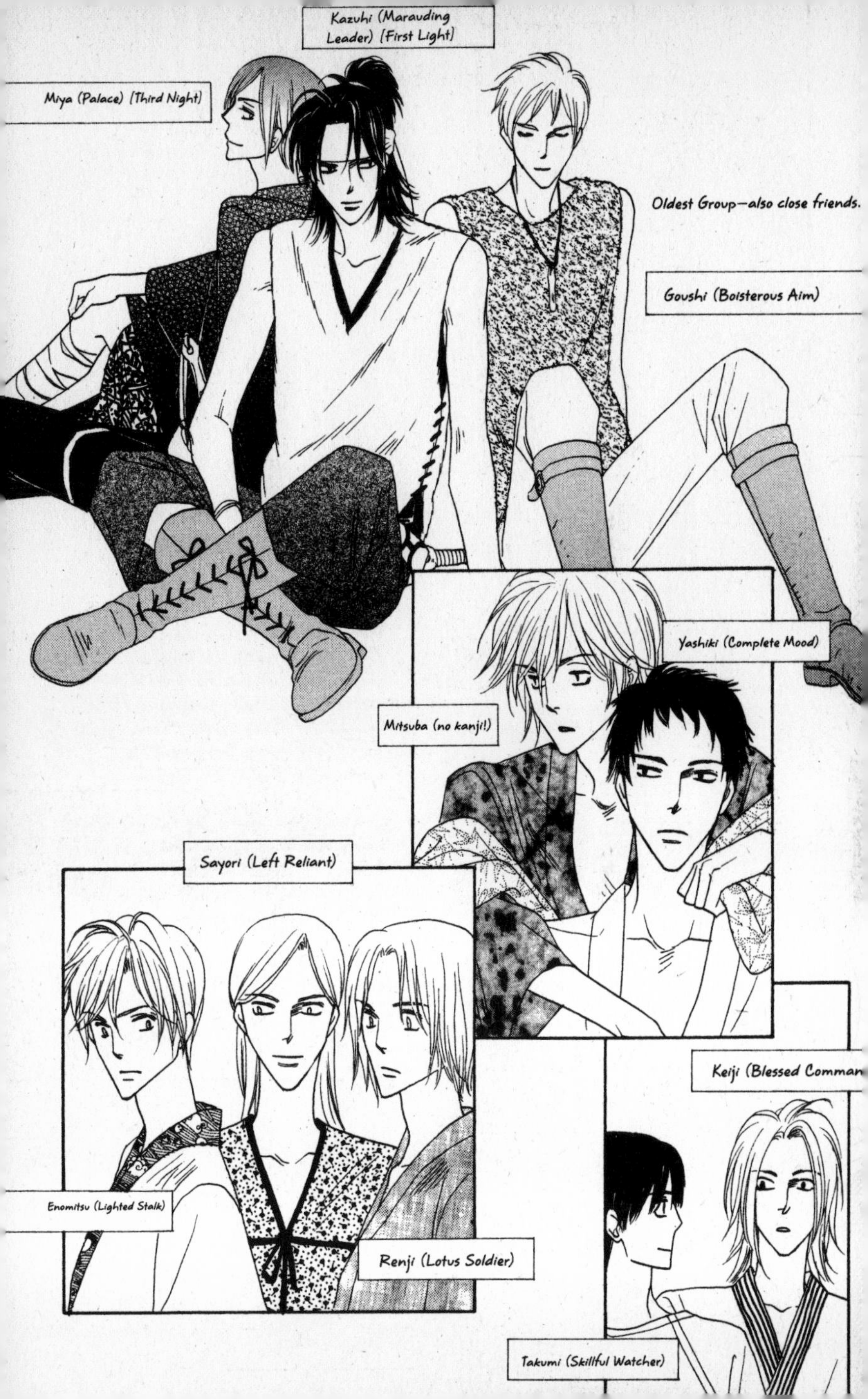
Kazuhi (Marauding Leader) (First Light)
Oldest Group—also close friends.
Miya (Palace) (Third Night)
Goushi (Boisterous Aim)
Yashiki (Complete Mood)
Mitsuba (no kanji!)
Keiji (Blessed Comman
Sayori (Left Reliant)
Enomitsu (Lighted Stalk)
Renji (Lotus Soldier)
Takumi (Skillful Watcher)

Well, I guess I'll finish up here this time.
Thank you for all the e-mails and letters
you send me! (Thank you to all the
people who send me your reviews of the
comic every month as well!) I'm sorry
that I can't reply to everyone, I will
continue focusing on drawing instead.

It doesn't really matter, but for some
reason Hakubi kept looking like a girl
to me. I wonder if it is because of his
hairstyle or attitude. Even though his hair
is tied the same way as Kazuhi's...Weird...

Well then--

See you
later!

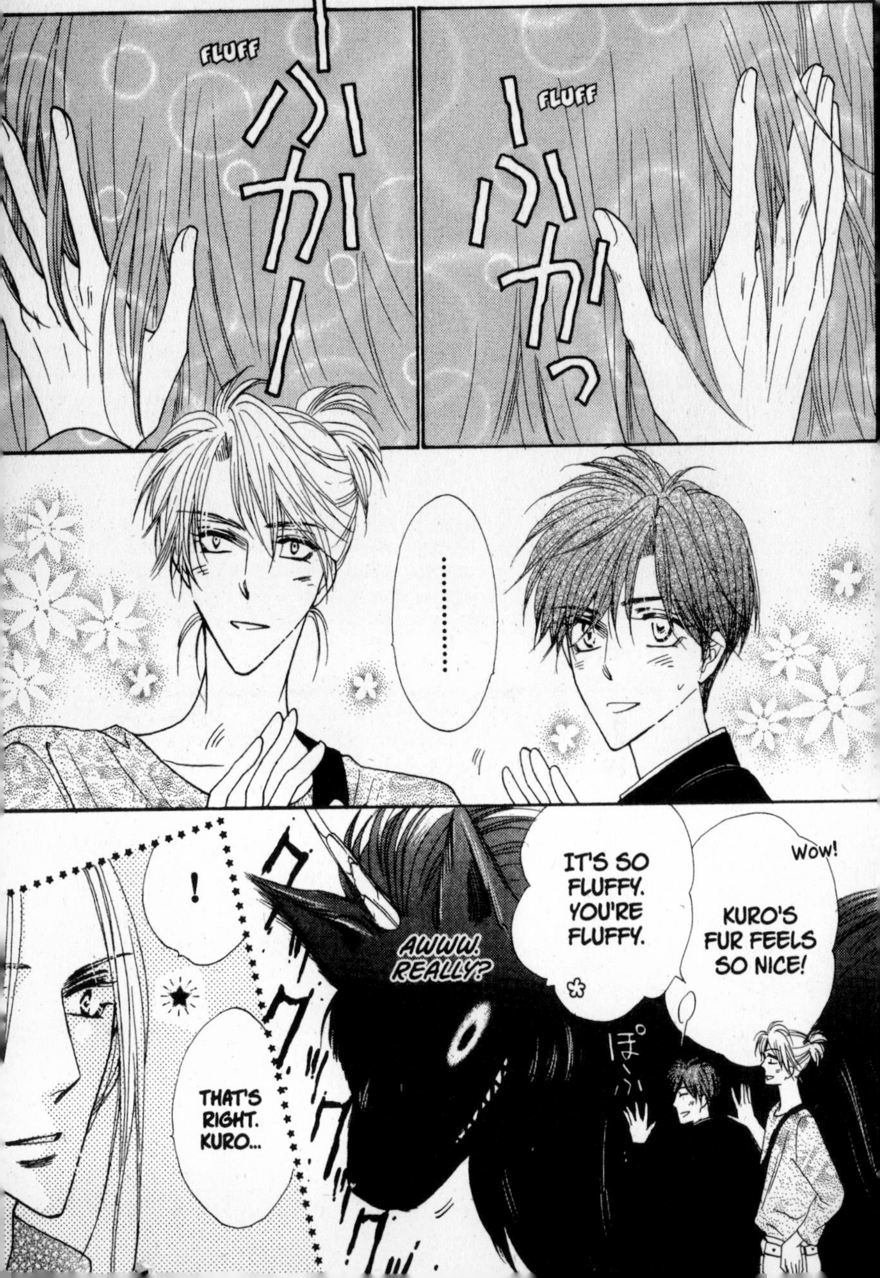
FLUFF
ふかっ
FLUFF
ふかー
......
WOW!
KURO'S FUR FEELS SO NICE!
IT'S SO FLUFFY. YOU'RE FLUFFY.
ぽふ
AWWW. REALLY?
!
THAT'S RIGHT. KURO...

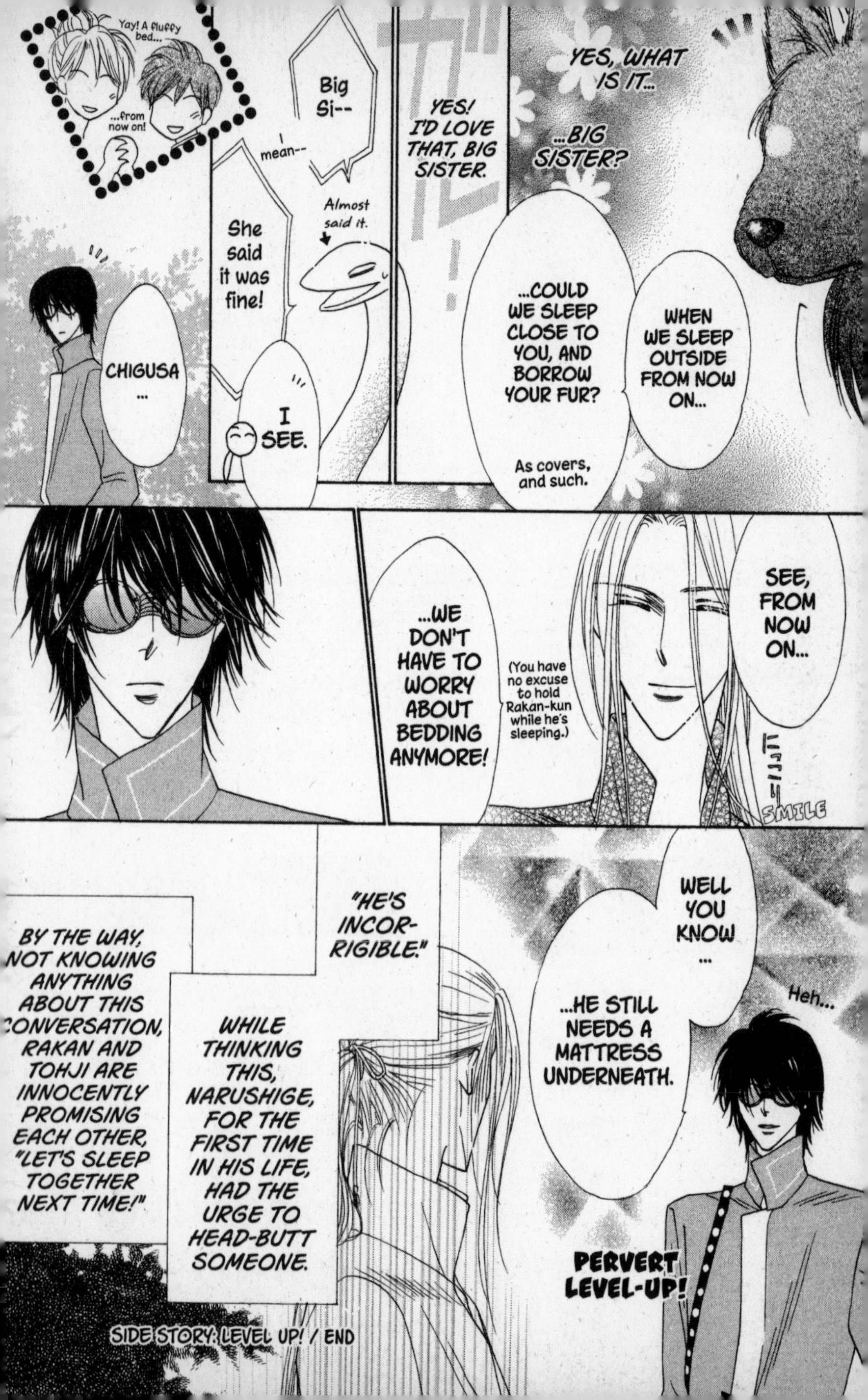
YES, WHAT IS IT...
...BIG SISTER?
WHEN WE SLEEP OUTSIDE FROM NOW ON...
...COULD WE SLEEP CLOSE TO YOU, AND BORROW YOUR FUR?
As covers, and such.
YES! I'D LOVE THAT, BIG SISTER.
Big Si--
I mean--
Yay! A fluffy bed...
...from now on!
Almost said it.
She said it was fine!
I SEE.
CHIGUSA ...
SEE, FROM NOW ON...
...WE DON'T HAVE TO WORRY ABOUT BEDDING ANYMORE!
(You have no excuse to hold Rakan-kun while he's sleeping.)
SMILE
WELL YOU KNOW ...
...HE STILL NEEDS A MATTRESS UNDERNEATH.
Heh...
PERVERT LEVEL-UP!
"HE'S INCORRIGIBLE."
WHILE THINKING THIS, NARUSHIGE, FOR THE FIRST TIME IN HIS LIFE, HAD THE URGE TO HEAD-BUTT SOMEONE.
BY THE WAY, NOT KNOWING ANYTHING ABOUT THIS CONVERSATION, RAKAN AND TOHJI ARE INNOCENTLY PROMISING EACH OTHER, "LET'S SLEEP TOGETHER NEXT TIME!"
SIDE STORY: LEVEL UP! / END

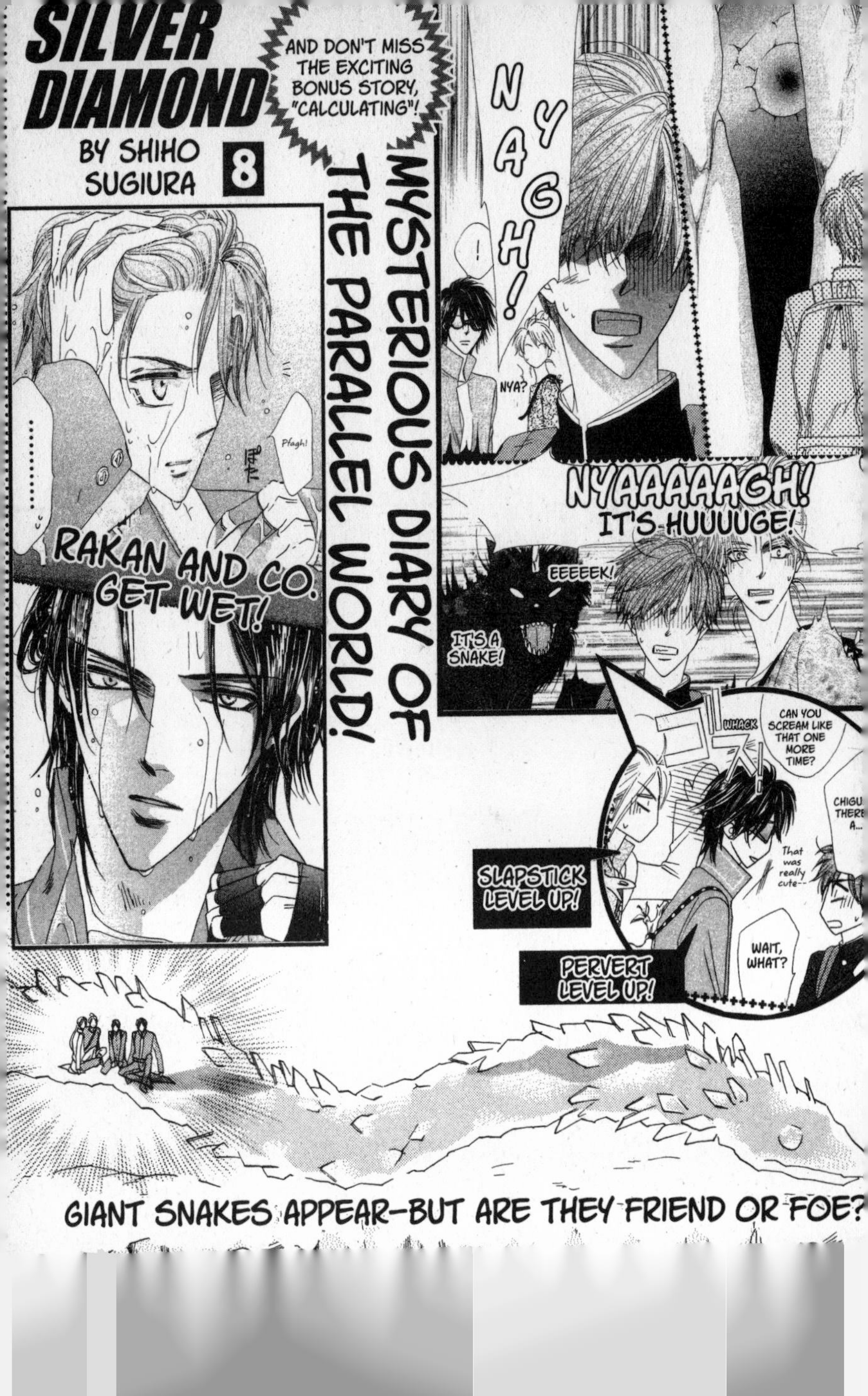

SILVER DIAMOND
BY SHIHO SUGIURA
8
AND DON'T MISS THE EXCITING BONUS STORY, "CALCULATING"!
MYSTERIOUS DIARY OF THE PARALLEL WORLD!
NYAGH!
!
NYA?
NYAAAAAGH!
IT'S HUUUUGE!
EEEEEK!
IT'S A SNAKE!
CAN YOU SCREAM LIKE THAT ONE MORE TIME?
WHACK
CHIGU THERE A...
That was really cute--
WAIT, WHAT?
SLAPSTICK LEVEL UP!
PERVERT LEVEL UP!
......
Pfagh!
RAKAN AND CO. GET WET!
GIANT SNAKES APPEAR—BUT ARE THEY FRIEND OR FOE?

Inside the World of...

SILVER DIAMOND

THIS SECTION HAS BEEN CREATED TO EXPLAIN AND ANALYZE THE COMPLICATED WORLD THAT IS *SILVER DIAMOND*. HOPEFULLY IT WILL SUCCESSFULLY COVER ALL THE CONFUSING CULTURAL AND LINGUISTIC ASPECTS OF THE SERIES AND HELP YOU ENJOY *SILVER DIAMOND* EVEN MORE!

honorifics JAPANESE USES HONORIFICS TO ADDRESS PEOPLE AND REFER TO THEM WITH RESPECT. SIMILAR TO "MR." AND "MRS." IN ENGLISH BUT THERE IS MORE VARIETY IN JAPANESE.

THE MOST COMMON HONORIFICS SEEN IN *SILVER DIAMOND* ARE AS FOLLOWS:
-SAN: VERY COMMON IN JAPANESE AND IS A SIGN OF RESPECT.
-KUN: INFORMAL HONORIFIC USUALLY USED FOR MALES WHEN ADDRESSING SOMEONE YOUNGER THAN YOURSELF.
-CHAN: INFORMAL AND USUALLY USED FOR FEMALES OR CHILDREN.
-SAMA: MORE FORMAL THAN "-SAN." USED FOR PEOPLE HIGHER IN RANK, LIKE THE PRINCE.

The seed boxes

IF YOU WERE WONDERING WHAT THE SEEDS ARE IN ALL THOSE DRAWERS, THEY ARE AS FOLLOWS, FROM LEFT TO RIGHT, TOP TO BOTTOM: TABLE, FENCE, FLOOR, BRIDGE, ROPE, ENVELOPE, CALTROP, AND IN THE NEXT PANEL, BAMBOO HAT.

Garnets

THIS IS ACTUALLY KIND OF A PLAY ON WORDS. GARNETS ARE "ZAKURO-ISHI" IN JAPANESE, WHICH IS PRESUMABLY HOW ZAKURO, THE STONE DOGGIE, GOT HIS NAME. "ZAKURO" ACTUALLY MEANS "POMEGRANATE," AND IF YOU'VE EVER SEEN THE LOVELY, GLISTENING INSIDE OF A POMEGRANATE, YOU CAN IMAGINE WHY GARNETS ARE "POMEGRANATE STONES" IN JAPAN. ☺

AND SPEAKING OF NAMES, WE'VE GOT A COUPLE OF NEW ONES IN THIS VOLUME:

白川白琵 : SHIRAKAWA HAKUBI
可岸律可 : KAGAN RITSUKA
夜橋夜明 : YORUBASHI YORUAKI

Kuro

KURO JUST MEANS "BLACK," AND IT'S ONE OF THOSE CLICHÉD PET NAMES, LIKE SPOT OR ROVER. WE REPLACED THE FLOATING TEXT BEHIND RAKAN, WHICH HAD BEEN JAPANESE EQUIVALENTS: "SHIRO," "KORO" AND "POCHI."

Rich-boy-Chan/Boku-chan/ 僕ちゃん

WHAT KAZUHI IS ACTUALLY REFERRING TO HERE IS THAT TO GO ALONG WITH HIS SNOTTY ATTITUDE, HAKUBI USES "BOKU," A PERSONAL PRONOUN GENERALLY ASSOCIATED WITH YOUNG BOYS, TO REFER TO HIMSELF. IT DEFINITELY GIVES AWAY SOME OF HIS HIGH-STATUS UPBRINGING, WHICH MAKES HIM MORE THAN A LITTLE SUSPICIOUS TO THE WARY GUARDS. BUT APPARENTLY MONEY DOESN'T BUY YOU CLASS! BY THE WAY, EVEN THE EVER-POLITE RAKAN USES "ORE," A MORE CASUAL (AND MORE MASCULINE) TERM, AND NARUSHIGE USES "WATASHI," A MORE GENTEEL, GENDER-NEUTRAL, AND NON-AGE-BASED PRONOUN.

Join us next time for more revealing tidbits in volume 8!

RightStuf.com asks...

"What kind of OTAKU are you?"

Naruto star Yuri Lowenthal is VAN VON HUNTER

Featuring

Shoji Kawamori

• Anime master
(Macross, The Vision of Escaflowne)

Stu Levy

• TOKYOPOP Founder and CEO
(Princess Ai, Juror 13)

PUTTING THE VAN IN VANQUISH
VAN VON HUNTER

Get ready for a hilarious, VANtastic adventure as the out-of-work evil vanquisher Van Von Hunter unravels the mysteries of manga, anime, and Japanese "pop" culture in order to save the world.

Get your DVD now at www.createspace.com/283456

f facebook
Van Von Hunter on Facebook
Become a Fan

To watch the trailer,
hear original music from the film,
become a VAN FAN, and more, visit:
www.facebook.com/vanvonhunter

AVAILABLE FOR PURCHASE ON DVD NOW
AND SCREENING AT FAN CONVENTIONS AROUND THE WORLD!

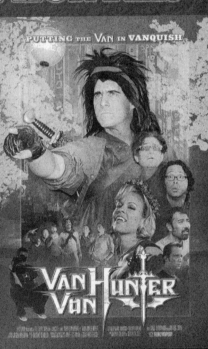

The second epic trilogy continues!

Princess Ai: The Prism of Midnight Dawn

Ai fights to escape the clutches of her mysterious and malevolent captors, not knowing whether Kent, left behind on the Other Side, is even still alive. A frantic rescue mission commences, and in the end, even Ai's magical voice may not be enough to protect her from the trials of the Black Forest.

Dark secrets are revealed, and Ai must use all her strength and courage to face off against the new threat to Ai-Land. But will she ever see Kent again...?

Princess Ai
The Prism of Midnight Dawn
2

"A very intriguing read that will satisfy old fans and create new fans, too." ~ *Bookloons*

KARAKURI ODETTE

カラクリ オデット

VOL. 2

KARAKURI ODETTO © 2005 Julietta Suzuki / HAKUSENSHA, Inc.

She's a robot who wants to learn how to be a human... And what she learns will surprise everyone!

Odette is now a sophomore at her high school. She wants to be as close to human as she can, but finds out she still has a long way to go. From wanting to be "cute" by wearing nail polish, to making a "tasty" bento that people would be happy to eat, Odette faces each challenge head-on with the help of her friends Yoko, Chris, the Professor and, of course, Asao!

FROM THE CREATOR OF AKUMA TO DOLCE

"A SURPRISINGLY SENSITIVE, FUNNY AND THOUGHT-PROVOKING SCI-FI SHOJO SERIES ... AS GENUINELY CHARMING AND MEMORABLE AS ITS MECHANICAL HEROINE." —ABOUT.COM

STOP!

This is the back of the book. You wouldn't want to spoil a great ending!

This book is printed "manga-style," in the authentic Japanese right-to-left format. Since none of the artwork has been flipped or altered, readers get to experience the story just as the creator intended. You've been asking for it, so TOKYOPOP® delivered: authentic, hot-off-the-press, and far more fun!

1
2
3
4
5
6
7
8
9
10

DIRECTIONS

If this is your first time reading manga-style, here's a quick guide to help you understand how it works.

It's easy... just start in the top right panel and follow the numbers. Have fun, and look for more 100% authentic manga from TOKYOPOP®!

THE MANGA REVOLUTION • LEADING
漫画革命